Intellectual Property Operations and Implementation in the 21st Century Corporation

Intellectual Property Operations and Implementation in the 21st Century Corporation

LANNING G. BRYER
SCOTT J. LEBSON
MATTHEW D. ASBELL

WILEY

John Wiley & Sons, Inc.

For general information on our other products and services or for technical support, please contact our Customer Care Department within the United States at (800) 762-2974, outside the United States at (317) 572-3993 or fax (317) 572-4002.

Wiley also publishes its books in a variety of electronic formats. Some content that appears in print may not be available in electronic books. For more information about Wiley products, visit our web site at www.wiley.com.

Library of Congress Cataloging-in-Publication Data

Bryer, Lanning G.
  Corporate intellectual property operations and implementation / Lanning G. Bryer, Scott J. Lebson, and Matthew D. Asbell.
    p. cm.
  Includes bibliographical references and index.
  ISBN 978-1-118-07587-6 (cloth); ISBN 978-1-118-14391-9 (ebk);
  ISBN 978-1-118-14392-6 (ebk); ISBN 978-1-118-14393-3 (ebk)
  1. Intellectual property. 2. International business enterprises—Law and legislation. I. Lebson, Scott J. II. Asbell, Matthew D. III. Title.
  K1401.B795 2011
  346.04'8—dc23

                                                          2011019564

Printed in the United States of America

10 9 8 7 6 5 4 3 2 1

To Gracie, man's best friend.
Lanning G. Bryer

To Mom, for everything.
Scott J. Lebson

In memory of Gidon Maidanik, for your unconditional love,
your passionate dedication to your work, and
your perseverance amidst life's challenges.
Matthew D. Asbell

Contents

Preface

"The Times They Are A-Changin'," wrote Bob Dylan, in the early 1960s, as a protest song characterizing the public sentiment, culture, and politics of that era. While some viewed the anthem as outdated by the very changes it predicted, the lyrics were prophetically timeless. In viewing Dylan's sentiments in the context of the modern era, his views could be applied to many important issues that affect not only the strategies employed by corporations to obtain and maintain competitive advantage, but also how those strategies are implemented on a day-to-day basis.

For instance, in asking us to "admit that the waters around [us] have grown" or we'll "sink like a stone," Dylan's words could be extrapolated in terms of the pressure market forces are placing on modern businesses to become or at least to appear "green." More corporations are investing in research and development of environmentally friendly products and processes, and governments are attempting to further encourage such investment. Simultaneously, more businesses are branding and marketing their products and services to take advantage of growing public interest in sustainability, and governments are exploring how to balance the reward of sustainability with the protection of consumers from false claims.

"The Times They Are A-Changin'" warned politicians that the "battle outside . . . [will] . . . soon shake your windows and rattle your walls," almost 50 years before the cultural changes brought about by security concerns and the availability of instantaneous information from across the globe. His words are as relevant to the earthquake victims in Japan, Chile, and Haiti and the revolutionaries in Egypt and Libya as they were to the "establishment" interests and hippies of the 1960s. The technological advances of the past decade or so and the resulting globalization have brought every battle and every natural disaster closer to home. In doing so, they have changed the ways in which companies do business, whether such business is with governments or their armed forces, manufacturers, or distributors in foreign nations, or with consumers in the companies' own stores. What do these businesses need to do to survive and prosper while they are "in the trenches" of a global economy?

Dylan recognized that tradition would have to give way when he advised the earlier generation that "your old road is rapidly agin'" and requested that they "please get out of the new one if you can't lend your hand." As globalization advances, traditional rules of the economic game are being challenged, and businesses need to determine how best to implement new strategies in practice.

Businesses must be in a position to adapt quickly to change as making decisions based on traditional considerations can be a dangerous premise. Moreover, even after the overarching policies are determined, companies must put them into practice with caution and foresight. Variables that impacted prior quarters and prior years may be different than those that will influence future financial performance. In the past, external conditions were considered a constant, and internal factors were used to predict organizational performance. That is no longer necessarily the case. It is dangerous, if not fatal, to create an economic or worldview rooted in the recent past. It may be even more dangerous to put that view into practice without careful consideration of the details.

Indeed, the 21st-century corporation can no longer rely merely on having been established long ago or the former success of its traditional forms of advertising and marketing. It must either get with the times or make way for a competitor who will. The modern era is less centralized, less hierarchical, and less private, with consumers publicly conversing and announcing to thousands of attentive listeners about their own experiences with products and services via social media web sites. Today's media reaches well beyond those listening to local radio or watching local television to the computers and smartphones of millions around the globe in an instant, and then spreads virally to all of their acquaintances. How do 21st-century corporations manage to protect their intellectual property rights and the competitive advantages arising therefrom when their secrets are so quickly and easily shared and their messages are enveloped by so much third-party commentary beyond their control?

How all intellectual property (IP) owners have historically chosen to acquire, develop, protect, maintain, leverage, and enforce their limited monopoly rights in intellectual property is a study and a book unto itself. However, the purpose of this particular series is to examine the decision-making processes, activities, and changes thereto of significant corporate IP owners in the new century and millennium. In this case, size matters.

Why not explore the decision-making processes and activities of all IP owners? Although similarities obviously exist between all IP owners, IP owners with significant portfolios have unique issues and challenges of scale, investment, oversight, law, and development. Moreover, the lessons to be learned from the processes and activities of large corporations can sometimes be applied with some modification to growing companies. As a result, we explore the corporate ownership and management of IP rights in this series of two books.

The first book in this series, *IP Strategies for the 21st Century Corporation*, published in April 2011, focused on the strategic decision making that occurs in this process. It was meant to be the view from 20,000 feet by senior decision makers, executives, general counsel, and IP counsel. What strategic, corporate, or tax issues involving corporate IP ownership need to be considered? How does a corporation expand markets or grow its IP portfolio? How does a corporation keep its IP pipeline full without incurring unnecessary expenses? How has the Internet changed business models and activities, and what are the related IP issues? These and other topics were explored in the first book as detailed in the contributions below:

Chapter Title	Authors	Affiliations*
Corporate Strategies, Structures, and Ownership of Intellectual Property Rights	Lanning G. Bryer & Deepica Capoor Warikoo	Ladas & Parry LLP
Properly Evaluating a Target with Intellectual Property Rights	David Drews	IP Metrics LLC
Growth through Acquisition or Merger	Diane Meyers	PPG Industries, Inc.
Penetrating New Markets through Extension of Goods or Product Lines or Expansion into Other Territories	Toshiya Oka	Canon, Inc.
Intellectual Property: From Asset to Asset Class	James Malackowski	Ocean Tomo, LLC
Strategic Patent Management after the Boom: Managing the R&D and Patent Pipeline	Marc Adler	Marc Adler LLC
Global Piracy and Financial Valuation of Intellectual Property Revisited	Robert Lamb & Randie Beth Rosen	Stern School of Business, New York University Formerly an associate at Orrick, Herrington & Sutcliffe
When to Litigate: the Rise of the Trolls	Raymond DiPerna & Jack Hobaugh	Ladas & Parry LLP Cooley LLP
Using Insurance to Manage IP Risk	Kimberly Cauthorn & Leib Dodell	Duff & Phelps Think Risk Underwriting Agency, LLC
Exploring Alternative Dispute Resolution	Alicia Lloreda	Jose Lloreda Camacho & Co.
Outsourcing and Offshoring of IP Work	Olga Nedeltscheff	Limited Brands, Inc.
Intellectual Property Legal Process Outsourcing	Marilyn Primiano	Pangea3, a Division of Thomson Reuters, Legal
Satisfying Ethical Obligations When Outsourcing Legal Work Overseas	Michael Downey	Hinshaw & Culbertson LLP
The Brave New World of Web 2.0 and the 3-D Internet	Steve Mortinger	IBM, Inc.
Managing "Green" Intellectual Property	Larry Greenemeier	Scientific American, a Division of Nature, Inc.
Accounting and Tax Policies as They Relate to Intellectual Property	Howard Fine & Andrew Ross	Gettry Marcus Stern & Lehrer, CPA, PC
IP Valuation Techniques and Issues for the 21st Century	David Blackburn & Bryan Ray	NERA Economic Consulting

*The views of the authors are not necessarily those of their employers or affiliates.

This second book, *IP Operations and Implementation in the 21st Century Corporation,* is equally important to the management of corporate IP rights. Having explored and understood better the strategic issues and decisions that companies make, this second book examines how companies are effectively implementing them. How does a corporation cost-effectively obtain or enforce its IP rights? How do corporations control expanded counterfeiting throughout the world? What technological developments are available today that did not exist in years past to help manage this process? How are IP searches and investigations more cost-effectively conducted? How are corporations using IP rights to drive increased revenues and profits? These and other subjects are explored as follows:

Chapter Title	Authors	Affiliations*
Conflicts: Causes, Prevention, and Controlling Counterfeiting	Joseph Gioconda & Joseph Forgione	Gioconda Law Group PLLC
Electronic Discovery in Intellectual Property Cases	Jennifer R. Martin	Symantec Corporation
Controlling Patenting Costs	John Richards	Ladas & Parry LLP
Trademark Costs: Trimming the Sails in Rough Economic Waters	Robert Doerfler & Matthew D. Asbell	SVP Worldwide Ladas & Parry LLP
Domain Names	Dennis S. Prahl & Elliot Lipins	Ladas & Parry LLP
Creating, Perfecting, and Enforcing Security Interests in Intellectual Property	Scott J. Lebson	Ladas & Parry LLP
Strategic and Legal View of Licensing Patents	James Markarian	Siemens Corporation
Monetizing IP Rights: Licensing In and Out	Kelly M. Slavitt	Reckitt Benckiser LLC
Working with Government	David J. Rikkers	Raytheon Company
Valuation, Monetization, and Disposition in Bankruptcy	Fernando Torres	IPmetrics LLC
Outsourcing of Branding and Marketing	Terry Heckler	Heckler & Associates
Trademark Searches	Joshua Braunstein	Corsearch (a Wolters Kluwer Business)
Investigations: Considerations for Selecting and Directing Outside Investigators	Jeremiah A. Pastrick	Continental Enterprises
Model Intellectual Property Internship Programs: Internship Programs within the Scope of Employment Law	Barbara Kolsun	Stuart Weitzman Holdings, LLC
Maximizing "Green" Brand Exposure and Minimizing Perceptions of Greenwashing	Maureen Beacom Gorman	Marshall, Gerstein & Borun LLP
The Financial Reporting Impact of Intellectual Property Activity	James Donohue & Mark A. Spelker	Charles River Associates, Inc. J. H. Cohn LLP

*The views of the authors are not necessarily those of their employers or affiliates.

Both books enjoy the perspective of different players in the process. We are fortunate to have a number of respected in-house professionals as well as outside practitioners, service providers, consultants, and academics. The intended purpose is to examine many of these issues from different vantage points. For example, on the topic of outsourcing, we have views from corporate counsel, outside IP counsel, and IP service providers. We are confident that looking at this issue with such a wide lens and from different angles provides greater understanding of the topic. Where possible, we have encouraged authors to consider their subjects from other perspectives and to speculate about changes in practice and attitudes that might yet occur in the future. We hope this approach will provide greater clarity and a deeper understanding of the issues that face everyone who has a role to play in the management and ownership of corporate IP rights in the 21st century and beyond.

In "The Times They Are A-Changin'," Dylan implored writers and critics not to "speak too soon" because "the wheel's still in spin," and indeed it is, perhaps moving faster than ever. While this book's quick snapshot of how corporations are managing their domain names, for example, may show up blurry amidst the speed of the changes in practice and policy that corporations are undergoing, we are hopeful that it will provide some helpful guidance as to where IP owners are and where they are headed.

Lanning G. Bryer
Scott J. Lebson
Matthew D. Asbell

Acknowledgments

The editors of this book owe significant debts of gratitude to many people, without whose time and effort this work would not have been possible.

We are deeply appreciative of the many contributors who submitted chapters, and sections of chapters, to make this work what it is. In addition to those who contributed to this book, we are also grateful for the significant contributions of the authors of the companion volume, *Intellectual Property Strategies for the 21st Century Corporation*. We further recognize the sacrifices of the various employers with which our contributors are affiliated, although the contents of this book do not necessarily reflect their views.

The editors wish to express their sincerest appreciation to the following law students and recent graduates for their tireless efforts in organizing, researching, drafting, critiquing, and handling necessary correspondence regarding this book: Ms. Ilaria Ferrarini, Mr. Ari Abramowitz, Ms. Marie Flandin, Ms. Caroline Camp, Mr. Alex Silverman, Mr. Jason Kreps, Ms. Shefali Sewak, Ms. Rachelle Fernandes, Ms. Olivia Ruiz-Joffre, Ms. Angela Lam, Mr. John P. Glowatz, Ms. Jennifer Baker, Mr. Eric Null, and Mr. John Kelly. Without their skill, energy, and dedication, this book would not have been possible.

We thank the splendid professional and trade editors of John Wiley & Sons, Susan McDermott and Judy Howarth, for their encouragement and assistance in making this book a reality.

We are indebted to our law partners and colleagues for their understanding and forbearance, and for believing in the value of this project.

Finally, we are grateful to our spouses and children, who patiently endured the lost evenings and weekends during the birth, development, and publication of this work.

Lanning G. Bryer
Scott J. Lebson
Matthew D. Asbell

CHAPTER 1

Conflicts

Causes, Prevention, and Controlling Counterfeiting

Joseph C. Gioconda, Esq., and Joseph M. Forgione
Gioconda Law Group PLLC

In the past decade, efficiently addressing brand protection issues within the corporate structure has evolved into a top priority for companies dedicated to protecting the goodwill associated with their brands. Counterfeit products are no longer seen as affecting only luxury brands on Canal Street in New York City. In fact, counterfeiting has grown to such an extent that it now operates as an entire industry, one that provides a constant stream of income to small-time infringers just the same as it does to members of organized crime and even terrorist groups.

While misappropriation of valuable company trademarks by counterfeiters has served as a means from which to realize this stream of income, the overall integrity associated with each brand subject to counterfeiting is now being put directly at stake. Controlling the consequences of this worldwide industry has become more challenging as technology and counterfeiters themselves have become more sophisticated. The Internet has grown into a major avenue of exploitation for counterfeiters,[1] without which many offenders would not have the refuge of anonymity and unaccountability. The corporate structure has quickly turned to online anti-counterfeiting enforcement strategies to supplement brick-and-mortar protections that have been utilized by brand owners seeking to protect their trademarks. By adapting to this anti-counterfeiting culture, companies provide a stronger barrier against notorious offenders operating in domestic and international spaces, and, in the same manner, recognize the relevancy of focusing on brand protection through a very modern approach.

The purpose of this chapter is to briefly discuss how the growth of counterfeiting as an industry has stimulated corporate responsibility to implement modern enforcement strategies needed to combat the problems that threaten the integrity of valuable brands. This chapter will address the importance of focusing on the burgeoning problem of online counterfeiting and how the development of a strategic online anti-counterfeiting enforcement program serves as a critical supplement to traditional brick-and-mortar enforcement protections. This chapter will also provide a focus on the importance of partnering with efficient and effective outside counsel to achieve complete brand protection, as well as discuss the benefits and risks associated with civil and criminal enforcement strategies currently being used to protect the intellectual property (IP) rights of brand owners.

In-House Enforcement Strategies on the Internet

Some corporations affected by recurring counterfeiting issues opt to retain full- or part-time attorneys, paralegals, and investigators to work in-house. In-house enforcement teams can conduct broad Internet searches and utilize domain-based research services (e.g., WHOIS) to uncover information necessary to construct a basic profile for a seller of counterfeit merchandise. Online investigative firms also provide additional assistance in this respect by undertaking test purchases, making purchases of infringing products, running trace investigations, and even monitoring auctions to further enhance the target profile.

After choosing a web site or group of web sites that pose the most immediate threat to the overall integrity of a given brand, brand owners may select any number of enforcement avenues available to them when seeking to protect their rights against a counterfeiter. Some of these avenues may include sending cease-and-desist letters themselves to counterfeiters directly or even implementing various notice and takedown programs that have the effect of helping to reduce the visibility of counterfeit products being offered on the Internet.

Reducing Counterfeit Visibility on Popular Search Engines

Depending on the magnitude of the counterfeiting problem relative to the particular brand, companies often begin their online anti-counterfeiting enforcement program by targeting counterfeit web sites that are most visible to the public. The volume of counterfeit sites operating on the Internet is overwhelming, and this fact is only complicated by the notion that most sellers of counterfeit goods have found it easier to perfect their trade by exploiting the anonymity that the Internet provides for them on a day-to-day basis. Counterfeiters expand the scope of their businesses to capture as many prospective customers as possible, even if that means operating a number of sites with different domain names and different content in order to increase product availability to the public. Counterfeiters also utilize the Internet to promote their merchandise through avenues such as sponsored links and comparison shopping sites found as listings on popular search engines to appeal to a substantially wider audience.

SPONSORED LINKS   Sponsored links are links to web sites that pay for strategic placement on a particular search engine (e.g., Google, Yahoo!, etc.). These links not only function as a means from which to access a particular site with ease, but they also serve an as important search engine marketing service through which sellers have the potential to purchase and maintain high levels of visibility for their businesses. Counterfeiters often bid on sponsored links offered by popular search engines in order to further promote their web sites and substantially increase the volume of their businesses. Consumers searching for particular terms or products on search engines encounter this advertising quite frequently—often featured on the border of the search engine itself—and counterfeiters exploit this avenue of promotion to target a particular customer base. Counterfeiters frequently bid on key terms for sponsored links promoting particular goods that best associate with the goods that they are in the business of selling. In addition to offering substandard goods and services to consumers, counterfeiters misappropriate company trademarks and diminish the goodwill associated with a particular brand by publicly advertising the sale of goods that are in no way authentic.

The growth of advertisements for counterfeit sites being promoted on popular search engine results pages has prompted many brand owners to focus more on protecting their rights on the Internet. In order to reduce the visibility of these advertisements, brand owners have the option of contacting search engine administrators and complaining about the infringing content being advertised as a sponsored link on the site. By requesting the removal of these links, brand owners take an important step toward implementing an enforcement strategy that aids in protecting the integrity of their valuable brands on the Internet.

COMPARISON SHOPPING SITES   Counterfeiters also utilize the Internet to promote their merchandise by offering infringing products on comparison shopping sites provided by popular search engines (e.g., Google Product Search, Bing Shopping). Comparison shopping sites are uniquely equipped with product listings, consumer reviews, store ratings, and personal shopping lists that offer creative shopping options to consumers on the Internet. Similar to the model of purchasing sponsored links, counterfeiters often place product listings on comparison shopping sites in order to further promote their web sites and increase the volume of their businesses. In doing so, counterfeiters create a presence in another important consumer arena and, at the same time, threaten brand owners by selling goods that have the overall effect of diminishing the reputation of authentic goods.

The growth of counterfeit products being listed on comparison shopping sites has also made brand owners more attentive to protecting their rights on the Internet. As such, brand owners may formally contact search engine administrators and complain about infringing content being listed on a particular comparison shopping site. In requesting the removal of these listings, brand owners take another important step toward controlling the counterfeiting problem and protecting the value of their brands on the Internet.

SEARCH ENGINE OPTIMIZATION   The goal of reducing counterfeit visibility on popular search engines has also led brand owners to participate in search engine optimization (SEO) strategies to give their web sites noticeable presence on the Internet. Brand owners interested in having their company web sites appear close to the top of "natural" or "organic" search results utilize SEO as a process to help increase the volume of web site traffic by means of inclusion in early search engine listings. In order to properly optimize a web site, companies edit content and coding to include brand and product-specific keywords for recognition by a search engine. Optimization efforts, whether conducted by in-house employees or outside consultants, have the overall effect of improving public recognition and access to a particular brand on the Internet by way of increasing visibility in prominent search engine listings.

Counterfeiters often take advantage of SEO by creating a vast number of spam blogs, which are a series of web logs with affiliated, interconnected hyperlinks, utilized in order to increase search engine rankings. If tagged with enough infringing content, spam blogs can rise to the top of search engine listings and even override the legitimate company web sites of brand owners. Companies focused on improving SEO for their particular brand can sue these infringers and, if successful, take ownership of all infringing sites, thus helping to decrease the visibility of counterfeit products in prominent search engine listings.

Monitoring Online Auction Sites and Internet Trade Boards

Companies have also begun to extend the reach of their online anti-counterfeiting enforcement program by monitoring online auction sites and Internet trade boards, as well as by contacting Web hosts and online service providers to take further action against counterfeiters. Counterfeiters utilize the Internet to promote their merchandise through avenues such as online auction sites (e.g., eBay and Yahoo! Auctions) and business-to-business (B2B) Internet trade boards (e.g., Tradekey, Ecplaza) in order to appeal to a wider audience. Though established legal precedent does not hold online marketplaces liable for trademark infringement on grounds of contributory liability,[2] business-to-consumer (B2C) online auctions and consumer-to-consumer (C2C) online auctions can be monitored quite effectively through the use of different online reporting programs. Since corporate trademark owners have the responsibility to protect their trademarks through individual acts of policing and enforcement, programs such as iOffer Reporting and the eBay VeRO (Verified Rights Owner) program enable brand owners to contact online auction sites directly and request the removal of individual infringing listings. Outside counsel may also provide creative options for auction monitoring and reporting services to brand owners seeking a more personalized and targeted campaign against wholesalers of counterfeit products operating on online auction sites and Internet trade boards.

Contacting Web Hosts and Online Service Providers

Though utilized by most web site owners in good faith, Web hosting services have also been the subject of exploitation by many counterfeiters looking for an avenue to sell their goods and promote their services. Web hosting services sell access to and provide web site owners and administrators with space on a server to position their web sites on the Internet. While host services may send takedown notices based on request, disable the IP addresses of infringing sites, or even block servers to prevent infringing conduct from occurring, counterfeiters will often change IP addresses and shift between host providers without notification. This activity makes it difficult at times for Web hosts to pinpoint the identity of counterfeiters and take appropriate action against them to protect the rights of frustrated brand owners.

While not traditionally subject to legal liability for infringing activity springing from counterfeit web sites operating on their servers, Web hosts recently have been found responsible for not terminating infringing uses when notified that web site owners in the business of operating counterfeit sites were residing on their servers. In *Louis Vuitton Malletier v. Akanoc Solutions Inc.*,[3] which was filed in the U.S. District Court for the Northern District of California, a jury found the defendants liable for contributory trademark and copyright infringement and awarded substantial statutory damages to the plaintiff in recovery, even despite arguments made by defendant that counterfeiters often changed IP addresses and shifted between host providers. The decision assigns new liability to Internet service providers for not acting—or failing to act—when notified by a brand owner that counterfeit or infringing merchandise is being offered by web sites hosted on their servers. This decision has had the effect of putting the entire online hosting community on notice that willful blindness will not be tolerated when counterfeit sites are reported as infringing and requested for removal by a brand owner.

This development in the law places companies in a better position to prohibit action, as well as nonaction, by Web hosting services not in the habit of combating counterfeiters that misappropriate IP rights after being notified by brand owners. The change in law affects corporate behavior substantially, in that takedown notices issued to Web hosting services by companies protecting their brands have much more command than they may have once possessed. It also provides a pathway for potentially extending the reach of liability onto services such as domain name registrars, Domain Name Service (DNS) name servers, and other online service providers that disregard counterfeiters in the business of abusing their services.

Monitoring Social Media and Networking Sites

In seeking compliance from online auction sites and Internet trade boards, as well as from Web hosts and online service providers, many companies have also begun to monitor social media and networking sites for ongoing counterfeit activities. Web-based social networking services provide a new, dynamic platform by which counterfeiters are positioned to reach across the expanse of the Internet and target potential consumers of their goods. Social networking sites often manifest in different forms, but, fundamentally, each platform attempts to serve the essential purpose of building an online community in order to better expand and refine relationships among people (e.g., Facebook, MySpace, Twitter, LinkedIn).

Most sites follow a similar model that provides users with the option of uploading a profile photo, listing personal information, and building a larger social network by inviting other members to join their networks. In order to join a particular network, the invited member must accept the networking request in order to bridge the gap between the two members. Once the request is accepted, both members are provided access to each respective profile, which often includes a list of contacts on each profile that can be utilized to build an even larger social network. Individual users are not the only parties that use social networking sites to expand their networks. Different industries and businesses alike also take advantage of social networking sites to market and promote their products and services, and they are uniquely equipped with their own networks to share their ideas and interests across other networks. This increased exposure not only allows established brands to build upon their reputation, but also provides an avenue for smaller brands to introduce their products and services to a large, available community of online consumers.

As social networking sites have started to become an essential part of the overall structure of the Internet, counterfeiters have also shifted their business strategy to begin promoting their goods in a unique and original manner through these sites. If available by the site, some counterfeiters utilize private groups to promote and sell their products. Members create groups in order to provide a venue for other members to meet and share interests and affiliations. Though some groups are not capable of being accessed unless approved by the group administrator, many groups are publicly accessible and any member of the site can access the contents of the group at will. With groups being so easily searchable and neatly organized according to subject matter, counterfeiters create groups and use them not only as a means to widely promote their products, but also to drive online traffic to any number of their counterfeit sites existing online. This can be accomplished by simply listing the URL for the counterfeit web site in the group page itself or by providing an actual link to the web site that contains the infringing merchandise. These groups are often utilized by counterfeiters to advertise purse parties as well, which are gatherings held at a host's or hostess's designated location to sell, distribute, and purchase counterfeit merchandise. With such avenues being exploited, it becomes crucial for brand owners to monitor this behavior and control counterfeiting in new and creative ways.

Though social networking sites can provide an innovative platform for brand owners to use in starting or continuing to promote goods or services, it is certainly in the best interest of a company to focus on the potential problems they pose. Corporate behavior has been adapting to the issues posed by social networking and taking charge of monitoring activity on sites where counterfeit sellers have been advertising or offering counterfeit products. Companies have started to exercise their right to draft weekly—or even daily—takedown notices to sites listing publicly available groups or profiles that advertise or sell counterfeit goods, in order to better protect their valuable IP rights. When subject to compliance by social networking service providers, these programs can be very effective at controlling the problem of counterfeiting and helping to reduce the overall visibility of infringing products on popular online platforms.

Partnering with Outside Legal Counsel

Along with the implementation of a strategic online anti-counterfeiting program, brand owners frequently partner with outside counsel to achieve comprehensive brand protection by assessing the benefits and risks of engaging in various enforcement strategies to protect their IP rights. In the United States, brand owners are often confronted with a recurring dilemma when choosing how to deal with specific counterfeiters who have been identified: whether to initiate civil litigation against the counterfeiter at the brand owner's own expense, or to attempt to secure law enforcement interest in pursuing the case at the public's expense. Each form of brand protection has its own benefits and drawbacks, and each case must be evaluated independently on its own facts and merits.

In recent years, brand owners have lobbied successfully for statutory mechanisms that permit the civil litigant to exercise a fair degree of control over potentially harsh remedies, including a form of "search and seizure" activity known as the "*ex parte* seizure" power. This power enables a brand owner to put counterfeiting at an immediate halt. However, while on paper these legislative enactments seem to impose heavy penalties on counterfeiters, in practice, they are often underutilized, misunderstood, or simply ignored by brand owners, in many cases because of expense and risk.

One of the key roles of outside legal counsel is to advise a brand owner by evaluating which targets are appropriate for civil litigation and which are most amenable to criminal prosecution. Experienced outside counsel can work with prosecutors and law enforcement officials to help prepare the case against the counterfeiter both before and after indictment.

Civil Action

The Lanham Act is the key federal statute governing civil trademark counterfeiting.[4] Sections 32 and 43 of the Lanham Trademark Act allow brand owners to pursue civil actions against trademark infringers and counterfeiters.[5] The Lanham Act provides several remedies to brand owners. These remedies include actual or statutory damages, preliminary and/or permanent injunctions, seizure and destruction of the counterfeit goods, as well as potential reimbursement for litigation costs and, in exceptional cases, reimbursement of attorneys' fees.[6] Additionally, federal courts may order the seizure of infringing goods and records relating to such goods through a proceeding initiated by the brand owner, without the adversary being given advance notice or warning.[7]

BENEFITS OF CIVIL ACTION   One of the primary benefits of initiating a civil action is that brand owners are able to exert a high degree of control over the course of the proceedings. Brand owners choose which counterfeiters to target in a civil action and can focus their resources on higher-priority targets. Brand owners also decide where and when to litigate, and also choose whether to settle once litigation has commenced.

Once a potential target is identified, before a civil action can be filed, brand owners and their investigators are responsible for investigating and collecting evidence.[8,9] In many cases, a private investigation may reveal additional targets as well as third parties that may be liable to the brand owner. Relevant third parties may include independent Internet sites trafficking in counterfeit goods, Internet service providers (ISPs), landlords, and/or flea markets that knowingly facilitate the sale of counterfeits or are "willfully blind" to such sales.[10] In cases where the real party responsible for the nefarious activity cannot be found or where the same third party repeatedly is involved, third-party claims may be appropriate and effective.

Initiating civil litigation also gives brand owners flexibility on the substantive merits of the claims that is unavailable in criminal proceedings. For example, a criminal complaint can be filed only against a counterfeiter who is imitating a registered trademark. However, to file a civil action, brand owners need not have a registered mark to claim trademark infringement under Section 43(a) of the Lanham Act.[11] Brand owners may also take action against two types of targets: (1) those who produce and sell *counterfeits*; and (2) those who produce and sell *knockoffs*. Counterfeit goods are those that bear a mark that is identical to, or substantially indistinguishable from, a registered trademark.[12] Knockoffs, however, are goods that are likely to cause confusion with the brand owner's goods when used in commerce, but either do not contain an identical mark or infringe unregistered "trade dress."[13] A brand owner, therefore, could take civil legal action against targets who infringe its registered trademarks or the trade dress of a product in a manner that is likely to cause confusion, whereas criminal laws are more circumscribed.

In civil actions, brand owners enjoy two benefits that may facilitate successful claims. First, a brand owner need not prove that a defendant intended to counterfeit goods or otherwise infringe on its IP rights in order to bring a successful claim.[14] Proving intent, however, entitles a brand owner to additional remedies such as treble damages, attorneys' fees, destruction of infringing articles, and elevated statutory damages (as discussed later).[15] Second, in civil actions, the evidentiary burden of proof is lower—brand owners must prove infringement by preponderance of the evidence, rather than beyond a reasonable doubt.[16]

Civil actions also afford brand owners numerous and flexible remedies that are unavailable in criminal proceedings. One major advantage of civil actions is that defendants pay monetary damage awards directly to the brand owner. In comparison, criminal defendants typically pay punitive fines directly to the government.[17] While recovery of restitution damages is available, it is not always the norm.

Under the Lanham Act, brand owners may claim either actual or statutory damages. Actual damages include the defendant's profits, any damages sustained by the brand owner, and the costs of the action.[18] If infringement is intentional, brand owners also may be entitled to treble profits or treble damages, whichever is greater, as well as attorney's fees.[19] The statutory damages provisions of the Lanham Act relieve the plaintiff of the burden of proving actual damages. Statutory damages range up to a maximum of $100,000 per mark infringed and, in cases of willful violation, up to $1 million per mark.[20] However, because so many counterfeiters are judgment-proof or have assets that are very well hidden, the most important remedy often may be injunctive relief.[21]

For defendants who are large-scale distributors, among the most potent remedies is the right to seize counterfeit goods and records documenting the manufacture, sale, or receipt of such goods and to impound devices that are used solely to make counterfeit goods. Seizure can sometimes be obtained on an *ex parte* basis, before the counterfeiter has a chance to destroy or hide helpful evidence.[22] Because *ex parte* seizure is an extraordinary remedy, there are stringent requirements for obtaining such relief. Seizure and other expedited remedies (such as asset freezes) are powerful weapons because they disrupt the offender's activities and make it more difficult for the counterfeiter to resume the activities elsewhere under a new name. Such *ex parte* seizures often involve federal law enforcement officials and may have a deterrent effect on targets.

Brand owners also can opt to use expedited civil remedies such as temporary restraining orders and preliminary injunctions. These remedies allow brand owners to take quick and decisive action against counterfeiters, whereas criminal investigations often may be protracted and slow moving.

Finally, a permanent injunction is a highly effective remedy against counterfeiting. If brand owners who have permanently enjoined a target from counterfeiting their goods discover that the target continues its activities, they can obtain fines and jail time for contempt of court. In a criminal action, brand owners would have to initiate additional, separate criminal proceedings to stop targets that have been found criminally liable from engaging in future counterfeit activities.

DRAWBACKS OF CIVIL ACTION The primary drawback of taking civil action against counterfeiters is that it is usually more costly to a brand owner than merely cooperating with a criminal proceeding. Because brand owners are responsible for the entire proceeding, they must pay for private investigators and outside legal counsel. Furthermore, the remedies available to brand owners in civil actions arguably have less of a deterrent effect on would-be counterfeiters than the criminal penalties they might otherwise face. That being said, in civil actions, monetary damage awards may be extremely high, and the potential effects on a target's pocketbook may be as great a deterrent as criminal penalties.

Brand owners should also be aware that when they bring civil actions, defendants may respond with counterclaims. In civil trademark actions, these counterclaims often include claims for declaratory judgment to cancel the brand owner's mark on grounds that the mark was procured by fraud or is invalid because it is generic or merely descriptive of the brand owner's goods.[23] Defendants may also allege that the brand owner is using the mark to violate antitrust laws. Antitrust counterclaims can be onerous and expensive to defend, and can open the brand owner up to far-reaching and intrusive discovery.

Criminal Action

With the Lanham Act functioning as the key federal statute governing trademark counterfeiting in the civil context, there are also various federal and state statutes governing anti-counterfeiting in the criminal context. The Trademark Counterfeiting Act of 1984[24] criminally punishes anyone who "intentionally traffics or attempts to traffic in goods or services and knowingly uses a counterfeit mark on or in connection with such goods or services."[25] Also noteworthy is the Anti-Counterfeiting Consumer Protection Act of 1996, which amended the Racketeer Influenced and Corrupt Organizations Act (RICO) to include criminal infringement of a copyright, trafficking in goods or services bearing counterfeit marks, and trafficking in counterfeit labels for phonorecords, computer programs, computer program documentation, or packaging and copies of motion pictures or other audiovisual works.[26] Additionally, each state has its own anti-counterfeiting criminal statutes. For example, New York has three criminal statutes ranging from third- to first-degree liability for trademark counterfeiting. First-degree counterfeiting is considered a class C felony.[27]

BENEFITS OF CRIMINAL ACTION Criminal prosecution of counterfeiters affords the brand owners numerous advantages. Unlike in civil actions, a defendant can be sentenced to prison if found guilty, in addition to being fined for his or her actions. The Trademark Counterfeiting Act of 1984, for example, carries with it a maximum term of imprisonment of 10 years for a given violation.[28] Imprisonment is a particularly effective deterrent to other counterfeiters or persons contemplating a similar violation, especially considering the possibility of such harsh sentencing if apprehended.

Further, criminal prosecutions require a relatively lower expenditure of time and resources on the part of the brand owner. In a criminal prosecution, the brand owner is a witness and not a party to the action. Therefore, pleadings, motion practice, and discovery efforts are all but eliminated in this context. Further, evidence gathering cannot be achieved via discovery, but instead through various investigative mechanisms accessible only to law enforcement (e.g., arrest, interrogation, search warrants). As such, criminal prosecution is largely within the hands of law enforcement officials, which substantially lessens the burden on the part of the brand owner.

Similar to a drug trade investigation, the less sophisticated counterfeiters often are only small players in large, heavily resourced counterfeiting operations. Prosecuting the small-scale offender, who often is easier to apprehend, puts pressure on the more sophisticated parties involved, and on their operation as a whole by interrupting cash flow and eroding isolated components of the greater counterfeiting mechanism. This process may lead to the identification and prosecution of those with greater power and authority within the criminal organization.

DRAWBACKS OF CRIMINAL ACTION   Notwithstanding its benefits, however, criminal counterfeiting prosecution presents a myriad of disadvantages from the brand owner's perspective. While having less control over criminal proceedings can eliminate the brand owner's burden significantly, by relinquishing control a brand owner also relinquishes its power to affect the prosecution's outcome. The U.S. attorney wields enormous power and authority over the result of a criminal investigation, as ultimately he or she decides whether to accept a defendant's plea. Further, the U.S. attorney decides whether to even proceed with a prosecution. Any lack of interest on the U.S. attorney's part may relegate a brand owner's concerns to little more than a filed complaint. This lack of control may also translate to an unwanted delay in criminal actions taken against an identified counterfeiter. Law enforcement and federal agencies may lack the requisite resources or interest necessary to pursue an investigation.

Further, it can be more difficult for a brand owner to obtain protection of its marks via criminal proceedings. The burden of proof is extremely high. To prevail, the government must demonstrate beyond a reasonable doubt that the defendant violated the governing statute. This is much greater than the preponderance of evidence standard adhered to in civil cases. What is more, some criminal statutes require a showing of criminal intent, also a greater burden than that required by the Lanham Act.[29] Finally, while a favorable ruling in civil court would effectively enjoin the infringer from future violations against the brand owner, a favorable outcome in criminal court usually will not result in an injunction. Instead, in the event that a previously convicted counterfeiter violates the statute, he or she must be prosecuted anew, as the prior conviction does not afford the brand owner any protection.

Pursuing a criminal conviction may present various obstacles that are not present in a civil context. For instance, law enforcement officials can prosecute counterfeit goods, but not goods that rise only to the level of infringement.[30] Therefore, despite the injury that these infringing items can cause a brand owner, the criminal justice system provides no protection and no recourse. Civil proceedings also may be substantially delayed by ongoing and concurrent criminal proceedings. For example, in the interests of justice, courts often will stay civil actions pending resolution of a criminal action.[31] Civil suits also may be hindered if defendants in a parallel criminal action invoke Fifth Amendment rights with respect to discovery demands made in the civil action.

While imprisonment is certainly an advantage unique to criminal prosecution, it also may have negative implications. Criminal lawsuits leading to convictions and/or imprisonment tend to generate an enormous amount of publicity for the brand owner. Although favorable publicity describing and promoting a brand is always welcome, numerous criminal prosecutions may shift focus from the product(s) itself, creating instead a public association of the brand with criminal prosecutions and/or convictions.

Finally, unlike in civil actions, a brand owner cannot collect damages or attorney's fees if an alleged counterfeiter is convicted in criminal court. While a convicted counterfeiter may be fined for his actions, fines are paid directly to the government and not to the brand owner. A brand owner may be entitled to restitution, but such recovery usually is limited to a brand owner's investigation costs (usually minimal since investigative tasks are primarily conducted by law enforcement) and any actual lost sales. Though recovery of lost sales may appear promising initially, it is extremely difficult to prove actual lost sales—particularly when dealing with a counterfeiter who more than likely did not maintain the comprehensive bookkeeping procedures of a legitimate, established business operation.

Conclusion

This chapter has reflected on the recent changes in corporate behavior as they apply to controlling counterfeiting, as well as the modern enforcement strategies being utilized by brand owners in the pursuit of protecting their trademarks on the Internet and beyond. The growth of counterfeiting as an industry has truly stimulated corporate responsibility to place emphasis on regulating the conduct of infringers by means of in-house enforcement and partnering with experienced outside legal counsel to combat the problems that threaten the integrity of their valuable brands. By incorporating and following a comprehensive enforcement program, brand owners provide insulation for their brands against the growth of counterfeiting throughout the world. The rapid development of the Internet has provided tremendous opportunities for counterfeiters to perfect their trade and expand their businesses far beyond the scope of what may have been intended originally. With corporate decision makers now recognizing the detrimental effects that these businesses have on the overall integrity of their brands, new and creative ways to control the problem of counterfeiting are becoming more necessary in order to successfully achieve the goal of complete brand protection.

Notes

[1] See also Dennis S. Prahl & Elliot Lipins, "Domain Names," Chap. 5.

[2] See *Tiffany and Company v. eBay, Inc.,* 2008 U.S. Dist. (S.D.N.Y., July 14, 2008) (holding that the online marketplace could not be held liable vicariously for trademark infringement based solely on the generalized knowledge that infringement is occurring as a result of sales made through that marketplace).

[3] See *Louis Vuitton Malletier, S.A. v. Akanoc Solutions, Inc. and Managed Solutions Group, Inc.* (N.D. Cal. 2007) (holding web site hosting companies liable for contributory and vicarious trademark infringement and contributory and vicarious copyright infringement for failing to disable or limit web site hosting services that customers were using to sell counterfeit goods).

[4] There are many state and local laws that address trademark counterfeiting.

[5] 15 U.S.C. §§ 1114, 1125.

[6] 15 U.S.C. §§ 1114, 1116–1118.

[7] 15 U.S.C. § 1116.

[8] See also Jeremiah A. Pastrick, "Investigations: Considerations for Selecting and Directing Outside Investigators," Chap. 13.

[9] Outside counsel frequently retain private investigators and supervise their investigation.

[10] See, for example, N.Y.Real.Prop. § 231 (holding a landlord liable for knowingly leasing real property that is used for any unlawful trade, manufacture, or business).

[11] 15 U.S.C. § 1125.

[12] 15 U.S.C. § 1116(d).

[13] 15 U.S.C. § 1125(a).

[14] 15 U.S.C. § 1117, 1125.

[15] 15 U.S.C. § 1117(b).

[16] See, for example, *Thane Int'l, Inc. v. Trek Bicycle Corp.,* 305 F.3d 894, 901 (9th Cir. 2002) (stating that a trademark owner bringing a claim under Section 43(a) of the Lanham Act must prove on a preponderance of the evidence that the alleged infringer's mark is likely to cause confusion, to cause mistake, or to deceive).

[17] Criminal proceedings may provide brand owners with restitution, which is generally limited to the costs of investigation and lost sales. Lost sales are difficult to prove. See discussion, *infra.*

[18] 15 U.S.C. § 1117(a).

[19] 15 U.S.C. § 1117(b).

[20] 15 U.S.C. § 1117(c).

[21] 15 U.S.C. § 1116.

[22] 15 U.S.C. § 1117(d).

[23] 15 U.S.C. § 1115(b).

[24] 18 U.S.C. § 2320.

[25] 18 U.S.C. § 2320(a).

[26] 18 U.S.C.A. § 1961.

[27] N.Y. Penal Law §§ 165.71–165.73.

[28]See *U.S. v. Hanna,* 2003 WL 22705133, at *2 (S.D.N.Y., November 17, 2003).

[29]See *U.S. v. Hon,* 904 F.2d 803, 806 (2d Cir. 1990).

[30]For example, the Second Circuit noted in *U.S. v. Hon* that the Trademark Counterfeiting Act of 1984 is "'narrower' than the Lanham Act provision [and] . . . proscribes only the use of counterfeits—marks 'identical with, or substantially indistinguishable from' a registered trademark—while Lanham Act liability may rest upon not only a 'counterfeit' but also a 'reproduction,' 'copy' or 'colorable imitation.'" 904 F.2d 803, 806 (2d Cir. 1990).

[31]"When a defendant in a civil case is facing criminal charges, a district court may, in its discretion, stay the civil action." *U.S. ex rel. Gonzalez v. Fresenius Medical Care North America,* 571 F.Supp.2d 758, 761(W.D. Tex. 2008), citing *United States v. Kordel,* 397 U.S. 1 (1970); see also *In re Ramu Corp.,* 903 F.2d 312, 318 (5th Cir. 1990) ("The stay of a pending matter is ordinarily within the trial court's wide discretion to control the course of litigation, which includes authority to control the scope and pace of discovery.").

CHAPTER 2

Electronic Discovery in Intellectual Property Cases

Jennifer R. Martin
Symantec Corporation

C ompany servers, databases, personal computers, backup tapes, handheld devices, and, most recently, the Internet "cloud" can contain a treasure trove of compelling evidence relevant in every type of investigation or litigation matter, big or small, criminal or civil. The information explosion and the concomitant escalation of costs associated with handling data during litigation is cause for significant concern among corporate litigants, in-house and outside counsel, and the judiciary, among others, and has resulted in untold numbers of conferences, workshops, articles, and legislative proposals to address the problems associated with electronic discovery. Indeed, growing litigation costs, coupled with concerns over the efficacy of current e-discovery practices and the gamesmanship of the parties during the discovery phase, have, in recent years, driven the evolution of the law in this area, and have arguably resulted in some dramatic paradigm shifts in long-standing notions governing the "adversarial process." Failures by parties to meet their discovery obligations also have resulted in serious sanctions against companies and sometimes their counsel for the resulting spoliation of evidence. Accordingly, it behooves all attorneys to stay abreast of the legal developments and their professional obligations in this area, and the very serious consequences that can result from a misstep during the electronic discovery phase. In addition to understanding their litigation obligations, however, smart litigants should also begin to think strategically about how best to economically and intelligently manage, store, and organize information relevant in their practice areas prior to litigation ever commencing.

This chapter provides an overview of the electronic discovery process for parties and their lawyers to prepare in advance for the electronic discovery phase of litigation. The key electronic discovery holdings and rules discussed herein apply to all types of cases; however, the information is presented within the context of intellectual property (IP) litigation. In addition, to the extent possible, essential e-discovery concepts and issues are illustrated through discussions of key IP cases; notably, many of the most important recent judicial holdings in this area have arisen in the context of contentious IP battles. This chapter also discusses some of the current legal and judicial trends intended to mitigate the mounting costs of electronic discovery.

Electronic Discovery Process

Although the electronic discovery life cycle, as described pictorially in Figure 2.1, really begins with managing information so that it is easily identified once a party's litigation obligations are triggered, the focus of this chapter is on parties' responsibilities during the discovery phase of litigation. As discussed more fully at the end of this chapter, however, many of the problems and concerns associated with electronic discovery can be mitigated through smart information management before litigation arises. From organizing data so that it is easily identified and collected, to destroying data that serves no useful business or legal purposes, an organization's decisions and policies governing the retention of information for business or other purposes will play a critical role in implementing cost-effective, defensible procedures during electronic discovery. Thus, the last section of this chapter provides some recommendations for managing information in the IP context.

Routine data retention and destruction policies necessarily change once litigation arises. By way of background, the Federal Rules of Civil Procedure, particularly the 2006 amendments addressing electronically stored information, provide the basic road map governing the electronic discovery process during litigation. In recent years, courts throughout the country have supplemented those rules through several key decisions that lay out a more comprehensive legal framework for conducting electronic discovery.

Trigger Event: Anticipation of Litigation

Although the Federal Rules of Civil Procedure do not explicitly spell out when the duty to preserve electronic information for litigation purposes is triggered,[1] it is well

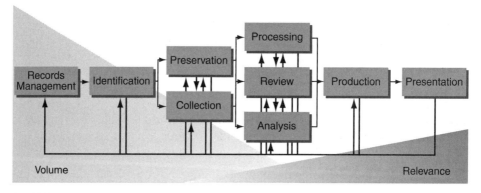

FIGURE 2.1 Electronic Discovery Reference Model

established under the common law that the duty to preserve commences when a party is on notice of a filed litigation or "reasonably anticipates" litigation.[2] Stated otherwise, the obligation to preserve evidence is triggered "when there is knowledge of a potential claim,"[3] or "a reasonable belief that litigation is foreseeable,"[4] or that "litigation is probable" but "more than a possibility."[5] Pinpointing that moment, however, is not always easy.

A series of patent infringement cases asserted by Rambus Inc. over the past decade against numerous potential competitors exemplify the difficulties the courts have had in determining when a plaintiff reasonably anticipates litigation. A lengthy description of Rambus's history and their activities in connection with their preservation obligations is provided in *Micron Technologies v. Rambus*, and may be insightful for the IP practitioner. Briefly, Rambus was founded in 1990 to develop a solution related to the speed with which dynamic random access memory (DRAM) transferred data to and from microprocessors. In April 1990, Rambus filed a patent application for its RDRAM solution, with the hopes of licensing that technology. By 1991, Rambus became concerned that competitors were using its RDRAM technology to develop DRAM solutions and, by the mid-1990s, began working with patent counsel to create a "patent minefield" by filing patent applications for various related technologies.

In February 1998, Rambus began developing a litigation strategy, which included instituting a new document retention policy. Critical to the spoliation challenges later lodged against Rambus, the retention policy included instructions for purging e-mail, called for regular document shredding, and instituted a three-month backup retention policy. Notably, Rambus also retained certain documents that would be helpful to potential patent claims and pulled one backup tape out of the rotation cycle because it contained evidence of invention dates. In April 1999, Rambus directed outside counsel to "clear out" the patent files such that only official documentation was retained, and that summer continued to hold "shred" days to destroy documents. During this same time frame, Rambus continued to prepare for litigation, although it did not yet target any one particular company for suit until later in the year. In the fall of 1999, Rambus obtained board approval to file suit, and in December it instituted a formal litigation hold. In January 2000, Rambus sued the first of its competitors, Hitachi, for patent infringement.

Thereafter, Rambus filed a series of suits against various companies for patent infringement. In one such case, the trial court ordered Rambus to turn over certain privileged documents based on its finding that the timing of the implementation of its retention policy, including the shredding, coincided with Rambus preparing for litigation.[6] In a similar case, however, the trial court held that Rambus had not spoliated by shredding documents because litigation at that time was only possible, and additional preparatory work had to be done before a suit could be filed.[7]

In the most recent case to analyze Rambus's prelitigation conduct, however, the District Court for the District of Delaware found intentional spoliation of documents by Rambus. In so holding, the court found that Rambus had anticipated litigation at least as early as December 1998. As a sanction, the court held that the Rambus patent was unenforceable against Micron.

Notably, the trial court acknowledged that there is nothing wrong under normal circumstances in establishing a retention policy that includes purging unnecessary e-mail and records, and explicitly noted that removing "all materials not part of the official record" from patent-related files is common practice; however, it found that the timing of the institution and execution of such policies in April 1999 exhibited bad faith on the part of Rambus. In particular, it held that Micron had likely been prejudiced by the shredding because documents related to patent misuse and unfair competition would have been destroyed in the process. The court further recognized that even in situations where a company has a well-established retention policy, all routine data destruction must be suspended upon that company anticipating litigation.[8]

In another recent patent infringement case, *Philip M. Adams & Assoc. v. Dell, Inc.,*[9] the court held that the defendant's had a duty to preserve even if it did not anticipate the *specific* litigation at issue. In particular, the court found that, given extensive litigation on the technical issues, including a previous class action, defendants were sufficiently "sensitized" to the issues and potential for litigation prior to notice of the instant suit.[10]

Other scenarios similarly raise tricky questions about when the obligation to preserve documents potentially relevant to litigation is triggered. For example, if a company is faced with foreign regulatory action, should that company, or potential claimant, reasonably anticipate U.S. or state regulatory action or civil claims? When an employee is terminated or leaves a company for a competitor's company, should in-house counsel foresee a potential employment or trade secrets claim? Does a copyright or trademark cease-and-desist letter trigger an alleged infringer's obligations?

Given the very significant sanctions imposed by courts for spoliation of electronic evidence and recent court decisions mandating early cooperation by litigants, attorneys are wise to advise their clients to err on the side of caution and pay early attention to preservation issues—usually earlier than when a complaint is filed or received.

IDENTIFYING RELEVANT "ELECTRONICALLY STORED INFORMATION"   The Federal Rules of Civil Procedure govern the basic obligations relating to the identification, preservation, and disclosure of electronic information once a party reasonably anticipates litigation. In particular, pursuant to Rule 26(b), a party "should produce electronically stored information that is relevant, not privileged, and reasonably accessible," but does not have to produce electronically stored information (commonly referred to as ESI) that it identifies as "not reasonably accessible because of undue burden or cost."[11] *Relevance* is generally assumed to have the same meaning it has under the Federal Rules of Evidence when identifying data to preserve.[12] However, in the spoliation context, the "relevance" of the lost data may be determined by a different standard: "the destroyed or unavailable evidence would have been of the nature alleged by the party affected by its destruction."[13]

The Federal Rules do not define the term *electronically stored information* nor provide guidance on what types of data are and required to be preserved. Clearly, active user-created documents, such as PDF files, Word documents, Excel spreadsheets, e-mail messages and their attachments, and text messages are ESI.[14]

In the copyright context, the term *ESI* has been broadly construed. In *Columbia Pictures v. Bunnell,*[15] for example, the court held that data stored temporarily in random access memory (RAM) could have been logged and preserved, and therefore was ESI within the scope of the Federal rules. The *Bunnell* case involved a copyright claim brought by Columbia Pictures against Bunnell for running a peer-to-peer file sharing system in which users could exchange copyrighted material. Bunnell, who ran the site from Holland, argued that he had no duty to preserve connection logs showing the Internet protocol (IP) addresses of the users who had used the system, in part because the logging system had not been configured to save those logs. The court held, however, that Bunnell could have, and should have, configured the system to retain the connection logs once the suit had been filed. Although the decision on spoliation was overturned on appeal, the trial court's ruling that the log information constituted ESI was not.

The *Viacom v. YouTube*[16] copyright infringement litigation, which was dismissed on summary judgment, also produced a series of rulings on the parties' obligations to preserve and produce various sorts of electronic data. In particular, the court ordered YouTube to produce millions of videos that it had made available to the public, and 12 terabytes of logging information including the unique login IDs and IP addresses for users viewing videos on YouTube. The *Viacom* court, however, rejected Viacom's discovery requests for video source code, which YouTube uses to search for potentially infringing videos, and YouTube's database schema used to track advertising revenues. In each of these cases, the court appears to have recognized that such materials constitute relevant ESI, but balanced the interests of the parties, including the burdens, needs, and proprietary concerns, in making its determinations.

Parties in litigation also are obligated to preserve certain types of latent data. For example, it is well established that, in most situations, the underlying metadata associated with electronic documents should be properly preserved and produced along with the documents.[17] Metadata can be critical to establishing original ownership and creation dates in all types of IP cases, and especially in cases alleging the misappropriation of valuable proprietary information.

Similarly, deleted data recoverable from a desktop or laptop hard drive may be essential in a theft of trade secrets case.[18] Besides recoverable deleted data, hard drives can contain other types of records of user activity relevant to an IP investigation, including records showing onward transmission of data to others, Web-browsing activity, the use of data destruction programs, and connection logs.

IDENTIFYING THE LOCATION OF RELEVANT ESI Identifying what kind of data should be preserved requires some basic knowledge as to where and what information is stored by an organization or individual, and how best to access and preserve it. Generally, data resides on the following digital media within an organization: local hard drives (desktops and laptops) and storage devices (thumb drives, external hard drives, DVDs), e-mail servers and e-mail archives, file servers, handheld devices, backup tapes, and databases.The make, manufacturer, and version of each piece of media vary from organization to organization, as do the various settings and policies. Because no two organizations have the same information technology (IT) infrastructures and data policies, it is incumbent on attorneys to work closely with IT personnel and others to understand the digital environment in each particular case.[19]

In addition, litigants are obligated to preserve data stored with third-party storage providers and vendors; indeed, as companies move their ESI into "the cloud" they should be cognizant of the complex legal and contractual concerns that may impact their ability to fulfill their e-discovery obligations. Finally, relevant ESI may also reside within custodians' personal devices and accounts, including social media accounts.

It is also essential for counsel, human resources, and IT personnel to work together to secure information that resides in legacy systems, as well as current systems, and from departing employees as well as active employees. Moreover, as previously noted, counsel must also educate themselves on specific technological features, procedures, and default settings of their clients' systems, and develop a detailed preservation plan with IT staff to ensure that data is not overwritten, auto-deleted, or recycled, and that the technical preservation routines capture the relevant data.[20] For example, backup tape rotation cycles must be understood so that backup tapes corresponding to key time periods and custodians are not destroyed,[21] and e-mail auto-delete settings generally must be turned off.[22]

LITIGATION HOLD NOTICES   Although the requirement to notify relevant custodians regarding their preservation obligations is well-established, in a notable 2010 Southern District of New York, *Pension Committee of the University of Montreal Pension Plan et al. v. Bank of America Securities, LLC,* the court held that "the failure to issue a *written* litigation hold constitutes gross negligence because that failure is likely to result in the destruction of relevant information."[23] Although it is not clear whether other jurisdictions will apply this arguably new *per se* standard,[24] companies and their attorneys are reminded to send clear written notice to custodians and key personnel, including designated IT staff, of their preservation obligations. Such notice should clearly describe the nature of the potential litigation and the types of relevant documents (both paper and ESI) that should be retained. It should also provide instructions for preserving those documents pursuant to sound technical means, and for labeling such documents for easy collection. Notice may be inadequate if "[i]t does not direct employees to *preserve* all relevant records—both paper and electronic—[or if it does not] create a mechanism for collecting the preserved records so that they can be searched by someone other than employees."[25] The litigation hold notice must be issued within a reasonable time of the event triggering the duty to preserve.[26] Moreover, reminders must be periodically issued, and certainly should be reissued after large time lapses in the prosecution of cases.[27] In *Pension Committee*, Plaintiffs retained counsel in 2003, and litigation was commenced in 2004 in Florida. Although the plaintiffs began to collect documents in late 2003, electronic discovery efforts were largely halted when a stay was initiated in 2004. The case was transferred to New York in October 2005, and the stay was lifted in 2007, at which time the plaintiffs also issued their first written litigation hold notice. The New York District Court held that the plaintiff's failure to issue a written litigation hold notice in 2005, when the case was transferred to New York, was grossly negligent.[28] Specifically, because the duty to issue such a notice had been established in the Southern District of New York as early as 2004, a written litigation hold notice should have been issued in 2005 despite the litigation stay.[29]

At least in the Southern District, relying on employees' self-collection and review also may be *per se* negligent, and companies are advised not to place "total reliance" on employees to find records that are responsive.[30] Moreover, counsel is obligated to oversee and monitor preservation and production of documents, and should instruct their clients not to destroy records before counsel has had the opportunity to adequately review and monitor compliance.[31]

As a practical matter, litigation hold strategies must be designed to cover employees, systems, and data sources that are reasonably likely to have information. In order to draft an adequate litigation hold notice, it is incumbent on attorneys to work closely with IT personnel and outside experts to understand, for example, where relevant data may reside, what default settings on data destruction need to be suspended, and what backup tapes should be pulled to prevent their being recycled. In short, counsel bears the burden not only to identify where relevant data might reside, but to actively supervise the preservation effort *beyond sending out notice.*[32]

NOT REASONABLY ACCESSIBLE ESI   As noted earlier, a party "does not have to produce ESI that it identifies as "not reasonably accessible because of undue burden or cost."[33] In most jurisdictions, determining whether data is reasonably accessible depends on multiple variables within the context of the particular litigation. Moreover, as technologies evolve, what was not reasonably accessible several years ago because of costs may now be readily accessed.

Notably, even if data is deemed "not reasonably accessible" for purposes of search, review, and production, such data often must still be preserved. Indeed, in cases where spoliation does arise, the preservation of such data often is critical to remediation efforts and to avoiding the most serious sanctions. The Committee Notes to Rule 26(b) recognize the obligation to preserve "not reasonably accessible" data in the first instance, and the potential need to resort to such data at a later time in the course of discovery:

> *A party's identification of sources of electronically stored information as not reasonably accessible does not relieve the party of its common-law or statutory duties to preserve evidence. Whether a responding party is required to preserve unsearched sources of potentially responsive information that it believes are not reasonably accessible depends on the circumstances of each case. It is often useful for the parties to discuss this issue early in discovery.*[34]

The Committee Notes further state:

> *Whether good faith would call for steps to prevent the loss of information on sources that the party believes are not reasonably accessible under rule 26(b)(2) depends on the circumstances of each case. One factor is whether the party reasonably believes that the information on such sources is likely to be discoverable* and not available from reasonably accessible sources.[35]

While the court in *Zubulake I* stated that whether something is reasonably accessible turns on the type of media at issue,[36] other courts have recognized that such a determination is instead dependent on the nature of the case and the resources of the party bearing the burden to produce the ESI.[37] Thus, litigants should not presume that certain ESI is not reasonably accessible just because it resides on a particular type of media; such determinations vary from jurisdiction to jurisdiction and case to case.

Generally, challenges to determinations on what types of ESI are "not reasonably accessible" are resolved in the context of a motion to compel, and the party from whom discovery is sought must show that the information is not reasonably accessible because of undue burden or cost. The party making such a claim must make some reasonable inquiry into the costs and burdens before claiming data is not reasonably accessible.[38] Certainly, bald assertions that discovery will be burdensome are insufficient.[39]

In deciding whether a party has carried its burden of defending an assertion of inaccessibility depends on the strength of its case, including the use of expert testimony. For example, in cases involving the accessibility of data stored on backup tapes, the same court on the same day came to two different conclusions on restoration of such tapes based, in part, on the lack of an expert opinion supporting the cost assertions in the case in which it ordered restoration.[40]

Even where a party carries its burden of showing that ESI is not reasonably accessible, a court may nonetheless order discovery, and shift costs upon a showing of "good cause." Although different courts consider different factors, generally courts consider the following in determining whether to order discovery:[41]

- Whether the data is obtainable from other less burdensome sources.
- Whether the benefits of the data to the litigation outweigh the burdens or production, considering
  - Amount in controversy.
  - Parties' resources.
  - Importance of issues.
- Whether the party seeking discovery delayed in trying to obtain the data at issue.

Whether a court decides to shift costs to reduce the burden may also depend on the actions of the parties during the discovery process. Of course, affirmatively deciding to preserve data in an inaccessible format will not relieve a party of its obligations to then produce that data.[42] It also may depend on whether the parties have been forthcoming in fulfilling their e-discovery obligations.[43]

Other Federal Rules Governing the Electronic Discovery Phase

Attorneys and their clients should be aware of all of the Federal Rules of Civil Procedure governing the electronic discovery process. For purposes of this chapter, some of the key provisions are briefly discussed here.

1. RULE 26(f): MEET AND CONFER Pursuant to Rule 26(f), the parties to a litigation must meet and confer "as soon as practicable" to "discuss any issues relating to preserving discoverable information" and other key ESI issues. Those issues may include the form of production, search methodologies and search terms, and issues relating to claims of privilege, including negotiating clawback agreements.

Given an increasing emphasis by the courts on parties' obligations to cooperate, parties should come prepared both legally and technicallyfor the meet-and-confer and take advantage of the opportunity to resolve any difficult discovery issues. Indeed, it inures to the benefit of the litigants to discuss ahead of time a proposed preservation strategy, develop search terms, and discuss the process for resolving technical problems or how difficult data will be handled. Presumably, early good faith discussions on the scope of the litigants' obligations and the handling of data will reduce the likelihood of spoliation challenges later. Another issue that might be discussed during an early meet-and-confer is any concern regarding what materials are "not reasonably accessible."

2. RULE 34(b): FORM OF PRODUCTION Rule 34(b) relates to the "form" in which ESI is produced. Specifically, in the absence of a request for a specific form of production, the responding party must produce the information "in a form or forms in which it is ordinarily maintained or in a form or forms that are reasonably usable." There are various formats in which to produce and receive data productions: "native" electronic files; load files for litigation support database systems (Concordance, Summation); and processed files loaded into Web-based review platforms, which generally allow for review in both native and image form. Parties should make clear up front the preferred format, but in any case should receive data in a format that preserves useful metadata and file path information. In this day and age, printouts of documents that are difficult to authenticate are arguably an unreasonable form of production.

3. RULE 37(F): SAFE HARBOR Rule 37(f) is referred to as the Safe Harbor provision, but can be dangerous for the unwary. Rule 37(f) provides: "Absent exceptional circumstances, a court may not impose sanctions under these rules on a party for failing to provide electronically stored information lost as a result of the routine, good-faith operation of an electronic information system." The systems to which it applies include e-mail auto-delete functions, backup tape rotation cycles, and normal data loss due to routine computer use.

Although framed as an exception, the rule does not permit a party to continue with business as usual if doing so will destroy information relevant to litigation. A failure to suspend an automated system that results in deletion may subject a litigant to a finding of negligence, and sanctions.[44] Moreover, a deliberate failure to intervene in routine information systems to prevent deletion where the party knows relevant information will be lost is not "good faith" and is subject to significant sanctions.

Spoliation

"Spoliation is the destruction or significant alteration of evidence, or the failure to preserve property for another's use as evidence, in pending or reasonably foreseeable litigation."[45] Generally, the sanctions for spoliation vary from jurisdiction to jurisdiction depending on the *mens rea* of the party charged with spoliation, and the prejudice to the other party.[46] Sanctions range from cost shifting to adverse inference instructions to entry of default judgment. Generally, the Fifth, Seventh, Eighth, Tenth,

Eleventh, and DC Circuits appear to require *bad faith* to impose adverse inference instructions; the First, Fourth, and Ninth Circuits require "severe prejudice"; the Second Circuit allows an adverse inference sanction for "negligent destruction of evidence"; and the Third Circuit balances degree of fault and prejudice.[47]

The court's power to sanction parties for spoliation emanates from its inherent powers, as well as from Rule 37, "Failure to Make Disclosure or Cooperate in Discovery: Sanctions." It is generally accepted that "a court should always impose the least harsh sanction that can provide an adequate remedy."[58] It is also widely accepted that default judgments are justified only in the most egregious cases.[59] Regardless of jurisdiction, however, damages resulting from spoliation can be significant: in *Zubulake V* the jury found for the plaintiff and awarded her $29 million in compensatory and punitive damages after an adverse inference instruction was given; in *Morgan Stanley*, the jury awarded Coleman Holdings $604 million in compensatory damages, and $850 million in punitive damages after default judgment sanction (although the case was overturned, the spoliation finding was not); and in *Qualcomm*, the court invalidated Qualcomm's patents and ordered Qualcomm to pay defendant Broadcom Corp.'s attorneys' fees and costs throughout the litigation—an amount totaling approximately $8.5 million.

Although a complete discussion of spoliation proceedings is beyond the scope of this chapter, to prevail on a spoliation claim a party must show the following:

- A duty to preserve evidence existed at the time of data loss.[48]
- Data loss.
- Culpability.
- The data lost was relevant and resulted in prejudice, although the burden to show prejudice may only apply if the culpability falls below some standard of gross negligence or willfulness, depending on the jurisdiction.

While the duty to preserve often will rest on whether a party "anticipated litigation" at the time of the loss, the other elements of a spoliation claim often require forensic expertise to prove. For example, although culpability can rest on a smoking gun or communication about destruction, more often than not it depends on circumstantial forensic evidence. Although the use of wiping utilities and reinstallation of operating systems is strong forensic evidence of intentional destruction,[49] more subtle forms of data destruction can result in sanctions. For example, in *Arista Records v. Tschirhart*,[50] the court ordered default judgment after a forensic examiner determined that a defragmentation program was run at key moments in litigation, and not on a routine basis. Similarly, in *Minnesota Mining & Mfg. v. Pribyl*,[51] the appellate court affirmed a negative inference instruction where defendant downloaded six gigabytes (GBs) of music the night before he was supposed to turn over his laptop, thereby erasing files.

The degree of culpability is critical to whether and which party bears the burden of proving relevance and prejudice. As noted previously, in the spoliation context, lost data is "relevant" "if it would have been of the nature alleged by the party affected by its destruction."[52] Most courts do not require proof of prejudice where intentional or willful destruction is found.[53] Where destruction is the result of negligence, the party seeking sanctions generally must prove prejudice.[54] However, in *Pension Committee*, the court held that relevance and prejudice is presumed where data destruction was the result of gross negligence.[55] Moreover, what constitutes negligence is highly dependent on common law precedents. In *Pension Committee*, however, Judge Scheindlin arguably drew some bright-line rules for application in the Southern District of New York. Those include:

- Gross negligence: failure to issue written litigation hold notice.
- Negligence: self-collection and review.
- Negligence: failure to image (*"all steps necessary"*).
- Gross negligence: loss of any e-mail.

Relevance and prejudice can be particularly difficult to prove when it is required. To the extent spoliation can be remediated through other sources, prejudice can be mitigated. However, in *Harkabi v. SanDisk Corp.*, although the court recognized that remediation through other sources had been largely successful, the court still ordered sanctions because of the delay caused by the spoliation, lack of attorney oversight, and the fact that the defendant's spoliation would not have been discovered but for the fact of plaintiff's perseverance.[56]

Remediation sources often include backup tapes and other inaccessible data stores, collection of data from noncustodians who might have been copied on e-mail, and collection from third parties. Where remediation is incomplete, a showing of relevance and prejudice can, in some circumstances, be shown by inferring the content of an e-mail in context of other e-mails, for example.[57] Typically, however, that is not possible if large volumes of data, rather than selective e-mails, are lost. In those situations, statistical analysis regarding e-mail loss may be used to show the sheer extent of the unremediated loss. Often, such analysis depends on comparing e-mail behavior and volumes before and after a litigation hold has been put in place. For other types of lost data, however, this kind of statistical analysis may not be possible, and more direct evidence of loss is necessary.

Recent Trends in Electronic Discovery

Given the enormous volume of data that must be preserved, searched, reviewed, and produced during discovery today, and the severe sanctions that can be imposed for failing to do so properly, the legal profession, judiciary, academics, and electronic discovery providers are looking for legal and technical solutions to address the concomitant increase in costs, time, and use of judicial resources. In the past couple of years, several dramatic trends have emerged, which may significantly change the course of litigation.

1. COOPERATION   More and more courts are mandating cooperation between parties during the discovery phase. While many lawyers may be surprised to learn that discovery is *not* part of the adversarial process, they should be aware that such cooperation is not only suggested by courts, but may be mandated under the law. Citing the Federal Rules, as well as the Sedona Conference's *Cooperation Proclamation*, several courts have held that electronic discovery is a "cooperative undertaking" required by law.[60]

In *Seroquel*, a products liability case, the court ordered spoliation sanctions, not simply for the loss of ESI, but because of the "purposeful sluggishness" in the production from AstraZeneca's self-chosen "custodians."[61] In imposing sanctions for discovery abuses, the court stated: "the posturing and petulance displayed by both sides on this issue [relating to the identification and production of relevant databases] shows a disturbing departure from the expected professionalism necessary to get this case ready for appropriate disposition."[62] It also noted that AstraZeneca's failure to allow contact between the opposing parties and individuals with the technical know-how to resolve the issues is an "inexplicable departure from the requirements of Rule 26. . . ."[63]

In short, although mandated cooperation may come as a surprise to many seasoned lawyers, it behooves counsel to consider opposing counsels' demands carefully, to respond to them in a timely fashion, and to be prepared to substantiate their legal and technical claims.

2. ADVANCED SEARCH AND REVIEW METHODOLOGIES   Second, courts also are beginning to explicitly challenge the reliability of traditional Boolean keyword searches.[64] In three notable decisions beginning in 2008, the courts recognized the technical and linguistic complexities associated with accurately filtering large volumes of data, and required the parties to support the defensibility of their selected search methodologies.[65] More explicitly, as Judge Grimm noted in *Victor Stanley*:

> *While keyword searches have long been recognized as appropriate and helpful for ESI [electronically stored information] search and retrieval, there are well-known limitations and risks associated with them, and proper selection and implementation obviously involves technical, if not scientific knowledge.*[66]

As a result, electronic discovery providers and corporate clients are working diligently to develop and use new technologies, and applying sampling methods, to automate the search and review processes in a defensible, cost-effective way.[67]

3. PROPORTIONALITY   At the same time that the court in *Pension Committee* was drawing bright-line rules to help litigants navigate the e-discovery landmines, other courts were recognizing the "proportionality" requirements of the Federal Rules of Civil Procedure. In particular, Rule 26(b) contains a rule of proportionality whereby the court *shall* limit discovery methods and scope if (1) the discovery sought is cumulative or duplicative or obtainable from more convenient, less burdensome, or less expensive sources; (2) the party seeking discovery has had ample opportunity to obtain the information; or (3) the burden or expense outweighs its likely benefit, taking into account the needs of the case, the amount in controversy, the parties' resources, the importance of the issues at stake, and the importance of the proposed discovery in resolving the issues.[68]

Thus, "[w]hether preservation or discovery conduct is acceptable in a case depends on what is reasonable, and that in turn depends on whether what was done—or not done—was proportional to that case and consistent with clearly established applicable standards."[69] Conversely, large, sophisticated corporations are expected to fulfill their obligations diligently and in a manner consistent with their litigation experience and resources.[70]

4. ATTORNEY SANCTIONS Courts are becoming more willing to impose spoliation sanctions not only on corporate litigants, but also on their attorneys for failing to diligently monitor the preservation process. As noted previously, in the seminal case describing counsel's role during electronic discovery, the court in *Zubulake* explained that an attorney's responsibilities do not end with the issuance of a litigation hold notice.[71] Rather, Judge Scheindlin warned:

> *[I]t is not sufficient to notify all employees of a litigation hold and expect that the party will then retain and produce all relevant information. Counsel must take affirmative steps to monitor compliance so that all sources of discoverable information are identified and searched.*[72]

Such steps must be "reasonably" calculated to ensure that sources of relevant information are identified and preserved.[73]

Moreover, Rule 26(g) requires attorneys to certify as to the completeness and accuracy of discovery responses.[74] The Advisory Committee Notes further state: "If an attorney makes an incorrect certification without substantial justification, the court *must* sanction the attorney, party or both."[75] The lawyer also is under a duty to supplement responses, and is under a continuing burden to periodically recheck all interrogatories and canvass all new information.[76]

The courts also are becoming less tolerant of finger pointing and whining by counsel, particularly about technical issues. As noted previously, the onus is directly on lawyers to understand the IT infrastructures in which discovery takes place and to provide substantive arguments for their decisions, supported by technical experts and appropriate IT witnesses as needed. The 2008 opinion in *Qualcomm Inc. v. Broadcom Corp.*,[77] is striking in this regard.

Although the sanctions against outside counsel were ultimately overturned because the court found that they had not acted in bad faith, the *Qualcomm* decision provoked extensive discussion among the legal community when it was issued because of the heavy sanctions imposed against counsel. Although the case law is replete with cases in which litigants have incurred heavy sanctions for e-discovery abuses and spoliation,[78] up until the *Qualcomm* decision the threat of sanctioning attorneys directly seemed to be simply that—a threat.

The underlying litigation in *Qualcomm* involved a patent infringement claim by Qualcomm against Broadcom. A key issue in the matter was whether Qualcomm participated in a standards-setting body for video coding (the joint video team [JVT]) in 2002 and 2003. Qualcomm repeatedly represented through its witnesses that Qualcomm had not participated in the JVT during that time frame, despite the fact that neither in-house nor outside counsel had ever searched the computers of the corporate witnesses it had produced for deposition.

While preparing for trial, however, one of Qualcomm's attorneys discovered a 2002 e-mail to a Qualcomm witness suggesting some level of participation in the JVT during the relevant time period. A subsequent search of the witness's computer revealed 21 related e-mails from 2002 that had not been produced in discovery.

Despite this finding, the Qualcomm trial team did not produce these e-mails; nor did it search for additional related e-mails. Indeed, an attorney for Qualcomm declared to the court that there were no such e-mails. During cross-examination, however, the witness in question admitted that she had received e-mails in 2002 relating to the JVT. Qualcomm then produced the 21 e-mails.

On January 26, 2007, the jury returned a unanimous verdict in favor of Broadcom in the underlying patent infringement case. Post-trial, Qualcomm searched the e-mail archives of 21 employees and found more than 46,000 responsive documents not previously produced during discovery. Broadcom subsequently moved for sanctions, including attorneys' fees.

In awarding Broadcom over $8 million in attorney's fees and referring six of Qualcomm's attorneys to the California State Bar for sanctions, the District Court found that Qualcomm's "counsel participated in an organized program of litigation misconduct and concealment throughout discovery, trial, and post-trial before new counsel took over the lead role in the case on April 27, 2007."

Although on remand the court declined to sanction outside counsel, it did note the "incredible breakdown in communications" and the failure to properly supervise the process. However, because of Qualcomm's employees' "incredible lack of candor," it held that outside counsel had not acted in "bad faith."

More recently, in *Green v. McClendon*,[79] the court found both the defendant and counsel negligent for the reinstallation of an operating system, which effectively wiped the hard drive and destroyed relevant evidence, and the failure to produce relevant documents earlier in the process. The court awarded costs and attorney fees to be divided between the defendant and defense counsel.

In short, recent cases make clear that attorneys are ultimately and potentially personally responsible for ensuring that their clients are truthfully and accurately meeting their e-discovery obligations, and are therefore advised to monitor and review decisions relating to the e-discovery process.

Safeguarding IP in Litigation

Many companies are rightly concerned that the documents responsive to an e-discovery request are also highly confidential, particularly in the intellectual property context. There are several mechanisms widely used by courts and counsel to protect the confidentiality of such information in litigation. For example, confidentiality agreements between the parties and "Attorney's Eyes Only" designations during production are commonplace. Moreover, parties are encouraged to craft and obtain protective orders from the courts.

From a technical and process point of view, there are ways to limit access to sensitive documents during the review process using secure computers without Internet connections. Indeed, online review platforms increasingly are used to segregate documents in accordance with access credentials allowing multiple people to review documents but under different access controls.

In addition, third-party vendors are often used as a sort of go-between or escrow for sensitive documents and to assist in *in camera* review when challenges do arrive. Electronic service providers often play this critical role in the context of "adverse acquisitions," which often arise in the IP context.

Rule 34(a), which governs adverse acquisitions, provides:

A party may serve on any other party a request to produce and permit the requesting party or its representative to inspect, copy, test, or sample the following items in the responding party's possession, custody, or control:

(A) any designated documents or electronically stored information . . . stored in any medium from which information can be obtained either directly or, if necessary, after translation by the responding party into a reasonably usable form.[80]

Rule 34 (a) does not create a "routine right of direct access to a party's electronic information system, although such access might be justified in some circumstances."[81] The party seeking an adverse acquisition order typically must present some reliable information that opposing party's representations during discovery are misleading or substantively inaccurate.[82]

Generally, adverse acquisitions are ordered in cases where (1) there is a discrepancy or inconsistency in the responding party's discovery responses that justifies a party's request to allow an expert to create and examine a mirror image of a hard drive; or (2) the computers in question were used to commit the wrong in question.[83] Thefts of trade secrets or other IP often require a neutral expert analysis regarding the dissemination of stolen information throughout a company's infrastructure.[84]

In *Quotient, Inc. v. Toon,*[85] the court ordered an expert to image defendant's computer in a contract matter involving a theft of trade secrets, even though there was no allegation that data had been concealed or destroyed. Citing the Sedona Principles, the court held that there was a "substantial probability" that relevant data "could be made less accessible to the parties merely by the defendant's normal course of computer use *regardless of his intentions and motive.*" The court further observed: "*unintentional destruction* of relevant evidence should be halted when it can be done so in a fashion that is minimally intrusive and where [the requesting party] is willing to bear the full cost of the process."[86]

Generally, an adverse acquisition order is executed by computer forensic experts—either neutral or the requesting party's expert—to image targeted computers and removable media, and to preserve server data and other evidence as required. Often, the protocol ordered by the court requires the expert to sign a confidentiality order, and provides for a right of first review of the producing party. Such review insures that privileged and otherwise confidential information is protected before the discoverable ESI is provided to the requesting party. To that end, any challenges on privilege or confidential designations can be argued before the court and reviewed *in camera.*

INFORMATION MANAGEMENT Finally, this chapter ends where the electronic discovery process begins—with information management. Almost all of the problems associated with the electronic discovery process, from identifying relevant sources of information to avoiding spoliation challenges to searching vast volumes of data can be avoided, at least in part, through well-informed information management practices. In-house counsel should work with their IT departments, outside vendors, human resource departments, and business units to plan and prepare for inevitable litigation. The records that an organization must keep in the ordinary course of business—either for business purposes or as mandated by law—should be identified, organized, and stored in a way that permits for easy identification, access, and searchability. There are a number of solutions on the market that permit for centralized document storage and archiving, tagging and labeling, and searching across repositories.

Often more important than smart organization and storage of necessary information is the eradication of data unlikely to be necessary for business or historical purposes, either because of age, content, or simply replication in multiple other locations. For example, employees generally should not be encouraged to archive old e-mails to their local hard drives if such e-mails are kept on an archive server. Backup tapes necessary for disaster recovery do not need to be kept for years, unless required under the law. For both security and management purposes, data should be accessible on a need-to-know basis, and computer use policies and technical solutions should be implemented to prevent replication of sensitive data to or through external storage devices, home computers, and personal e-mail accounts.

More and more companies are taking affirmative steps to limit the volume and replication of data, particularly e-mail communications. Some of the actions involve technological solutions such as implementing mailbox volume or age restrictions, and the use of auto-delete to enforce those policies. Companies also are restricting the use of thumb drives and other storage media to prevent the propagation of data and the potential disclosure of sensitive information. Still others are using aggressive education tactics, including conducting regular training on e-mail use and language, and conducting spot checks, to sensitize their employees as to the nature of their communications.

With respect to intellectual property, in particular, organizations should consult with outside IP lawyers to understand what information might be necessary to prove or disprove IP claims. For example, in a trade-secrets litigation, any documents showing the extent to which a trade-secret owner tried to keep a concept, process, or other sensitive information "secret" is relevant. Such materials might include documents and logs related to "need-to-know" access limitations, employment agreements, and e-mails and public information regarding ideas or "crown jewels." A trade secret also must have some value associated with its being kept secret; thus, any financial projections or discussions about competition or the market may be relevant and should be retained.

Similarly, the measures taken to protect copyrights, or not protect them, may be relevant in mounting or defending a copyright challenge as it was in the *Viacom v. YouTube* litigation. Patent cases are highly dependent on the context of how and when an invention was created. Thus, scientific notebooks and discussions about ideas, for example, may be highly relevant. As noted in the *Micron* case, however, it is common practice to remove "all materials not part of the official record" from prosecution files *when not in a litigation hold posture*.

In short, businesses should limit what they retain to those items necessary to conduct their business, to protect their critical assets, and to defend against challenges to their rights. To the extent that we depend on electronic communications to conduct our businesses, employees should be educated on good e-mail management practices and be cautioned that their e-mails and other records, including Internet surfing habits, are not private and may be subject to close scrutiny in the litigation context. And businesses should be aware of the significant costs associated with having to collect, search, and review substantial volumes of data, most of which could have been simply discarded in the normal course of business.

Conclusion

Electronic discovery is a time-consuming and expensive component of litigation, and poor management of the process can have disastrous consequences to litigants and their attorneys. Thus, it behooves all parties and attorneys, regardless of their practice areas, to stay abreast of the evolving law and technology in this area. More important, parties should institute e-discovery action plans and thoughtful data management programs well before litigation is ever anticipated.

Notes

[1] Regulated industries, such as medical and financial institutions, are required under the law to retain particular types of data for specified periods of time. The use of the term *preservation* in this chapter refers to the obligations of unregulated and regulated industries to preserve data in the context of litigation.

[2] *Zubulake v. UBS Warburg LLC*, 220 F.R.D. 212, 216 (S.D. N.Y. 2003) ("Zubulake IV"); see also Fed. R. Civ. P. 37(f), Advisory Committee Note to Fed. R. Civ. P. 37(f).

[3] *Winters v. Textron, Inc.*, 187 F.R.D. 518 (M.D. Pa.1999).

[4] *Micron Technologies v. Rambus*, 2009 WL 54887 (D. Del. 2009).

[5] *Hynix Semiconductor Inc. v. Rambus, Inc.*, 591 F. Supp. 2d 1038, 1061 (N.D. Cal. 2006).

[6] *Rambus Inc. v. Infineon Technologies AG*, 222 F.R.D. (E.D. Va. 2004).

[7] *Hynix Semiconductor Inc. v. Rambus Inc.*, 591 F. Supp. 2d 1038, 1061 (N.D. Cal. 2006).

[8] *See also Mosaid Technologies Inc. v. Samsung Electronics Co.*, 348 F. Supp. 2d 332, 335 (D. N.J. 2004).

[9] 2009 WL 910801 (D. Utah 2009).

[10] Id.

[11] Fed. R. Civ. P. 26(b).

[12] Fed. R. Evid. 401 ("relevant" information is that which has a "tendency to make the existence of a fact or consequence to determination of the action more or less probable").

[13] *Pension Committee of the University of Montreal Pension Plan, et al. v. Banc of America Securities, LLC*, 2010 WL 184312 at *5 (S.D. N.Y. 2010).

[14] *PSEG Power NY, Inc. v. Alberid Constructors, Inc.*, 2007 WL 2687670 (N.D. N.Y. Sept. 7, 2007) (e-mail and attachments); *Flagg v. City of Detroit*, 2008 WL 787061 (E.D. Mich., Mar 20, 2008) (text messages).

[15] 245 F.R.D. 443 (C.D. Cal, Aug. 24, 2007).

[16]Nos. 07-Civ-2103 (LLS), 07-Civ-3582 (LLS).

[17]See, for example, *Williams v. Sprint/United Mgmt Co.*, 230 F.R.D. 640 (D. Kan. 2005).

[18]*Ameriwood Ind., Inc. v. Liberman*, 2006 WL 3835391 (E.D. Mo., Dec. 27, 2006) ("It is generally accepted that deleted computer files are discoverable."); see also *Gates Rubber Co. v. Bando Chemical Indus., Ltd.*, 167 F.R.D. 90 (D. Col. 1996) (holding that the entire computer drive should be imaged to preserve all recoverable data).

[19]*Zubulake v. UBS Warburg LLC*, 229 F.R.D. 422 (S.D. N.Y 2004) (attorneys have an affirmative obligation to understand technical environment and assure compliance with discovery obligations).

[20]*See Harkabi v. SanDisk Corp.*, 2010 WL 3377388 (S.D. N.Y. 2010) (in determining culpability, court noted that in-house counsel were "notably absent at critical junctures" in collection process).

[21]*Zubulake v. UBS Warburg*, 220 F.R.D. 212 ("Zubulake IV") (S.D. N.Y. 2003).

[22]*Mosaid Technologies Inc. v. Samsung Electronics Co.*, 348 F. Supp. 2d 332, 335 (D. N.J. 2004).

[23]*Pension Committee of the University of Montreal Pension Plan, et al. v. Banc of America Securities, LLC*, 2010 WL 184312 at *3 (S.D. N.Y. 2010).

[24]See *Adorno v. Port Auth. Of NY & NJ*, 258 F.R.D. 217, 228-29 (S.D. N.Y. 2009) (holding that defendants were negligent only where they instituted some form of limited litigation hold).

[25]Id.

[26]*Pension Committee* at *3.

[27]Id.

[28]Id. at *10.

[29]Id.

[30]Id.

[31]Id.

[32]*See Harkabi v. SanDisk Corp.*, 2010 WL 3377388 (S.D. N.Y. 2010) (in determining culpability, court noted that in-house counsel were "notably absent at critical junctures" in collection process).

[33]Fed. R. Civ. P. 26(b).

[34]Advisory Committee Note to Fed. R. Civ. P. 26(b) (emphasis added).

[35]Advisory Committee Note to Fed. R. Civ. P. 37(f) (emphasis added).

[36]*Zubulake v. UBS Warburg LLC*, 217 F.R.D. 309, 318 (S.D. N.Y. 2003) ("Zubulake I") (holding that backup tapes are inaccessible).

[37]Compare, for example, *Ameriwood Industries, Inc. v. Liberman* (E.D. Mo. 2006) (holding that imaging hard drives and recovering deleted data constituted "undue burden and cost" where defendants are individuals and defendants submitted affidavits describing costs) with *Mikron Ind., Inc. v. Hurd Windows & Doors* (W.D. Wash., Apr. 21, 2008) (hard drives and active e-mail servers treated as presumptively "reasonably accessible" ESI).

[38]*Kelly v. Montgomery Lynch & Assoc.*, 2007 WL4412572 (N.D. Ohio, Dec. 13, 2007).

[39]*City of Seattle v. Prof'l Basketball Club*, 2008 WL 539809 (W.D. Wash., Feb. 25, 2008); see also *Auto Club Family Ins. Co. v. Ahner*, 2007 WL 2480322 (E.D. La., Aug. 29, 2007) (mere statement of an attorney is insufficient to prove that requested ESI is not reasonably accessible).

[40]*Compare Bank of Amer. Corp. v. SR Int'l Bus. Ins. Co.* (N.C. Super. 2006) (court refused to compel production of deleted e-mails from 400 backup tapes held by nonparty, *after*

expert stated such recovery would cost $1.4 million) with *Analog Devices Inc. v. Michalski* (N.C. Super. 2006) (*noting that discovery costs were unknown*, court ordered production of e-mails from over 400 backup tapes held by plaintiff and split costs between the parties).

[41] See Fed. R. Civ. Proc. 26(b)(2)(C)(iii); *Zubulake v. UBS Warburg LLC*, 217 F.R.D. 309 (S.D. N.Y. 2003) ("Zubulake I").

[42] See *Quinby v. WestLB* (S.D. N.Y. Sept. 5, 2006) (holding that a producing party does not have a duty to preserve evidence in an accessible form; however, the court refused to shift the costs of producing inaccessible data because the defendant converted the data to an inaccessible format after litigation was reasonably anticipated); *Farmers Ins. Co. v. Peterson*, 81 P.3d 659 (Okla. 2003) ("unilateral decision on how it stores information cannot, by itself, be a sufficient reason for placing discoverable matter outside the scope of discovery").

[43] See, for example, *Coleman (Parent) Holdings, Inc. v. Morgan Stanley & Co.*, 2005 WL 679071 (Fla. Cir. Ct.).

[44] See *Mosaid Technologies v Samsung Electronics* (D. N.J., Sept. 2004) (in a patent case court found negligence and prejudice for party's failure to turn off e-mail auto-delete, and granted adverse inference sanction).

[45] *Kounelis v. Sherrer*, 529 F.Supp.2d 503, 519 (D. N.J. 2008) (citing *Mosaid Tech. Inc. v. Samsung Elec. Co.*, 348 F. Supp. 2d 332, 335 D. N.J. 2004).

[46] See *Monsanto Co. v. Ralph*, 382 F.3d 1374, 1380 (Fed. Cir. 2004) (In patent cases, the imposition of sanctions for spoliation is controlled by regional circuit law.)

[47] See *Rimkus Consulting Group, Inc. v. Cammarata*, 688 F. Supp. 2d 598, 614 (S.D. Tex. Feb 19, 2010).

[48] *Kounelis v. Sherrer*, 529 F. Supp. 2d 503 at 518–19 ("spoliation occurs when a party has intentionally or negligently breached its duty to preserve potentially discoverable evidence," and cannot occur in the absence of such a duty).

[49] See, for example, *AdvantaCare Health Partners, LP v. Access IV, Inc.*, 2005 WL 1398641 (N.D. Cal., June 14, 2005); *Anderson v. Crossroads Capital Partners*, 2004 WL 256512 (D. Minn., Feb. 12, 2004).

[50] 2006 WL 2728927 (W.D. Tex., Aug. 23, 2006).

[51] 259 F.3d 587 (7th Cir. 2001).

[52] *Pension Committee*, at *5.

[53] See, for example, *Micron v. Rambus*, 2009 WL 54887 (D. Del. 2009) (holding low burden to prove prejudice where destruction of evidence was intentional); *Arista Records, Inc. v. Sakfield Holding Co SL*, 314 F. Supp. 2d 27 (D. D.C. 2004) (in copyright infringement case, court held that "destruction of evidence raises the presumption that disclosure of the materials would be damaging"); but see *Condrey v. SunTrust Bank of Ga.*, 431 F.3d 191, 203 & n.8 (5th Cir. 2005) (even if bad faith is shown, an adverse inference instruction is not appropriate absent a showing that the lost data would be relevant).

[54] *Zubulake IV*.

[55] Id. at *5.

[56] Harkabi, 2010 WL 3377388 (S.D. N.Y. Aug. 23 2010).

[57] See, for example, Zubulake V.

[58] Pension Committee, at *6.

[59] Id.

[60] *In re Seroquel Products Liability Litigation,* 2007 U.S. Dist. LEXIS 61287 (M.D. Fla., Aug. 21, 2007) ("Identifying relevant records and working out technical methods for their production is a cooperative undertaking, not part of the adversarial give and take."); *Mancia v. Mayflower Textile Servs. Co.,* Civ. No. 1:08-CV-00237-CCB (D. Md. Oct. 15, 2008) (J. Grimm); *Qualcomm Inc. v. Broadcom Corp.,* 2008 WL 66932 (S.D. Cal. Jan 7. 2008), vacated in part, *Qualcomm, Inc. v. Broadcom Corp.,* 2008 WL 638108 (S.D. Cal. March 5, 2008) ("For the current 'good faith' discovery system to function in the electronic age, attorneys and clients must work together to ensure that both understand how and where electronic documents, records and emails are maintained and to determine how best to locate, review, and produce responsive documents."). See also *The Sedona Principles, Second Edition: Best Practices, Recommendations & Principles for Addressing Electronic Document Discover,* Principle 3 (The Sedona Conference Working Group Series, 2007).

[61] *In re Seroquel Products Liability Litigation,* 2007 U.S. Dist. LEXIS 61287 at XX.

[62] Id.

[63] Id.

[64] The concern over the reliability of using traditional Boolean searches in the legal context, both in terms of overretrieval and underretrieval of documents, was first questioned in a study conducted in 1985. In that experiment, lawyers and paralegals were asked to develop keyword terms to search approximately 40,000 documents for materials relevant to an accident. Although the attorneys estimated that they had found approximately 75 percent of the relevant documents using this traditional search methodology, the study showed that, in fact, their keyword searches had identified a mere 20 percent of the relevant materials within the document sample. See David Blair & M. E. Maron, *An Evaluation of Retrieval Effectiveness for a Full-Text Document Retrieval System,* 28 Com. A.C.M. 289 (1985). More recently, such studies have been conducted by TREC Legal Track, which is sponsored in part by the National Institute of Standards and Technology (NIST), to evaluate search methodologies in the context of electronic discovery.

[65] *William A. Gross Construction v. American Manufacturers Mutual Insurance Co.,* 256 F.R.D. 134 (S.D. N.Y. 2009); *Victor Stanley, Inc. v. Creative Pipe, Inc.,* 250 F.R.D. 251, 260, 262 (D. Md. May 29, 2008); *United States v. O'Keefe,* 537 F. Supp. 2d 14, 24 (D. D.C. 2008).

[66] *Victor Stanley,* 250 F.R.D. at 19. See also *William A. Gross Construction,* 256 F.R.D. at 134 ("This Opinion should serve as a wake-up call to the Bar in this District about the need for careful thought, quality control, testing, and cooperation with opposing counsel in designing search terms or "keywords" to be used to produce emails or other electronically stored information ["ESI"].")

[67] Judge Facciola and Jonathan Redgrave have proposed a new, groundbreaking model for parties in litigation to preserve claims of privilege without having to perform document-by-document review and logging. See Hon. John M. Facciola and Jonathan M. Redgrave, *Asserting and Challenging Privilege Claims in Modern Litigation: The Facciola-Redgrave Framework,* 2009 Fed. Cts. L. Rev. 4 (November, 2009) (hereinafter "Facciola-Redgrave Framework").

[68] Fed. R. Civ. Proc. 26(b)(2)(c).

[69] *Rimkus v. Cammarata,* 07-cv-00405 (S.D. Tex., Feb. 19, 2010), J. Rosenthal.

[70] See *Magana v. Hyundai Motor,* 167 W.2d 570 (Wash. Sup. Ct. 2009) (court entered $8 million default judgment for deliberate and willful discovery violations, in part because Hyundai had not maintained an adequate document retrieval system to respond to discovery requests).

[71] *Zubulake v. UBS Warburg LLC,* 229 F.R.D. 422 (S.D. N.Y. 2004).

[72] Id.

[73] Id.

[74]Fed. R. Civ. Proc. 26(g)(1).

[75]Advisory Committee Note to Fed. R. Civ. Proc. 26(g).

[76]Fed. R. Civ. Proc. 26(e) and the 1966 Advisory Committee Note to Fed. R. Civ. Proc. 26(e).

[77]2008 WL 66932 (S.D. Cal., Jan 7. 2008), vacated in part; *Qualcomm, Inc. v. Broadcom Corp.,* 2008 WL 638108 (S.D. Cal., March 5, 2008).

[78]See, for example, *Coleman (Parent) Holdings, Inc. v. Morgan Stanley & Co., Inc.,* 2005 WL 679071 (Fla. Cir. Ct. 2005); *Mosaid Technologies, Inc. v. Samsung Electronics Co., Ltd.,* 2004 U.S. Dist. LEXIS 23596 (D. N.J. July 7, 2004); *Zubulake v. UBS Warburg,* 2004 WL 1620866 (S.D. N.Y. July 20, 2004).

[79]2009 WL 2496275 (S.D. N.Y., Aug. 13, 2009).

[80]Fed. R. Civ. Proc. 34(a).

[81]Advisory Committee Notes to Rule 34. See *Calyon v. Mizuho Securities USA, Inc.,* 2007 WL 1468889 (S.D. N.Y. May 19, 2007) (finding that direct access "not justified").

[82]*Williams v. Mass. Mut. Life Ins. Co.,* 226 FRD 144 (D. Mass. 2005). *Scotts Co. LLC v. Liberty Mut. Ins. Co.,* 2007 WL 1723509 (S.D. Ohio, June 12, 2007) (mere suspicion that party may be withholding discoverable information is not enough to support adverse inspection).

[83]*Ameriwood Industries, Inc. v. Liberman,* 2006 WL 3825291 (E.D. Mo., Dec. 27, 2006).

[84]*Cenveo Corp. v. Slater,* 2007 WL 442387 (E.D. Pa., Jan. 31, 2007) (allowing inspection of ex-employees' hard drives in misappropriation case despite defendant's willingness to do own inspection and production because of "close relationship between plaintiff's claim and defendant's computer equipment."); *Experian Info. Solutions, Inc. v. I-Centrix, LLC* (N.D. Ill. 2005) (In misappropriation case, court ordered "an independent expert [to] review the bit-stream copy [of mirrored drive] for contextual information and metadata" relevant to plaintiff's discovery request.).

[85]2005 WL 4006493 (Md. Cir. Ct. Dec. 23, 2005).

[86]Id. at *3. See, for example, *Keithley v. The Home Store.com, Inc.,* 2008 U.S.Dist.LEXIS 61741 (N.D. Ca. 2008) (holding that dismissal requires willfulness; adverse instruction does not require bad faith; and belated compliance does not preclude sanctions).

CHAPTER 3

Controlling Patenting Costs

John Richards
Ladas & Parry LLP

N ow more than ever one needs to ensure value for money in creating and maintaining a patent portfolio. Not only are budgets decreasing or stagnant, but the
number of countries that need to be considered is increasing. Who today can afford
the risk of ignoring the potential of Brazil, Russia, India, and China (the so-called
BRIC countries) in addition to the traditional list of countries of the North American
Free Trade Agreement, Japan, the Europe Patent Office (EPO), and Korea?

Key steps to accomplishing this are the following:

1. A clear understanding of the objective that is desired to focus on productive
   goals.
2. Preparing properly in advance of incurring costs.
3. Avoiding duplication of effort.
4. Being ruthless in cutting costs if it seems that the objectives cannot be achieved
   and there is no other reason for continuing.

This chapter discusses ways in which such steps may be implemented. This
chapter does not address the costs of patent litigation. This is, of course, a factor to
be borne in mind, but since one can derive benefit from a patent without actually
litigating it, such costs are normally a subsidiary factor at the filing and prosecution
stages.

Defining the Objective

Realistic assessments of the potential benefit of securing patent protection are
needed early. Not every invention requires a patent to protect actual or potential
products.[1] Neither does every invention have the potential to be licensed or
cross-licensed, nor is every invention for which patent protection is justified
equal. Some will justify maximum effort to secure the broadest possible claims. In

other cases, relatively narrow claims directed to a specific embodiment may be all that is needed to achieve the applicant's objective, for example, if the applicant already has patent protection for related inventions. A proper assessment involving research, financial, and marketing management is needed at an early stage to make such a determination.

In making such assessment, it should be borne in mind that the main value of a patent is to enable one to exclude others from doing what is patented. As a corollary, this gives the right to license others to use the patented technology and to charge them for such use. In both contexts, it is important to identify the actual activity for which one needs to secure patent protection in order to achieve the desired degree of control. This may not necessarily mean that one has to secure patents for every feature of a product one intends to sell. If there is one key element that is necessary, it may suffice to secure patent protection for that element alone. Before deciding on this course, however, it would be prudent to consult an expert as to exactly what type of protection is likely to be obtained in any given country. Some jurisdictions require more detail than others to secure broad protection. It is therefore helpful, even at this early stage, to make a tentative decision as to the countries of interest.

In some cases, one may be seeking patent protection not so much to protect one's own investment but to provide bargaining counters for use in cross-licensing deals. In such cases, a similar analysis applies, but one would be looking to determine what are likely to be key elements in a competitor's product.

University and nonprofit research organizations may have other factors to bear in mind, for example, the need to be able to establish their reputation in a field by securing patent protection in it as well as the need to establish a licensable portfolio.

In other cases, the impetus for seeking protection for an invention in a country derives not so much from the legal right to exclude others but from other considerations. These include marketing, the desire to have a statutory intellectual property (IP) right to anchor what is otherwise know-how, or a consulting agreement. In some such cases, alternative cheaper forms of protection such as utility models, designs, or even copyright protection may suffice.

A proper assessment of these factors will also assist in determining whether any additional experimental work is needed before filing. In the chemical and biochemical fields, the scope of obtainable protection will, in many countries, depend on what experimental data are presented in the application and what one can plausibly argue would be expected to function in the same way as what one has exemplified. If one's objectives call for broad protection, it may be that an application is not ripe for filing until such experimental work has been carried out. Simply filing a narrow application based on the original experimentation, and then filing a later application to broaden it out when further experimental results are available, may be a feasible option if one is interested only in countries that provide protection against "self-collision" such as the United States and Japan. However, it is of no help if the countries under consideration include Europe or China, because if the prior registration is citable against the new registration, the lack of protection against "self-collision" would preclude the latter registration. Therefore, such an approach may be a waste of money.

As noted earlier, there can be situations where a narrow claim is as valuable as a broad one. In such a case, further experimental work may not be needed. In any case, irrespective of whether additional experimental work is contemplated, it is a good idea to try to make an assessment as soon as possible of what breadth of protection is needed. It is, unfortunately, all too easy to spend significant sums of money on patent prosecution in pursuing broad protection where narrower protection may meet the objective and be much cheaper to obtain. Deciding early on as to what scope of protection is necessary can have an effect on the way in which the application is drafted.

The other situation in which one may wish to delay filing until experiments have been completed is where the patentability of the invention is likely to depend on being able to show some superiority over what has gone before. Most countries will permit comparative data to demonstrate this later; however, there are some countries—Japan in particular—where the presence of such information in the application at the time of filing may greatly simplify prosecution later in view of the heavy emphasis that Japanese practice places on showing advantages to overcome obviousness rejections. Also, one has to be able to show to the Japanese examiner that the application as filed demonstrates that a problem has been solved. Without comparative data, this can sometimes be difficult, especially in the field of biochemistry.

Deciding Where to File

Filing decisions will depend on the nature of the invention, location of the competition, markets for one's products, and possibly where one manufactures one's own products. If there is natural dominance in one country, there may be less need for patent protection there than in a market into which one is trying to gain access. All of this requires a clear understanding of objectives at an early stage.

In considering where to file, a primary consideration will always be the location of one's competitors and potential competitors.

Deciding what and where to file is a key ingredient in cost control. Assuming the invention to be patentable in the country under consideration, the following decision tree sets out some of the factors to be considered. If there are concerns as to whether a particular invention is patentable under the laws of any country, additional factors come into play, for example, it is easier to obtain patents for business method–type and software-related inventions in the United States, Australia, and Japan than it is in the European Patent Office or China.

The decision tree shown in Figure 3.1 may be of assistance in considering the issues to be evaluated when deciding where to file a patent application for a product invention. The considerations for a process invention are similar, but one also needs to take into account the question of how easy or difficult it will be to determine whether someone is actually infringing the patent. In countries such as Germany and Japan where there is no effective discovery, this may be difficult.

A further factor that needs to be taken into account, and that is more difficult to quantify, is the health of the patent system in any country. This includes issues such as the quality and speed of examination, the impartiality of the courts and their attitude to patents, and a number of less tangible factors. Unfortunately, these tend to change over time, so predicting what the situation will be when a patent is examined in countries where there are long delays in examination, or when a patent needs to be enforced, may be difficult.

Patent Filing Decision Tree for Product Patent

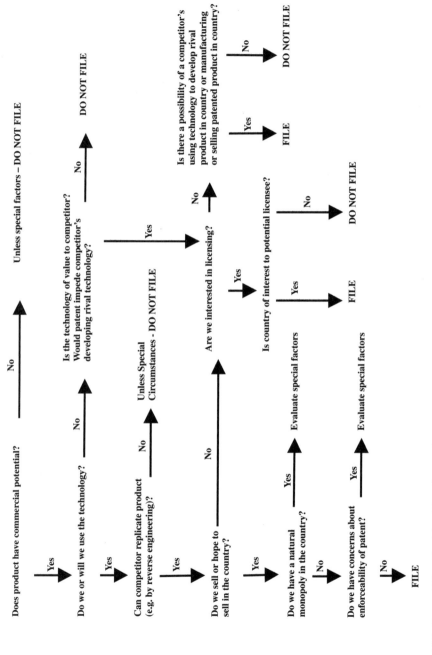

FIGURE 3.1 Patent Filing Decision Tree for Product Patent

Source: Ladas & Parry LLP. All rights reserved.

TABLE 3.1 U.S. Application Filing Figures

	GDP 2009 $US billion	U.S. Applications Originating From	Approximate Lifetime Cost	Ratio GDP:Cost
Argentina	307	146	18,500	16.6
Australia	924	3,699	27,000	34.2
Brazil	1,594	464	31,500	50.6
Canada	1,336	10,309	21,000	63.6
Chile	163	66	10,500	15.5
China	4,985	6,879	27,500	181.3
France	2,649	9,331	27,000	98.1
Germany	3,330	25,163	39,000	85.4
India	1,377	3,110	17,000	81
Indonesia	540	18	28,500	18.9
Israel	195	4,727	13,500	14.4
Italy	2,112	3,940	29,000	72.8
Japan	5,068	81,982	34,500	146.9
Korea	832	23,950	31,500	26.4
Mexico	874	220	18,000	48.5
Netherlands	792	4,203	34,500	23
Russia	1,231	552	25,500	48.3
Saudi Arabia	375	147	49,000	7.6
Singapore	182	1,225	20,000	9.1
South Africa	285	318	12,000	23.7
Spain	1,460	1,162	27,000	54.1
Sweden	406	3,515	28,500	14.2
Switzerland	492	3,508	24,500	20.1
Turkey	614	85	33,000	18.6
United Kingdom	2,174	10,568	23,000	94.5
United States	14,119	224,912	25,000	564.8
EU	16,378	67,578		

It is, however, always worthwhile looking to see what one will get for one's money. Table 3.1 sets out information that may be helpful in a more general context when deciding on where to file. The table is for the G-20 countries and a few others where patent filings are common. Two general factors to bear in mind can be deduced from this information, namely, (1) the size of the economy in the country measured by its gross domestic product (GDP); and (2) the inventivity of the country measured by the number of U.S. patent applications filed that originate from the country. We also compare the GDP with our best guess as to the total cost of obtaining a modest patent and maintaining it for 20 years in the country assuming that one does not encounter serious difficulties in prosecution. By doing so, we obtain a ratio that gives some indication as to the countries that provide the greatest amount of economic protection for the lowest cost (the higher the ratio, the better the value for money). The U.S. filing figures provide a basis for projecting which countries are likely to prove to be competitors in the future so that it is desirable to obtain patent protection there now.[2]

Delaying Costs

Filing a "provisional-type" application may be useful as a holding operation while assessments on filings outside one's own country are made. However, even this requires the use of resources that may be better used elsewhere, since in order for such a "provisional" application to serve its "date-holding" purpose, it must properly describe the invention to provide basis for a claim to priority from it later.[3] On the other hand, if the invention is still undergoing development, use of the provisional may enable one to secure a date for what has already been realized while avoiding the need to fix the final form of application for a year so as to permit inclusion of later developments without the need to file a separate application.[4] This does, however, require close monitoring of developments by the patent attorney involved so as to make sure that nothing is missed. In appropriate cases, foreign applications may be filed on the basis of a combination of different provisionals, as long as the subsequent national application or a Patent Cooperation Treaty (PCT) application designating the country of interest is filed within one year of the first such application.[5]

Alternative Means of Protection

In assessing what and where to file, it is worth bearing in mind that in some countries, lower-cost protection may be available by way of utility model or even registered design or copyright protection for some types of inventions. Additionally, in many countries the nonobviousness requirements are lower and the examination simpler for these types of protection than for patents. It should, however, be noted that utility model protection is not available in some countries, including Canada, the United Kingdom, and the United States. Table 3.2 lists the countries in which utility model–type protection is available.

Filing utility model applications in countries prone to patent racketeering may also be helpful in avoiding business disruption later, and so, filing for utility model protection early can avoid future costs. In countries where invalidity of an IP right can be asserted only in proceedings before the patent offices, Russia and China being commonly quoted examples, it is not unknown for unscrupulous local businesspeople to secure utility model protection for products from other countries and then use such utility models to disrupt importation of legitimate goods. Such businesspeople rely on delays in proceedings based on proving prior use and the like by the legitimate owner to delay the foreigner's product coming into the market. It is much easier to deal with this situation, or even to avoid it, if one has first secured one's own utility model or design protection for the article.

Design protection is available in most countries, and some, such as the European Union (for which a single registration covers the entire EU), permit up to 100 designs to be included in a single application, although there is an additional charge for each included design. Most countries now provide for design protection for a period of at least 15 years, and in Europe the norm is 25 years. Many, but not all, countries permit design protection for parts of articles. In general, however, design protection is not available for features whose shape is dictated by their function. In a few countries, France and the Netherlands being among the most liberal, copyright protection may

TABLE 3.2 Countries Providing Utility Model Protection

Country	Novelty Requirement	Subject for Protection	Duration
Andean Community (Colombia, Ecuador, Peru only)	Same as patents	Device, tool, implement, mechanism, or other object or part thereof, etc.	10 years
Australia	Same as patents	Same as for patents	8 years
Austria	6-month grace period	Products, devices, machines, processes, and programming logic, therapy for animals	10 years
Belgium	Same as patents	Same as for patents	6 years
Brazil	Same as patents	Tool, working instruments, utensils, etc.	10 years
Bulgaria	Same as patents	Shape, etc. of products, tools, apparatuses, etc.	10 years
Chile	Same as patents	Instruments, apparatuses, tools, devices, parts	10 years
China	Same as patents	Shape or structure of product	10 years
Czech Republic	6-month grace period for own publications	All tangible items including chemicals	10 years
Denmark	Same as patents	All tangible items including chemicals	10 years
Finland	Same as patents	Shape or design of a device	10 years
France	Same as patents	Same as for patents	6 years
Germany	Use outside Germany not a bar; 6-month grace period	All inventions except processes and methods (note new uses are covered)	10 years
Greece	Same as patents	3D object with definite shape or form	7 years
Guatemala	Same as patents	Device, tool, implement, mechanism, etc.	10 years

(*continued*)

43

TABLE 3.2 (*Continued*)

Country	Novelty Requirement	Subject for Protection	Duration
Hungary	Use outside Hungary not a bar	Form, structure, etc. of an object	10 years
Indonesia	Same as patents	Same as for patents	5 years
Ireland	Same as patents	Same as for patents	10 years
Italy	Same as patents	Machines, machine parts, tools, etc.	10 years
Japan	Same as patents	Shape, construction, etc. of an article	10 years
Korea	Same as patents	Shape, construction, etc. of an article	10 years
Malaysia		Similar to patents	15 years
Mexico	Same as patents	Objects, utensils, apparatuses, or tools	10 years
Netherlands	Same as patents	Same as for patents	6 years
Philippines	Local novelty only required	Noninventive new form, etc. of tools or products	15 years
Poland	Same as patents	Shape, construction, etc. of an object	10 years
Portugal	Same as patents	Tools, utensils, containers, etc.	15 years
Russia	Use outside Russia not bar	Construction of production means/articles	8 years
Slovakia	6-month grace period for own publications	All tangible items including chemicals	10 years
Spain	Unlike patents; local novelty only	Utensils, instruments, tools, apparatus, etc.	10 years
Thailand	Same as patents	Similar to patents	10 years
Turkey	12-month grace period	Anything patentable except for processes and chemical products	10 years
Ukraine	Same as patents	Devices	8 years
Vietnam	Same as patents	Anything patentable	10 years

provide valuable protection for useful articles, and for countries that are members of the Berne Convention, such protection may come into being simply as a result of creation of the work without the need for any type of registration or additional cost. However, in some countries, such as the United States, registration may be necessary to effect enforcement.

Proper Preparation

Proper preparation is the key to controlling costs in patent procurement. The most important factor in securing good patent protection is that the person drafting the patent application has a good understanding of what the invention is and how it is distinguished from the prior art. Once the draftsperson understands the broad concept of the invention, it is essential that a proper search of the prior art is carried out to see what limitations this places on the original broad concept. Desirably, such a search will cover not only American and European art but also East Asian and Russian art, among others.[6] It is sometimes said that there may be advantages in not carrying out a search before filing to avoid the risk that one will have to advise the United States Patent and Trademark Office (USPTO) and possibly other patent offices about the results of that search.[7] This is taking a gamble that no patent office finds the art in question. If it does find such art while the U.S. application is still pending, one will have to disclose it and, if it turns out to be pertinent, hope that there is basis in the specification for drawing a distinction. Had one known about it before filing, one could have made a clear distinction up front.

If the nature of the invention is one where different countries have different criteria as to patentability, a proper assessment needs to be made as to what an application requires in order to present patentable subject matter in all countries of interest.[8] Internal due diligence also is required at this point to see whether there have been any disclosures of the invention or external testing or offers for sale that might affect patentability in one or more of the countries of interest.[9] Additionally, if one contemplates filing in countries where it is necessary to include the best method for carrying out the invention in any patent application,[10] information on this also has to be collected.

Once these steps have been taken, the draftsperson can start drafting. The single most important step that can be taken to reduce the total cost of obtaining a patent is to begin with a good set of claims. Consideration of patenting costs too often focuses on the cost of filing rather than the overall cost of securing patent protection. In most countries, the cost of patent prosecution exceeds that of filing. The key to avoiding significant prosecution costs lies in minimizing objections that an examiner can raise. First and foremost is making sure that the claims are clear of all of the art that can readily be found.

The concept of a "global patent application" that is perfect for filing everywhere remains elusive. Statements of advantage that may be beneficial in Japan can cause problems if stated in the form of "object" clauses in Australia or the United States.[11] Discussing the failings of the prior art may be useful in establishing the problem to be solved and therefore advantageous in an application filed in the EPO, but can have unexpectedly limiting effects of the claims if incorporated in a U.S. application.[12] This can mean that in some cases it may be preferable to use a different specification for the United States than the rest of the world. This can be done either by filing a separate application in the United States or by entering the U.S. national phase under the PCT as a continuation or continuation-in-part application.

However, there are many steps that one can take that are common to all good patent applications. Writing the specification and claims in a manner that satisfies such requirements can save money later and indeed can even be the key to securing any effective protection at all. Writing an application with a broad definition of the invention, perhaps with some of the features defined in functional terms, and then proceeding directly to a specific embodiment, can often lead to problems. Particularly, jurisdictions such as the EPO and Japan have rules on amendment during prosecution that are strict. A couple of paragraphs setting out intermediate generalizations can sometimes be worth their weight in gold. If the invention is conceived of in functional terms, it should be borne in mind that many countries, including Japan and the EPO, are reluctant to accept functional definitions unless there is no other way to define the invention and that if such language is permitted, it has its natural meaning. It is therefore desirable to include descriptions of structures that will perform the function in the claims not only to fulfill the requirements of 35 USC §112(6),[13] but also to provide for fall-back positions in other countries should it be found that something falling within the broad functional definition already exists.

Filing an application for a medical use invention in Japan or Korea (where such inventions are typically claimed as use-limited pharmaceutical compositions), without including data is likely to be a complete waste of money. These factors should be considered and balanced up front, and competent advice should be obtained.

Translation costs form a large part of the filing costs in multi-country filings. Simply filing in the countries noted in the introduction to this chapter would require translation into Japanese, Korean, Spanish (for Mexico), Portuguese (for Brazil), Russian, and Chinese. Translators charge by the word, and therefore the draftsperson should engage in rigorous pruning of unnecessary language. There is no need to repeat definitions and/or descriptions throughout the specification. Overly elaborate descriptions of the prior art beyond what is necessary to understand the invention add little. Again, advice from an experienced professional can help in deciding what to put in and what to leave out.

Other ways to reduce costs include proper use of the International System of Units (SI), and limiting the number or type of claims to avoid excess claim fees in, for example, Australia, Brazil, EPO, Japan, Russia, South Korea, and the United States (in Japan and Korea such fees affect not only examination and grant fees, but also maintenance costs).

Additionally, the new rules that took effect in the EPO on April 1, 2010, make proper preparation of the claims for filing there even more important than previously. It is desirable that, before entering the EPO (either as a direct application or through the PCT), one makes sure that the claims are limited to 15 or fewer,[14] except under the following very limited circumstances: when one includes only a single independent claim in each claim category;[15] and when one makes sure that anything that is likely to be needed in the ultimate claim set is present in a claim that is presented originally.[16]

Similarly, if one opts for protection by way of design patent registration, proper preparation can save money later. Some countries, such as the United States and Japan, permit the use of broken lines to disclaim features that are not essential to the design; others, such as China, do not. In some, such as Israel, one may have to show the whole drawing in solid lines, but use a statement of novelty to effect a disclaimer. Some countries, including China, following its 2009 law change, require a written description of the design as well as drawings.[17] Addressing these issues ahead of dispatching a case for filing can save costs in the short and long run.

Proper preparation is not, however, confined to drafting of the specification. One should also check to make sure that one has the correct applicants and inventors since errors in these can cause major problems and costs later.[18] This is particularly true in cases of joint ownership. In most countries, joint owners of a patent can exploit the patented invention themselves without consideration of the other owners, but cannot license the invention without the consent of their co-owners.[19] This is not so in China or the United States, where co-owners may not only use the invention themselves but also license it to others without consent, although in both countries, all co-owners must participate in infringement actions. In China, however, they must share the proceeds with their co-owners.[20]

Logistics of Filing

Once one has a good specification and claim set or sets, the question often becomes PCT, or not PCT? There are other logistical choices that may need to be made, in particular whether to take advantage of various regional patent systems that are available. These include the EPO, the African Intellectual Property Organization (known from its initials in French as OAPI), African Regional Intellectual Property Organization (ARIPO), the Eurasian Patent Convention, and the Gulf Cooperation Council (GCC).[21]

The EPO, with its headquarters in Munich, Germany, carries out examination of patent applications that could give rise to patents in all member states of the convention.[22] Once an application has been found grantable by the EPO, however, it morphs into individual patent rights for each of the countries for which the necessary formalities are carried out and the fees paid.

OAPI was originally created to take over responsibility for intellectual property matters in countries that had formerly been part of the French Union, but to which French patents ceased to apply when the countries became independent. Unlike the European system, it provides for a unitary right that is effective throughout all of its member countries without additional formalities. The organization has its headquarters in Yaoundé in Cameroon.

ARIPO operates a common patent office in Harare, Zimbabwe, which examines patent applications on behalf of its member countries. Unlike the European system, however, the ARIPO system allows member countries a period of six months after examination is complete to determine that an application does not comply with its own laws, for example, having regard to protection for pharmaceutical products. Like the European system, however, national rights remain after grant, and applicants can select the countries in which they wish protection.

The Eurasian Patent Convention was set up following the dissolution of the Soviet Union to provide a common means for applying for IP protection in many of the former Soviet republics. In many aspects, the convention was modeled on the European Patent Convention so that a Eurasian patent application is examined by the Eurasian Patent Office in Moscow and can give rise to rights that can be effective in each of the member countries. Unlike the European Patent Convention, however, there is no need to translate the granted patent into any other language (the initial filing must be in Russian) and no national formalities need be complied with for the patent to be effective in all member states. After grant, the patent owner does, however, have the right to indicate that it is no longer interested in protection in one or more of the countries initially covered and to cease paying for maintenance of the patent in such country.

The GCC has set up its patent office in Riyadh, Saudi Arabia. Unlike the other regional patent offices, however, the GCC office does not at present carry out its own substantive examination on patentability. This is normally contracted out to the patent office of a European country such as Austria. Once granted, a GCC patent is effective throughout the whole GCC region without further formalities.

Additionally, there remain a few countries where one can simply register a patent that has been granted elsewhere.

The countries that are members of various agreements relating to patents are set out in the following web site: http://www.ladas.com/Patents/Treaties.html.

In recent years, use of the PCT to defer costs has resulted in most applicants interested in international filing using it as their normal modus operandi for securing protection in all but the few countries that are still not members of the PCT, such as Taiwan, Kuwait, Saudi Arabia, and Argentina and a few other countries of South America. This can become a trap for the unwary—because it is easy to file a PCT application at the last minute, there is a tendency to delay foreign filing decisions and simply file the same text as a corresponding home country application as the PCT filing. Unfortunately, one is then effectively locked into this text for all countries without taking account of the requirements of the specific countries where protection is desired. Furthermore, under the PCT, there is a risk that in some countries only the first presented independent claim will be searched without payment of extra fees, which makes the order that claims are presented important for obtaining the best value for one's money. If cost deferral is not an issue and if one is confident in the search that has been carried out, proceeding directly with international filing can expedite the grant of a patent in some jurisdictions and also reduce costs.

Conversely, if one lacks confidence in one's own search, the PCT search can be valuable to avoid wasting money on filings that can never result in patents that meet the intended objective. In this case, one has to make a determination as to where to have the international search carried out. Although this will depend on options open to applicants in different countries,[23] in most countries one has a choice, and if obtaining a European patent is one of the objectives, having the search carried out by the EPO and then obtaining a refund of the EPO's search fee can often be the optimal way to proceed.[24] However, if immediate cost control is the primary objective, having the international search carried out in Korea,[25] the United States,[26] or Australia[27] may be more appropriate.[28] The value of the PCT search should increase over the next few years as the number of options for a supplementary international search increases.[29]

PCT Formality Advantages

A big advantage of the PCT, which can result in cost savings by avoiding duplication of effort, is taking advantage of the possibility under PCT Rule 51*bis*2 of filing declarations that may be needed later in national patent offices at the time of filing the PCT request. Declarations that are permitted under this provision are:

- Identity of the inventor.
- Applicant's entitlement to file the patent application.
- Applicant's entitlement to claim priority from an earlier application.
- Applicant's entitlement to claim inventorship.[30]
- Nonprejudicial disclosures or exceptions to lack of novelty.

It should be noted that failure to use the prescribed wording for a declaration could result in its being ineffective to avoid the need for further formalities when entering the national phase. It will be possible to correct declarations of this type up to sixteen months from the claimed priority date.

Not only does use of this possibility minimize the risk that one may have "lost" the inventor by the time national phase entry occurs, but it also means that the clerical staff handling these matters do not themselves have to get up to speed again later. This is useful in controlling costs.

Another useful facet of the PCT procedure is the ease with which formal corrections may be effected under Rule 92*bis*. Under this rule, many corrections can be effected by simply submitting a letter to the International Bureau setting out the correction required. It is open to national patent offices later to ask for more information if they wish, but in practice few do.

Further points to bear in mind if one is interested in protection in Europe are the subtle differences that exist between the European Patent Convention as it is applied by the EPO and the way in which virtually identical national laws are applied by the national patent offices of the member states of the EPO. Thus, where there may be issues as to obviousness or where one suspects that significant amendment may be necessary during prosecution, it may be worthwhile to consider whether national applications, for example, in Germany and the United Kingdom, might be preferred to filing at the EPO. Similar issues can arise if the application is one to which the increasing number of hurdles presented to applicants by the EPO noted earlier are applicable. Such problems are either nonexistent or much easier to deal with in, for example, the United Kingdom, German, French, and Italian patent offices, so that additional costs of filing may be offset by reduction of costs during prosecution, and this will result in patents that are better focused on the applicant's business objectives. One problem with such a strategy is that for France and Italy, proceeding through the EPO is mandatory if one uses the PCT; so, to use the national route for these countries, one must make a decision early and not rely on PCT to delay it. For Italy, however, this problem can, to some extent, be avoided by filing an application under the PCT in San Marino, which has a treaty with Italy providing for reciprocal enforcement of each other's patents.

For those outside the United States seeking patent protection in it, again a decision needs to be made as to whether to use the PCT. There are a number of factors to consider:

- If one proceeds with national-phase entry out of PCT, one is locked into the text of the PCT application (unless entering the U.S. national phase as a continuation-in-part application), whereas an application claiming only Paris Convention priority from the foreign application could be amended if any changes are desirable and priority claimed only for what is described in the PCT application.
- If the PCT application is published in a language other than English, its publication will not be effective under 35 USC §102(e) as prior art against other inventions. Once national-phase entry occurs, however, the application will be republished under 37 CFR §1.211(b). Logically, it might seem that once this has occurred, the reference would then be citable; however, the United States Manual of Patent Examining Procedure (MPEP) takes the opposite view, and so far as we are aware no case law has addressed the issue. To date, § 706.02(f)(1) of the MPEP, relating to Examination Guidelines for Applying References under 35 U.S.C. §102(e) [R-5], under Clause II, Example 5, reads as follows:

    > *References based on the national stage (35 U.S.C. 371) of an International Application filed on or after November 29, 2000 and which were not published in English under PCT Article 21(2):*

    > *All references, whether the WIPO publication, the U.S. patent application publication or the U.S. patent, of an international application (IA) that was filed on or after November 29, 2000 but was not published in English under PCT Article 21(2) have no 35 U.S.C. 102 (e) prior art date at all. According to 35 U.S.C. 102 (e), no benefit of the international filing date (nor any U.S. filing dates prior to the IA) is given for 35 U.S.C. 102 (e) prior art purposes if the IA was published under PCT Article 21(2) in a language other than English, regardless of whether the international application entered the national stage. Such references may be applied under 35 U.S.C. 102 (a) or (b) as of their publication dates, but never under 35 U.S.C. 102 (e).*[31]

- The USPTO will normally only commence processing national-phase PCT applications 30 months after the claimed priority date. If desired, it is possible to request earlier processing.

Avoiding Duplication of Effort

Every time a different person has to confront the same task, whether in a patent office or on the applicant/attorney side, there is a duplication of effort and ultimately an increase in costs. As noted earlier, avoiding duplication of effort commences at the drafting stage. Other ways to avoid duplication are to deal with formality issues only once, for example, by taking advantage of the PCT formalities simplifications previously noted.

On the patent office side, a number of steps have been taken that could open the doors to lower prosecution costs for applicants. These include the so-called patent

TABLE 3.3 Countries Participating in Patent Prosecution Highways by September 30, 2010

	AT	AU	CA	DE	DK	EP	FI	GB	HU	JP	KR	RU	SG	US
AT									X	X				
AU														X
CA					X					X	X			X
DE										X				X
DK			X							X	X			X
EP										X				X
FI								X	X	X			X	
GB										X	X			X
HU	X						X			X	X			X
JP	X		X	X	X	X	X	X	X		X	X	X	X
KR		X			X		X	X		X		X		X
RU										X	X			X
SG										X				X
US		X	X	X	X	X	X	X	X	X	X	X	X	

prosecution highways (PPHs), new routes, and triway collaborations between patent offices. Another patent office collaboration that also reduces the applicant's costs is the cooperation between the U.S., Japanese, Korean, and European patent offices with respect to supply of Convention documents. If requested, they will secure these themselves from each other electronically rather than requiring the applicant to file such copies in each case.

PPHs exist between several pairs of patent offices, as set out in Table 3.3.

An applicant who has received a ruling from the patent office of one member of the highway pair that at least one claim in an application is patentable, may request that the patent office at the other end of the highway accelerate the examination of corresponding claims.[32] This PPH extends to patent offices in PCT countries that serve as an International Search Authority or International Preliminary Examination Authority.[33] This should, hopefully, not only accelerate prosecution but also reduce prosecution costs.[34]

On the applicant's side, duplication of effort can be avoided by coordinating prosecution so that a single person having a good grasp of all of the relevant laws can consider all of the issues while deciding an appropriate overall strategy. What happens in one country may or may not have an impact on what can be accomplished elsewhere because of the differences in laws in different places. Thus, prior art that is highly pertinent in the EPO may, because it was a publication of the same inventor that occurred within one year prior to the filing of a corresponding U.S., Australian, or Korean application, be irrelevant in the United States, Australia, or Korea.

Prosecution Issues

In addition to consideration of the use of PPHs where current evidence indicates that prosecution costs may be reduced, although at the expense of commencing examination in the second country with what has been found acceptable in the first, many countries permit deferment of costs by allowing the applicant to delay examination. This, of course, delays the grant of the patent, but in some areas of technology where there are high capital investment costs, competitors are likely to treat a published patent application[35] as being just as effective a "keep off the grass" sign as a granted patent; as long as they deem that it is likely that a patent will ultimately issue, there is no great need to expedite the grant. Such deferment of examination is possible in, for example:

- Brazil for three years from filing.
- Canada for five years from filing.
- China for three years from priority.
- Japan for three years from filing.
- South Korea for five years from filing.
- Russia for three years from filing.
- Taiwan for three years from filing.

Other ways in which prosecution costs may be controlled include being willing to accept more limited claims than originally presented if the examiner indicates some subject matter to be allowable, and using modified examination in countries such as Israel and Singapore if patents have already been granted in the United States or Europe and the claims of such patents are suitable.

Particular Issues in the United States

In the United States, restriction requirements in which examiners assert that there is more than one distinct invention present in an application are common. If a restriction requirement is raised, opting for the easiest subject matter to prosecute (often a method claim), rather than the most encompassing, may be a way to delay costs until the first application is close to grant. Then, one could file a divisional application on the more difficult subject matter.

Typically, the second official action issued by the USPTO will be indicated to be "final." Issue of such a final rejection means that examiners are not required to look at any arguments that may raise new issues unless the applicant pays the fees for a Request for Continued Examination. If this is done, the applicant typically will receive a further "ordinary" official action. If the response to this official action does not result in allowance of the application, it will be followed by a "final rejection." Under the present rules, the applicant can file as many requests for continued examination as he or she wishes, as long as the responses filed to the official action show that the applicant is making a proper effort to respond to the issues raised. However, such repeated requests for continued examination can become expensive. Recent information from the USPTO indicates that, on average, at least one such request for continued examination is filed on each granted patent. If the application is one where broad protection is not essential, it may be that making some concession to the examiner in response to the first action represents a cheaper way to reach one's objective than the traditional view that one should argue for broad protection at least once. In the days when one had the possibility of substantive dialogue after a final rejection, this may have been sensible; but today, it is rare that much can be achieved by responding to a final rejection (indeed, some practitioners have reputedly given up filing response to final rejections at all). In reality, one has only one chance to satisfy the examiner before needing to pay fees for requesting continued examination.

Particular Issues in the EPO

Two big problems exist in prosecution in the EPO. Both relate to what is permitted by way of amendment to the claims.

The first is the EPO's rigid approach to amendment. The case law indicates that amendments must be directly and unambiguously derived from the original text. Unfortunately, many examiners regard this as meaning that the language used in an amendment must be identical to the original text. Furthermore, examiners typically will not permit one to take a feature from one embodiment or example and attempt to use this in a claim in a more general way unless the original text indicates that the feature is of general applicability. Much time and effort can be wasted in trying to persuade examiners that these rules should not apply in any given case. They rarely succeed, and the way to avoid these problems is to draft the application with appropriate language providing basis for intermediate generalizations if one's broad claims turn out to be unpatentable.

The second problem lies in the new rules that came into effect on April 1, 2010. Under these rules, unless the claims are directed to:

a. a plurality of interrelated products,
b. different uses of a product or apparatus, or
c. alternative solutions to a particular problem, where it is inappropriate to cover these alternatives by a single claim,[36]

only a single independent claim is permitted in each category. Following the rule changes of April 1, 2010, unless one of the above-noted exceptions applies, the EPO will now search only the one independent claim in each category (the applicant will be able to choose which, but not amend the language of the claims at this point) and will not thereafter permit amendments that introduce unsearched subject matter into a claim. This means that one must make sure that the claims are in the best format before entering the EPO. In any case, the last date on which voluntary amendment will be permitted is before the application is taken up for substantive examination. The situation is further complicated by the limitations that have been placed on filing divisional applications, which in most cases must now be filed within 24 months of the first substantive official action on any application in the family of applications to which the application being divided belongs. This places considerable limitations on one's ability to redirect the application easily should the search results indicate such redirection to be desirable. It is therefore important to ensure that the claims are in the best possible form before filing or regional phase entry under the PCT.

As previously noted, use of the EPO is not the exclusive way in which to obtain patent protection in Europe, and national filings in individual countries are still possible. Traditionally, however, it has been the view that the costs of proceeding nationally will outstrip those of using the EPO when the applicant seeks protection in more than two or three countries, depending on which countries they are and the translation costs involved. However, the increasing difficulties in the EPO have led to a small but steady increase in the number of applicants who are bypassing the EPO and filing directly in, for example, the United Kingdom, Germany, and France,[37] thereby trading off increased initial filing costs for what are often lower costs in prosecution.

Particular Issues in Japan

Japanese practice is very reluctant to permit functional definitions in claims, and prosecution can be made easier if such language is replaced by something more concrete before examination is commenced. Japan has also adopted compact prosecution, with the second action typically being a final rejection. It is not possible to broaden or change the scope of claims after receipt of a second office action.[38] Unlike the United States, there is no possibility of filing a request for continued prosecution, although filing a divisional application is possible to preserve one's rights, should an appeal fail. Amendment may be possible during appeal, but only if the appeal board agrees. The effect of these provisions is therefore that, as in the United States, it may be desirable to try to compromise with the examiner in responding to the first action because if one does not do so, costs can increase rapidly. In this context, it should be borne in mind that when dealing with the obviousness issue, Japanese examiners tend to be less impressed by arguments based on motivation than they are by data showing that the difference from the prior art has some real-world advantage.

Pruning the Portfolio

Regular reviews as to the current and potential value of each patent and application in a portfolio is desirable for avoiding waste. When doing this, it should be borne in mind that patents of the same family may have different values, depending on the country in which they exist. It should also be borne in mind that in several countries[39] refunds of at least some of the fees may be possible if a case is abandoned before the examiner has commenced examination.

The decision tree shown in Figure 3.2 may be of help in making determinations on where to maintain any particular patent.

Licenses of Right

If one is not commercializing an invention in a given country oneself, but is willing to grant a license, many European countries provide that maintenance fees may be cut in half by endorsing the patent as being open to licenses of right. A typical provision is found in Section 46 of the U.K. Patent Act, which provides:

Patent Renewal Decision Tree for Product Patent

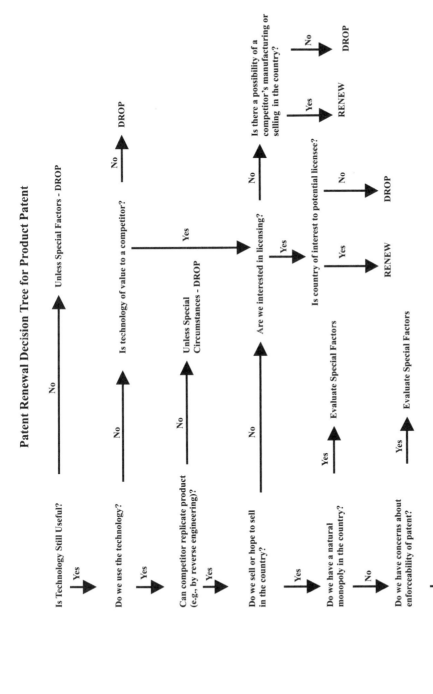

FIGURE 3.2 Decision Tree on When to Maintain a Granted Patent

Source: Ladas & Parry LLP. All rights reserved.

Any person shall, at any time after the entry is made, be entitled as of right to a license under the patent on such terms as may be settled by agreement or, in default of agreement, by the comptroller on the application of the proprietor of the patent or the person requiring the license.

Section 47 permits the patent owner to remove the endorsement by paying up the full amount of the annuity fees for the years during which such fee payments had been reduced. Similar provisions exist in the laws of, for example, Germany and Spain, so that use of such provisions can provide a means for maintaining rights in these countries at reduced cost for the time being and reinstating full rights later if no licenses have been granted in the meantime.

Conclusion

It is critical to ensure that one has a clear idea of what is important to start with and that one has the best possible understanding of the relationship between the invention and the prior art before drafting a patent application. Be ruthless about cutting losses if the desired objectives cannot be achieved, and seek advice early if in doubt.

Notes

[1]See also James Markarian, "Strategic and Legal View of Licensing Patents," in Chap. 7.

[2]More detailed information as to the countries of origin of inventions in particular areas of technology can be found at www.uspto.gov/web/offices/ac/ido/oeip/taf/tecstc/clstc_gd.htm. Another indicator of future trends may be the percentage of GDP that a country spends on research and development. At present, the leaders are Israel, Sweden, Finland, Japan, South Korea, Switzerland, the United States, Germany, Taiwan, and Denmark.

[3]Use of a "provisional-type" or other internal-priority application may be useful to delay the expiration of any patent granted, but it also inevitably delays the grant of a patent for a year. In some industries, this delay is important. Such applications are not necessarily called provisional applications. Many countries today have provision for internal priority where one can claim priority from an earlier-filed national application as long as the application claiming priority is filed within one year of the application from which priority is claimed.

[4]If this is done, it should, of course, be borne in mind that one is entitled to priority only for that which is disclosed in the original application, and care should be taken to ensure that one includes claims in the final application that are clearly entitled to claim the date of the provisional application. If priority is claimed from more than one application, then claims based on each of such applications must be incorporated with appropriate supporting language for them in the final text.

[5]Paris Convention Article 4F. It should be noted that Article 4C(4) of the Paris Convention in effect limits the filing of an application claiming Convention priority to a period of one year from the filing of the first application describing the invention, unless the true first application is totally dead and no rights have been or will be claimed from it before the filing of the application from which priority is actually claimed.

[6]There is increasing competition in the market for prior art searching between traditional search firms, Indian entrepreneurs, and even the Danish Patent Office. Consequently, the price of a good search has decreased in recent years.

[7]For example, at present, Canada and Israel have such a requirement. It will become a requirement in the EPO in 2011.

[8]For example, if filing in the EPO is desired, there must be a technical problem that is solved. If the invention relates to a pharmaceutical composition or use and protection in Japan or Korea is desired, there must be data available. For inventions of this type where protection is desired in Canada, one must make sure that there is appropriate data or sufficient theory of the invention set out to meet the requirements for "sound prediction."

[9]This may include checking on what grace periods are available for one's own disclosures. Although these are not available in Europe, except, for example, in Germany where one may have a grace period within which to file a utility model application, grace periods are available in several countries, including Australia, Canada, Brazil, Japan, Korea, Mexico, and the countries of the Andean Community. However, details of the requirements in each jurisdiction differ; for instance, the filing may need to be as soon as six months after the disclosure, or patent publications may be excluded from the type of publication for which a grace period is available. Furthermore, some of these countries will require submission of details of the publication promptly after filing the application.

[10]These include Argentina, Australia, Brazil, China, India, Mexico, New Zealand, the United States, and the countries of the Andean Community.

[11]See, for example, the adverse effect object clauses had in cases such as *On Demand Machine Corp. v. Ingram Industries Inc.*, 78 USPQ2d 1428 (Fed. Cir. 2006).

[12]In addition to the *On Demand* decision mentioned in note 010, a number of decisions of the Federal Circuit have used statements in the introductory portion of the specification to give unexpected meaning to the claims. See, for example, *Edwards Lifesciences LLC v. Cook Inc.*, 92 USPQ2d 1599 (Fed. Cir. 2009), *Alza Corp. v. Mylan Laboratories Inc.*, 73 USPQ2d 1161 (Fed. Cir. 2004), *Honeywell International Inc. v. ITT Industries Inc.*, 79 USPQ2d 1294 (Fed. Cir. 2006).

[13]This provision permits the use of "means plus function" language to define an element of a U.S. claim but requires that such language is construed as being limited to a structure defined in the specification for performing that function and "equivalents" thereof.

[14]Fees are currently 210 euros per claim above 15, and 525 euros per claim for claims above 50.

[15]EPC Rule 43.

[16]EPC Rule 137(5) provides that claims may not be amended during prosecution to include unsearched subject matter. One may be able to file a divisional application to address this problem, but this is expensive and under new Rule 36, voluntary divisionals must be filed within two years of the first official action on the application from which division is desired or any earlier European application from which it is itself divided.

[17]Chinese Patent Law Article 59.

[18]In some countries, it may even be irremediable after grant. See, for example, the Australian decision in *Davies Shephard Pty Ltd v. Stack*, 51 IPR 153 (2001).

[19]See, for example, German Civil Code Articles 743–745; Japanese Patent Act Article 73(3) and UK Patents Act Section 36(3).

[20]Chinese Patent Law Article 15.

[21]At present, Kuwait and Saudi Arabia, which are members of the Gulf Cooperation Council, are not members of the PCT, which may add a complication in deciding which filing routes to use. Qatar will join the PCT on August 3, 2011.

[22]However, it should be noted that the EPO does not have the exclusive right to examine patent applications for these countries; national patent offices remain in existence in all of them.

[23]Patent offices with competent searching ability can be appointed as International Search Authorities (ISAs) by the World Intellectual Property Organization. Once appointed, a patent office will look to its capabilities in terms of both size and linguistic ability and may make agreements with other countries to search patent applications of that other country's nationals or residents. The result is that where one can have an application searched depends on the nationality or residence of the applicants and inventors.

[24]The EPO's International search fee is 1,785 euros as of April 1, 2010. Although the EPO search fee is higher than search fees for other ISAs, it should be noted that the EPO's own search fee after entry into the regional phase is waived if the international search was carried out by the EPO. If the international search was carried out by the Austrian Patent Office, the Finnish Patent Office, the Nordic Patent Institute, the Spanish Patent Office, or the Swedish Patent Office, the EPO search fee is reduced by 940 euros. If the international search was carried out by the USPTO or certain other international searching authorities, the European search fee is reduced by 190 euros. It should be noted that, according to the EPO rule changes that came into effect on April 1, 2010 (new Rule 70a(2)), if the EPO carries out the international search, it may require the applicant to make a final decision on how to deal with cited prior art sooner than would otherwise be necessary.

[25]The cost of an international search in Korea is currently $1,092. The cost of an international search in Korea for a PCT application filed in the United States is currently $1,157.

[26]The cost of an international search in the United States is currently $2,080. The cost of an international search in the U.S. for a PCT application filed in the United States is currently $2,680.

[27]The cost of an international search in Australia is currently approximately $2,035. The cost of an international search in Australia for a PCT application filed in the United States is currently $1,837.

[28]Applicants from countries other than the United States may have other options based on the arrangements that their national patent office has made with the World Intellectual Property Organization.

[29]At its implementation on January 1, 2009, a supplementary search is available only from the Russian, Swedish, and Nordic searching authorities. A supplemental international search became available from the EPO on July 1, 2010, and from the Austrian Patent Office on August 1, 2010.

[30]This is of particular importance when the intention is to seek protection in the United States, where the use of a declaration in the correct form signed by the inventors is very important. It should, however, be noted that even if one takes advantage of the PCT rules to have a declaration executed early in the proceedings, it will still be necessary to file a power of attorney to enable one's attorneys to prosecute the application before the USPTO.

[31]As originally adopted, use of a PPH was dependent upon obtaining approval of a claim in the country where the application was first filed and there were fears that having to commence examination in the second country, based on the claims that might already have been limited during prosecution in the first country, might be disadvantageous. In a modification adopted in July 2011, several countries agreed to use of a PPH based on results in the first country to examine an application rather than only on the application in the country where it was filed

first. Since some countries carry out examination more quickly than others, this change should make a greater number of applications eligible for PPH treatment than was the case originally. However, fears still exist in some areas of technology that modifications made in the claims to meet the requirements of one country may impose unnecessary limitations on the claims that are desired in the second country. PPHs have been used most widely in the computer and tele-communications industries, and those who have used them have found that they do indeed speed up prosecution and that there is a good chance of a speedier allowance.

[32]Initially, there were fears that having to commence examination in the second country, based on claims that might already have been limited during prosecution in the first country, might be disadvantageous. These fears still exist in some areas of technology. PPHs have been used most widely in the computer and telecommunications industries, and those who have used them have found that they do indeed speed up prosecution and that there is a good chance that claims granted in the second country will be similar to those allowed in the first. The agreements of the U.S., European, Japanese, and Korean patent offices that work product created during international searches under the PCT should also increase use of PPHs at least between these patent offices.

[33]Current PCT countries whose searches and/or examinations are recognized by Japan as eligible for PPH treatment include the following: United States, E.P., Finland, Spain, Sweden, and Mexico; Current PCT countries whose searches and/or examinations are recognized by the United States as eligible for PPH treatment include the following: Austria, E.P., Finland, Japan, Korea, Russia, and Spain.

[34]For example, using the United Kingdom or Danish Patent Office as the office of first filing may result in a quick and relatively cheap initial search and examination that can then be used as the basis for expediting prosecution in Japan and the United States.

[35]Not only are PCT applications published 18 months from their priority date, but so are applications in most other countries.

[36]EPC Rule 43(2).

[37]If one wishes to obtain protection in France in this way, it is not possible to use the PCT for the French application.

[38]Under Article 17*bis* (4), amendments at this stage are restricted to cancellation of a claim or claims, restriction of a claim or claims (as long as this does not change the nature of the problem to be solved by the claimed invention), correction of errors in the description, and clarification of any ambiguities in the description that have been raised by the examiner in the notice of rejection of the application.

[39]Including the U.S., European, and Japanese patent offices.

CHAPTER 4

Trademark Costs
Trimming the Sails in Rough Economic Waters[1]

Robert Doerfler
SVP Worldwide

Matthew D. Asbell
Ladas & Parry LLP

During tough economic times, businesses often must make critical decisions about their trademark portfolio. The choices may be determined by a priority to generate profit while maintaining long-term viability of the business. The lofty standard of "best practice" to an in-house legal department becomes subject to the limited immediate resources of a sluggish economy. The trick with any trademark portfolio is not so much to cut back, but rather to be vigilantly efficient with your resources in good times and in bad. When the chips are down, brand equity may be all you have. For many companies, it is the primary company asset, but particularly in bad economic times, brand equity can significantly help carry you through. A brand is a trademark, or family of trademarks, that influences consumers' choices and sets apart your unique business from that of your competitors.

The value of a company is maximized when the goodwill associated with the company's trademarks and other intellectual property provides a competitive advantage in the marketplace. When efficiently maintained and enforced, your trademark portfolio is your primary asset generating brand equity. This is predicated on the assumption that the commitment of customers to a brand creates a marketing asset that can be developed. Brand equity is developed through the skillful use of trademarks to define the products in the minds of customers, and the successful positioning of trademarks in the marketplace enhances the equity. Unlike other types of intellectual property, trademark rights exist in perpetuity provided they are continuously used and maintained. In order to benefit from a trademark portfolio, the properties must be well documented and protected.

Trademark rights are created either upon adoption ("first to use") or upon filing ("first to file"), depending on the country in which they are sought. While some jurisdictions, such as the United States, provide for common-law rights based on use of a distinctive trademark, a majority of territories require the filing of a trademark application, and subsequent registration thereof, to acquire trademark rights. These "first-to-file" countries are often viewed as the genesis of trademark litigation war stories of bad-faith trademark applications filed by competitors, counterfeiters, and unsavory business colleagues, all of whom may beat a client in the race to the trademark office for protection.[2] And you often cannot anticipate innocent infringement: the independent adoption of an identical or confusingly similar trademark, especially where the selected mark is only a common term or variation thereof.[3]

Registrations evidence or provide certain exclusive rights in connection with the exploitation of the trademark. They provide a relatively clear description of the metes and bounds of these intangible rights, which can otherwise be difficult to identify. They help identify the parameters of the subject matter in both geographic and substantive terms. In many countries, registration of a trademark is a prerequisite to enforcement.

A trademark registration serves two primary purposes. The first is to provide the registrant with evidence of its trademark rights[4]; the second is to provide notice to third parties of existing rights. A trademark registration will save considerable expense and time in the defense of a trademark because it acts as title to the trademark for the specification of goods listed in the registration in the jurisdiction or territory where the registration is granted. Otherwise, you will spend significant resources trying to prove your trademark rights to the authorities at a time when, quite likely, time is of the essence and any ambiguities may jeopardize your ability to act efficiently and protect your brand. For instance, when Chinese Customs has stopped a suspicious container, which they can hold for only a limited amount of time, and they need to confirm the authenticity of potentially counterfeit goods, the lack of documented trademark rights could leave Customs without lawful authority to seize the counterfeit goods. Here, a window of opportunity to stop the distribution of goods bearing your company's brand would be missed and your market affected. Further, as notice to third parties, a trademark registration announces to the world your claim to a particular trademark. This allows third parties who diligently screen their own trademark development to identify potential risks that they may wish to avoid and reduces the amount of litigation associated with the trademark. A registered trademark in some common-law jurisdictions also enjoys additional damages in litigation if the original trademark owner can show that a third party knew about a valid trademark registration and yet adopted a confusingly similar or identical mark in spite of the existing registration.[5]

Companies that do not have a formal process in place for developing and managing trademarks may not be fully capturing and capitalizing on the value of their intellectual assets. Every day, marketing and sales teams are creating new ways to promote their products or services. Many of those ideas are unique, and a sense of propriety may often develop over a concept that is adopted and developed in the marketplace; however, without a procedure to oversee the adoption, registration, use, and maintenance of the trademarks, the value of the intellectual property is easily lost. These companies are potentially missing out on significant business opportunities, and exposing themselves to unexpected litigation or other costly liabilities.

This chapter will address cost-saving techniques useful in trademark management in the context of (1) evaluating and organizing a trademark portfolio; (2) selecting and clearing a trademark; (3) filing and pursuing registrations; and (4) using, monitoring, and enforcing trademark rights.[6]

Evaluating and Organizing a Trademark Portfolio

The following section discusses strategies for cost-effective trademark portfolio management, including the importance of taking inventory, evaluating the importance of existing brands, prioritizing the maintenance of registrations, and organizing trademark records.

Taking Inventory

Companies that do not yet have appropriate policies in place or have lost track of their rights over time as a result of inattention can begin or renew the process of taking control of these rights and saving, or even profiting therefrom, by conducting an inventory. To inventory existing trademark rights, identifying and cataloging the properties owned by the company is an essential first step. This may require conducting worldwide searches of registrations owned by the company or its affiliated entities and a review of marketing materials and product packaging by an intellectual property (IP) specialist, who can identify existing unregistered trademarks, investigate the history of use of the trademarks, and assist in the registration process. Moving forward, engaging a trademark specialist in the product development and marketing process can establish a proactive procedure to clear and record trademark rights. A business cannot effectively exploit or protect what they do not know they have, and law enforcement officers and courts cannot efficiently assist in the defense of vague, undocumented trademark rights. Further, any attempt to enforce such rights may cost significantly more than a trademark that has been properly registered and maintained.

Evaluating Importance

Many companies have a surplus of trademark registrations. Whether due to projects that were once hot but abandoned before they went to market, products that hit the market and found themselves no longer of interest, or corporate acquisitions, trademarks that at one point in time were sought after and secured may be unused or otherwise unimportant to the company. During weak economic times, companies should review existing trademark applications and registrations that may have been acquired for a project but not used, both to determine whether some may be abandoned or canceled to avoid the costs of maintaining them and to consider the possibility of recycling old brands instead of developing new ones. As discussed later in this chapter, maintaining an organized electronic database of trademarks, including those that are available for reuse, can facilitate the selection and adoption of brands for new products and result in savings related to clearance and registration. Recycling these trademarks may generate savings for your company. During down economic times, review existing trademarks in your company's portfolio that may have been acquired for a different project but not used. The list of available trademarks could be reviewed before a new list of candidates is generated.

Prioritizing Trademarks

Large corporations that have hundreds or thousands of trademarks worldwide should consider a strategy for prioritizing the maintenance of their trademarks within a smaller budget. Categorizing trademarks and markets by importance as primary, secondary, and tertiary helps to identify priorities and can assist in identifying registration and enforcement strategies based on each category.[7] For example, infringement of a primary trademark in a primary market would certainly require action, but you have to balance the costs to protect a tertiary trademark in a tertiary market. A periodic review of existing global trademark applications and registrations prevents overprotection, where the same trademark is registered multiple times, or instances of underrepresentation, where strategic trademarks do not have required protection in key markets or for an appropriate scope of goods/services. Often, companies will file trademark applications for trademarks that are used for only a relatively short period. In countries where the trademark application process can take years, a company may be prosecuting trademark applications for marks that are no longer in use. At other times, the scope of goods or services identified or the number of classes covered in the registrations may be over- or underinclusive. Periodic review of your current trademark portfolio identifies and eliminates these excess costs.

Knowledgeable attorneys and marketing departments that have a history with a company and have seen the branding trend over many years can offer insight into the strategy that initiated a trademark registration; however, with turnover and reorganization, the people who were involved in the original product development can be far removed from these positions years later and yet prosecution and maintenance of the trademark applications continues. Key members from marketing and sales should review and influence the decision-making process for maintaining trademark applications and registrations that are secondary or tertiary or that protect products that are no longer at the core of a company's business model. Many players are involved in the effort to protect trademark rights, and it is essential to work with key management personnel to evaluate the priorities of how to spend the trademark budget before one realizes it has been exhausted.

Organizing the Portfolio

Managing an IP portfolio requires organization of information. Investing money in a database management system and appropriate human support to keep accurate account of basic information for a trademark portfolio can save a company a significant amount of money in missed deadlines and late fees, duplicative registrations, maintenance of unused trademarks, and time spent gathering simple yet significant evidence for prosecution or litigation.[8] In addition to creating up-to-date schedules of marks listing correct statuses; registration numbers; dates of filing and registrations; goods, services, and class identifications; and first-use dates for the marks worldwide, a database should help organize information on past infringers and other conflicts, licensing commitments, upcoming trademark renewals, and current uses. The ability to access accurate, updated information is extremely cost efficient (and stress minimizing) for creating schedules to include in license agreements and when facing an objection to an application or registration or an imminent threat of trademark infringement or counterfeit action. For example, documentation supporting an applicant's *bona fide* intent to use a mark at the time of filing, such as reports and budget proposals, may be helpful or necessary to defend against efforts by third parties to invalidate registrations. Advertising and sales figures may be needed for purposes of determining damages that may have resulted from an infringement.

A central database of records maintains history better than any individual employee might do so. Counterfeiters are often reoccurring offenders or past business partners. For instance, you receive an alert reporting suspect counterfeit goods detected in transit in South Africa. Your investigator was able to identify the exporter of the goods, which originated in China. The exporter happens to be a former original equipment manufacturer (OEM) supplier who has continued to produce product bearing your company's brand since the related contract expired five years ago. The ability to quickly connect the export to your former OEM relationship, together with efficient access to the related agreements and documents, would fortify your claim of willful infringement against the manufacturer and potentially increase your leverage or the infringer's liability for damages.

A searchable database of actions taken also will help support action in other territories. You learn about a pending trademark application in the Czech Republic for a third-party registration of your brand but with a minor variation on your brand by merely adding the word *super* to the beginning of your brand so that the resulting trademark is SUPER BRAND. You commence with an action in the Czech Republic against the pending trademark application for SUPER BRAND. Four months later, your sales team in Canada reports evidence of SUPER BRAND products being sold in their territory. Six weeks later, Chinese Customs detains a container of goods bearing the SUPER BRAND trademark. You are able to link all the cases together, but local counsel in each action needs to be advised of the activities taking place in other territories, and a galvanized strategy to contain further distribution of the goods and encroachment of your IP rights is necessary. The organization of information required to combat the spread of such infringement determines just how quickly and cost effectively you are able to react.

A well-managed database will also organize due dates in advance of the specific deadlines in docket reports. Discipline in reviewing the docket reports reduces costly errors in missed deadlines or in hasty, last-minute filings, and it eliminates the costs of filing unnecessary extension requests or petitions to revive abandoned applications, for example. Furthermore, an awareness of your existing registrations in each jurisdiction may allow for replacement of multiple national registrations by a single, less costly registration.[9]

Easy access to information is also helpful when making a claim of status as a "well-known" trademark. In countries that are members of the Paris Convention,[10] a trademark holder may qualify for additional protections for its trademark if they can establish that the trademark is well known. The volume of information required to support such a claim of well-known status can be daunting and cost prohibitive (many foreign law firms will also include additional charges for organizing arguments in support of a claim of well-known status due to the volume of infor-mation required), but if successful, the additional protection provided to a trade-mark that is declared well known significantly increases the value of the brand equity. When seeking protection as a well-known trademark, maintaining orga-nized information that establishes first-use dates and is frequently updated to include declarations by other tribunals of well-known status, magazine and newspaper articles, photographs, advertisements, blog mentions, and public inter-views that show the notoriety of the trademark will relieve a company of the cost of organizing this information quickly when it is urgently needed for litigation. Well-known trademark claims require significant evidence of history, costs, and marketing information. Proactively collecting and organizing information in an easily accessible manner related to each jurisdiction and establishing public recognition can save time and money.

Selecting and Clearing a New Trademark

Just as proper management of your existing portfolio can save substantial costs, effi-ciency in the selection and clearance of new trademarks can also conserve funds in both the short and long term. Developing new marks on a budget is accomplished through educating your personnel, involving counsel in the selection process, and adopting appropriate search strategies.

Educating Personnel

Marketing, sales, and product development personnel can be trained to assist in identifying, clearing, and securing trademark rights, and somewhat regular training sessions should occur to keep the subject matter fresh in the minds of these decision makers. In the absence of a common understanding of how the process for obtaining trademark protection should work, a company's trademark portfolio could suffer when simple, appropriate, and inexpensive steps are not taken to clear and secure trademark rights. The individual expense of a trademark registration can be nominal, but when aggregated across a number of product categories in multiple countries, the costs add up, so a well-constructed strategy and regular review of a trademark portfolio ensures that limited resources are not wasted.

A primary function of counsel, both in-house and outside, is to educate com-pany management and marketing teams on the value of properly selecting, clearing, and filing trademark registrations and avoiding costly errors. While review of market-ing materials by trademark counsel or a trademark specialist may seem excessive and time consuming, problems can be identified and prevented and costs may be saved by having a trademark professional review marketing materials before they are printed for public use. Review of marketing materials may also help capture trade-mark rights that are developed unexpectedly as marketing materials are created. The review process should include feedback to the marketing and management teams that provide an explanation in lay language for the suggested changes. The explanation will provide a heightened understanding of trademark principles to non–trademark specialists and will cultivate sensitivity to trademark issues within the ranks. Some in-house counsel also make a point of regularly meeting with key marketing personnel to ensure open and easy communication, and to reduce the misperception that the legal department is obstructionist.

In the selection process, communicating and demystifying the concept of distinctiveness helps a marketing department learn to adopt stronger trademarks. Trademarks are not created equally. Stronger trademarks enjoy stronger protection under the law. The more distinctive the trademark, the greater the protection it is afforded, the easier it is to register and enforce, and the less likely it is to conflict with others' rights. Therefore, more distinctive trademarks are generally less expensive, in particular during the prosecution of the application. In U.S. trademark law, we observe three categories of trademark strength that enjoy protection merely upon use of the mark. These three categories, in order of least to most strength, are: "suggestive," "arbitrary," and "fanciful" marks.

Other categories are limited in their protectability, if they are protectable at all. Generic terms by themselves usually cannot be registered as trademarks. For example, the generic mark Mattress.com for services identified as "online retail store services in the field of mattresses, beds, and bedding" and the generic mark Tires Tires Tires for services identified as "retail tires store[s]" describe the entire class of goods or services in connection with the use of the marks and are therefore not registrable in the United States.[11]

Trademarks that are classified as descriptive do not automatically receive trademark protection until they have achieved a level of secondary meaning, or "acquired distinctiveness" as used in many territories. Ice-Pak, the phonetic equivalent of "ice pack," is considered merely descriptive for a freezer pack and therefore not registrable in the United States without evidence of secondary meaning.[12] Similarly, the number 1,000 is considered devoid of distinctive character for *inter alia* periodicals containing crossword puzzles in the European Community because consumers will perceive the mark as an indication that it contains 1,000 puzzles."[13] Sometimes grouped together with descriptive marks, common surnames, known geographic terms, product packaging, and other forms of trade dress may also be considered weak or nondistinctive when not combined with other matter.[14]

By comparison, The Soft Punch is considered suggestive, rather than merely descriptive, of noncarbonated soft drinks because it "possesses a degree of ingenuity in its phraseology which is evident in the double entendre that it projects."[15] Other examples of nondescriptive marks include Veuve—meaning "widow" in English—which is considered arbitrary for champagne and sparkling wine because it is a known word used in an unexpected or uncommon way,[16] and Kodak, which is considered fanciful for film because it does not exist as a word with significance in any language.[17] The more that a marketing or product development team understands the relative strength of trademarks, the more likely they are to choose trademarks that fall higher on the spectrum of strength. As a result, the prosecution of the corresponding trademark application may be less expensive because it may require fewer responses to questions or objections relating to descriptiveness and it may encounter fewer potential conflicts with coexisting marks. Stronger trademarks are also easier and cheaper to enforce.

Developing New Trademarks

The creative process from which potential trademarks are borne can be performed by your marketing department or outsourced to branding agencies.[18] In either case, engaging legal counsel in the brainstorming process is emerging as a trend away from the traditional practice of using trademark attorneys only for isolated, specific tasks (e.g., clearance searches and registration applications), and towards engaging them in the initial conversation and the business process. Instead of committing to a potential mark prior to consulting legal counsel, a more cost-effective strategy may be to collaborate with them early in the development of potential marks, and then provide a prioritized list of desired marks for searching. By allowing a trademark attorney to evaluate potential marks in context, the prioritized list can enable a single analysis and report that compares the relative risks involved in adopting each of the new marks of interest. Such a comparative analysis and report can often be prepared at substantially less expense than the aggregate cost of several separate searches. It bears repeating that before one embarks on a selection process for a new mark, one should consider the possibility of adopting any older marks that the company has ceased to use or acquired.[19]

Where new brands incorporate logo designs or other matter, companies should take the precaution to ensure they will own any corresponding copyrights before attempting to clear such marks and adopting them for use or registration since the costs associated with copyright infringement, invalidation of trademark registrations, and rebranding a product can be very substantial.[20]

Sometimes, trademarks or another form of IP protection may be desirable and available, but it may not be sufficiently obvious to the creative or marketing personnel that legal advice should be sought. For example, an unusual product shape, packaging, or even a distinctive building or other design may be protectable and worth protecting under trade dress or other design protection. Identifying such matter can be a benefit of regular meetings between creative and marketing personnel and the in-house legal department.

Searching

Either during the development of a candidate trademark list or after its inception, searches can be executed. Before using or attempting to register a new trademark or product name in any country, a company should identify the countries where the new product is expected to be sold and establish a timeline in which the new product offering is expected to occur. Searches generally should be initiated in the countries where the product will be launched within the current year, or in the order of business priority to avoid potentially substantial costs that may arise as a result of disputes with prior rights holders. It is also generally a good idea to conduct searches where the product will be manufactured or its original components are sourced. If a conflicting mark is disclosed, the search process may sometimes need to begin again, so providing a list of prioritized marks at the outset can serve to streamline the clearance search process. Limiting searches to only those potential marks on the agreed-upon list can be an efficient way to manage resources for developing new trademarks. Additionally, providing legal counsel with considerable information regarding the exact nature of at least the primary goods and services to be used in association with the candidate trademarks, the specific countries of commercial interest, and the commercial launch timetable will serve to facilitate the prioritization of efforts and empower the attorney to provide more meaningful and timely results. This information often helps to minimize the cost of searching and to spread the cost of filing and registration processes over a period of several years, which will also reduce costs in the event the project is aborted.[21]

Preliminary Searches

Where hiring legal counsel for searching is cost prohibitive and the company is not highly risk averse, your marketing department or branding agency may initially decide to perform a cursory Internet keyword search, domain name and social media username checks, and even their own trademark office database search for the identical mark, all of which can help avoid costly problems before substantial funds and efforts are committed to using a mark.[22]

However, personnel should be cautioned that such searches are imperfect and further that the company cannot rely, for example, on mere registration of an available domain name as the basis for the company's claim of trademark rights. The benefits of utilizing legal expertise to perform a traditional preliminary search at this stage should not be discounted. Trademark clearance searches in general are subject to a number of inherent limitations of which legal counsel will be aware, including the relatively subjective nature of trademark law and the types of marks that will likely be deemed confusingly similar, the accuracy and completeness of the official records of countries searched, the fact that not all existing trademark rights are registered, and the common-law rights created by use even if an application has been abandoned or a registration has been canceled. Therefore, even where your marketing department or branding agency has conducted a search, a trademark attorney should perform at least a preliminary search on the candidate trademark list and provide a brief analysis of the relative strengths and registrability of the potential marks.

During this early screening process, the attorney will search relevant trademark registries in territories of interest for identical and highly similar trademarks, which can sometimes be done online, often without expense on the respective country's trademark registry web site. However, each trademark registry has its own search formats and protocols, and considering the results are limited to the respective territories, this process can become time-consuming and require a significant amount of care to produce accurate results.[23] In recent years, many of the vendors providing comprehensive searches have also developed online interfaces that enable preliminary searching in numerous jurisdictions simultaneously.[24] Some offer these services free of charge, while others charge on a per-record or a subscription basis. By aggregating data across multiple trademark registries, vendor-provided search interfaces have changed the nature of the various search options, creating a uniform search protocol across multiple territories. For example, a trademark attorney can search the registries of the United States Patent and Trademark Office (USPTO) and the several states, Canada, Mexico, the European Community Trademark Office (Office for Harmonization in the Internal Market [OHIM]), and 24 of the 27 European Community member states simultaneously.

In some cases, the search report will make immediately clear that the company will not be successful in registering a potential trademark. Other times, the chances of failure are not certain, but fairly high. Some businesses proceed with the trademark process after a preliminary search, or even after a mere cursory search, and have successfully registered a trademark after resolving oppositions and other barriers, but they may expend significant resources in doing so. Therefore, the best candidate for a cost-efficient trademark is one where success seems likely based on the results of a comprehensive search, though the higher cost of obtaining same should be considered.

It is worth noting that technological and economic factors have blurred the lines between the various search options in recent years. In the past, the traditional U.S. preliminary search was often limited only to identical marks revealed in the federal registry, but the availability of online access to state registries, algorithms for finding phonetically similar marks, increased sophistication of attorneys conducting the searches, and access to domain name and social media username searches across numerous registries and sites have facilitated more extensive preliminary searches that begin to rival the traditional comprehensive searches discussed below. As a result, some less risk-averse companies elect to proceed with applications to register a mark without obtaining a comprehensive search.

Comprehensive Searches

Even with the assistance of legal counsel, concluding that a mark is clear and available based on a preliminary search only can still be a costly mistake that is otherwise preventable by performing a comprehensive search, at least in common-law jurisdictions. While there are significant costs associated with domestic and international comprehensive searches, both can save a company a significant amount of money and risk by identifying avoidable conflicts, particularly where substantial expenditures will go into the production and marketing of the goods or services under the adopted mark. A comprehensive search in the United States typically covers more variations and similar marks than might be disclosed by a preliminary search. Moreover, it typically casts a wider net by searching not only national registries, but also state registries and common-law uses found in periodicals and other publications, Internet sites, domain names, business names, and elsewhere. Comprehensive searches are carried out for a fee by search firms, which traditionally have provided their results in the form of a bound hardcopy book. Typically, attorneys would review a copy of the book by affixing colored adhesive notes to the pages that contained marks of concern. Then, they would draft a letter to their client referring to the relevant pages and enclose a clean copy of the book. These can be obtained by corporations directly, but outside counsel may be able to obtain them at substantial discount based on volume and its relationship with the vendor. Today, most vendors have online services or downloadable software to enable effective paperless review of the results where desired. However, comprehensive searches take time: depending on the scope and nature of the specific search requested, the turnaround time can be up to two weeks. Of course, if clearance is required urgently, the search can be conducted within a day at hyperinflated fees of sometimes two to three times the normal cost.

Traditionally, companies undertaking comprehensive searches followed an ul-tra-conservative search process that sometimes consisted of hiring multiple, independent search vendors to research the same mark in the same jurisdiction. With regard to domestic searches, many smaller companies now rely solely on slightly extended preliminary searches performed by legal counsel, and proceed with applications for registration, assuming the risks that result therefrom. However, the practice of obtaining clearance based on a comprehensive search after the top priority marks are identified and sometimes also preliminarily cleared is alive and well. A cost-saving approach is to limit requests for comprehensive searches to one or two of the preliminarily cleared marks.

With regard to international searches, worldwide searches costing in excess of $10,000 to $20,000 appear to be less common in the wake of the somewhat more "surgical," cross-market knockout searches (CMKOs), which provide what local counsel perceive to be the closest results in more than 50 key economies and markets throughout the globe at a fraction of the cost. Having legal counsel assist in a U.S. comprehensive search combined with a CMKO after a mark has been preliminarily cleared is cost efficient and may be a sufficient strategy for clearing marks. Where rebranding would be a very costly endeavor, comprehensive searching is more or less essential.

Filing and Pursuing Trademark Registrations

This section discusses various filing systems and strategies to consider when pursuing trademark registrations and their respective benefits and limitations.

Electing to Use a Trademark without Seeking Registration

In the United States, trademark owners can enjoy protection through a federal registration, state registration(s), or at common law. One element of prioritizing costs and rights is the decision to simply use the mark, relying solely on common-law protection, versus filing an application for federal (or state) registration. For tertiary trademarks, relying on common-law rights might make sense. Just how willing and able a company is to protect a tertiary trademark, in particular during a down economy, may justify relying solely on common-law rights provided the company understands the limitations of such rights and the risks associated therewith. It may be advisable for companies electing only to use a tertiary mark to schedule periodic reviews of the use and reevaluation of whether to pursue registration.

National versus Treaty-Based Filings

When pursuing trademark registrations in territories where a product will be marketed, another element of prioritizing costs and rights is the decision to file nationally or by using an international treaty-based system of registration. Trademark protection has conventionally been sought through national trademark applications country by country, where obstacles and unexpected costs can be encountered during each step of the process in each country. The trademark owner employs a trademark attorney or agent in each country of interest, although one "primary" counsel, often in the owner's home country, may serve to manage local counsel in other countries. The territoriality attribute of trademark law requires local legal counsel for complex matters, and trademark registries usually correspond only with local attorneys or agents. The owner or primary counsel then corresponds with each local attorney or agent to provide the filing requirements. An emerging practice that has been successful in containing costs is the appointment of primary counsel, not as a middle man between the company and local counsel, which has historically been the practice, but instead as a strategic adviser on domestic and foreign trademark issues reported from local counsel directly to both the primary counsel and in-house corporate counsel simultaneously.

The individual trademark process can be beleaguered with communication and translation problems, significant backlogs at trademark offices, outdated online databases, and difficulties that arise from incoming invoices in various currencies and a foreign exchange rate that can change from the time the work is completed to the time the invoice is received. Also, in order to maintain, renew, or record a change in ownership, name, or address, the procedure is repeated for each trademark registration in each country. Problems aside, the country-by-country approach is still commonly used to secure foreign protection, and may be the only or, ultimately, the least expensive option in some countries.

However, some treaty-based systems, such as the Community Trade Mark (CTM) registry[25] and the Madrid System,[26] allow a single trademark registration to be extended to multiple countries simultaneously, decreasing at least the initial costs related to registering and maintaining trademark rights. A CTM registrant establishes trademark rights in all member states of the European Union. An international registration under the Madrid System extends applications for protection to each of the member states designated by the applicant and accepted in the international registration. Both systems provide for a means to consolidate rights of preexisting national trademark registrations into a single trademark registration under the respective registry system, provided (1) the trademarks in the national registration are identical to the CTM or international registration, (2) the registered owners of the affected registrations are the same, and (3) the goods and/or services of the national registration are covered by the CTM or international registration.

As an example, the CTM registry allows for a "seniority claim" of preexisting national-level trademark registrations from any or all of the European Union countries. Hypothetically, your company has held trademark registrations for your primary trademark in Germany, Italy, Poland, Sweden, and the United Kingdom, each since the 1950s. The rights associated with the registrations are limited to the respective territories of each country. The CTM registry provides protection in all European Union member states, including the five countries above. Accordingly, your company can obtain a single CTM registration for your primary trademark, which presently provides protection across 27 countries,[27] and then subsequently file for a seniority claim based on the existing national registrations. Alternatively, a seniority claim may be made at the time of filing of the CTM application, but not during prosecution. Once the seniority claim has been accepted, the national trademark registrations can be abandoned; the seniority claim allows the CTM to enjoy recognition of trademark rights dating back to the filing dates of the earlier national registrations within the respective territories, and the single CTM provides protection across a significantly larger territory at a lower cost.

By way of example, the Singer trademark for sewing machines and related products has been registered in many European countries since the early 1900s. In 2007, the Singer Company Limited registered a CTM for the Singer trademark and subsequently claimed seniority to 39 preexisting national trademark registrations.[28] The seniority claims were all accepted, and the registrant may now allow the 39 national registrations to lapse in lieu of the single CTM registration for Singer, which significantly reduces the costs of maintenance and administration of the trademark portfolio. Instead of 39 renewals every 10 years, the Singer Company Limited has only one CTM to renew, and after the national registrations have been abandoned, the single CTM may be assigned to a subsequent owner at a significant reduction of the cost of assigning all 39 national registrations.

Similarly, the Madrid System provides for a "replacement" of national trademark rights under an international registration. The Madrid System, however, does not require a formal filing or acceptance of the replacement rights. The replacement automatically takes place when protection of an international registration is granted in the respective country. This system has been criticized for its lack of documented approval of the replacement rights and the weak enforceability of the Madrid replacement system should a national court choose to not apply the replacement provision in a litigation action.[29]

The Madrid System is governed by two treaties: the Madrid Agreement Concerning the International Registration of Marks ("Madrid Agreement")[30] and the Protocol Relating to the Madrid Agreement ("Madrid Protocol").[31] With the Madrid System, many trademark owners have the option of obtaining and maintaining foreign trademark protection through a process that is designed to make filing and postregistration procedures easier and more cost efficient.[32] An international registration under the Madrid System is based on an applicant's home registration and requires that the applicant's home country is a Madrid System member. For instance, a U.S. trademark applicant can file a single trademark application with the USPTO and have that application serve as a basis (called the "basic mark") for an international registration, which may be extended for the same goods and services to other Madrid System member states designated by the applicant. Choosing to initially file an application through the World Intellectual Property Organization (WIPO) does not make a trademark any more likely to register, since the substantive review of trademark registration applications under the Madrid System generally remains the same as an independent national application in each respective country. Enabling a trademark owner to file an application for registration in multiple jurisdictions simultaneously, as well as to renew and maintain the subsequent registrations through WIPO, are primary benefits of utilizing the Madrid System for protecting trademarks internationally.

Another advantage of the Madrid System is that it imposes time restrictions on the examination process in an effort to expedite applications. Designated countries have 12 months to either refuse registration or to register the trademark; otherwise, the Madrid System application is considered registered. In countries such as China, where a national trademark application can take over three years to register, the Madrid System essentially provides an expedited procedure for granting protection within the territory.

However, the Madrid System has its limitations. First, any change during the first five years to the basic application or registration used as the filing basis of the international registration similarly modifies the corresponding international registration and corresponding foreign extensions of protection (i.e., applications and registrations resulting from the international registration). Under this procedure, an international registration may be at risk for third parties to challenge the owner's registrations by attacking the original, local registration that was used as the filing basis for the international registration. This strategy for canceling an entire international registration (i.e., a "central attack") is successful when the basic application or registration is challenged before the fifth anniversary of the international registration. This is an important risk to consider when devising a strategy for securing a new trademark internationally. If an international registration is successfully challenged by a central attack, the Madrid System provides a procedure to proceed with corresponding national applications in the designated countries; however, costs escalate when converting the international registration into national applications and the process for prosecution is repeated from the beginning.

Second, the restrictive approach of the USPTO to specifications of goods and services can be disadvantageous for U.S.-based entities looking to extend protection abroad through the Madrid System. As a result of the narrow specifications of goods and services that must be used when registering U.S. trademarks, corresponding international registrations obtained on the basis of a U.S. registration are similarly limited in their protection. For instance, the USPTO would require that "clothing" be narrowed so as to describe which specific types of clothing are intended to be protected. But, in contrast, a CTM registration may cover an entire class heading. A U.S. registrant utilizing the Madrid System may be limited by the specificity of its U.S. basic registration and unable to obtain the desired breadth of protection in many foreign jurisdictions.

Third, the Supplemental Register, the means by which the USPTO allows applications for less distinctive marks to reserve rights and acquire distinctiveness over time, is unavailable to foreign entities looking to extend protection to the United States through the Madrid System. Therefore, unless the mark is registrable on the Principal Register, registration will be refused.[33] This may include attempts to register surnames and marks that are merely descriptive, where there is insufficient support for a claim of acquired distinctiveness. The issue also arises where foreign companies seek to extend protection of an international registration for a product package design or other trade dress in the United States.

In the modern world of mergers and acquisitions and private equity, a significant consideration in a filing strategy may be the transferability of a trademark.[34] International registrations under the Madrid System have their advantages and disadvantages when it comes to assignment of the registrations. The significant advantage is the centralized and low-cost procedure to assign a single international registration that may affect the registration in a number of territories. Under a country-by-country filing strategy, this procedure must be done locally at each registry. However, for an international registration, the country of origin of the receiving party in an assignment of trademark rights must be a member of the Madrid System in order to assume ownership of an existing international registration filed under the Madrid System.[35]

When deciding the most cost-efficient strategy for filing new trademark applications, the length of time the mark will be used, the likelihood of changes to the ownership information, and possible changes of the mark and its use in other countries should be considered. While a company can save money in the beginning of the process by filing for protection using the Madrid System instead of individual national applications, more significant savings through the Madrid System may not be seen until it is time to renew or transfer the international registration. Therefore, if the trademark is going to have a life longer than the renewal period, where one fee for the renewal of the international registration will be paid instead of individual country renewal fees, the Madrid System cost savings are more noteworthy. Likewise, updating ownership information is easier, quicker, and less costly if done through the Madrid System. Thus, this system may be preferable to national filings if the trademark owner knows it will be transferring ownership to new owners that are domiciled in a Madrid System member state, changing its name, or changing its address in the near future.

However, national filings may be a better choice if there will likely be alterations to the trademark or if it will be used slightly differently in foreign countries, or if there is uncertainty about the long-term future of the mark. Many trademarks carry minor variations from country to country to accommodate differences in language or culture. While some countries permit owners to amend a change that is immaterial to a registered mark,[36] the Madrid System does not allow for these changes regardless of how minor the difference may be. A single international registration application must present the mark exactly the same in all the designated jurisdictions.

Awareness of the differences between trademark practice in the United States and abroad is also essential when ensuring the proper description and classification of goods and services. The USPTO follows a fairly stringent approach when reviewing the description of goods and services, as noted above, whereas many trademark offices in other countries are more willing to accept broader descriptions, such as the entire heading of an international class. For example, a CTM application may cover "clothing, footwear, headgear" in Class 25,[37] whereas the USPTO would surely object to such a description as indefinite and require further specification. The USPTO would also likely object to an application for "clothing, including shirts (tops)" because of certain formal rules. Instead, a proper description in the United States might be "clothing, namely, T-shirts, shirts, caps, pants; and shoes, namely, leather boots, running shoes."[38] A seasoned trademark attorney would be aware of these nuances in practice and thus could help to avoid the expenses involved in later filing amendments to the description of goods and services.

Similarly, differences in practice between jurisdictions can be significant to the ultimate cost of registering trademark rights as desired within a complex corporate structure. For instance, when a corporation seeks to own trademark registrations for similar marks in the names of related entities, the strategy for doing so may differ by country. While the USPTO will allow registration by related entities where there is a unity of control,[39] the Mexican trademark office typically considers related companies as totally different entities such that previous marks in the name of one company could become potential obstacles for similar marks filed by the sister company, and letters of consent between the related companies are not always accepted.[40] Accordingly, it may be more cost effective to file Mexican applications for similar marks in the name of one entity, and upon registration, proceed to assign marks to their appropriate owners.

Whichever system is used for filing new applications, searches in individual countries usually should be sought for the availability of a trademark. An opinion rendered by local counsel may be invaluable when deciding whether to proceed with a mark. Simply filing for worldwide protection without prior knowledge of potential conflicts can be a costly mistake that affects an entire portfolio. For example, if an international registration is filed for a primary trademark, and then, in Japan, the Trademark Examiner finds a conflict, the mark may not be registrable in that territory. Although some conflicts can be overcome by litigation, straw man actions, or monetary settlements, they may be costly. Such conflicts can often be avoided and consistency maintained worldwide if a search reveals the prior mark before the international registration is filed. Another costly shortcut of not conducting a local search is the loss of local counsel's knowledge of market climates and negative cultural connotations.

It is notable that certain changes to the Madrid System that are being proposed may also affect the decision and corresponding costs of seeking international protection.[41] Proposed changes include the deletion of the "basic mark" requirement entirely, which would delete the five-year dependency feature and the central attack feature. From a U.S. perspective, eliminating the basic mark requirement means that U.S. holders may no longer be internationally bound by stringent U.S. specification requirements, as previously discussed. Also, usage of the Madrid System might be an easier option for brand owners who have markets exclusively outside of their home country. Without the basic mark requirement, there may no longer be a risk that cancellation of a basic registration in the home market will result in cancellation of the downstream registrations.[42]

We certainly will see more countries join the Madrid System. In 2010, Sudan, Israel, and Kazakhstan joined as parties to the Madrid Protocol.[43] Presently, however, the system lacks membership from key regions, including Central and South America.[44] Mexico and Canada are missing as well (Canada is also not a party to the Nice classification system of goods/services). But implementation is not easy, particularly for Canada, where the nuance of use requirements presents challenges. While the United States was able to structure implementation into the Madrid System to accommodate its use requirements, the Canadian system will require its own procedural approach to fulfill its unique statutory use requirements.

Knowing Potential Markets

When developing both a registration and enforcement program, the market influences strategy. Identifying key geographic markets and manufacturing locations is fundamental, but the unanticipated distribution of your goods as gray market and the potential distribution of infringements forces intellectual property holders to expand priorities in a registration strategy to countries that are hubs in international trade. What are the likely international trade routes for your goods and your markets? Free trade zones, which allow for the free movement of goods within the territories that comprise the zone, cannot be ignored. The European Union is perhaps obvious, but many other free trade zones exist, such as the Andean countries in South America (consisting of Colombia, Ecuador, Peru, and Bolivia) and South African Development Community (which includes South Africa, Lesotho, Swaziland, Namibia, and Botswana). The EU simplifies the concern of free trade zones and provides an inexpensive alternative to national registrations through the CTM registry. In contrast, in the Andean and southern African countries, individual national registrations or member designations under an international registration are necessary to provide complete protection.

Litigation is not cheap, and it may create an unexpected budget expense if the market is producing an unexpected surge in counterfeit and gray market goods and bad-faith or good-faith encroachment of your IP rights. They can strain resources in both time and money. Modern technology and communications can easily make a small, domestic problem into a complex international web overnight. Some companies have created innovative ways of addressing gray market goods through combined use of trademarks, copyrights, and other means.[45]

Claiming Priority

Many companies take advantage of provisions of the Paris Convention, which enable them to follow an initial trademark application filing in their home country with applications for the same mark in foreign jurisdictions. As a result of membership of the home and foreign jurisdictions in the treaty, the companies can claim priority back to the original application filing date in the foreign applications filed up to six months later. While this process enables companies to defer foreign filing costs sometimes into the next budget cycle, it may actually increase costs as a result of the numerous formalities to which a priority claim must adhere. These may include obtaining original certificates of registration in the home country, notarization, legalization, and/or translation. As a result, unless the benefits of deferring the costs of filing outweigh the additional costs associated with a claim of priority and the priority claim is needed to avoid a refusal or objection, it can be more cost effective either to file the foreign applications concurrently with the home application or to file later without claiming priority and take a risk that an application filed in the interim may prevent registration in the foreign jurisdiction.

Avoiding Domain Name and Social Media Username Conflicts

Traditionally, companies have considered domain names to be somewhat isolated from their trademark portfolio. Some, at their peril, have even registered domains before clearing and seeking trademark registrations for the corresponding marks. However, with the increased number of generic and country-code top-level domains and the anticipated availability of "vanity" top-level domains in the foreseeable future,[46] it may be more cost effective to register domain names concurrently with new trademarks in order to avoid the potential expenses involved with disputing such registrations by third parties at a later date. Moreover, the growing number of social media sites on which users can adopt usernames, handles, or page titles; the availability to search and register names across multiples social media sites; and the difficulty of obtaining such names when third parties have already registered them suggest that it may be more cost effective to register a mark as a username on important social media sites concurrently with seeking registration with the various trademark offices and domain registries.

Avoiding Self-Help Services

Filing applications without the help of knowledgeable trademark professionals is a costly shortcut that many inexperienced companies choose when filing and pursuing registrations. For instance, although self-service web sites may superficially appear to provide a less expensive alternative to apply for trademark rights, their use may result in substantially higher costs in the long run. While self-help may initially decrease costs by lowering the barriers to entry that result from a limited budget, it may be shortsighted to do so. Some pitfalls that may accompany such self-help include pushback or complete rejection from the Patent and Trademark Office (PTO), the omission of information that can leave an application open to opposition, or the subsequent cancellation of a registration for fraud or other reasons. By researching the particulars and investigating the use of a mark, knowledgeable trademark professionals may be able to determine means to inexpensively overcome objections by the PTO, sometimes *ab initio*. Overcoming these objections may prove difficult without legal advice, removing the perceived economic benefit of self-help. An experienced trademark attorney, whether in-house or serving as outside counsel, can maximize the chances for successful results by addressing issues both before the application is filed and when complex issues arise thereafter.

Supporting Registrations with Use

For marks filed in the United States, it is essential to ensure that the mark is in fact used on each and every good and service listed either at the time of filing or at the time that use is alleged. The goods and services identified in a U.S. application should be characterized as accurately and broadly as possible to anticipate change in use of the mark down the road, but cannot include, at the time that use is alleged, goods or services simply to preserve a company's future right in the absence of actual commercial use. For example, claiming use in connection with "wine," which is an acceptable description according to the Trademark Office ID Manual,[47] is much safer than claiming "wine, namely white wines and red wines." If the mark is used only for white wine, despite any initial intentions, the registration may be considered fraudulent and vulnerable to cancellation.[48] Although cancellation based on fraud is generally limited to the class of goods and services in which the fraud occurred, some still advocate against filing multiclass applications in the United States.[49] Those who do may elect to file separate trademark applications for each class of goods and services, which, when filed on one's own, do not differ in cost. The official filing fee remains the same, though outside counsel may charge differently for their services.

A benefit of isolating classes within separate applications is that examiners are less likely to be influenced by materials submitted for other classes when evaluating use in a particular class. For instance, in a multiclass application covering goods and services in two classes, the examiner may consider the use specimen in one class in light of the goods or services in the other class and refuse the application on grounds that the services are "merely incidental."[50] Similarly, when two single-class applications are filed on different dates, both may not always be refused based on likelihood of confusion with a prior third-party mark. Since a multiclass application in the United States is generally reviewed by one examiner, he or she may be more likely to perceive all the goods/services in multiple classes to be sufficiently related to refuse the application across all of the classes. However, resorting to separate applications for each class of goods and services can be cumbersome and more costly to manage and maintain.

With intent-to-use applications in the United States, it is essential, at the time of filing the statement of use, to confirm that the goods and services are accurate and that the mark is indeed in use for all identified goods and services. It is also important that the dates of first use are correct for every class of goods and services listed in the application.[51] Finally, it is important to ensure that any and all specimens of use accurately reflect the use of the mark. It should be noted that the availability of multiclass applications and the need to show use are nuances of practice and vary by jurisdiction.

Using and Enforcing Trademark Rights

This section discusses the use of brand guidelines and strategies for engaging in due diligence in connection with trademark filings and usage.

Brand Guidelines

Brand guidelines encourage the proper use of trademarks and any trade dress associated therewith. They fortify the rights associated with trademarks by providing consistent and detailed guides for use of the trademarks by the many groups within an organization, both internal within the registrant and related entities, and external within licensees who use the trademarks. Keeping branding guidelines updated guards against misuse or inconsistent use of a trademark by one's own personnel, which can dilute the strength of the mark or make it vulnerable. Such guidelines should also include marking requirements for use of the ™ and ® symbols and IP attribution statements for use on marketing materials and product packaging. An emerging practice is the creation and distribution of policies and guidelines regarding use of marks by employees and licensees on social media web sites.[52]

Due Diligence

The enforcement of trademark rights can become costly, particularly if not addressed at an early stage. With regard to trademark owners actively engaging in due diligence in connection with ongoing trademark usage, it is equally important to review registrations prior to becoming a party to a Trademark Trial and Appeal Board proceeding to identify any potential problems before they may come under attack. Companies that are proactive in both attempting to prevent others from applying for similar marks and cutting off counterfeit operations quickly can preserve a substantial amount of their legal budget.[53] These proactive efforts may include: (a) the use of watch services, which help reduce expenses by promptly identifying potentially conflicting applications filed throughout the world; (b) customs recordals; (c) educating customs officials; (d) educating and mobilizing consumers and the general public to properly reference the mark and to identify and prevent infringements; (e) participating in provider-based notification services (e.g., eBay's VeRO program); and (f) the announcement through appropriate media of actions taken in order to demonstrate the company's attentiveness and responsiveness as a warning to other parties. By learning of a potential conflict early on, a company has the possibility of investigating the business more in depth to form a better opinion as to whether it is worthwhile to litigate. At the end of the day, due diligence will ensure solid trademark rights.

Conclusion

Whether a company is managing its existing rights or selecting, clearing, registering, and using new ones, trademarks can be costly enough to tempt decision makers to ignore such matters or take shortcuts to cut expenses in a difficult economy. But companies should recognize that trademarks are not mere expenses in the liability column of their books. Rather, they are also assets that can have substantial value when they are properly maintained. Accordingly, companies should not haphazardly cut their trademark budgets or their portfolios in hard times. Rather, they should review and prioritize the marks they have and make careful, strategic decisions before adopting new brands in order to preserve and efficiently use their vital funds.

Notes

[1] The authors gratefully acknowledge the diligent efforts of Jason Kreps and Angela Lam in preparing this chapter.

[2] For example, in Thailand, a "first-to-file" country, a Thai manufacturer of motorcycle roller chains was no doubt surprised in 1997 when it learned that not one but two of its local distributors in Thailand had filed trademark applications before it for the manufacturer's trademark in their home country of Thailand. The company, Thai Roller Chain Industry Ltd. ("Thai Roller Chain"), had used the trademark DAI since 1970 in connection with its products. Presumably with bad-faith intent, both distributors of Thai Roller Chain filed the trademark applications without notifying the brand owner. Thai Roller Chain was able to negotiate a settlement with one distributor, but the other was determined to maintain its hold on the DAI trademark. After the trademark registrar and the Board of Trademarks sided with the distributor under observance of the "first to file" rule, Thai Roller Chain pursued civil litigation in Thailand's specialized Intellectual Property and International Trade Court, which again affirmed the distributor's title in the DAI trademark. Only after they took their case to the Supreme Court of Thailand was Thai Roller Chain successful in securing their rights to the DAI trademark. The cost of filing a trademark application early on would have saved Thai Roller Chain the expense of years of litigation. For a full case study, see: www.tillekeandgibbins.com/publications/event_articles/IP_NOV05/trademark_hijacking.pdf.

[3] See further below on selection of marks.

[4] Lanham Act § 7(b), 15 U.S.C.A. § 1057(b); Lanham Act § 33(a), 15 U.S.C.A. § 1115(a). See *J. C. Hall Co. v. Hallmark Cards, Inc.,* 340 F.2d 960, 144 U.S.P.Q. 435 (C.C.P.A. 1965) (registration on the Principal Register is prima facie proof of continual use of the mark, dating back to the filing date of the application for registration).

[5]See 15 U.S.C. §1117(a).

[6]For further discussion of ways to control costs in the trademark registration process, see Allan S. Pilson, Sebastian Lovera Reso, and Matthew D. Asbell, "Tips on Acquisition and Enforcement of Trademark Rights on a Tight Budget," May 14, 2009, www.mondaq.com/unitedstates/article.asp?articleid=79550.

[7]For instance, primary marks may be company names, logos, and other marks that are used globally across entities, departments, divisions or markets. Secondary marks may be those that can be substituted for a primary mark in certain areas of use, for practical or marketing reasons. Tertiary marks are those that may be for products that are limited to specific markets or short-term usage.

[8]Such database management systems can be implemented by developing or purchasing them for in-house use (e.g., proprietary or purchased software), outsourcing them through your law firm or IP services vendor, or utilizing third-party Web-based database services (e.g., trademarkia.com), which have certain limitations.

[9]See "National v. Treaty-Based Filings" following.

[10]Current contracting parties to the Paris Convention are available at www.wipo.int/treaties/en/ShowResults.jsp?lang=en&treaty_id=2.

[11]*In re 1800Mattress.com IP, LLC,* 586 F.3d 1359 (Fed. Cir. 2009); *In re Tires, Tires, Tires, Inc.,* 94 U.S.P.Q.2d 1153 (T.T.A.B. 2009).

[12]*In re Stanbel Inc.,* 16 U.S.P.Q.2d 1469 (T.T.A.B. 1990).

[13]*Agencja Wydawnicza Technopol sp. z o.o. v. Office for Harmonisation in the Internal Market,* E.C.J. Case C-51/10 P., March 10, 2011, available at http://eur-lex.europa.eu/LexUriServ/LexUriServ.do?uri=CELEX:62010J0051:EN:NOT.

[14]See *In re P. J. Fitzpatrick, Inc.,* 2010 WL 2513861 (T.T.A.B. 2010).

[15]*In re Delaware Punch Co.,* 186 U.S.P.Q. 63 (T.T.A.B. 1975).

[16]See *Palm Bay Imports, Inc. v. Veuve Clicquot Ponsardin Maison Fondee En 1772,* 396 F.3d 1369, 1372 (Fed. Cir. 2005).

[17]TMEP § 1209.01(a).

[18]For a discussion of outsourcing to branding agencies, see Terry Heckler, "Outsourcing of Branding and Marketing," in Chap. 11.

[19]But see 15 U.S.C. § 1127 ("If the mark has not been in use for three consecutive years and the owner has done nothing to try to resume use of the mark, the Office may presume that the owner has abandoned the mark."); see also Michael S. Denniston, "Residual Goodwill in Unused Marks—The Case Against Abandonment," 90 *Trademark Reporter* 615 (2000).

[20]See Matthew D. Asbell and Barbara Kolsun, *Back to the Drawing Board: How Your Graphic Designer's Ignorance of the Law May Cost Your Company,* ACC Docket, Association of Corporate Counsel, forthcoming September 2011.

[21]For a discussion of outsourcing of searches from the vendor perspective, see Joshua Braunstein, "Trademark Searches," in Chap. 12.

[22]See KnowEm.com for a useful social media web site search service.

[23]Moreover, an attorney in one jurisdiction may not be able to recognize marks that would be considered problematic in other jurisdictions, in view of differences in language, cultural significance, and the practice of trademark law.

[24]See *supra* Note 20.

[25]The registry administered and managed by the Office for Harmonization in the Internal Market (OHIM).

[26]The system of international registration of trademarks administered and managed by the World Intellectual Property Organization (WIPO).

[27]European Union member states available at http://europa.eu/abc/european_countries/eu_members/index_en.htm.

[28]CTM Reg. No. 005867759.

[29]P. Jay Hines and Jordan S. Weinstein, "Using the Madrid Protocol After U.S. Accession," *Trademark Reporter,* Vol. 93, No. 5, pp. 1023–1024 (September–October, 2003).

[30]Madrid Agreement Concerning the International Registration of Marks, April 14, 1891, 828 U. N.T.S. 389, 1 Basic Docs. International Econ. L. 781 (CCH 1994). (The Madrid Agreement was launched in 1891 as a special arrangement within the scope of the Paris Convention, and only countries party to the Paris Convention may join the Agreement.)

[31]Protocol Relating to the Madrid Agreement Concerning the International Registration of Marks, 15 U.S.C. § 1141a(b) (2004) (hereinafter Madrid Protocol). (The Madrid Protocol was instituted in 1996 to address issues raised by the many countries that had refused to join the Madrid Agreement previously [including the United States] for procedural reasons. In 2003, the Madrid Protocol became effective in the United States.)

[32]Over 80 countries participate in the Madrid System, having become party to the Madrid Agreement, the Madrid Protocol, or both.

[33]See TMEP § 1904.02(f).

[34]For a discussion of intellectual property considerations in mergers and acquisitions, see Diane Meyers, "Growth through Acquisition or Merger," in *IP Strategies for the 21st Century Corporation.*

[35]If the country of origin of the receiving party is a member of the Madrid Agreement and not the Madrid Protocol, the registration may only be assigned in those territories designated in the Madrid Protocol registration that are members of the Madrid Agreement. For example, Canada is not a member of the Madrid Protocol. If a Canadian company wants to acquire the trademark portfolio of a U.S. entity that has an international registration, the U.S. company could not record the assignment of the international registration to the Canadian company. The international registration cannot be transferred since Canada is not a member of the Madrid Protocol.

[36]See TMEP § 807.13.

[37]See EUROACE (http://oami.europa.eu/euroace/euroaceservlet?action=search&langid=en), an online search engine service provided by OHIM where applicants can perform searches on goods and services descriptions and the corresponding class numbers.

[38]See TMEP § 1402.04; See the U.S. Acceptable Identification of Goods and Services Manual (http://tess2.uspto.gov/netahtml/tidm.html): Class 25.

[39]See TMEP §1201.03.

[40]E-mail correspondence of August 23, 2010, from Mexican counsel.

[41]Description of proposed Madrid System revision, available at www.uspto.gov/trademarks/notices/madrid_feedback.jsp.

[42]An alternative proposed change is that if the "basic mark" requirement remains, holders of international marks may be able to designate their own office of origin after the expiration of the five-year dependency period.

[43]See WIPO web site, "Madrid Agreement Concerning the International Registration of Marks and Protocol Relating to the Madrid Agreement Concerning the International Registration of Marks, Status on March 17, 2011," available at www.wipo.int/export/sites/www/treaties/en/documents/pdf/madrid_marks.pdf.

[44]However, as of May 31, 2011, the Colombian Congress approved a bill calling for the country's accession to the Madrid System. As of the last edit date of this chapter, the bill is awaiting presidential sanction and Constitutional Court approval. See "Colombian Congress Approves Madrid Protocol," *INTA Bulletin,* Vol. 66, No. 11, June 15, 2011. (www.inta.org/INTABulletin/Pages/Colombian%20Congress%20Approves%20Madrid%20Protocol.aspx).

[45]See *Omega S.A. v. Costco Wholesale Corp.,* 541 F.3d 982 (9th Cir., 2008), *affirmed by* 562 U. S. (Dec. 13, 2010), Case No. 08-1423.

[46]See Dennis S. Prahl and Elliot W. Lipins, "Domain Names," in Chap. 5.

[47]Available at http://tess2.uspto.gov/netahtml/tidm.html.

[48]But see *In re Bose Corp.,* 580 F.3d 1240, 1245 (Fed. Cir. 2009) ("We hold that a trademark is obtained fraudulently under the Lanham Act only if the applicant or registrant *knowingly* makes a false, material representation with the *intent to deceive* the PTO. Subjective intent to deceive, however difficult it may be to prove, is an indispensable element in the analysis.") (emphasis added).

[49]But see J. Thomas McCarthy, *McCarthy on Trademarks and Unfair Competition* § 31:73 (6th ed., 2010) ("'[W]e find that each class of goods or services in a multiple class registration must be considered separately when reviewing the issue of fraud, and judgment on the ground of fraud as to one class does not in itself require cancellation of all classes in a registration.'") (quoting *G&W Laboratories, Inc. v. G W Pharma Limited,* 89 U.S.P.Q.2d 1571, 1574 (T.T.A.B. 2009)).

[50]See TMEP § 1301(a).

[51]But see J. Thomas McCarthy, *McCarthy on Trademarks and Unfair Competition* § 31:74 (6th ed., 2010) ("the Trademark Board has repeatedly held that for a use-based application, an erroneous date of first use does not constitute fraud so long as there was some valid use of the mark prior to the filing").

[52]Matthew D. Asbell & Christopher Lick, presentation on the Use of Trademarks on Social Media Websites, Benjamin N. Cardozo School of Law, March 17, 2011. Though the provisions may vary by company and an attorney familiar with trademark and social media marketing issues should be consulted regarding any proposed policy, some key provisions of such a policy might include: (1) requiring approval of licensees' social media web site employment policy; (2) requiring that license must be in effect for the duration of the use on a social media web site and that pages must be deleted upon nonrenewal or termination of the license; (3) requiring that royalties and other payments under the license must not be overdue to the licensor; (4) requiring that trademark terms be used as adjectives, capitalized, and immediately followed by the appropriate symbol ® or ™; (5) requiring that any page on a social media site must include an attribution statement; and (6) requiring that a prominent hyperlink to the web site/page of the licensor be included on the social media page.

[53]For a discussion on the use of private investigation to protect intellectual property rights, see Jeremiah A. Pastrick, "Investigations—Considerations for Selecting & Directing Outside Investigators," in Chap. 13.

CHAPTER 5

Domain Names

Dennis S. Prahl and Elliot Lipins
Ladas & Parry LLP

T he Internet and domain names have created one of the largest challenges to the protection of trademarks since the end of the 20th century. It is essential for every trademark owner to understand the nature of domain names, the threats posed to trademarks by domain names, and the options available to prevent and act against abuses by other parties.

An Overview of the Internet

The Internet is a large number of interconnected computer networks located across the globe, which collectively offer a vast amount of information to other people on the network. At the end of 2009, an estimated 1.8 billion people were using the Internet.[1] The World Wide Web specifically refers to a network of hyperlink documents that users access via an Internet browser on their computer. The Internet and, most prominently, the World Wide Web have become wildly popular and offer companies great opportunities to establish and expand their brands. The Internet and World Wide Web also pose significant opportunities for trademark infringement and misuse by third parties.

The Internet has also presented a challenge internally to brand owners and companies, forcing a convergence of assets across the legal, marketing, communications, and information technology (IT) departments. The most successful companies in this area are those who have recognized this convergence and established protocols for strategy, budgeting, and communications across these internal departments, resulting in proactive policies to capitalize on the opportunities and address the challenges. Others have simply left it to an ad hoc and inconsistent approach that achieves neither an effective message, a productive legal strategy, nor IT best practices. Either way, brand owners have had to devote more personnel and monetary resources to their Internet strategies and coordination among the three key departments yields the greatest cost-benefit.

A basic understanding of the Internet and careful monitoring of a company's trademarks on the Internet is necessary in order to establish and maintain effective policies and the goodwill and value of a company's trademarks.

Domain Names

Brand owners need to understand how domain names function and how they are allocated and used in order to grasp the risks they present to brands.

The Function of Domain Names

Organization of large numbers of computer networks that comprise the Internet is accomplished largely by the Internet protocol (IP) address system. Under the IP system, each network on the Internet is assigned a unique IP address in the form of a 32-bit number, or a number string such as 123.234.345.456, which can be analogized to a telephone number. Computers rely on the IP address of a network to identify and connect to specific web sites on that network.

Domain names provide a simplified naming system to associate with IP addresses so that users do not need to remember long number strings. A domain name is an alphanumeric identifier that is used to designate a particular 32-bit Internet protocol Web address. The use of meaningful, informative language to direct a user to a particular domain name greatly simplifies the task of locating particular web sites. The use of language within a domain name allows domain owners to define their web site in a manner that helps users find and remember the domain name. For instance, Ladas Domains, LLC has registered ladasdomains.com to provide information and a Web commerce site for its services. Internet users simply type www.ladasdomains.com in the address bar of their Internet browser to find the web site rather than typing 69.20.67.17, which is the IP address for the same web site.

Domain name servers (DNSs) associate the specific numeric IP address with the corresponding domain name and provide the technical framework to allow the domain name system to function successfully. DNSs ensure that an Internet user who types a specific domain name in his Internet browser is routed to the proper IP address. Notably, they also allow a domain name holder to modify the domain name/IP address relationship at any time. As a result, if the domain owner's server or server location is changed, the domain owner or its network administrator can update the IP address on the DNS and an Internet user typing the domain name will then be directed seamlessly to the new location or new server. A domain name's function as an unchanging designator for a domain owner's server allows physical changes of server locations to go unrecognized to a visitor of the owner's web site.

The Anatomy of a Domain Name

A web address such as http://www.internet.com is comprised of numerous parts. The most relevant components of a domain name for intellectual property owners are the portions following the "www." The rightmost portion immediately following the rightmost period is known as the top-level domain (TLD). The TLD defines the register on which the domain name is listed and has several legal ramifications, which will be discussed in detail later in this section.

The component to the left of the TLD, immediately preceding the rightmost period, is known as the second-level domain. This portion of the address consists of a string of alphanumeric characters that provides a context to the purpose of the web site. This portion is the most relevant component of a brand owner's intellectual property as domain name disputes typically arise from allegations that the alphanumeric content of the second-level domain infringes another party's trademark. A domain name may also have third-level domains, which are additional alphanumeric strings immediately preceding the period before the second-level domain. In the web address http://www.my.internet.com, "internet" is considered the second-level domain and "my" is the third-level domain.

The leftmost portions of a domain name are primarily technical terms that have little relevance to intellectual property issues. The leftmost portion normally consists of "http://" or "https://". These designations specify the communication protocol that an Internet browser should use to obtain requested information. "http://" denotes that the Hypertext Transfer Protocol should be used. "https://" refers to usage of the Hypertext Transfer Protocol Secure, which creates a secure channel over an unsecure network, and is typically used for sensitive transactions like online payments.

The prefix "www" indicates the World Wide Web. This prefix is not instructional to the Internet browser and is mainly placed in a domain name due to an established practice of naming the domain location according to services provided on that server. Many Internet browsers automatically add the "www" if the second-level and top-level domains are entered by the user.

Top-Level Domains

There are two categories of TLDs: country-code top-level domains (ccTLDs) and generic top-level domains (gTLDs).

ccTLDs Country-code top-level domains are two letter extensions that are intended for specific countries or territories. The specific name of the ccTLD for each country or territory is an abbreviation for that country or territory. In all but a few historical exceptions, the country code corresponds to the International Organization for Standardization (ISO-3066) two-letter abbreviation for that country or territory.

As of June 2010, there were 248 ccTLDs. The countries/territories with 10 of the most popular ccTLDs at that time were: China (.Cn), Germany (.de), United Kingdom (.uk), Netherlands (.nl), European Union (.eu), Russia (.ru), Brazil (.br), Tokelau Islands (.tk), Italy (.it) and Poland (.pl).[2]

Many ccTLDs have introduced subdomain ccTLDs in an effort to apportion additional space in the domain name system based on the function of the domain name. For example, the .UK domain itself is unavailable for domain name registrations. Instead, the registry offers domains in the .co.uk subdomain for commercial domain names, .ac.uk for academic domain names, .gov.uk for government domain names, and so forth.

Some ccTLDs no longer bear any connection to their country-code roots, such as .tv (Tuvalu), .co (Colombia) and .me (Macedonia), which were delegated to commercial operators and opened for any users.

INTERNATIONALIZED DOMAIN NAMES   Traditionally, the ccTLDs were restricted to Latin characters corresponding to the ISO two-letter country codes. More recently, an emerging area in the domain name system that particularly affects ccTLDs is the introduction of domain names in non-Latin characters. The character-encoding scheme used to represent text in computers is called the American Standard Code for Information Interchange (ASCII), which is based on the English alphabet. Internationalized domain names (IDNs) have been introduced that have local language characters that are from non-ASCII scripts, such as Chinese, Arabic, and Cyrillic. Applications for such domain names were accepted starting in November 2009. In April 2010, the Internet Corporation for Assigned Names and Numbers (ICANN) board accepted the IDN ccTLD delegation requests for Egypt, Russia, United Arab Emirates, and Saudi Arabia.[3] The IDNs will allow domain names to be more accessible to more than half of the estimated 1.6 billion Internet users that speak languages having non-Latin alphabet scripts.

Although this development opens up opportunities for millions of new domain names intended for specific linguistic markets, it also opens up additional opportunities for cybersquatting and trademark infringement in these domains. A common practice, for example, in the area of trademark infringement is for a would-be infringer to use and/or register the local language translation or transliteration of a foreign brand name. The introduction of IDN domain names allows this practice to expand to use of such translated or transliterated brands to the Internet.

gTLDs   Generic top-level domains are top-level domains having three or more characters that are not country/territory specific. gTLDs are comprised of unsponsored TLDs and sponsored TLDs (sTLDs). Unsponsored gTLDs include restricted and unrestricted domains while sTLDs are normally restricted. Unrestricted domain names may be registered by any individual or corporation for any purpose. The current unsponsored gTLDs are .biz, .com, .info, .name, .net, .pro, and .org.[4] Notably, .info is the only unsponsored gTLD that was not planned for a specific purpose. The .com, .net, and .org gTLDs were originally intended specifically for commercial entities, organizations involved in networking technology, and nonprofit organizations, respectively. However, widespread registration of these TLDs for purposes outside the scope of the intended purposes resulted in these domains being treated as unrestricted.

The current restricted, unsponsored gTLDs are .biz, .name, and .pro.[5] The .biz gTLD is intended for use solely by businesses and must be for a "bona fide business or commercial use." The .name gTLD is intended solely to be used by individuals and the domain must comprise their legal name or nickname. The .pro gTLD is intended for use solely by licensed professionals in furtherance of the provision of their services.

Sponsored gTLDs are specialized domains sponsored by private agencies or organizations for specific purposes and usage is restricted to specific communities. The current sponsored gTLDs are as follows: .aero, .asia, .cat, .coop, .edu, .gov, .int, .jobs, .mil, .mobi, .museum, .tel, and .travel.[6] As an example of the communities served by sponsored gTLDs, .aero is run by the Société Internationale de Télécommunications

Aéronautique (SITA) for use by companies and individuals in the field of aviation. Other examples of popular sponsored gTLDs are .edu, which is sponsored by Educause for academic institutions recognized by the U.S. Department of Education, and .gov, which is sponsored by General Services Administration, an agency of the U.S. government, for domains used by the U.S. government.

On March 18, 2011, the sponsored gTLD .xxx was approved by ICANN for domains used by the adult entertainment industry. The .xxx sponsored gTLD is expected to launch later in 2011.

PLANNED EXPANSION OF gTLDs In June 2008, ICANN announced its intention to expand the number of open and sponsored gTLDs available. Under the plan, which was approved by the ICANN Board of Directors on June 20, 2011, a company will be able to purchase its own gTLD for an application fee of approximately $185,000. The company would then have the responsibility of operating a registry for that gTLD and to manage and monitor domains on the registry. As of August 2010, it was rumored that as many as 113 new gTLDs are under contemplation for possible submission,[7] including geographic domains such as .nyc and .berlin,[8] and keyword domains such as .shop and .eco.

The expansion of gTLDs to cover a company's brand name offers a plethora of potential benefits and problems for trademark owners. A branded gTLD may offer a company with the necessary funds a great opportunity to market its brand online, organize a community concerning its company and provide greater security for its online branding. However, the relatively high costs associated with applying for and operating a gTLD will disadvantage smaller companies that do not have the resources for a gTLD. Additionally, there may be many instances of companies with identical trademarks in different fields seeking a particular gTLD, with only one company able to acquire it. Descriptive and generic terms, such as .shop, are likely to be very valuable gTLDs as well, with many companies having an interest in a particular generic or descriptive TLD and only one company able to own the TLD.

Allocation of Domain Names

The Internet Assigned Numbers Authority (IANA) is the organization that is responsible for the creation and delegation of TLDs. The IANA handles several vital technical requirements for the Internet to run efficiently, including assignment of ccTLDs and gTLDs, maintaining numbers and codes in many different IPs, and coordination of the IP addressing system.

Since 1998, the IANA has been a function of ICANN.[9] After approving the formation of a TLD, the IANA's duty is to assign an operator for the TLD.[10] The domain registry operator, referred to as a Network Information Center (NIC), handles the allocation of domain names and maintains a registry of all domain names registered under the TLD. The IANA does not take an active role in managing TLDs aside from the creation of the TLD and assignment of a capable operator for the TLD.

Registration of Domain Names

A company may "register" a domain name, which provides them an exclusive right to use the domain name for a specific period of time but no actual ownership interest. A domain owner generally has the right to transfer or assign its domain name to another company.

The sale of domains is handled by registrars. Domain names are sold on a first-come, first-served basis. Domain names are purchased for a finite number of years, and annual fees must be paid for each registration. The application for registering a domain name usually requires that the following information be provided: administrative contact, technical contact, billing contact, and name servers. There is a requirement that the information provided is accurate. Some or all registration information is made available in a public "whois" database unless the domain holder uses a privacy service that provides generic information for the whois database in order to protect the domain holder's identity from publication in a public database. A privacy service is generally available for most gTLDs, although not for most ccTLDs.

Independent registrars accredited by ICANN are able to sell domain names in many different TLDs. At present, there are no exclusive registrars for a particular TLD. The domain name applicant purchases the domain at the registrar. The registrar then notifies the operator for that TLD of the registration and sends them a fee for the registration. The operator then updates its registry to reflect the new owner of the domain name. As of April 2011 there were nearly 1,000 registrars accredited by ICANN.

Unrestricted domain names may be purchased by any individual or company. However, restricted gTLDs have specific eligibility criteria that must be satisfied. The majority of ccTLDs also have specific eligibility criteria that must be satisfied. For instance, to purchase an Australian .com.au domain name, the applicant must be an Australian company or have a registered business name or association, and the domain name must be an exact match of the company's business name, a close abbreviation or acronym, or have a close and substantial relationship to the company's business.[11] Similarly, in order to register the domain name .ac.uk, the applicant has to have a permanent physical presence in the United Kingdom, and it must have central government funding to provide teaching at a tertiary level; or part of its core activities must be to conduct publicly funded academic research where a reasonable proportion of the results are placed in the U.K. public domain; or its primary purpose must be to provide support for organizations that work with tertiary level educational establishments; or it should have the status of a Learned Society, which is a society that exists to promote an academic discipline or group of disciplines.[12] France has a subdomain, .tm.fr, that requires the proprietor to show evidence of a corresponding trademark application or registration effective in France for eligibility.[13]

A registrar customarily will scrutinize the eligibility requirements before approving a registration. A registrar will typically register the domain name even if all of the eligibility requirements are not met. However, registrants for domain names that do not meet the eligibility requirements risk losing the domain name if they are challenged by a third party.

Regulation of Domain Name Disputes

All gTLDs and many ccTLDs have a policy in place to regulate disputes regarding domain names within that TLD. ccTLDs may have specific policies that reflect the local laws of the specific territory or country covered by the ccTLD. For instance, disputes under the .us domains are governed by the usTLD dispute resolution policy.[14]

In contrast, most gTLDs (including all open gTLDs) are governed by ICANN's Uniform Dispute Resolution Policy (UDRP). The UDRP currently applies to disputes that arise for domains with the following TLDs: .com, .net, .org, .aero, .asia, .biz, . cat, . coop, .info, .jobs, .mobi, .museum, .name, .pro, .travel and .tel.[15] Some countries have adopted the UDRP as the policy applicable to their ccTLD domain name disputes. These countries include Armenia,[16] Bermuda,[17] Colombia,[18] Ecuador,[19] Pakistan,[20] Puerto Rico,[21] Romania,[22] and Venezuela.

UDRP In 1999, ICANN adopted the UDRP in order to provide a uniform process and set of rules to protect trademark owners from abusive registrations.[23]

Registrants of domain names falling under the UDRP automatically consent to the terms and conditions of the UDRP policy as a condition of purchasing the domain name. Registrars that sell these domain names are required to agree to the terms of the UDRP. The mandatory consent to the UDRP by domain registrants and registrars ensures that the UDRP will be applicable and binding on domain disputes of TLDs that the policy is intended to govern.

The UDRP provides that an owner of a domain name that is governed by the UDRP is required to submit to an administrative proceeding conducted before an approved administrative dispute resolution service provider.[24] The arbitration hearing prescribed by the UDRP is intended to provide a cost-effective and quick resolution to domain name disputes.

Currently, complainants under the UDRP may submit their claims to the ICANN-approved providers, namely, Arbitration and Mediation Center of the World Intellectual Property Organization (WIPO), the National Arbitration Forum (NAF), the Asian Domain Name Dispute Resolution Centre (ADNDRC), and the Czech Arbitration Court (CAC).[25] The UDRP Rules establish the rules of procedure.[26] Additionally, each administrative dispute resolution provider has its own supplemental rules of procedure. For instance, the ADNDRC follows the Supplemental Rules to ICANN's Uniform Domain Name Dispute Resolution Policy and the Rules for the Uniform Domain Name Dispute Resolution Policy[27]; the NAF follows the Supplemental Rules to ICANN'S Uniform Domain Name Dispute Resolution Policy[28]; WIPO has its own Supplemental Rules for Uniform Domain Name Dispute Resolution Policy[29]; and the CAC follows the UDRP Supplemental Rules of the Czech Arbitration Court.[30]

UDRP decisions are rendered within about two months from the institution of the proceeding.[31] A complainant institutes the proceeding by filing a complaint along with the required fee. A respondent then has a specific period of time to file its response. Each party can then file one additional submission, which may cost an additional fee. The panel (composed of one or three members, depending on the request of the parties) then makes a decision based on the record before them.

The sole remedy for a complainant in a UDRP proceeding is the cancellation of the domain name or transfer of the domain name to the complainant. After the panel has made a decision, if the decision was for transfer or cancellation of the domain name, the registrar will be notified and is obligated to transfer the domain name to the complainant or cancel the domain name registration unless the losing party provides notice within 10 days after the decision that a lawsuit challenging the decision has been commenced. Such a lawsuit would have to be instituted in a specified Mutual Jurisdiction, generally being either the location of the principal office of the registrar (provided the domain-name holder has submitted to such jurisdiction in its registration agreement), or the domain-name holder's address as indicated in the registration of the domain name in the registrar's whois database at the time the complaint is submitted to the provider.[32]

Disputes under the UDRP require that the complainant asserts that:

1. The contested domain name is identical or confusingly similar to a trademark or service mark in which the complainant has rights; and
2. The domain owner has no rights or legitimate interests with respect to the domain name; and
3. The domain name has been registered and is being used in bad faith by the domain name owner.[33]

Where domain name disputes do not satisfy each of these criteria, they are considered to be outside the scope of the UDRP. Therefore, the UDRP will assist a trademark owner that has a valuable domain taken by a third party only when the registration is a bad-faith, abusive registration within the circumstances specified by the UDRP. Unrestricted domain names are still available on a first-come, first-served basis, and many domain disputes are outside the specific cybersquatting-type problems that the UDRP seeks to redress.

Under the UDRP, a panel will find any of these three circumstances to constitute bad-faith registration and use:

1. Circumstances indicating that the domain owner has registered or acquired the domain name primarily for the purpose of selling, renting, or otherwise transferring the domain name registration to the complainant who is the owner of the trademark or service mark or to a competitor of that complainant, for valuable consideration in excess of its documented out-of-pocket costs directly related to the domain name;
2. The domain owner registered the domain name in order to prevent the owner of the trademark or service mark from reflecting the mark in a corresponding domain name, provided that the domain owner has engaged in a pattern of such conduct;
3. The domain owner has registered the domain name primarily for the purpose of disrupting the business of a competitor; or
4. By using the domain name, the domain owner has intentionally attempted to attract, for commercial gain, Internet users to the web site or other online location, by creating a likelihood of confusion with the complainant's mark as to the source, sponsorship, affiliation, or endorsement of the web site or location or of a product or service on the web site or location.[34]

The UDRP provides that a respondent to a complaint may show one of the following circumstances to prove rights to and legitimate interests to a domain name:

1. Before any notice to the domain owner of the dispute, the domain owner used, or made demonstrable preparations to use, the domain name or a name

corresponding to the domain name in connection with a bona fide offering of goods or services;

2. The domain owner has been commonly known by the domain name, even if it has not acquired any trademark or service mark rights; or

3. The domain owner is making a legitimate noncommercial or fair use of the domain name, without intent for commercial gain to misleadingly divert consumers or to tarnish the trademark or service mark at issue.[35]

While a dispute falling under the UDRP is usually resolved via an administrative proceeding, the UDRP specifically permits either party to commence litigation in court before the UDRP proceeding is commenced or within 10 business days after a decision is rendered.[36]

THE ANTICYBERSQUATTING CONSUMER PROTECTION ACT In the United States, litigation of domain name disputes is governed by a federal statute enacted in 1999 entitled the Anticybersquatting Consumer Protection Act (ACPA).[37] A trademark owner can sue a domain name registrant in federal court pursuant to the ACPA.

The ACPA provides in relevant part that a person shall be liable for "cyberpiracy" to an owner of a trademark if they have a bad-faith intent to profit from that mark and they register, traffic or use a domain name that is (i) identical or confusingly similar to a mark that is distinctive as of the time the domain name is registered or (ii) is identical or confusingly similar or dilutive of a mark that is famous at the time the domain name is registered.

The ACPA lists the following factors to consider when determining if a domain name registrant had the necessary bad faith:

1. Whether the domain owner has trademark or other intellectual property rights in the domain name;

2. The extent to which the domain name consists of the legal name or a commonly used name to identify the domain owner;

3. Whether the domain owner has prior use of the domain name in connection with a bona fide offering of any goods or services;

4. Whether the domain owner is using the domain name in connection with a bona fide noncommercial or fair use of the mark;

5. Whether the domain owner intends to divert consumers from the mark owner's online location to a site accessible under the domain name that could harm the goodwill represented by the mark, either for commercial gain or with the intent to tarnish or disparage the mark, by creating a likelihood of confusion as to the source, sponsorship, affiliation, or endorsement of the site;

6. Whether the domain owner has offered to transfer, sell, or otherwise assign the domain name to the mark owner or any third party for financial gain without having used, or having an intent to use, the domain name in the bona fide offering of any goods or services, or the domain owner's prior conduct indicating a pattern of such conduct;

7. Whether the domain owner provided material and misleading false contact information when applying for the registration of the domain name, intentionally

failed to maintain accurate contact information, or has prior conduct indicating a pattern of such conduct;

8. Whether the domain owner has registered or acquired multiple domain names that the domain owner knows are identical or confusingly similar to marks of others that are distinctive at the time of registration of such domain names, or dilutive of famous marks of others that are famous at the time of registration of such domain names, without regard to the goods or services of the parties; and

9. The extent to which the mark incorporated in the domain name registration is or is not distinctive and famous within the meaning of subsection (c).

The ACPA further provides that bad faith shall not be found if the court determines that the domain registrant "believed or had reasonable grounds to believe that the use of the domain name was a fair use or otherwise lawful."

While the ACPA is substantively similar to the UDRP, the ACPA has several important differences as compared to the UDRP. Most notably, the ACPA provides relief to a plaintiff in the form of monetary damages in addition to transfer or cancellation of the domain name registration.[38] The plaintiff under the ACPA may recover its actual damages.[39] Alternatively, in lieu of actual damages, the plaintiff may elect statutory damages which the court has discretion to award in an amount from $1,000 to $100,000 per domain name.[40] Costs and attorney's fees may also be awarded under the ACPA.[41]

However, monetary damages are limited for domain names containing living personal names. The only monetary damages a plaintiff may recover if the domain name comprises a living person's name is attorney's fees and costs.[42]

If the domain registrant cannot be located, such as instances where false information was provided when registering the domain name, the ACPA provides that a plaintiff may file an *in rem* proceeding.[43] The venue for an *in rem* action is the judicial district in which the domain name 'registrar, domain name registry, or other domain name authority that registered or assigned the domain name is located.' Monetary damages are unavailable to a plaintiff in an *in rem* ACPA proceeding and the plaintiff's relief is limited to transfer or cancellation of the domain name.[44]

Litigation under the ACPA is normally much longer than a UDRP proceeding and can also be much more expensive, depending on how vigorously it is defended. However, the availability of monetary damages makes ACPA proceedings appealing to complainants. Furthermore, a party may prefer such proceeding since litigation under the ACPA is more extensive and may provide a fairer determination on the merits than a streamlined UDRP proceeding, especially in difficult, fact-intensive cases. However, where delay in taking action is an issue, the ACPA proceeding, which may be subject to equitable considerations of laches and acquiescence,[45] may be less attractive than a UDRP proceeding where such principles are given less deference. Since Paragraph 4(c) of the UDRP does not mention laches and acquiescence among the defenses that may be asserted by a respondent, most panelists deem these grounds to be unavailable in a UDRP proceeding.[46]

For action against domain name holders located outside the United States, whose identity and location can be identified, a complainant who does not wish to, or cannot, use the UDRP, may be limited to judicial action within the domain holder's jurisdiction under the classic trademark infringement, passing off, and unfair competition laws of that locale.

Domain Watch/Enforcement of Intellectual Property

Abusive domain name registrations present serious threats to trademark rights, but there are a number of courses of action and strategies brand owners can employ to minimize the damage.

ABUSIVE REGISTRATIONS   In order for a company to protect its valuable trademarks, continuous monitoring of domain name registrations containing terms relevant to a company's intellectual property is necessary, as well as the activities on those domains.

There are many different types of problematic registrations that threaten to infringe, dilute, or otherwise misappropriate a company's trademark. A domain name infringer or "cybersquatter" will normally seek domain names that are similar to a company's trademark either because the domain name has a second-, third-, or fourth-level domain containing a company's trademark or a typographical error for a company's trademark. An example of a problematic domain name registration is a domain having a second-level domain comprising the company's trademark by itself that the company failed to register. This often occurs when a company focuses on specific TLDs and leaves valuable TLDs available for registration by others. In addition, sometimes a company inadvertently permits a domain registration to lapse. The existence of "domain sniping" services allows a third party to automatically register the domain immediately after the domain name expires.

Often, a cybersquatter will register a domain name that contains the company's trademark in combination with a generic or descriptive wording for the company's goods and/or services ("combosquatting"). These combosquatting registrations may be particularly valuable because they place high in the results on an Internet search engine.

Misspellings of a company's trademark ("typosquatting") is another type of domain name commonly registered by cybersquatters. For instance, a cybersquatter may seek to register the domain wwwgoogle.com or gooogle.com to divert Internet users seeking Google.com but accidentally leaving out the period after "www" or adding an extra "o" to the popular second-level domain "google."

The .co ccTLD for Colombia was recently opened to any registrants[47] and has many companies concerned that this ccTLD will be used by cybersquatters to attract customers that mistakenly leave out the "m" in the .com TLD. Therefore, the .co ccTLD is expected to be a hotbed of activity that will attract the interest of many companies that have few or no business interests in Colombia.

Cybersquatters have different modes of conduct after they attract consumers to a web site at an infringing domain name. Many times, a cybersquatter will provide numerous links to e-commerce web sites that generally relate to the trademark owner's goods and services, that is, web sites offering the company's or its competitor's goods and/or services. These links are usually provided by automated services such as Google's AdSense. The cybersquatter generates "click-through fees" for Internet users that visit the web sites at the provided links and purchase products at those web sites. Other times, a domain name is registered by a cybersquatter solely to resell the domain name for a substantial sum. The web site associated with the domain name may display a parking page and may include links to an auction site that allows visitors to bid on the domain name.

A serious misuse occurs when the infringing domain name has an e-commerce site that offers competitors' products or counterfeit goods. This type of abusive registration requires immediate action.

Another very critical misuse occurs when the domain owner places a counterfeit web site at the domain name, which appears to be the company's real web site. Often, the forged web site is used to acquire an Internet user's confidential information including credit card numbers, Social Security numbers, usernames, and passwords ("phishing"). While the company may have been unaware of the "phishing" site, customers who are duped by such web sites may lose loyalty and trust in the company. Accordingly, this is another situation where swift action is imperative.

STRATEGIES TO PROTECT TRADEMARKS   There are several steps trademark owners can take to reduce the number of domain name infringements it faces. To begin, when adopting a trademark, a comprehensive domain name search should be performed so the company can determine how many domain name registrations already exist reflecting that trademark. A trademark that has few available domain names containing this term may significantly decrease the potential value of that trademark.

Before introducing a trademark or as soon as possible after a trademark is adopted, the trademark owner should implement an appropriate plan to purchase relevant domain names containing that trademark in (1) all available gTLDs, (2) sTLDs for which the trademark owner is eligible, (3) ccTLDs that are highly cybersquatted (.cn, .com.cn, .tv, etc.), and (4) ccTLDs that match the commercial plans for the trademark (ccTLDs for countries of sale and interest). It is also important when considering registration of ccTLDs that consumers in countries outside the United States usually look first for a trademark owner's web site at their country's own ccTLD. Therefore, a company should try and register the domain name for ccTLDs in countries/territories in which a company is currently doing business or intends to do business in the future.

The registration of domain names that a company is not particularly interested in using but that they want to hold mainly to prevent a cybersquatter from registering the domain is known as acquiring "defensive registrations." The proactive step of purchasing defensive domain names that a cybersquatter is likely to register such as typosquatting or combosquatting names is a prudent strategy. While a gTLD domain registration costs anywhere from $10 to $30 a year, an infringement action even under the UDRP will result in exponentially larger costs. Therefore, even if the number of defensive registrations a company purchases is quite large, this strategy normally will be a more cost-effective solution than leaving the domain names available and enforcing the company's intellectual property rights against third-party registrants afterwards.

Once a domain portfolio relating to a trademark is initiated, a domain watching service that conducts a weekly or periodic comprehensive search of all new domain name registrations containing a company's trademark is an invaluable tool for detecting potentially conflicting registrations. The Internet is so vast that it is not feasible for most companies to conduct a diligent Internet search of problematic domain names in a cost-effective, efficient manner. An enforcement policy should also be adopted at the outset in order to prioritize action against the various types of domain names and uses that are detected and ensure that appropriate and cost-effective action is taken against them.

Trademark owners also need to maintain their registrations carefully. This requires proper internal administrative procedures to ensure that notices are received, domain name renewals are attended to, and the information provided for the domain registrations remains accurate and contacts remain accessible. It also means that domain names in the portfolio are used to resolve to the trademark owner's web site(s) and not to their domain name registrar's parking or search engine optimization pages, which drive traffic elsewhere.

A trademark owner that learns of an abusive registration should take swift action in order to preserve its trademark rights. Each domain name requires an analysis of the degree of conflict involved, the seriousness of the use, the profile of the domain holder, and the rights and remedies that are available. A typical initial step is to send a letter from counsel demanding that the domain owner cease and desist all use of the domain name and transfer the domain to the trademark owner. If the domain owner does not comply with the request, or where the desired level of compliance appears unlikely, the trademark owner may consider instituting available administrative action, such as a UDRP proceeding in the case of gTLD domain names. The institution of a lawsuit under the relevant laws, such as the ACPA in the United States, is also an available option. Many consider that ACPA lawsuits have a greater deterrent effect than UDRP proceedings on prospective cybersquatting situations.

Alternatively, trademark owners can also consider attempting to purchase conflicting domain names from their owners, but may wish to do so through an unconnected third party, using dissemblance, in order to keep the asking price reasonable.

If a trademark owner suspects that a domain owner has created a phishing site, they should contact the Federal Trade Commission to seek criminal charges[48] against the domain owner in addition to other enforcement measures.

Although the UDRP is applicable to gTLDs and a number of ccTLDs that have also adopted it as their own, such as Cyprus (.cy),[49] the Republic of Moldova (.md),[50] and Belize (.bz),[51] certain TLD registries have adopted their own dispute policies, such as the ccTLD registries in the United Kingdom,[52] China,[53] and Canada.[54] Each of these have different rules, venues, and procedures that apply to domains in their ccTLDs but serve as another weapon in the trademark owner's arsenal against cybersquatting. Unfortunately, many more ccTLDs have no dispute resolution policies and procedures, such as Russia (.ru), where trademark owners are left to initiate court action in order to enforce their rights against abusive domain name registrations.

ENFORCEMENT AFTER THE NEW gTLD PROGRAM IS IMPLEMENTED   Many trademark owners are concerned that the approved expansion of gTLDs,[55] which is anticipated to increase greatly the number of new top-level domains, also will greatly increase infringement problems and the costs of protecting trademarks on the Internet. Each new gTLD poses the risk of many new instances of problematic registrations for a company. A company seeking to reduce cybersquatting by purchasing defensive registrations at each new gTLD may have thousands of new domains to purchase. Furthermore, companies are concerned that registrars for the new gTLDs may charge excessive fees to register domains.

In order to allay the fears of many trademark owners concerning escalation of infringement issues on the Internet when the new gTLDs are introduced, ICANN appointed an Implementation Recommendation Team,[56] which proposed new systems designed to prevent bad-faith registrations and make enforcement of intellectual property easier. Some of these proposals were formally adopted in the new gTLD program and have the potential to dramatically change the practice of protecting and enforcing intellectual property rights on the Internet.

The mechanisms proposed by ICANN's Implementation Recommendation Team[57] included an intellectual property clearinghouse,[58] which will act as a database for validated common-law and registered trademark rights on a worldwide basis. Additionally, a global protected marks list[59] was considered, although rejected by ICANN, for famous trademarks that are subject to a large number of worldwide trademark registrations and are considered the biggest targets for cybersquatters.

The new gTLD program has incorporated the intellectual property clearinghouse. Trademark owners may deposit proof of their trademarks with the clearinghouse, and the new gTLDs will advise both the trademark owner and the domain registrant that the domain name being registered is identical to the deposited trademark. In addition, each new gTLD will need to incorporate a sunrise period whereby owners of previously registered trademarks will be given priority for registering corresponding domain names in the new gTLDs.

Another procedure that will supplement the UDRP is a uniform rapid suspension system (URS).[60] The URS would allow a trademark owner to quickly obtain a suspension of a domain name registration if the owner provides clear and convincing evidence that it is an abusive domain name registration. The suspension will eliminate all web sites from being associated with the domain name during its registration period and will in essence act as an injunction stopping the trademark owner from being further harmed by the domain name registration. The rights to the suspended domain name can then be challenged in a UDRP proceeding or litigation in order to achieve the transfer or cancellation of the domain name. Additional systems are proposed to ensure that the registrars and registry operators do not operate a new gTLD in a manner that infringes a company's trademark rights and that the whois records offered by registrars of the new gTLDs provide sufficient information.

The final mechanism to protect trademark owners in the new gTLD program is the Postdelegation Dispute Resolution Procedure (PDDRP) whereby a trademark owner may file a complaint against a domain name registrar for engaging in a pattern of bad-faith exploitation of domain names that conflict with the owner's trademark. The PDDRP can potentially suspend a registrar's business for such activity.

Adoption of the new gTLDs will mean that trademark owners will need to regularly review their registration, defensive registration, and maintenance policies, as well as their enforcement policies, in order to ensure that their policies keep pace. It is hoped that some of the additional systems incorporated in the new gTLD process will also be useful for trademark owners.

Conclusion

The importance of the Internet in modern commerce means that domain names are now an integral part of intellectual property and they should be protected and defended. The increase in Internet usage coupled with the coming explosive growth of top-level domains means successful brand owners need to implement policies across their marketing, legal, and technology departments to capitalize on the benefits of domain names, while also protecting their brands from the threats domain names present.

Notes

[1] See www.internetworldstats.com/stats.htm, www.internetworldstats.com. Copyright © 2000–2010, Miniwatts Marketing Group.

[2] World Statistics on Domain Names, *DomainesInfo*, www.domainesinfo.fr/statistiques.php, accessed on August 31, 2010.

[3] Tina Dam, "IDN ccTLD Delegations Approved by the ICANN Board," *ICANN Blog*, April 27, 2010, http://blog.icann.org/2010/04/idn-cctld-delegations-approved-by-the-icann-board/, accessed on August 10, 2010. See www.icann.org/en/topics/idn/ for current status.

[4] About gTLDs, *ICANN*, www.icann.org/en/registries/about.htm, accessed on August 12, 2010.

[5] Business Constituency Position Paper, *ICANN*, http://forum.icann.org/gtld-plan-comments/general/pdf00000.pdf, accessed August 12, 2010.

[6] Root Zone Database, *IANA*, www.iana.org/domains/root/db/, accessed on August 9, 2010.

[7] New TLDs, *newTLDs*, www.newtlds.tv/newtlds/, accessed on August 31, 2010.

[8] Antony Van Couvering, "What Cost New gTLD Trademark Infringement to Brands," *Minds & Machines*, February 17, 2010, www.mindsandmachines.com/2010/02/what-cost-new-gtld-trademark-infringements-to-brands/, accessed on August 10, 2010.

[9] Introducing IANA: Baltic Region and Eastern European International Seminar, *IANA*, www.iana.org/about/presentations/davies-riga-igf-061004.pdf, accessed on August 9, 2010.

[10] Save Vocea, "ccTLD Best Practices & Considerations," *ICANN*, June 30, 2008, www.pacnog.org/pacnog4/presentations/save-cctld-best-prac.pdf, accessed on August 9, 2010.

[11] "Domain Name Eligibility and Allocation Policy Rules for Open 2LDS," Policy No. 2008-05, publication date May 30, 2008, *The Australian Domain Name Administrator*, www.auda.org.au/policies/auda-2008-05/, accessed on August 9, 2010.

[12] "Eligibility Guidelines for a Name under ac.uk," *JANET, The UK's Education and Research Network*, www.ja.net/services/domain-name-registration/register.ac.uk/eligibility-ac.html, accessed on August 9, 2010.

[13] "Naming Policy for .fr Registration: Rules for .fr Domain Names, Version in Force Starting March 16, 2010," *AFNIC*, www.afnic.fr/data/chartes/charter-fr-2010-03-16.pdf, accessed on August 31, 2010.

[14] usTLD Dispute Resolution Policy, *.US*, www.nic.us/policies/docs/usdrp.pdf, accessed on August 31, 2010.

[15] Uniform Domain Name Dispute Resolution Policy, *ICANN*, www.icann.org/en/udrp/, accessed on August 9, 2010.

[16] Application Form for Non-Residents, *Armenia Network Information Center*, www.amnic.net/register/, accessed on August 9, 2010.

[17] Domain Name Dispute Resolution Policy, *BermudaNIC; The Bermuda Network Information Center*, www.bermudanic.bm/, accessed on August 9, 2010.

[18] CO Launch and Registration Rules for Grandfathering, Sunrise and Landrush, *.CO Internet S.A.S*, www.cointernet.co/sites/default/files/documents/CO_Sunrise_Launch%26Registration_1.4.pdf, accessed on August 9, 2010.

[19]Dispute Resolution Policy, *Domain Registry EC – Ecuador*, www.nic.ec/info/eng/resolution. htm, accessed on August 9, 2010.

[20]Internet Domain Registration Policy, *PKNIC*, http://pk5.pknic.net.pk/pk5/pgPolicy.PK, accessed on August 9, 2010.

[21]PR Domain Name Registration Agreement, *PR Puerto Rico Top Level Domain*, www.nic.pr/ registration_agreement.asp, accessed on August 9, 2010.

[22]Registration Agreement, *Romania Top Level Domain*, http://portal.rotld.ro/pages/en/1/, accessed on August 9, 2010.

[23]Special Meeting of the Initial Board Minutes October 24, 1999, *ICANN*, www.icann.org/en/ minutes/minutes-24oct99.htm#99.112, accessed on August 9, 2010.

[24]Uniform Domain Name Dispute Resolution Policy, *ICANN*, www.icann.org/en/dndr/udrp/ policy.htm, accessed on August 9, 2010.

[25]List of Approved Dispute Resolution Service Providers, *ICANN*, www.icann.org/en/dndr/ udrp/approved-providers.htm, accessed on August 9, 2010.

[26]Rules for Uniform Domain Name Dispute Resolution Policy, *ICANN*, www.icann.org/en/ dndr/udrp/uniform-rules.htm, accessed on August 9, 2010.

[27]Asian Domain Name Dispute Resolution Center Supplemental Rules to the Internet Corporation for Assigned Names and Numbers Uniform Domain Name Dispute Resolution Policy and the Rules for the Uniform Domain Name Dispute Resolution Policy, *ADNDRC*, www.adndrc. org/hk_supplemental_rules.html, accessed on August 9, 2010.

[28]Dispute Resolution for Domain Names, Supplemental Rules, *NAF*, http://domains.adrforum. com/users/icann/resources/UDRP%20Supplemental%20Rules%20eff%20March%201%202010. pdf, accessed on August 9, 2010.

[29]Supplemental Rules for Uniform Domain Name Resolution Policy, *WIPO*, www.wipo.int/ amc/en/domains/supplemental/eudrp/, accessed on August 9, 2010.

[30]UDRP's Supplemental Rules of the Czech Arbitration Court, *Arbitration Center for Internet Disputes*, www.adr.eu/arbitration_platform/udrp_supplemental_rules.php%20, accessed on August 9, 2010.

[31]Guide to WIPO Domain Name Dispute Resolution, *WIPO Arbitration and Mediation Center*, www.wipo.int/freepublications/en/arbitration/892/wipo_pub_892.pdf, accessed on August 9, 2010.

[32]Rules for Uniform Dispute Resolution Policy, *ICANN*, Paragraph 4(k), www.icann.org/en/ dndr/udrp/policy.htm, accessed on August 9, 2010.

[33]Uniform Dispute Resolution Policy, *ICANN*, www.icann.org/en/dndr/udrp/policy.htm, accessed on August 9, 2010.

[34]Id.

[35]Id.

[36]Id.

[37]15 U.S.C. § 1125(d).

[38]15 U.S.C. § 1117(d).

[39]15 U.S.C. § 1117(a).

[40]15 U.S.C. § 1117(d).

[41]15 U.S.C. § 1117(a) and (b).

[42]15 U.S.C. § 1129(2).

[43]15 U.S.C. § 1125(D)(d)2(A)&(C).

[44]15 U.S.C. § 1125(D)(d)2(D).

[45]*Southern Grouts & Mortars, Inc.*, S.D. Fla, No 0:07-cv-61388 (Sept. 19, 2008), *Flentye v. Kathrein*, 485 F. Supp. 2d 903, 916 (N.D. Ill. 2007), *Ford Motor Co. v. Catalanotte*, 342 F.3d 543, 550 (6th Cir. 2003).

[46]*Tropicana Products, Inc. v. Dunne*, FA0811001235498 (NAF Jan. 13, 2009).

[47]CO Launch and Registration Rules for Grandfathering, Sunrise and Landrush, *.CO Internet S.A.S*, www.cointernet.co/sites/default/files/documents/CO_Sunrise_Launch%26Registration_1.4.pdf, accessed on August 9, 2010.

[48]15 U.S.C. § 45(b).

[49]Domain Name Registration Agreement, *Country Code TLD Registrar for .CY,* www.nic.cy/rulesreg.htm, accessed on August 10, 2010.

[50]Domain Name Registration Agreement, *Registration under .MD Top Level Domain*, www.register.md/terms.php, accessed on August 10, 2010.

[51]Registration Guideline, *Dot BZ*, www.belizenic.bz/index.php/home/regguidelines, accessed on August 9, 2010.

[52]Dispute Resolution Service Policy, *NOMINET,* www.nic.uk/disputes/drs/?contentId=5239, accessed on August 10, 2010.

[53]Rules for CNNIC Domain Name Dispute Resolution Policy, *CNNIC,* www.cnnic.net.cn/html/Dir/2006/03/15/3655.htm, accessed on August 10, 2010.

[54]CIRA Domain Name Dispute Resolution Policy, *Canadian Internet Registration Authority (CIRA)*, www.cira.ca/assets/Documents/Legal/Dispute/CDRPpolicy.pdf, accessed on August 10, 2010.

[55]New gTLD Program, Draft Applicant Guidebook, Version 4, *ICANN*, www.icann.org/en/topics/new-gtlds/draft-rfp-clean-28may10-en.pdf, accessed on August 10, 2010.

[56]http://icann.org/en/announcements/announcement-6-06mar09-en.htm.

[57]Introduction: Implementation Recommendation Team (IRT), *ICANN*, www.icann.org/en/topics/new-gtlds/irt-draft-report-trademark-protection-24apr09-en.pdf, accessed on August 10, 2010.

[58]IRT Recommendation for an IP Clearinghouse, a Globally Protected Marks List, and other Top and Second-Level Rights Protection Mechanisms, *ICANN*, www.icann.org/en/topics/new-gtlds/irt-draft-report-trademark-protection-24apr09-en.pdf, accessed on August 10, 2010.

[59]Id.

[60]Draft Uniform Rapid Suspension System (URS), *ICANN*, www.icann.org/en/topics/new-gtlds/irt-draft-report-trademark-protection-24apr09-en.pdf, accessed on August 10, 2010.

CHAPTER 6

Creating, Perfecting, and Enforcing Security Interests in Intellectual Property

Scott J. Lebson
Ladas & Parry LLP

In November 2006, Ford Motor Company was featured prominently in the business sections of many major newspapers and financial media outlets for offering nearly all its domestic assets as collateral in exchange for US$18 billion in secured loans.[1] Among the key assets included in this refinancing were all of Ford's patent and trademark rights. Foreseeing difficult times ahead, Ford strategically leveraged the full value of its intellectual property (IP) rights as part of the overall collateral. The resultant liquidity ultimately allowed Ford to weather the height of the global economic recession and become the only major U.S. car company to avoid declaring bankruptcy in 2009.[2] Ford CEO Alan Mullaly stated, "During the worst economic recession in 30 or 40 years, because of the strength of the plan we put in place a few years ago, we were not only able to survive but also to create a foundation that is delivering now profitable growth."[3] Undoubtedly, the Ford name and technology were critical components of this successful refinancing strategy.

The Ford example is indicative of how far IP has evolved in not just the protection of inventions, brands, and other intangible assets, but as a dynamic and dominating factor in commercial transactions. In fact, it could be argued that the driving force behind a majority of mergers and acquisitions completed during the last two decades has been the acquirer's desire to obtain the target's IP assets. Lenders[4] and other professionals in the investment community have come to recognize that a company's IP may be its most valuable asset. Secured transactions[5] are an ideal method in which to capture the true value of IP rights. This chapter will discuss the creation, perfection, and enforcement of security interests in the United States and worldwide.

U.S. Securitization of Intellectual Property

Both in the United States and in most other countries, there are three separate and distinct legal components that must be taken into account during the securitization process. These three components are:

1. Creation
2. Perfection
3. Enforcement/release

Source of Law: Application of Uniform Commercial Code Article 9[6]

Most IP rights created in the United States, in particular, patents, trademarks, and copyrights, are creatures of *federal* law, deriving from powers granted by the U.S. Constitution or federal legislation.[7] However, the *creation* of a security interest in IP is governed by the law of the individual *states*, which is typically set forth in that state's principal commercial statutory framework known as the Uniform Commercial Code (UCC). Article 9 of the UCC, which governs secured transactions, explicitly provides that it applies to *any* transaction, regardless of its form, that creates a security interest in *personal property*.[8] More specifically, Article 9 of the UCC governs security interests in "general intangibles,"[9] and general intangibles are considered *personal property* for purposes of UCC interpretation.[10] It is important to note that there is no specific mention of patents, trademarks, and copyrights in Section 9-102. However, upon a more in-depth review of this section, the *Official Comment* utilizes the catch-all term "intellectual property" as an example of a general intangible,[11] and it is well settled that patents, trademarks, and copyrights fall within the definition of intellectual property.[12]

Federal versus State Law: When Does Federal Law IP Law Trump State Law

As previously mentioned, the law with respect to the *creation* of security interests in IP is governed exclusively by state law and is fairly uniform across the fifty states under their respective versions of the UCC.[13] However, in terms of *perfecting* (i.e., filing and recording) a security interest in IP, state law does not exclusively control.[14] Depending on the type of IP being securitized, preemption by federal law could be encountered when secured parties are seeking to perfect their liens so as to obtain priority and make certain their rights are protected and enforceable if foreclosure is subsequently necessary. It is critical for borrowers, lenders/secured parties, and their respective counsel to be aware of some potential pitfalls that currently exist when securitizing IP in the United States.

Section 9-109(c)(1) of the UCC states:

> *This article does not apply to the extent that: a statute, regulation or treaty of the United States preempts this article.*[15]

For IP rights that are governed exclusively by state law, such as common-law trademarks used in intrastate commerce and trade secrets, Article 9 is clear that no federal rules need to be followed or federal filings made. The creation, perfection, and enforcement of IP security interests in these common-law properties are governed by state law. The issue becomes less clear when discussing perfection of IP rights governed by federal law, such as patents, copyrights, and federally registered trademarks. Unless and until such time as there is a federal statute governing the perfection of security interests in IP, the type of IP subject to a security agreement will determine where perfection should take place.[16]

Proper Creation of a Security Interest under State Law

The UCC explicitly requires that a security interest is created in the form of a written instrument, at least with respect to securitizing certain property, including IP. The specific source of the law can be found at Section 9-201(a) of the UCC, which provides:

> *Except as otherwise provided in this chapter, a security agreement is effective according to its terms between the parties, against purchasers of the collateral and against creditors.*

In addition, Article 9 sets forth certain basic requirements that must be met in order to create a valid security interest. Article 9-203 states that:

> *A security interest* attaches *to collateral when it becomes* enforceable against the debtor *with respect to the collateral, unless an agreement expressly postpones the time of attachment.*[17]

ATTACHMENT　　The term *attachment* generally means "enforceable against the debtor."[18] In order to be enforceable against the debtor, Article 9 sets forth three basic requirements for creating an enforceable security interest in collateral. Article 9-203(b) states:

> *Except as otherwise provided . . . a security interest is enforceable only if:*
>
> *value has been given;*
>
> *the debtor has rights in the collateral or the power to transfer rights in the collateral to a secured party; and*
>
> *the debtor has authenticated a security agreement that provides a description of the collateral.*

A description of personal or real property is considered sufficient, whether or not it is specific, if it reasonably identifies what is described.[19] When all three of the preceding elements exist, that is: *value, debtor's rights in the collateral,* and a *signed agreement with an evidentiary requirement* (the "description"), a valid security interest has been created between the parties and attaches to the collateral.[20]

Perfection of a Security Interest in the United States

Upon proper creation of a security interest in IP, it is critical for secured parties to take appropriate measures to make the lien public record. *Perfection* is of critical importance in that a secured party with a perfected security interest has greater rights than those of an unperfected secured or unsecured party.[21] This is especially true in the event of bankruptcy. To "perfect" a security interest, the secured party must provide public notice of the existence of such interest by filing a lien notice with the applicable local, state, or federal agency. With respect to IP, the applicable jurisdiction and law depends on the type of IP involved.

PERFECTION OF IP UNDER STATE LAW (UCC FILING)   In order to properly perfect a security interest under the UCC, a secured party must first determine (1) where to perfect and (2) how to perfect.

WHERE TO PERFECT   The general rule under the UCC discussing where security interests should be perfected is stated in Section 9-301, which provides:

> *Except as otherwise provided in this section, while a debtor is located in a jurisdiction, the local law of that jurisdiction governs perfection, the effect of perfection or non-perfection and the priority of a security interest in collateral.*[22]

Filing under the law of the debtor's location is the general rule governing the perfection of security interests in both tangible and intangible collateral.[23] This, of course, includes security interests against certain types of IP. If the debtor has more than one "place of business,"[24] its location for purposes of perfection shall be considered its chief executive office.[25] If the debtor's location changes, the security interest is considered perfected for a period of four months, after which a new financing statement must be filed in the debtor's new location.[26] The filing generally takes place in either the secretary of state's office where the debtor is located or in the county clerk's office.[27] In certain states, dual filings at the state and county level may be necessary.

HOW TO PERFECT   With respect to general intangibles, perfection cannot take place automatically, such as in the case of a "purchase money security interest"[28] or by simply handing over possession. Rather, in order to perfect a security interest in general intangibles, this must take place by filing what is known as a "financing statement."[29] The financing statement must adequately describe the collateral that is the subject of a lien.[30] If only certain IP is serving as collateral, then that collateral must be separately identified.[31] If, however, all general intangibles are to serve as collateral, there is no requirement under the UCC that they be separately identified.[32] Language to the effect of "all general intangibles now owned or hereinafter acquired by the debtor" is usually considered a sufficient statement.[33]

There have been cases, however, such as *In re 199Z, Inc.*, wherein a California bankruptcy court held that the mere description of collateral as "general intangibles" was insufficient to describe the IP and the security interest was not properly perfected.[34] Unfortunately for the creditor in this case, its attempt to perfect with the United States Patent and Trademark Office (USPTO) was also deemed insufficient and they were relegated to unsecured creditor status.[35]

As will be discussed in more detail herein, there are certain exceptions to perfection by filing under the UCC. The most notable exception regarding IP is found in UCC 9-310(b)(3) and 9-311(a)(1), which provides:

> *The filing of a financing statement is not necessary to perfect a security interest in property subject to a statute, regulation or treaty of the United States whose requirements for a security interest's obtaining priority over the rights of a lien creditor with respect to the property preempt Section 9-310(a).*

This subsection exempts from the filing provisions of Article 9 those instances where a system of federal filing has been established under federal law. This subsection makes clear that when such a system exists, perfection of a relevant security interest can be achieved only through compliance with that federal system; that is, filing under Article 9 is not a permissible alternative.[36]

Perfection of Security Interests in Trademarks in the United States

In order to consider how a security interest in a trademark is perfected, it is first necessary to discuss certain limitations on trademark transfers, which have a secondary effect on the creation of a security interest.

Limitations on Assignment and Relevance to Perfection

Unlike most assets, including patents and copyrights, special statutory restrictions exist on the form that a transfer of a trademark may take.[37] 15 U.S.C. §1060 provides that:

> *A registered mark or a mark for which an application to register has been filed shall be assignable with the **goodwill** of the business in which the mark is used, or with that part of the good will of the business connected with the use of and symbolized by the mark.*[38]

Trademarks function to identify and distinguish the owner's goods from those of others and to indicate the source of those goods.[39] As such, they cannot exist separate and apart from the ongoing business with which they have become associated.[40] If a mark were separated from that business, it could no longer function to identify the source of the goods to which it was attached and it would therefore cease to be a trademark.[41] The situation sought to be avoided is customer deception resulting from abrupt and radical changes in the nature and quality of the goods or services after assignment of the mark.[42]

Merely taking a security interest will not in and of itself violate the rule against an assignment "in-gross," or without goodwill, inasmuch as a security interest is not an assignment.[43] If, however, the debtor defaults and the creditor tries to take title to the mark pursuant to a security agreement, the prohibition against assignments in-gross may be triggered.[44] Therefore, taking a security interest in a trademark without the associated goodwill could result in the trademark's being canceled upon foreclosure if the subsequent assignment takes place without goodwill.[45] In order to avoid this consequence, secured parties are advised to take a lien on other related assets associated with the products marketed under the trademark, such as accompanying trade dress, to make certain that in the event of foreclosure, the mere act of assignment would not in and of itself destroy the value of the collateral.[46] The secured party need only acquire those assets necessary to ensure that a mark will continue to be connected with substantially the same products with which it has become associated.[47]

UCC Filing Required

The general rule with respect to trademarks, whether registered or unregistered, is that perfection of a security interest in a trademark should be accomplished under Article 9 as a general intangible. Although the UCC provides that any federal filing scheme would preempt its provisions, Section 1060 of the federal Lanham Act addresses only the issue of *assignment* of trademarks, not liens on federally registered marks.[48] There is no specific mention or reference to mortgages, hypothecation, collateralization, or any other synonym associated with taking a security interest in U.S. federal trademark law. The case of *In re 199Z Inc.* reinforced the distinction between assignments and security interests. In that case, the defendant/creditor argued that its security interest had been properly perfected at the state level under the UCC *and* at the federal level at the USPTO.[49] The bankruptcy court discussed how the assignment of a trademark is an absolute transfer of the entire right, title, and interest to the trademark and that the grant of a security interest is less than an outright transfer.[50] The court summarized that a security interest is merely what the term suggests, namely, a device to secure indebtedness and only an agreement to assign in the event of default by the debtor. Since a security interest in a trademark is not equivalent to an assignment, the filing of a security interest is not covered by the Lanham Act.[51] Much to the dismay of the creditor, the court also held that its security interest was not properly perfected under the UCC due to an insufficient description of collateral.[52] This case illustrates the potential pitfall for secured creditors because of improper filing.

A subsequent bankruptcy case further delineated the relationship between federal and state law as it pertains to trademark security interests. In *Trimarchi v. Together Development Corp.*, a Massachusetts bankruptcy court rejected the notion that the Lanham Act created an exemption to state and local filing requirements under the Supremacy Clause[53] and did not preempt the UCC's filing requirements to perfect a security interest.[54] Additionally, the filing of a security interest was not the equivalent of an assignment and the Lanham Act makes no specific mention of security interests in its recording statute.[55] It has been repeatedly held that for federal law to supercede the UCC, the federal statute itself must provide a method for perfecting the security interest.[56]

Dual Filings Recommended

Notwithstanding that the current state of the law dictates that perfection of security interest in trademarks are properly filed and recorded at the state level, the USPTO will accept and record security interests in trademarks. Thus, it has become common knowledge and practice for secured parties to file and record such security interests with the USPTO. This, in turn, has led to the common misconception that recording with the USPTO will be sufficient. This misconception has caused confusion among secured parties who believe that they have taken the appropriate measures to properly protect their interests. Several courts have noted the dichotomy in how this area of the law has developed, which has been referred to by one judge as a "trap for the unwary."[57]

Notwithstanding the foregoing, even though filing with the USPTO will have no legal effect in and of itself, it is still advisable to make such a filing. While filing with the USPTO will not perfect the lien, the filing will serve as notice to a subsequent purchaser, who in the course of due diligence would be well advised to search the USPTO records for security interest recordals. Any purchaser who has notice of an unperfected lien would take the property subject to such lien.[58]

Intent-to-Use Applications

U.S. trademark law requires that trademarks be used in order to maintain validity and continued registration. Generally, a trademark owner acquires common-law rights in a trademark before it is entitled to registration of that mark under federal law. However, it is permissible to apply for registration at the USPTO as an "intent-to-use" (ITU) trademark. As such, a trademark owner may "hold its place" at the USPTO before acquiring common-law rights through actual use.[59] However, a mere ITU application without use does not confer upon the trademark owner sufficient "rights in the collateral" as required by Article 9 to properly create a security interest. In fact, Section 10 of the federal Lanham Act provides that no ITU application shall be assignable prior to the filing of an amendment to allege use or a verified statement of use unless the assignee succeeds to all or part of the assignor's business.[60]

In *Clorox v. Chemical Bank*, the Trademark Trial and Appeal Board held that an outright pre-use assignment of an ITU application to a lender as part of a security agreement was prohibited,[61] and the Board subsequently invalidated the debtor's trademark.[62] However, the Board observed that the grant of a mere Article 9 security interest in a mark would not be considered an assignment and would not provoke a penalty for trademark trafficking.[63] They did not opine on whether the security interest was properly created under state law. However, without use, the trademark owner will not have obtained sufficient rights in the collateral. Parties to a secured transaction should be cautious if considering taking ITUs as collateral as trademark rights could be jeopardized, harming both the trademark owner and secured party. Whether an ITU mark can be assigned to a creditor will depend on whether commercial use has actually been made.

Perfection of Security Interests in Patents in the United States

The general rule with respect to patents is that perfection of a security interest should be accomplished under Article 9 as a general intangible. Similar to the Lanham Act, the relevant assignment provision of the federal Patent Act does not specifically address the issue of perfection of security interests in patents.[64]

UCC Filing Required

Historically, patent liens were recorded at the USPTO, a practice that stemmed from the U.S. Supreme Court case of *Waterman v. McKenzie*.[65] The Court in *Waterman* held that a recorded lien on a patent was tantamount to a delivery of possession, thereby permitting the secured party to sue for infringement.[66] The Court opined that:

> *A patent right is incorporeal property, not susceptible of actual delivery or possession; and the recording of a mortgage thereof in the Patent Office, is equivalent to a delivery of possession, and makes the title of the mortgagee complete towards all other persons, as well as against the mortgagor.*[67]

Of course, while *Waterman* provided that perfection under the USPTO was proper, it could not specifically exclude the UCC method of perfection since the UCC did not exist in the 1890s. Subsequent to *Waterman* and with the advent of the UCC, there was a divergence in the lower courts as to whether UCC perfection is proper. Leading this divergence were cases emerging from the bankruptcy courts. In *In re Cybernetics, Inc.,* the 9th Circuit held that state UCC recording requirements were not preempted by Section 261 of the Patent Act concerning assignments in that the Patent Act did not speak specifically to "security interests" and, therefore, recordal at the USPTO was not required in order to properly perfect.[68] Therefore, the bankruptcy trustee as a hypothetical lien creditor could not avoid a lien on a patent that had been perfected under the UCC, but not with a federal filing.[69] In the case of *In re Transportation Design*, the U.S. Bankruptcy Court for the Southern District of California entertained the question of whether a mere filing of a UCC-1 Financing Statement was sufficient to perfect the security interest in a patent. In finding that the recordal at the USPTO was not required, the court reasoned that with the advent of the UCC, it is no longer necessary to create a security interest by an assignment or transfer of title.[70] In sum, filing under the UCC is proper and a subsequent filing at the USPTO is advisable.

Perfection of Security Interests in U.S. Copyrights

In considering perfection of security interests in copyrights, it is important to understand that registration, or lack thereof, will determine the proper method of securitization.

Federally Registered Copyrights

Of the three most prominent forms of intellectual property, namely, patents, trademarks, and copyrights, only the Copyright Act currently provides for a federal perfection scheme. Section 205 of the Copyright Act provides:

> *Any transfer of copyright ownership or other document pertaining to a copyright may be recorded in the Copyright Office if the document filed for recordation bears the*

actual signature of the person who executed it, or if it is accompanied by a sworn or official certification that it is a true copy of the original, signed document.[71]

At first glance, Section 205 does not appear to discuss securitization of copyrights in any manner whatsoever. However, on closer scrutiny of the Copyright Act, the definition of a "transfer of copyright ownership" is defined under Section 101 as:

An assignment, mortgage, exclusive license, or any other conveyance, aliena-tion, or hypothecation of a copyright or of any of the exclusive rights comprised in a copyright, whether or not it is limited in time or place of effect, but not in-cluding a nonexclusive license.[72]

Case law under this section, including the leading case in this area, *In re Pere-grine Entertainment*, has emphatically rejected any notion that federally registered copyrights are properly perfected under the UCC or that a UCC filing is an acceptable alternative method.[73] The *Peregrine* court opined that even in the absence of express language, federal regulation will preempt state law if it is so pervasive as to indicate that Congress left no room for supplementary state regulation.[74] In view of the com-prehensive scope of the Copyright Act's recording provisions, along with the unique federal interests they implicate, the *Peregrine* court held the view that federal law preempts state law in the context of registered copyrights. As such, the current state of the law dictates that, with respect to registered copyrights, perfection should take place by filing at the U.S. Copyright Office.

Unregistered Copyrights

Although security interests in registered copyrights can only be properly perfected by recording with United States Copyright Office, it has been held in cases such as *In re World Auxilary Power Co.*, that a bank's security interest in *unregistered* copy-rights was properly perfected pursuant to Article 9 of the UCC, as no other way existed for a secured creditor to preserve priority in an unregistered copyright.[75] The U.S. Copyright Office has no means of indexing a recordal against an unregistered copyright. In *In re World Auxilary Power*, whereby the 9th Circuit Court of Appeals rejected the notion that *Peregrine* could be extended to unregistered copyrights, the court stated that the effect of such an extension would be to make registration of copyrights a necessary prerequisite of perfecting a security interest.[76] The court con-tinued that such a requirement would effectively render unregistered copyrights use-less as collateral, which was not the intent of the statute.[77] However, other cases decided subsequently to *Peregrine* have extended *Peregrine*'s holdings to include unregistered copyrights as well, finding that only a federal filing with the Copyright Office was the proper method and if registration was required, then this was a neces-sary prerequisite to perfection.[78] In *In re AEG Acquisition Corp.* and *In re Avalon Software, Inc.*, both courts held that perfection could only be obtained by first regis-tering the copyrights and thereafter recording the security interest with the Copyright Office. A prudent creditor/secured party may want to insist on registration and recordal at the federal level at the U.S. Copyright Office while simultaneously record-ing at the UCC level against any unregistered rights.

Perfection of Security Interests in Domain Names

Domain names, although not necessarily a "new" form of IP anymore, have quickly become a critical component of any IP portfolio. A domain name[79] may be registered and/or acquired not only for commercial purposes, but for defensive purposes as it relates to a company's overall trademark protection and enforcement strategy. Thus, corporate domain name portfolios can become considerably large in a short period of time and accrue substantial value in terms of goodwill related to the company's business. As a result, domain names are typically included in an IP securitization transaction.

UCC Filing Required

To date, there have been no statutes, regulations, or case law to suggest that the creation and perfection of security interests in domain names should occur in any other manner than at the state level under the UCC under the rules set forth for general intangibles. The filing of a financing statement setting forth a description of the domain names to be used as collateral should ensure proper perfection.

Are Domain Names "Property"?

There is a minority view among some legal scholars and practitioners as to whether domain names are in fact a type of "property." Some argue that a domain name is not property and that a domain name registrant receives only the conditional contractual right to the exclusive association of the registered domain name for the term of the registrations.[80] Under the minority view, the registrant does not, through its contract with the registry, obtain any rights against any other person other than the consequent exclusivity resulting from the fact that an identical domain name cannot be used during the term of registration.[81] Thus, this view likens the legal status of domain names to that of telephone numbers.[82]

In the United States, the Anticybersquatting Consumer Protection Act (ACPA) authorizes *in rem* civil action against a domain name, suggesting that a domain name is indeed a form of intangible property, especially since *in rem* actions are brought specifically against property.[83] Cases decided under the ACPA have held that the U.S. Congress intended for domain names to be treated as property, at least with respect to the ACPA.[84] Notwithstanding the minority view, domain names have nonetheless routinely been treated as property and made subject to security interests created and perfected under the UCC.

Attempts to Harmonize Perfection Laws in the United States as It Relates to Intellectual Property

As the adoption, protection, and enforcement of IP rights have evolved to represent a critical aspect of a company's overall asset portfolio, it is important to understand how to exploit their full financial potential. Recognizing this fact, several bills were proposed in the U.S. Congress in the past decade to harmonize state and federal law in the United States as it pertains to IP securitization. Such bills included the Intellectual Property

Security Interest Coordination Act and the Intellectual Property Security Act. Both bills were very similar in that they recognized the shortcomings in the current system and the unsettled nature of the law in this area. It is this author's opinion that predictability and uniformity in the treatment of security interests in IP on a federal level would minimize the risks to lenders and simultaneously create greater access to capital for IP owners, especially start-up companies. Unfortunately, the bills discussed above were not passed and parties to commercial transactions should continue to look to the current state of the law for guidance in the financing and securitization of IP.

Default

Default by the borrower will have significant implications for all parties to a securitization transaction. The course of action taken by the parties, especially by the secured party, will generally be governed by the security agreement and state law. Federal bankruptcy law can also play a significant role in determining how secured property is treated.[85]

Events of Default

Events of default are typically established between the parties and memorialized in the security agreement. Events of default could include, but are not limited to:

- Payment-related default.
- Performance-related default.
- Failure to properly maintain (abandonment) or enforce (infringement) the IP rights.

Remedies for Default

The UCC provides a few different ways in which defaults can be remedied by a secured party.

REPOSSESSION WITHOUT JUDICIAL INTERVENTION   Remedies for default are provided for under state law under Article 9 of the UCC. Generally, Article 9 allows for "repossession" (as opposed to foreclosure) of IP collateral without having to resort to legal or equitable forums should the parties agree.[86] So, for example, if the borrower in default agrees to assign the securitized IP to the lender, initiating foreclosure procedures in a traditional court of law may not be necessary.[87] In certain circumstances, the secured party may be able to effect transfer of title to the IP collateral unilaterally by means of a "transfer statement."[88] A power of attorney provided for by the security agreement may be helpful in this regard. The secured party may thereafter be required to dispose of the collateral in a commercially reasonable manner as further required by UCC.[89]

FORECLOSURE AND AVAILABLE JUDICIAL PROCEDURES   In addition to nonjudicial remedies, Article 9 allows for the secured party to resort to any available judicial procedures.[90] This could include obtaining a judgment and writ of execution by a court of law.[91] Additional remedies could include obtaining a writ of replevin, sequestration, or a bill in equity.[92] Other remedies may be available, depending on the particular state in which the security interest is attempting to be enforced, and counsel should be consulted in this regard.

International Creation and Perfection of Security Interests

With globalization increasing the value of IP on a worldwide scale, prudent planning requires that companies continue to place a premium on the protection and enforcement of these rights. Companies with substantial *worldwide* IP portfolios are in the unique position of being able to not only offer their domestic IP rights as security, but increasingly, their international rights as well.

Identifying Markets

For lenders/secured parties to these transactions, it is important to seek perfection of these security interests at the relevant IP registries in the major world markets. Of course, not all jurisdictions recognize the creation of security interests in IP, thereby rendering perfection impossible or impracticable in many instances. Some jurisdictions may recognize the concept of securitizing IP as personal property, but do not offer a mechanism for perfection of same at the relevant IP registry. As such, IP counsel familiar with international securitization of IP should be consulted with respect to analyzing and identifying costs, markets, and procedures for worldwide IP perfection programs.

Sufficiency of Documentation

Subsequent to identifying those jurisdictions which offer a mechanism for perfecting a security interest in IP, it is critical to determine whether the security agreement will be accepted by the local authorities for recordal. Many major market jurisdictions will accept a standard commercial security agreement, assuming the parties do not mind disclosing sensitive financial or other confidential terms dictated by regulation. In some instances, it may be necessary to make certain amendments to the security agreement in order to create a valid security interest under local law. A common example of this would be changing the "governing law" provisions to that of the jurisdiction under which perfection is sought. In some instances, it may be necessary for the parties to execute entirely new security agreements tailored specifically for creating and perfecting liens in certain jurisdictions. These "short-form" agreements usually omit sensitive financial and/or other confidential terms. Local counsel may need to be engaged to determine whether the short-form security agreement will suffice for purposes of creating and perfecting a valid IP security interest under local law.

Opinions of Local Counsel

In order to make certain that the secured party is not blindly undertaking the ministerial act of perfecting the security interest, it may be worthwhile to obtain a formal opinion letter of local counsel discussing some or all of the following issues:

- Whether any prior liens or encumbrances have been recorded against the rights;
- Whether a valid security interest is created by the security agreement under local law;
- Whether the security interest is capable of being perfected at the local Patent and Trademark Office; and/or
- Whether the security interest is capable of being enforced against third parties.

Costs Assessment

Beyond simply determining which jurisdictions recognize perfection of security interests and identifying what supplemental documentation (e.g., powers of attorney) is needed, a cost analysis of perfection across multiple jurisdictions may be worthwhile. For example, it may not be worthwhile to perfect a security interest in a jurisdiction where sales of the products associated with the IP are nominal or do not exist. Factors to consider in this determination are:

- The number of pending or registered intellectual property rights subject to the security interest.
- The government fees in perfecting the security interest, which are usually assessed on a per unit basis.
- Local counsel fees in preparing an amended or new security agreement, providing supplemental documentation (e.g., powers of attorney), opinion letters (if requested), and filing the security interest documentation.
- The value of the rights as determined by notoriety and/or sales of the products.
- The sophistication of the jurisprudence in a particular jurisdiction.
- Other standard valuation benchmarks in determining the value of IP rights.

Time Considerations

In addition to cost considerations, time is also a factor when considering perfection of security interests internationally. While certain jurisdictions can typically record the security interest at the relevant registry within three to six months, there are still many jurisdictions (e.g., Italy) that typically require several years before recordal is officially reflected on the register. Therefore, in terms of obtaining the benefits of perfection by providing notice to third parties, proceeding in some of these jurisdictions may not be in the parties' interest.

Major Markets

Recording (or attempting to record) security interests against IP varies in degree of difficulty depending upon the jurisdiction.[93] Some major market countries that recognize the concept of security interests in IP and offer a quick and cost-effective mechanism for recording include Australia, Canada, France, Germany, Mexico, and the United Kingdom. Countries for which recordal of a lien may be more challenging, but still desirable from a secured-party perspective include Austria, Brazil, China, India, Italy, Japan, Korea, Spain, and Taiwan. Other countries should be considered on a case-by-case basis.

Madrid Agreement and Protocol

A registrant who furnishes their international registration as security may notify the national trademark office of the jurisdiction in question to inform the World Intellectual Property Organization (WIPO) or inform WIPO directly, which will then record the security interest in the WIPO Register. It should be noted, however, that a security interest in a trademark may not be recognized under the laws of some of the national jurisdictions to which an international registration has been extended, even if WIPO records the security interest effective against all designated jurisdictions.[94] As a result, the national laws of the particular jurisdictions to which the international registration has been extended should be reviewed.[95] It is also important to consider that filing at WIPO could result in unintentionally making the security interest public record in a designated extension country, which may not have been targeted for protection. Parties should be cautious before recording a security interest against international registrations, and trademark counsel should be consulted prior thereto.

European Patent Office

While the European Patent Office (EPO) will accept and record security interests against pending European patent applications, parties should be cautious in doing so to avoid such rights being encumbered upon entry into the national phase in jurisdictions where perfection was not intended.

Default

In the event of a default, a secured party should be aware of what steps may need to be taken locally (if any) in order to enforce the security interest and foreclose on the IP rights. If the defaulting party challenges the forfeiture of rights upon default, it is theoretically possible (albeit unlikely) that the secured party may need to bring a court action under local commercial law in the jurisdiction in question.

Conclusion

In today's rapidly changing global economy, intellectual property has taken on a new and dynamic role in commercial lending transactions. Uncertainty with respect to securitizing IP can result in those rights not being exploited to their fullest potential. Both IP owners and lenders would benefit from harmonization of federal and state law in the United States and from increased worldwide recognition of perfection schemes relating to secured IP assets. Without the foregoing, both IP owners and lenders will continue to absorb unnecessarily high transaction costs.

Notes

[1]Nick Bunkley, "Ford Pledges Major Assets in Financing," *New York Times*, November 28, 2006.

[2]Sharon Silke Carty, "Ford Earns $2.7 Billion in 2009, First Profit in Four Years," *USA Today*, January 28, 2010. See also Fernando Torres, "Valuation, Monetization, and Disposition in Bankruptcy," in Chap. 10.

[3]Id.

[4]See also Diane Meyers, "Growth Through Acquisition or Merger," in *Intellectual Property Strategies for the 21st Century Corporation*.

[5]See also Kimberly Klein Cauthorn & Leib Dodell, "Using Insurance to Manage Intellectual Property Risk," in *Intellectual Property Strategies for the 21st Century Corporation*.

[6]All references to the Uniform Commercial Code (UCC) are to that version enacted by New York State, which is fairly typical of the UCC provisions of most of the fifty states.

[7]Some IP rights, such as common-law trademarks and trade secrets, are creatures of state law.

[8]UCC 9-109(a)(1). "Except as otherwise provided . . . this Article applies to: 1) a transaction, regardless of its form, that creates a security interest in personal property or fixtures by contract. . . . "

[9]U.C.C. 9-102(42).

[10]Section 9-102(42) of the UCC defines *general intangibles* as "any personal property, including things in action, other than accounts, chattel paper, commercial tort claims, deposit accounts, documents, goods, instruments, investment property, letter of credit rights, money and oil, gas, or other minerals before extraction." The terms include payment intangibles and software.

[11]Official Comment, 9-102(d) providing that "general intangible" is the residual category of personal property, including things in action, that is not included in the other defined types of collateral. Examples are various categories of *intellectual property* and the right to payment of a loan that is not evidenced by chattel paper or an instrument. As used in the definition of general intangible, "things in action" includes rights that arise under a license of intellectual property, including the right to exploit the intellectual property without liability for infringement."

[12]But see Fernando Torres, "Valuation, Monetization, and Disposition in Bankruptcy," in Chap. 10. The bankrupcty code does not include Trademarks within its definition of intellectual property.

[13]Karl Llewellyn led development of the UCC in the 1930s and 1940s. Congress formalized and adopted the UCC in 1952. Since then, the UCC has been adopted by the 50 states and the District of Columbia and has undergone several revisions. In New York and several other states, the most recent revisions to Article 9 became effective on July 1, 2001.

[14]In the United States, *perfection* is a legal term of art that generally means to file and record a security interest against a particular form of collateral at the appropriate governmental office so as to become public record and provide constructive notice to third parties of the existence of such lien.

[15]Official Comment, 9-109(c)(1), Official Comment 8, providing that Subsection (c) (1) recognizes explicitly that this "Article defers to federal law only when and to the extent that it must—i.e., when federal law preempts it."

[16]U.C.C. 9-201(a).

[17]UCC 9-203(a) (emphasis added).

[18]Id.

[19]UCC 9-108(a). See also Section 9-108(b) for specific examples of what is considered a reasonable identification.

[20]UCC 9-203, Official Comment.

[21]Baila H. Celedonia, "Intellectual Property in Secured Transactions," *Trademarks in Business Transactions,* p. 108, 2002.

[22]See UCC 9-301(a).

[23]See UCC 9-301, Official Comment (4).

[24]UCC 9-307(a) where a *place of business* is defined as "the place where a debtor conducts its affairs."

[25]UCC 9-307(b)(3).

[26]UCC 9-316(a)(2).

[27]UCC 9-501.

[28]"Purchase money security interests" usually attach to consumer goods sold at the retail level.

[29]UCC 9-310(a).

[30]UCC 9-502(a)(3). See also Baila H. Celedonia, "Intellectual Property in Secured Transactions," *Trademarks in Business Transactions Forum,* p. 109, 2002.

[31]Baila H. Celedonia, p. 109.

[32]Id.

[33]Id.

[34]*In re 199Z, Inc. v. Valencia, Inc.,* 137 B.R. 778 (C.D. Cal. 1992).

[35]Id. As discussed in the following, trademarks are not properly perfected at the USPTO, although there may be benefits to such recordal.

[36]UCC 9-311(a)(1); Official Comment (2).

[37]Stuart M. Riback,"Trademark Issues in Bankruptcy," *The Trademark Reporter,* July–August, 2003.

[38]15 U.S.C. § 1060.

[39]Melvin Simensky, Howard A. Gootkin, "Liberating Untapped Millions for Investment Collateral: The Arrival of Security Interests in Intangible Assets," in Melvin Simensky & Lanning Bryer, *Intellectual Property in the Global Marketplace* (New York: John Wiley & Sons, 1999), 29.25.

[40]Id.

[41]Id. See also J. Thomas McCarthy, *Trademarks and Unfair Competition,* vol. 1 (New York: Clark Boardman Callaghan, 1995), 18-5.

[42]Id., p. 18-16. See also Simensky and Gootkin, 1999, p. 29.25.

[43]Id.

[44]See, e.g., *Haymaker Sports, Inc. v. Turian,* 581 F.2d. 257 (C.C.P.A.1978). The United States Court of Customs and Patent Appeals (now known as the U.S. Court of Appeals for the Federal Circuit) noted that the assignees never played an active role in the assignor's business, never used the mark themselves, and never acquired any tangible assets or goodwill of the assignor. Therefore, the court concluded that the assignment was invalid as an assignment-in-gross.

[45]See *Marshak v. Green* 746 F.2d 927 (2d Cir. 1984); *Clark & Freeman Corp. v. Heartland Co. Ltd.*, 811 F. Supp. 137 (S.D. N.Y. 1993).

[46]Riback, 2000, p. 16. See *Matter of Roman Cleanser Co.*, 802 F.2d (6th Cir. 1986).

[47]Simensky, and Gootkin, 1999, p. 29.25.

[48]See *Matter of Roman Cleanser Co.* 43 B.R. 940 (Bankr. E.D. Mich. 1984) *aff'd*, 802 F.2d 207 (6th Cir. 1986); *In re Together Dev. Corp.*, 227 B.R. 439, 441 (D. Mass. 1998); *In re 199Z, Inc.*, 137 B.R. 778 (Bankr. C.D. Cal. 1992). Lanham Act § 1060 provides: "An assignment shall be void against any subsequent purchaser for valuable consideration without notice, unless the prescribed information reporting the assignment is recorded in the Patent and Trademark Office within 3 months after the date of the assignment or prior to the assignment."

[49]*In re 199Z, Inc.*, 137 B.R. 778, 782.

[50]Id.

[51]Id.

[52]Id.

[53]U.S. Const. Art. VI., cl. 2.

[54]*Trimarchi v. Together Development Corp.*, 255 B.R. 606 (D. Mass. 2000).

[55]Id.

[56]*In re America's Hobby Center v. Hudson United Bank*, 223 S.D. N.Y. 275, 286 (1998). *See also Roman Cleanser v. National Acceptance*, 43 B.R. 940, 944 (E.D. Mich. 1984) (finding that the Lanham Act covered only assignments of trademarks and not security interests and holding that a security interest in a trademark is governed by Article 9 of the U.C.C.); *Creditors Committee v. Capital Bank*, 41 B.R. 128, 131 (Bankr. C.D. Cal. 1984) (finding that it was not the purpose or intent of Congress in enacting the Lanham Act to provide a method for the perfection of security interests in trademarks, trade names, or applications for the registration of same).

[57]*In re Together Dev. Corp.*, supra, 227 B.R. at 439.

[58]UCC 9-301(1)(d).

[59]15 U.S.C. §1051(b). See also "Intellectual Property as Collateral," *Journal of Law and Technology*, Franklin Pierce Law Center, 41 Idea 481 (2002). The term *inchoate* generally refers to an impartial or imperfect right. For example, in patent law, the right of an inventor to his invention while his patent application is pending is inchoate, until such time as the patent issues and the right matures as a full property right. See *Mullins Mfg. Co. v. Booth*, 125 F.2d 660, 664 (6th Cir. 1942).

[60]Id. See also 15 U.S.C. § 1060.

[61]40 U.S.P.Q. 2d 1098 (1996).

[62]Id.

[63]Id.

[64]Section 261 of the Patent Act provides: "Subject to the provisions of this title, patents shall have the attributes of personal property. Applications for patent, patents, or any interest therein, shall be assignable in law by an instrument in writing."

[65]*Waterman v. McKenzie*, 138 U.S. 252 (1891).

[66]Id.

[67]Id.

[68]*In re Cybernetic Services, Inc.*, 252 F.3d 1039 (9th Cir. 2001), *cert. denied*, 534 U.S. 1130 (U.S. 2002). See also *In re Pasteurized Eggs Corp.*, 296 B.R. 283 (Bankr. D.N.H. 2003) (holding that "the Patent Act does not contain any language regarding security interests, and therefore does

not preempt state law. As such, perfection of a security interest in a patent requires filing a UCC-1 in accordance with state law. Filing a security agreement with the PTO does not perfect the security interest.").

[69] *See In re Cybernetic Services, Inc.*, 252 F.3d 1039 (9th Cir. 2001), *cert. denied,* 534 U.S. 1130 (U.S. 2002); see also *In re Transportation Design & Tech., Inc.* 48 B.R. 635 (Bankr. S.D. Cal. 1985); *City Bank & Trust v. Otto Fabric, Inc.* 83 B.R. 780 (D. Kan. 1988).

[70] *In re Transportation Design,* 48 B.R. at 639.

[71] 17 U.S.C. §205.

[72] 17 U.S.C. §101.

[73] *In re Peregrine Entertainment, Ltd.*, 116 B.R.194 (C.D. Cal. 1990).

[74] Id. at 199. See also *Hillsborough County v. Automated Medical Laboratories, Inc.*, 471 U.S. 707 (U.S. 1985).

[75] *In re World Auxiliary Power Co.*, 303 F.3d 1120, 1128 (9th Cir. 2002).

[76] Id. at 1130.

[77] Id.

[78] *See AEG Acquisition Corp.* 127 B.R. 34 (Bankr. C.D. Cal. 1991), *aff'd* 161 B.R. 50 (9th Cir. BAP 1993); *In re Avalon,* 209 B.R. 517 (Bankr. D. Ariz. 1997).

[79] See also Dennis S. Prahl & Elliot Lipins, "Domain Names," in Chap. 5.

[80] Sheldon Burshtein, "A Domain Name Is Not Intellectual Property," World E-Commerce & IP Report, November 2002, p. 9. See also *Dorer v. Arel,* 60 F. Supp. 2d 558 (E.D. Va. 1999).

[81] Id. at 9.

[82] Id.

[83] Id. at 10. See also 15 U.S.C. § 1125(d).

[84] Sheldon Burshtein, p. 10. See also *Porsche Cars North America v. Porsche.Net,* 302 F.3d 248 (4th Cir. 2002).

[85] See also Fernando Torres, "Valuation, Monetization, and Disposition in Bankruptcy," in Chap. 10.

[86] UCC §9-609.

[87] Other nonjudicial remedies such as accepting the collateral in satisfaction of the debt or collection of receivables are also expressly provided for by the UCC. See UCC 9-608 to 9-622.

[88] UCC § 9-619.

[89] UCC § 9-620 to 9-622.

[90] UCC 9-601 (providing that a secured party may "reduce his claim to judgment, foreclose or otherwise enforce the security interest by any available judicial procedure.").

[91] Thomas M. Ward, *Intellectual Property in Commerce* Eagan, MN: WEST, (Belmont, Thomson/ West, 2004), 3:37.

[92] Id., p. 3:40.

[93] This discussion should not be viewed as an exhaustive treatment of commercial and intellectual property law as it pertains to securitizing and perfecting intellectual property and counsel should be consulted in a particular jurisdiction as needed.

[94] Ian Jay Kaufman and Lanning G. Bryer, *Worldwide Trademark Transfers*, Montgomery & Taylor, at III.D.8. (2002).

[95] Id.

CHAPTER 7

Strategic and Legal View of Licensing Patents

James Markarian
Siemens Corporation

Over the past 20 years, patent licensing revenue has grown in leaps and bounds with companies pushing their intellectual property (IP) departments to generate revenues by licensing out their patents. That trend seemed to accelerate during the past 10 years with the release of Rivette and Kline's book, *Rembrandts in the Attic: Unlocking the Hidden Value of Patents,* which brought patent licensing a more widespread awareness among corporate executives.[1] During this recent period, licensing activity has further been increased through the growth of entities whose sole purpose is to develop licensing revenue from patents ("trolls" or "nonpracticing entities [NPEs]"),[2] and by academia taking a more aggressive approach to licensing its patents through the establishment, or expansion, of university technology transfer offices (TTOs).

In the present challenging economic times, there is even a greater sense of urgency and pressure on corporate IP departments to generate additional revenues from corporate assets. Companies are using these revenues to offset downturns in their core business or to try and help transition into more lucrative fields of endeavor.[3] In addition to revenue generation, corporate IP departments are further being tasked to handle licensing-in activities by limiting the payouts to third parties who are looking to license their own patents such as other companies, university TTOs, and NPEs. However, there has been a reaction in the courts to moderate all this increased patent licensing activity. As a result, court rulings over the past few years have made it more difficult to license patents and created more risks for the licensor. Conversely, these recent court rulings have benefited licensees by providing them with greater defenses and tools to ward off a licensor. These rulings are also being reflected in the America Invents Act presently pending in Congress.[4]

What this chapter will explore is practical strategies and best practices from an "in the trenches" view, which will assist corporate IP departments to maximize licensing-out revenues, while limiting risks, and will also discuss how to best handle, and if possible reduce, licensing-in claims.

Nomenclature

Before further exploring the practices and suggestions for licensing out and licensing in, it is useful to go over some of the nomenclature in the field; for instance, what is a license, and what are the different types of licenses?

- A *patent license* is simply a contract between an owner, or holder, of patents, and a third party who wants to acquire rights to those patents. Since a patent gives its owner or holder ("licensor") the right to exclude others from the use of the patented subject matter, a patent license amounts to an understanding that the patent owner, or holder, will not assert its right to exclude against a third party ("licensee") that acquires a license to the owner's, or holder's, patent rights. Depending on the negotiations between a licensor and licensee, the license may provide the licensee with the right to manufacture, use and/or sell the patented apparatus, article of manufacture, process, and/or method, and could be limited as to geography or field of use.
- A *licensor* is a person, company, or entity who is transferring some or all of its patent rights.
- A *licensee* is a third party that obtains some or all of the patent rights held by the licensor.
- A *sublicense* is a right that can be granted to the licensee by the licensor, which allows the licensee to transfer some or all of its rights licensed patent rights to another person, company or entity ("sublicensee"). A license should explicitly state whether or not sublicense rights are granted to the licensee.
- An *opportunity* or *outreach* refers to the situation in which a single person, company, or entity, who has the potential to be a licensee, is, or will be, contacted about taking a license under a single patent, or a collection of patents having a common technology. The person, company, or entity contacted is referred to as a *potential licensee*.
- A *program* is a collection of opportunities or outreaches, wherein two or more persons, companies, or entities are, or will be, contacted about taking a license under a single patent, or collection of patents having a common technology.
- A *royalty audit* is a when a person or entity, hired by or working for the licensor, reviews the records of a licensee to make sure they are paying the amounts owed under the license.
- There are three types of patent licenses—an exclusive license, a nonexclusive license, and a cross-license.
  - An *exclusive license* is a type of license wherein the licensor agrees to license only one licensee for a particular technology. In an exclusive license, the licensee is provided with the right to sue third parties for infringing the licensed patents, and may have the right, depending on the terms of the exclusive license, to sublicense others. To have the right to sue, the licensor must have transferred to the licensee "all substantial rights" in the licensed

patents. What that essentially means is that the transfer must be tantamount to an assignment.[5]

- A *nonexclusive license* is a type of license that permits the licensor to enter into many license agreements for the same technology.
- A *cross-license* is a license in which two companies act as both licensor and licensee, so that each company is granted rights to the other company's patents. Cross-license agreements are typically entered into by competitors, in certain fields, so that all parties have the freedom to operate without constantly being in court defending lawsuits. Typically, cross-license agreements do not compensate either party, but when one party has a qualitative and/or quantitative advantage in patents over the other party, and/or one party's financial exposure in connection with a potential patent lawsuit is substantially greater than the other party, there can be arrangements wherein the party with the advantageous position regarding patent rights, and the smaller financial exposure, can demand royalties from the other party while being protected from the assertion of the other company's patents through the cross-license.
- *Trolls,* or the new politically correct term, *nonpracticing entities* (NPEs), are companies, persons, or other entities that acquire patents from other parties, by license or purchase, for the sole purpose of generating income, and have not, and will not, themselves use the technology they are trying to license.
- An *amalgamator* is a variant of an NPE who acquires patents from various sources, but in the same technical field, and then puts together a portfolio that can be later sold or enforced.
- A *stick* licensing opportunity refers to the situation in which a patent owner, or possibly an exclusive licensee (with sublicense rights), or their representatives, alleges that a potential licensee is infringing the patent owner's, or exclusive licensee's, patents, which means that each and every element in a patent's claims can be found in a product, article of manufacture, process, or method, which is made or used by a potential licensee.
- A *carrot* licensing opportunity refers to the situation in which no infringement currently exists, but there are persons, companies, or entities that may benefit from using the patent owner's, or exclusive licensee's, patents. Stick licensing is generally more effective in patent licensing than carrot licensing. One of the reasons for this difference is that if a patent is infringed, the potential licensee is on notice that it possibly has financial exposure, and may be involved in litigation (which can be distracting, expensive, and the results uncertain), so it must act with a sense of urgency should it want to avoid litigation. Whereas a carrot license for a patent is generally offered to a company for enhancing its products, so the teachings and know-how of that patent needs to be incorporated into the potential licensee's business and production line, which generally involves a significant undertaking and expense to the potential licensee. Hence, there is not the same sense of urgency to respond to a carrot license unless the technology licensed is groundbreaking, for example, if the technology is like the "Mr. Fusion Energy Reactor" from the *Back to the Future* movie series, or can be easily and inexpensively incorporated into the potential licensee's business. In contrast, carrot licensing can be extremely effective in relation to trademarks.[6]

- A *practicing entity* is a company, person, or entity who itself uses, or has used, its patents in its business and/or manufacturing.
- A *patent holding company* is a separate company, generally set up by a practicing entity, to hold, license, or enforce the parent entity's patents, but the patent holding company does not itself practice the technology, as the patents continue to be practiced by the parent entity. Patent holding companies can be created to shelter significant patent royalty income from state or federal taxes, or as a separate business entity whose sole focus is licensing, and thereby sheltering the parent entity from countersuit in the event of litigation. A problem with patent holding companies is that they are generally not deemed practicing entities so, under current case law, they will not be granted injunctive relief for patents they are looking to enforce. Consequently, many practicing entities retain the most valuable patents to their business, and do not place them in their patent holding companies, so they can get injunctive relief to stop a potential infringer. In this hybrid arrangement, the practicing entity ends up placing its less critical patents in the patent holding company, which are then used by the patent holding company to generate licensing income.

State of the Law

Over the past few years, decisions by the United States Supreme Court and Court of Appeals for the Federal Circuit (CAFC) have made it much harder and riskier to license patents and, in turn, made it easier for licensees to defend against license requests or challenge existing patent licenses. Many of the changes in the law seem to be a reaction to increased activity and success by trolls or NPEs over the past 10 years. From 1995 to 2001 (before and right after the Revitte and Kline book), the median damage award in patent infringement cases brought by NPEs and practicing entities was nearly identical at a little over $5 million. However, from 2002 to 2008, the difference widened, with the NPE cases resulting in a median damage award of $12 million. For practicing entities the median award was only $3.4 million (see Figure 7.1).[7]

Some of the key Supreme Court cases during this period, which have had an impact on licensing, include *eBay, Inc. v. MercExchange, LLC* (making it much harder for a patent holder to get an injunction);[8] *Medimmune, Inc. v. Genentech, Inc.* (allowing a licensee to challenge the validity of a licensed patent while still being licensed);[9] *KSR Int'l Co. v. Teleflex Inc.* (making it easier to invalidate patents since a mere incremental improvement would not be patentable);[10] and *Quanta Computer, Inc. v. LG Electronics, Inc.* (making it easier to find patent exhaustion).[11] The CAFC has also issued many decisions that have affected licensing, including *SanDisk v. STMicroelectronics* (making it easier for a potential licensee to file a declaratory judgment);[12] *In re Seagate Tech, LLC* (making it harder to prove willful infringement, and collect enhanced damages, since a patent holder now must show recklessness, not mere negligence by an infringer);[13] and *Hewlett-Packard Co. v. Acceleron LLC* (expanding on *SanDisk* by making it even easier for a potential licensee to find a basis for bringing a declaratory judgment action, particularly against an NPE, so that just about any correspondence received from an NPE offering a license

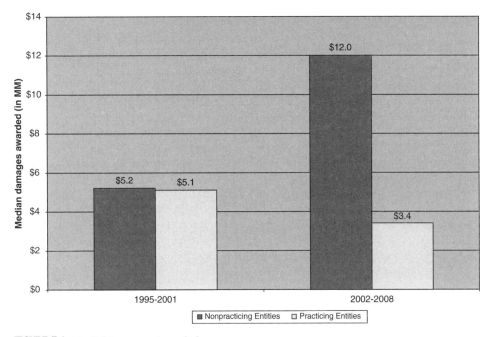

FIGURE 7.1 Medial Damages Awarded

can be the basis for a declaratory judgment countersuit by a potential licensee).[14] The strategies of how to navigate this new legal landscape will be discussed later in this chapter.

Basic Principles for Licensing

There are five overriding principles that will be helpful to both licensors and potential licensees in licensing patents (or any IP), whether it involves licensing out or licensing in. These principles are the following: (1) do your due diligence, (2) be prepared, (3) zealously represent your client/company and believe in your positions, (4) be realistic and constantly evaluate your positions, (5) understand the leverage points between the parties, and (6) be professional and act in a civil manner. So what does that mean?

The first principle, doing one's due diligence, from both a licensor's and potential licensee's perspective, involves the licensor or potential licensee making an independent determination if the patents to be licensed are valid and enforceable, and that infringement exists. Some practical steps that should be undertaken are to make sure all maintenance fees are current, all the assignments or transfer of rights are in order so that the licensor knows it has all the rights it is looking to transfer, and there is nothing in the file wrapper for the patents that would be catastrophic for licensing. From a licensor's prospective, if there are any problems, these problems should be fixed before going out and licensing any patents. Two possible tools available to a licensor are reissue and reexamination proceedings at the United States Patent and Trademark Office (USPTO). From a potential licensee's perspective, finding any such deficiencies can be grounds to dismiss a licensing outreach or provide leverage to negotiate better terms.

Due diligence also involves putting in the time to understand the other party's business, which might be useful during negotiations, and making sure that one's actions do not cause harm to one's own company. For example, if a potential licensee has a portfolio of patents that could be used against the licensor, and the impacted sales of the licensor are greater than those for the potential licensee, then it does not make sense to approach that potential licensee. Also, if the impacted sales of the potential license are small, say $10,000, then it also does not make sense to try and license to that company since the time and effort by the licensor will exceed what it could recover from a license.

A further aspect of due diligence is to learn about the people whom you will be negotiating against. For example, it can be useful, as an ice breaker, to know someone's educational or employment background. It is also helpful to keep a log of what they have communicated in the past, so one can readily bring up, during negotiations, any contradictory statements or positions. Remember, although companies are involved, you are still negotiating with a person.

The next principle is preparation. Preparation in the licensing context takes many different forms. In one form, it means that before telephone conferences or meetings, one is prepared to anticipate the other side's positions, and then respond to advance one's own positions. Another aspect of preparation is understanding what your company's business objectives are and how licensing can help those objectives. For example, it is critical for the licensor to make sure its actions enhance, and do not harm, its company's business interests. Unlike an NPE or amalgamator, where its business is licensing or selling assets, a practicing entity's primary concern is the operation and profitability of its business, not licensing activity. So nothing should be undertaken by the licensor that might jeopardize its company's business by putting its company at risk of countersuit from the potential licensee's patents, or damaging existing or potential business relationships by using an aggressive approach to licensing. From a potential licensee's prospective, it is critical to try and avoid paying any license fees, and if it ends up paying any fees, to reduce those fees as much as possible. By being prepared, the potential licensee may uncover deficiencies in the licensor's arguments, which can then allow the potential licensee to leverage those deficiencies to push for favorable terms, or to avoid altogether having to take a license.

Like litigation, licensing involves persuasion, but instead of convincing a court or jury of the merits of one's position, a licensor or potential licensee is trying to persuade the other side that there is merit in one's position. For both the licensor and potential licensee, the level of persuasion needs to be sufficient to convince the other side that taking a license (the licensor's objective), or dropping the demand for a license or minimizing royalty payments (the potential licensee's objective), is a better solution to settling the matter than enduring the cost, distractions, and uncertainties of litigation. It is also important to believe in one's position and zealously argue one's position so as to persuade the other party. Such belief, conviction, and zealousness stems from doing one's due diligence and being prepared.

During most license negotiations and during litigations, there come different points where one receives information that is detrimental to one's position, or the negotiations have stalled. It is at these points during a license negotiation when the licensor and potential licensee must reevaluate their positions in view of the positions and information provided by the other party. In evaluating one's position, it is critical that one be realistic regarding what is demanded, both from its side and what is being demanded by the other side. Also considered in the evaluation should be the costs of litigation if the parties are not able to find an amicable settlement to the matter. By making these evaluations, and reevaluating one's positions, a course of action can be chosen.

Sometimes, a potential licensee presents a licensor with good arguments regarding why a license is not necessary. At that point, the licensor can decide to withdraw the outreach, lower the royalty demands, or possibly look to bring other patents into the licensing discussions. On the other side, sometimes the licensor's arguments seem unassailable, at which point the potential licensee can look to mitigate its exposure by trying to negotiate favorable terms, or trying to get in a most-favored-nation clause so that it does not pay more than other licensees. Another option for a potential licensee would be to look at business connections that might exist with a licensor and try to exploit those relationships to gain more favorable terms.

It is also critical to understand the leverage points of each party. What that means is that in every negotiation the facts and circumstances generally favor one party over the other. For example, if the licensor has a particularly strong case that the potential licensee is infringing its patents, and the potential licensee does not have strong arguments for invalidity, noninfringement, or unenforceability, the licensor will be able to dictate the terms and conditions for a license. However, the more doubt regarding the licensor's position, and strength regarding the potential licensee's defenses, the more freedom the potential licensee has to resist the licensor's terms, and to insist on the inclusion of more terms favorable to the licensee. Getting a grasp of these leverage points comes from doing one's due diligence, and preparation, and then exploiting these leverage points by zealously arguing one's position.

The final principle is that one needs to be professional and act in a civil manner, no matter the actions of the other party. Remember, the licensing community is a small one, and people move around. One day you may be negotiating against a person, and months later you may be on a panel with them discussing licensing, or you may be interviewing with them for your next job. Also, reputations get around. Therefore, it is advisable to act in a professional and civil manner, as one would want to be treated, and to remember that licensing is ultimately about a business decision, and should not be made into a personal decision or vendetta—remember the saying from the movie *The Godfather*, "[i]t's not personal, . . . [i]t's strictly business."

How Does One Go About Licensing Out Patents, and What Are Some Strategic Considerations?

Licensing-out activity can take a few different arrangements. In one form, the company tasks its IP department to itself directly license or sell the company's patents. Sometimes, as mentioned earlier, this can also involve the company's setting up a separate patent holding company just for monetizing patents. Another arrangement is for the company, or IP department, to enter into contractual relationships with outside law firms or third-party entities (like NPEs or amalgamators), who themselves license or sell the company's patents. The problem with using third parties is that the company loses control of the process, while its patents are at risk of being invalidated, or declared unenforceable, or being sold at a cut-rate price. Another problem with using third parties is the reduction of income to the company due to the percentage demanded by these third parties to license or sell patents.

Regardless of what approach is taken, the first step to licensing or selling a company's patents is to get the relevant businesspeople, those with the authority to allow a company's assets to be licensed or sold, to get behind the idea of monetizing these assets, and also to provide sufficient resources (financial and human) to accomplish the monetization. The businesspeople must also understand that there are risks of countersuit for infringement, invalidity, or enforceability, and if an impasse occurs in the negotiations, the company might have to bring a lawsuit. Furthermore, the businesspeople need to understand that it takes time to monetize patents—typically in excess of one year. In addition, expectations about success, and how much income can be realized from monetization, must be managed and be realistic. Without such up-front notification and understanding, corporate support can diminish over time, ending up with poor results.

If the monetization of patents is to be handled in-house, the next step is to find patents that can be licensed or sold. Here is where corporate support is critical, since the best way to find assets that can be monetized, and targets for those assets, is to assemble a team of business and legal people to review the company's patent portfolio. From the business side, the team should include a technical adviser with a general understanding of the technology to be licensed or sold, and a financial analyst who knows, or can find out, the financial information concerning this technology, including information on potential licensees. The legal people on the team would include a patent attorney to review and opine on the scope of patents, and a licensing attorney (or licensing professional), who will coordinate all the resources, direct the strategy, and conduct the negotiations. If qualified, that person can also draft agreements. As the need arises, the team can also include many other resources, including but not limited to transactional attorneys, tax counsel, outside law firms, accountants, technical experts, damages experts, and experts on governmental contracts.

The team should first try and find patents that are "diamonds in the rough," that is, those patents that have relatively broad claims, so that they can be used against many potential licensees. Also, it is preferable to have a portfolio of patents to license or sell, rather than just one patent, so the team should look to group similar patents together. It can also be helpful to have the patent attorneys prosecuting the company's patents to try and push for broad claims, which go beyond the company's core products. Such patents will be quite useful for licensing later.

The next step for the team is to look at the portfolio and find potential licensees who are infringing the company's patents. If the potential licensee is a direct competitor of a practicing entity, then litigation counsel should be brought in immediately since it may make more sense, with respect to a direct competitor, to try and get an injunction through a lawsuit, rather than license them under the practicing entity's patents. The best potential licensees will be companies who are not direct competitors, who have sufficient sales to make a licensing outreach worthwhile financially, and who do not have a sizeable patent portfolio that could be asserted against the licensor. Monetizing patents is all about making money, so if the potential royalties are low or the risks high for a successful countersuit by the potential licensee under its own patents, then it is probably not a worthwhile endeavor to contact that company. This brings back the principle of doing one's due diligence. In addition, if possible, a practicing entity should look to set up a licensing program to contact as many potential licensees as possible so that revenue can be maximized.

There are many services and software programs available to help companies evaluate patent portfolios.[15] For instance, it can be helpful to look at the comparison between the forward and backward citation trees for a patent, and if there are many forward citations compared to few backward citations, that can indicate a patent with broad scope, and identify potential licensees as the owners of the patents in the forward citation tree.[16] Also, comparing international patent codes (IPCs) for patents related to a technology can be helpful in evaluating the strength of one portfolio versus another (see Figure 7.2).

Even though these tools can be helpful, skilled patent professionals must still go through the patent claims, file wrappers, and the products of potential licensees to see if there appears to be infringement.

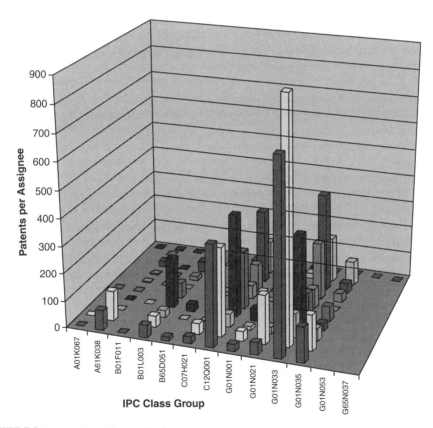

FIGURE 7.2 International Patent Codes

To estimate the revenue that might be generated from a licensing program, the licensor must perform an initial analysis. There are three typical approaches to evaluating licensing revenue—the market method, the cost method, and the income method.

Using the *market method,* one looks at what comparable technologies have licensed for recently. There are books, articles, organizations, and web sites to find various royalty rates, for example, Licensing Executives Society (LES), Association of University Technology Managers (AUTM), reported case settlements, and so forth. Generally, the market method is the most reliable since it looks at comparable arm's-length negotiations or settlements, but the difficulty is finding a comparable situation. The second approach is the *cost method,* in which one looks at a licensor's costs and expenses incurred in developing the patented technology, and then determines a royalty rate that will recover these costs plus a reasonable profit margin. The advantage of the cost method is that the licensor knows this information before ever contacting a potential licensee; however, using this approach can cause a licensor to substantially undervalue a royalty since the ultimate worth of the license can be greater than just the cost to obtain the patented technology. The final approach is the *income method,* in which one determines the net present value of the potential licensee's projected income for the licensed product/method/process, with the licensor looking to obtain an appropriate percentage of those profits. If the income approach is used, courts and parties have in the past sometimes used the so-called 25% Rule to determine what is the appropriate royalty rate percentage, and which involves coming up with a royalty that is twenty-five percent of the potential licensee's profit margin. To use this method, a licensor needs to know, or estimate accurately, the potential licensee's profit margin. Although, in 2011, the CAFC held that the use of the 25% Rule in an expert's testimony was not permissible, many in the licensing profession continue to use the 25% Rule in their licensing negotiations, and still view it as a viable methodology.[17]

Having done its due diligence, the licensor will know that the prosecution history is free from any catastrophic deficiencies, there are no substantive issues regarding ownership of the patents, and the maintenance fees are up to date. So the next step, after a portfolio of patents to license has been put together and potential licensees identified for a licensing program, is to prepare claims charts of the patents to be licensed and the potential licensee's products. Much care must be taken in the preparation of these claims charts since they must be sufficiently persuasive to make a potential licensee take a license. Also, if the license negotiations fail, these same claims charts could end up in a patent litigation between the parties, so they must be of the quality that one would use in a patent litigation.

After all this groundwork has been done and the claims charts prepared, it is time for the licensor to decide which potential licensees to contact. If the licensor is embarking on a licensing program, it is critical to think first about the order that potential licensees are to be contacted. For example, an infringing product may exist at both the original equipment manufacturer (OEM) and retailer levels, but if one licenses the OEM first, exhaustion will prevent royalties from the retailer. Another consideration is momentum and being able to use one or multiple licensees as leverage for further potential licensees. So a licensor might want to consider initially picking a potential licensee that appears easier to license to, and then build up a group of licensees before contacting those potential licensees who the licensor perceives might be more difficult or riskier to license to. There is no standard approach, but by doing one's due diligence, one will get a better sense of the leverage points for the different potential licensees, and what approach is best to use under the circumstances.

With the prenegotiation steps accomplished, care must be taken in drafting the initial communications to potential licensees. The *Hewlett-Packard* decision, as previously mentioned, makes it much easier for a potential licensee to find a basis for bringing a declaratory judgment action when contacted about taking a license. It seems that under the *Hewlett-Packard* case, any contact from an NPE can trigger a declaratory judgment action by a potential licensee, and just about any communication from a practicing entity, with the possible exception of an offer for a cross-license, can also trigger a declaratory judgment action. That said, the fact is that if a practicing entity contacts a potential licensee who is not direct competitor, there is not as great a risk that the potential licensee will file a declaratory judgment action. Companies are generally risk and litigation averse, so they are not inclined to start litigation in which they will be countersued for patent infringement. However, if a practicing entity licensor contacts a direct competitor, then there is a high likelihood that a declaratory judgment may be brought, since the stakes are much higher under those circumstances. A possible way to lessen the chance of a declaratory judgment action is to contact the direct competitor about a cross-license, and then during negotiations try to negotiate a balance of payments that favors the licensor.

Another potential ramification of the *Hewlett-Packard* decision is that although the licensor's communication with a potential licensee may be sufficient to trigger a declaratory judgment, it is nonetheless insufficient to trigger statutory notice of infringement under 35 USC § 287. Such notice is critical, since for patent infringement lawsuits involving apparatus claims, the time period for calculating damages starts with the alleged infringer's receipt of a notice letter if there is no marking.[18] To satisfy the notification requirements of section 287, a licensor at a minimum needs to identify the patents that it is looking to license in the initial communication with a potential licensee. It is also recommended that the initial letter contain an offer to enter into a nondisclosure agreement (NDA), and that such an NDA be provided with the initial letter. Claims charts and financial offers should not be provided to the potential licensee until the parties have executed an NDA. Even at this stage, the licensor should also have a draft license agreement prepared that can be provided to the potential licensee at a moment's notice once the NDA has been executed.

So who should this initial communication be sent to? That depends on the type and size of company, for instance, whether it is a publicly traded company, closely held company or partnership, a foreign company, a small company, a large company, and so on. Generally, if the company has a chief IP counsel, that is the person who should first be contacted since he will either handle the matter or forward it to the person who will be handling the matter. Sources for the names of chief IP counsel include the membership directories of the American Intellectual Property Law Association (AIPLA), LES, American Bar Association (ABA), and Association of Corporate Patent Counsel (ACPC). If one cannot find the chief IP counsel, the next person to contact would be the general counsel for a company. For publicly traded companies, you can find a company's general counsel name in the company's 10Q or 10K Securities and

Exchange Commission (SEC) filings. For foreign companies, it is recommended that the licensor contact the company's top representative in the United States, and for small companies the licensor is probably best served by contacting the CEO.

Some Legal Considerations for a Patent Licensor

With the potential licensee having been contacted and negotiations progressing toward a license, it is worthwhile to keep in mind some legal considerations when it comes time to draft a license agreement. First, remember that a patent license cannot last for longer than the life of the licensed patents; otherwise, the license can violate U.S. antitrust laws. So if the licensor wants to expand a license beyond the patent terms, a solution is to include other IP in the license, like know-how or trademarks, but if a licensor follows that approach, then the royalties need to be lowered when the patent terms expire.

Another legal consideration for the licensor is to include so-called *Medimmune* defenses in their license agreement. As mentioned earlier, the decision in *Medimmune* allows a licensee to challenge the validity of a licensed patent while still being licensed. Some *Medimmune* defenses include:

- A clause in the license agreement wherein royalty payments are accelerated or increased if the licensee unsuccessfully challenges the validity of the licensed patents.
- Front-loading the royalty payments by requiring a nonrefundable, up-front, lump-sum payment of the royalties instead of payments over time, or possibly demand higher royalty payments during the earlier portion of the license term.
- A clause terminating the license agreement if the licensee challenges the validity of the licensed patents.
- Having venue and choice-of-law clauses favorable to the licensor.

For a further list of *Medimmune* defenses, as well as courses of action for potential licensees, it is suggested that both licensors and potential licensees read the May 2008 article, "Patent Licensing Strategies after *Medimmune*," by Michael J. Cavaretta and Howard Zaharoff, which appears in the *IP News* bulletin from the firm of Morse, Barnes-Brown & Pendleton, PC.[19]

A licensor should also consider pushing for a grant-back license from any potential licensee, which would cover the technology owned by the licensee during the license term and which might cover the licensor's products by generally concerning the technology licensed by the licensor. By having such a grant-back license, the licensor protects itself from later being approach by the licensee for a license concerning the same technology. It is also important for the licensor to have strong termination provisions for breach of the license agreement by the licensee, or for a change in control of the licensee, and have strict restrictions regarding the assignability of the license agreement. Also, the licensor should base royalties on the gross price of the licensed product, not the net price, and try to avoid many offsets. At the end of this chapter is a checklist that can help the licensor and licensee focus on some of the legal issues involved in a license agreement.

Strategic and Legal Considerations for a Patent Licensee

A potential licensee's goal is first to avoid paying any royalties for a license, and if that is not possible, extracting the best deal possible. Therefore, it is critical for the potential licensee to do its due diligence and try to invalidate, show noninfringement, or declare unenforceable any patents asserted against the potential licensee. Also, the potential licensee should demand that the licensor prove, as it would have to prove to a judge or jury, that the potential licensee's products infringe the licensor's patents.

The potential licensee should also review its own portfolio to see if there are any of its patents that can be asserted against the licensor. If so, that can provide leverage to cause the parties to enter into a no-fee cross-license agreement, or possibly extract more money from the licensor than the licensor was trying to collect from the potential licensee. In addition, if the potential licensee has any other business dealings with the licensor, it should look to see if it will be possible to leverage those dealings to put pressure on the licensor to drop its outreach since failure to do so will otherwise jeopardize existing and future business relationships.

If a potential licensee cannot invalidate, show noninfringement, or declare unenforceable any patents asserted against the potential licensee, or find some other business leverage against the licensor, and the licensor has sufficiently proved their case of infringement, the potential licensee can still push for a most-favored-nation clause in the license agreement, so that the royalties it pays will not be greater than any other licensee. A most-favored-nation clause is most likely to occur if the potential licensee is one of the first licensees, and the licensor is interested in signing up other licensees with even greater exposure.

A potential licensee also should push for strong representation and warranties by the licensor as to ownership of the patents, and try to negotiate favorable venue and choice-of-law clauses. If possible, the potential licensee should try to make sure that it has sublicense rights, especially if it uses an OEM, and that the license agreement is freely assignable. If the license agreement is an exclusive license, the potential licensee must be sure that license transfers "all substantial rights" as discussed earlier. Also, if possible, a licensee should try and reduce the royalty basis by having royalty offsets (e.g., returns, shipping costs, taxes) subtracted from the initial royalty price. The potential licensee also needs to watch for licensor's imposition of any *Medimmune* defenses and to avoid burdensome reporting and royalty audit provisions.

Royalty Audits

Often overlooked in licensing negotiations and after a license has been entered into are the royalty audit provisions. Once a license has been entered into, the licensor often fails to closely monitor the royalties paid by the licensee. The problem is generally not that the licensee is purposely trying to hide royalties (although that does happen), but that there are mistakes in what products or combination of products are subject to royalties, or there could be misunderstandings regarding the scope of the license. Moreover, there are also instances of simple miscalculations by the licensee.

That is why it is critical that any licensor include robust royalty audit provisions in its license agreements, that it monitor royalty income for dramatic deviations, and, particularly early in the license, undertake an audit to make sure appropriate royalties are being paid. The first audits typically can identify significant additional royalties not timely reported by the licensee, which would otherwise get overlooked without an active contract management program. Other benefits of an active contract management program are that, once audited, a licensee is going to be more careful in calculating royalties due in the future, it signals to other licensees to be correct and accurate in their reporting and, if there is underreporting, can provide a justification for a licensor to terminate an existing agreement due to noncompliance by the licensee.

In setting up royalty audit provisions in a license agreement, it is important that the licensor include a severability clause, since typical audit provisions provide some interest penalty for underreporting, and various jurisdictions have different standards about how much interest can be accessed. From a licensee's perspective, it is important to limit how many audits can be conducted in one year and make sure that whoever is conducting the audit is under an obligation to maintain that information as confidential. The leverage points of the parties will have an impact, as on everything else, on the degree upon which the licensor's requirements, or the potential licensee's push back, will ultimately prevail in their negotiations concerning the terms and conditions of the royalty audit provisions.

Conclusion

This chapter provides licensors and potential licensees with a basic road map sense for what is involved in licensing patents and what are some of the best practices. Both licensor and potential licensees are best served by sticking to the principles enunciated in this chapter, namely, (1) do your due diligence, (2) be prepared, (3) zealously represent your client/company and believe in your positions, (4) be realistic and constantly evaluate your positions, (5) understand the leverage points between the parties, and (6) be professional and act in a civil manner. Following those principles will help both licensor and licensee be as successful as possible in their license negotiations.

Patent License Agreement Checklist of Important Legal Considerations

1. License (grant):
   a. Exclusive versus nonexclusive (exclusivity can vary by product, field, territory, time).
   b. Transferable versus nontransferable.
   c. Revocable versus irrevocable (can be contingent on time, payment of money).
   d. Royalty bearing versus fully paid.
   e. Royalty base (e.g., system, licensed product, specified part, implementing method).
   f. Sales and manufacturing territory, use location restrictions.
   g. Time periods (length of agreement, limits on confidentiality and grants).
   h. Licensed technology.
   i. Grant backs.

    j. Markets (licensed field of use, or licensed programs).
    k. Have made rights (OEM).
    l. Options (to expand agreement, to maintain exclusivity, to limit licensed field).
    m. Rights to licensor's improvements—new products.
    n. Reversions (loss of exclusivity, narrowing of licensed field).
    o. Sublicense rights.
2. Patents and/or proprietary data rights:
    a. Infringement.
    b. Indemnity.
    c. Warranties.
    d. Disclaimers.
    e. Confidentiality.
    f. U.S. government requirements (unlimited rights, government rights, options).
    g. Representations.
    h. Marking.
3. Compensation:
    a. Lump sums (initial payments, additional payments, installment payments).
    b. Prepayments (against future royalties, purchase of products, developments).
    c. Fixed versus variable royalty (percentage, specified dollars).
    d. Purchases from licensor.
    e. Stock.
    f. Minimums, maximums (yearly, over life of agreement, sales volume, number of products).
    g. Royalty offsets (e.g., returns, shipping costs, taxes).
4. Manufacturing rights:
    a. All versus portion.
    b. Assembly from kits.
5. Technology transfer and assistance:
    a. Technical data package (complete, exclusions).
    b. Timing.
    c. Continued assistance (time, location, level).
    d. Updating, configuration control.
6. Considerations for royalty payments and manufactured item prices:
    a. U.S. dollars.
    b. Currency fluctuation.
    c. Audit—royalties, price, reports.
    d. Reasonable and competitive.
    e. Quoted, invoiced, or NTE (not-to-exceed) prices.
    f. Mechanism and understanding of price concessions during best and final offer (e.g., front-end investment).
7. Length of agreement:
    a. Number of years.
    b. Life of program.
    c. Time limitations for reasons specified in the agreement (default, loss of control, bankruptcy).
    d. Rights after termination.
    e. Life of licensed patent(s).

8. Repair, maintenance, and product support issues.
9. Government contract clauses—mandatory flow-down provisions (e.g., patents, data, audit, challenge to restrictive markings, certification).
10. Export control laws (hardware, software, technical data, technical assistance agreements, manufacturing licenses):
    a. Commerce.
    b. Reporting.
11. Antitrust law consideration.
12. Venue/governing law.
13. Enforcement of IP/joinder.
14. Miscellaneous provisions—assignablity/severability/waiver.
15. Other types of agreements:
    a. Teaming.
    b. Manufacturing, use, and sales license.
    c. Joint development.
    d. Subcontract.
    e. Joint venture.
    f. Technical assistance.
    g. Coproduction.
    h. Consulting.
    i. Research.
    j. Distribution, sales or purchase.
    k. Service.
    l. Option.
    m. Proprietary information.
    n. Escrow.
    o. Software.
    p. Cross-license.
    q. Combinations thereof.

Notes

[1]Kevin G. Rivette and David Kline, *Rembrandts in the Attic: Unlocking the Hidden Value of Patents* (Boston: Harvard Business Press, 2000).

[2]See also Raymond DiPerna & Jack Hobaugh, "When to Litigate: Rise of the Trolls," in *Intellectual Property Strategies for the 21st Century Corporation*, at 143-58.

[3]Eastman Kodak Company is an example of how licensing revenues are helping a company offset a drop in its core business and helping it transition its business into seemingly more lucrative areas. In a June 25, 2010, *Wall Street Journal* article entitled, "Kodak Chief Perez Plans to Curtail Patent Lawsuits," by Dana Mattioli, Kodak's CEO, Antonio Perez, is quoted as saying "We need [cash flow from patents] right now because we're investing too much for the size of the company in these new businesses." But Kodak's experience also provides a cautionary tale, in that by taking a very aggressive approach to licensing, through litigation, Kodak has alienated potential business partners and is now looking to cut down on its use of litigation in the future. As Mr. Perez is also quoted as saying in that same article, "[g]oing to Court is expensive, it creates a lot of publicity, and nobody benefits from it" and that "[w]e'll find more value

getting into business relationships that generate revenue working with some other partner rather than asking for cash."

[4]S.23 & HR 1249; previously named the Patent Reform Act of 2011.

[5]For a discussion about different scenarios where courts have held there was, or was not, a transfer of "all substantial rights," it is suggest that both licensors and potential licensees read Jeffrey Newton's article in the December 2009 issue of *Les Nouvelles,* entitled "Assuring All Substantial Rights in Exclusive Patent Licenses," pp. 235–254.

[6]Carrot licensing of patents is a completely different endeavor than the carrot licensing of trademarks. With trademarks, there is not that same involved technical undertaking to incorporate the licensed IP into one's business, so carrot licensing is much more common with trademarks. For example, one can see the Coke® or Coca-Cola® mark on a wide variety of licensed products, and most likely just about all, if not all, of those licenses were entered voluntarily by potential licensees wanting to use these marks on their products, rather than as a result of the Coca-Cola Company's first suing, or threatening to sue, these potential licensees, for using these marks without first getting permission.

[7]See PricewaterhouseCoopers' 2009 "Patent Litigation Study," pp. 6–7 (August 2009).

[8]547 U.S. 388 (2006).

[9]549 U.S. 118 (2007).

[10]550 U.S. 398 (2007).

[11]553 U.S. 617 (2008).

[12]480 F.3d 1372 (Fed. Cir. 2007).

[13]497 F.3d 1360 (Fed. Cir. 2007).

[14]587 F.3d 1358 (Fed. Cir. 2009).

[15]Examples of Web-based software that can help evaluate patent portfolios include Aureka and Innography.

[16]Backward citations are those patents cited during prosecution of a patent as prior art, and forward citations are patents issued after the patent of interest, and which the patent of interest has been cited as prior art.

[17]Under *Uniloc USA, Inc. v. Microsoft Corp.*, 632 F.3d 1292 (Fed. Cir. 2011), the CAFC specifically rejected the use of the "25% Rule" in an expert's testimony regarding patent infringement damages as not comporting to FRE 702. Nonetheless, many licensing professionals still view this methodology as a viable and useful tool in licensing negotiations by providing an initial idea of an applicable royalty rate, when it is otherwise difficult, expensive, or time consuming to ascertain through other approaches, and then refining the calculations using further financial information about the parties and the marketplace. See Robert Goldscheider, "The Classic 25% Rule and the Art of Intellectual Property Licensing," *2011 Duke L. & Tech. Rev.* 006 (May 30, 2011).

[18]For method claims, there is no obligation to mark, so damages can be calculated from when the patent issued, not when the notice letter was received by the alleged infringer. Marking generally requires the patent number to be placed on the product or packaging of the product covered by the apparatus claims.

[19]The URL for the article is www.mbbp.com/resources/iptech/patent_medimmune.html.

CHAPTER 8

Monetizing IP Rights

Licensing In and Out

Kelly M. Slavitt, Esq.
Reckitt Benckiser LLC

A license is a contract[1] between the owner of the intellectual property (licensor) and the party that wishes to use the intellectual property (licensee).[2] Intellectual property (IP) owners license "out" their IP to increase revenue and reap the rewards of its earlier efforts: the research and development (R&D) has already been done, the goodwill has already been generated, and/or the content has already been created. In contrast, companies license "in" IP owned by a third party to save on R&D expenses and leverage another company's expertise by combining it with its own brand.

A poorly constructed license agreement can damage a company's reputation with customers (current and potential) and put a company in the headlines and possibly the courtroom. Examples in recent years were the licensing disputes between (1) the makers of the Blackberry and the owners of patented IP used in the Blackberry[3]; (2) retired NFL players and their union over licensing their names, images, and biographies, and claims of failure to pursue licensing opportunities[4]; (3) New York City and its licensee for the sale of New York City Police Department (NYPD) and Fire Department, City of New York (FDNY) merchandise[5]; (4) Topps and their exclusive South American bubble gum manufacturer, seller, and distributor[6]; and (5) the owner of Martha Graham's choreographic works and her non-profit dance center.[7]

There are many types of licenses for IP in many different industries,[8] since there are many types of IP with their own special concerns. Types of IP include copyrights (including for music,[9] application service providers,[10] and software), trademarks, patents,[11] trade dress, and trade secrets. Types of IP licenses include for use, sale (including retail), promotion, manufacturing, and distribution. The common formats for a license are a license agreement, a clickwrap,[12] a browsewrap, a shrinkwrap, and terms and conditions on a web site. This chapter describes licenses broadly and notes issues to be considered in all licenses.

In considering whether to license IP "in" or "out," or both, a company must do an audit of its IP. A potential licensor needs to see what it has that may be of value to others in the market. Some of licensor's IP may already be covered by IP protections, but some of it may not, and so a potential licensor should look closely at what they have that can be trademarked, copyrighted, patented, and/or covered by trade secret[13] protection. Conversely, a potential licensee should see what "gaps" it has in its IP that are keeping it from monetizing products and/or services it already has because filling the gap by "licensing in" the IP can save the time and money needed to develop the IP internally.

The price to be set for use of the IP can be determined after an evaluation of the demand in the market. Through valuation, it may be determined that selling the IP is a preferable option, depending on how costly the license in would be over time and how critical the IP is to your company's business. Valuation is discussed in greater detail in Chapter 10.

When selecting a company with which to enter into a license, each party should conduct due diligence about the other. Particular issues to research include finances, reputation, past track record, other products in the market, and whom the company's other license agreements are with (to ensure they will devote sufficient time and energy to you, as well as what volume, level of quality, and countries the other party has done business in previously). Particularly in foreign countries, references should be checked. In addition, the licensor should investigate if the licensee has a conflict of interest in a particular market or for particular goods. Before negotiations begin, each party should sign a confidentiality agreement.

The written license is designed to protect IP ownership (licensing out) and how the IP is used (licensing in). The key concepts to be considered in a written license are the rights to be granted, key defined terms (IP, licensed products, territory, distribution channel, royalties), quality control of the IP, term of the agreement and termination rights, confidentiality, and managing risk and costs. Each of these is discussed in more detail below.

Grant of Rights

The grant of rights sets out which of its rights the licensor is granting to the licensee. This is the essence of the purpose for the license agreement and can be critical to the licensee where the IP is necessary to the functioning of its business and/or critical to the licensor where the license is a primary revenue stream for it. The parties should also be extremely clear about what rights are being granted, such as to use, sell, promote, manufacture, and/or distribute the licensed products or services. A license must address each of the rights available under the law for the underlying IP. For example, a copyright license should address each of the five bundled rights cited in the Copyright Act because if not specifically granted by licensor, the licensee is not entitled to them.

Typical grant language addresses who can use the IP, for how long, where, and the payments. The legal language used is some variation of the following terms: *nonexclusive, nonsublicensable, nontransferable, irrevocable, perpetual, worldwide, and royalty-free or royalty-bearing.*

A *nonexclusive* license grants licensee a right to use the IP along with others who also have this right. Software is a good example where many consumers have a nonexclusive right to use software and would not need or want an exclusive right to use, for example, Microsoft Word. In contrast, an *exclusive* license prevents others from also using the IP.[14] It also prevents the owner itself from using its own IP unless it reserves a right for itself in the written license. Exclusivity is a monopoly of sorts and should be granted only after careful consideration of other potential opportunities being forgone as a result. Payments in return for exclusivity are usually substantially higher than for nonexclusivity. Exclusivity is frequently carved up among licensees with expertise in a particular area, such as manufacturing or distributing.

A *nonsublicensable* license prohibits licensee from allowing others to use the license it has been granted by licensor. As an example, if licensee has the right to manufacture products, it would not be permitted to contract with a third party to have them do the actual manufacturing.

A *nontransferable* license is for only the named licensee and cannot be transferred to another party. An *irrevocable* license is not for a specific term but rather cannot be revoked by the licensor.[15] A *perpetual* license is similarly not for a specific term and lasts forever.[16] A *worldwide* license has no geographic limitations, and, as a note of caution, both parties should ensure that if this word is used in the grant of rights there are no conflicting limitations on geography elsewhere in the written license that could cause ambiguity. Finally, a *royalty-free* license is a free license, and a *royalty-bearing* license is a paid license.

Drafters should be cautious when placing conditions on a grant of rights. If a condition (as opposed to a covenant) is being placed on the license grant to limit the rights being granted, this should be explicitly stated in the written license using "provided that" language[17] (i.e., licensor grants X to licensee provided that licensee does Y).

Key Defined Terms

There are several key defined terms that the parties should explicitly spell out in writing in great detail. These are the *intellectual property,* the *licensed products* (or *licensed services*), the geographic area in which use is permitted (*territory*), through which channels the products/services are to be distributed (*distribution channels*), and the payment (if any) in return for the use of the IP (*royalties*).

A definition of what constitutes the intellectual property for purposes of the license is critical. Each party must be clear about who owns what, not only upon entering into the license but also upon termination of the license.[18] In some agreements, the parties will differentiate between IP owned by one or both of the parties prior to the license (*prior IP*) and IP that is developed or becomes known during the course of the license (*new IP*). If at the end of the license period the parties decide to allow each other to use certain new IP for internal noncommercial purposes (perhaps even *royalty-free*), they can explicitly state such in the license.

The license must also define what the licensed products or licensed services are. This is often a highly negotiated provision of the license. For instance, "jewelry" is not very specific. "Earrings" is more specific. "Gold earrings" is even more specific. And finally, "gold earrings for pierced ears" is most specific.

The licensed products or licensed services definition should also address collateral services related to the licensed goods. This would include, for example, any repair or maintenance of the products or services. Any related fees should be addressed in the payments/royalties section of the written license.

The definition of territory may be "worldwide" or carved up more narrowly. For example, a licensor may grant one party the right to manufacture its products and then several licensees to distribute and/or sell the products in different territories because they have networks and expertise in certain territories. The parties should be clear on what the territory includes. For example, "United States" may or may not include the U.S. territories and/or military bases and "eastern Europe" may include geographic boundaries that change during the term of the license.

The definition of *distribution channel* specifies where licensor is permitting licensee to sell or distribute its products, such as in retail stores or on the Internet. This definition should take into account how licensor wants its brand to be perceived by consumers, which may be "consistent with licensor's past practice" but ideally should specifically spell out where sales are permitted and where they are prohibited. For example, a licensor of high-end luxury goods may not want them sold in certain developing countries or to mass merchandisers, warehouse stores, outlets, or discounters. The definition may carve out *reserved channels* for the licensor where licensee has no rights to sell the product, such as on the Internet.

The payments are also a highly negotiated section of the written license, and should include the definition of *royalties*. The valuation of the IP will be tied in with the fee structure, and is generally whatever the market will bear. While some of the older industries have guidelines as to what typical royalty rates are, newer industries have to set a value and convince others their products/services are worth such value. The fee structure can be usage based (number of copies or users, such as with software licenses), a flat rate, an annual fee, or a royalty (typically, this rate is paid quarterly based on a percentage of net sales). Since royalties are the most common payment structure for licenses, this section will refer to all payments with the term *royalties*.

In addition to royalties, payments can include an *advance,* marketing commitment, maintenance fee, support fee, and/or fees for improved versions of the IP. An advance is an up-front payment frequently sought by licensors, particularly in the publishing industry. It may be applied against royalties or be a stand-alone guaranteed payment to the licensor in advance of products/services to be provided. This fee is not typically tied to the quantity of goods and/or services sold by licensee.[19] A marketing commitment may be sought by licensor as a dollar amount to be spent by the licensee on marketing the products and/or services as a type of insurance that the licensee will commit a certain level of its resources to making the products/services successful in the marketplace. Maintenance and support fees may be sought by licensee for maintaining software over time or providing customer support, as just two examples. If improvements and new versions of software are not explicitly included in the written license, licensee will charge an additional fee to licensor.[20]

Royalties can vary depending on the length of time of the license. While one party may want to "lock in" a royalty rate in a long-term license because it can help predict costs and revenues, it may disadvantage the other party if costs rise or if the seller does not meet anticipated targets. Compromise positions can include a lockstep provision that ties royalties with the quantity of products/services sold, or a requirement that the parties reevaluate and renegotiate the license at certain time intervals.

Another important term in the payments section that should be defined is what constitutes sales, as this will impact payments. The defined term *sales* (or *sold*) should state whether wholesale or net sales, and when the products/services are "considered "sold" such as when they are "billed, invoiced, delivered, or paid for, whichever occurs first." *Net sales price* should specify computation of the royalty due based on the gross sales price less certain allowances and discounts for cash payments, early payments, allowances or discounts related to advertising, shipping, returns, samples, promotions, and uncollectible accounts.

Licensor will typically require licensee to provide reports and records, most commonly a quarterly report of royalties. This allows licensor to monitor sales volume and locations as well as earned royalties. Licensor will also typically reserve the right to inspect licensee's books and records upon reasonable notice, and if a deficiency in the royalties paid by licensee is over a certain percentage (typically 3 to 5 percent), licensor will require licensee to pay the owed royalties as well as the cost of the audit.

Quality Control

Licensor, as the owner of the IP, should be responsible for its protection (including registrations and recordation of licenses); however, licensor should place obligations on licensee to protect licensor's IP—including its reputation and goodwill in its name—from a decrease in value. This is particularly important for trademarks where licensor can lose trademark rights if it fails to monitor usage of its trademark by licensee.[21] Among the standards licensee may be held to are the same quality level as licensor uses or a level comparable to that of competitive products. These are subjective standards, however, and so licensee should seek to be held to a more specific standard such as licensor's branding guidelines and style guide, or an industry certification or testing body's standards.

Licensor should reserve a right for its approval of all uses of its name/trademark in connection with licensee's use of licensor's IP. This includes all printed and digitally reproduced (i.e., web sites) uses in materials related to marketing, advertising, promotion, and display of its name/trademark in connection with the licensed products. In addition, the license should address whether licensee may cobrand licensor's trademark with its trademark or that of a third party, or use licensor's trademark in licensee's web site name or URL.

Manufactured products raise additional quality control concerns. Where the license covers products to be manufactured by licensee, the licensor must inspect the products manufactured as well as the manufacturing process. Licensor should require licensee to send it two to five free samples of the products from each geographic market for licensor approval. Licensor should also conduct factory inspections periodically, not only to inspect the products and process, but also to ensure proper safety requirements are being followed and that the factory is in compliance with human rights standards (i.e., child labor).

Approvals by licensor can delay licensee's time frame for manufacture, distribution, and/or sale of the products/services. Therefore, a time frame for approval should be specified so that licensee is not held responsible for delays caused by licensor. Licensee may seek a provision deeming that licensor's approval is given if licensee receives no response from licensor within a certain number of days of licensee providing licensor with the materials.

The license should specify which party is responsible for customer support. Typically, a licensee provides customer support, since it is more familiar with the products/services. However, licensor may want licensee to provide it with all data regarding consumer complaints so that it can modify its products or services as necessary. For products, licensor should require that licensee provide it with all data regarding consumer safety–related complaints and reserve the right to require a recall of products. Licensee should specify that any recall be at licensee's cost, and whether recall can be only when required by the government or also if licensor reasonably requests it.

Once quality control provisions are negotiated and put in writing in the license, Licensor must ensure compliance by Licensee. In addition to inspecting Licensee's chosen factory, as noted above, Licensor should also proactively investigate how its products are being advertised and sold in the marketplace.

Although protection and enforcement of rights in licensor's IP is licensor's responsibility, licensee is closer to the products and services in the market and must be part of the protection program. Licensee's obligation should be to report any potential infringements or counterfeits it learns of to licensor. Licensor should then take over enforcement (control of and payment of fees incurred in connection with protection of its IP), but require licensee to provide reasonable cooperation in assisting licensor with IP protection.

Term and Termination

The length of time of a license varies. A license to reproduce copyrighted material may be a one-time license, whereas a license to bring a new product to market may be a multiyear license.

In deciding on the appropriate length of time (i.e., the *term* of the license agreement) the parties should consider whether having short terms that are renewable is preferable to a longer term with the ability to terminate under specific written conditions. For example, if the license is a new relationship, the parties likely do not want to be locked into a long term if the relationship is not working out. Conversely, a licensee who has to prepare his factory to manufacture products will likely not want to commit the resources for only a short-term contract. A compromise solution can be a license with short terms that can be renewed automatically if certain milestones are achieved.

The conditions under which each party can end the relationship are essential. These are called *termination rights* because they allow for termination of the license agreement if certain events occur. Termination rights are critical for both parties: licensors will be concerned with tying their brand and reputation to licensee's actions, and licensees will be concerned with committing resources to a relationship that may end (and also because their business may depend on the use of licensor's IP).

Typically in contracts, certain events will allow for immediate termination, while other events allow for termination after notifying the other party of the breach and desire to terminate, and then allowing a period of time to "cure" the breaching event. For example, nonpayment of royalty payments for one month is unlikely to be such an egregious event that either of the parties would want to immediately terminate the relationship after all the time and resources have been devoted to the relationship. However, nonpayment of three or more consecutive royalty payments in any 12-month period may be egregious enough that the licensor may want the right to terminate.

Also typical in contracts are rights to terminate *for cause* or *for no cause* (also referred to as *without cause*). A termination without cause means the party can terminate without giving a reason. When granting such a broad right, the grantor should at least make sure they have a long notice period for termination so that they can wind down this relationship and seek a replacement partner. A termination for cause should specify in writing the reasons that the party can terminate the license agreement (such as for bankruptcy, as discussed further later).

In addition, contract termination provisions typically include termination for breach but because a literal breach of contract can include being one day late with a royalty payment, the parties should clarify the major breaches (called a *material breach*) that allow for termination. Sometimes material breaches allow for immediate termination, while nonmaterial breaches allow for a notice and cure period before termination is permitted.

Nearly all contracts allow for termination in the event one of the parties to the contract becomes insolvent. This can be an assignment for the benefit of creditors, or a voluntary or involuntary bankruptcy event.

In license agreements in particular, licensors will typically seek termination rights for licensee's nonpayment of royalties and fees, failure to follow license limitations, failure to meet quality control obligations, and failure to meet ship, launch, or delivery dates. An additional termination provision sought by licensors may be termination for poor sales, because this may demonstrate that the licensee did not use its "best" or "reasonable" efforts to sell or distribute the products as explicitly required of the licensee in the license agreement. This is difficult for a licensor to prove, however, even where defined sales targets are stated in the license agreement.

Licensors may seek to include a termination right based on a breach of ethics/ morality by licensee (perhaps referencing licensor's written corporate policy), which may include extending such right to any celebrity that may be endorsing licensor's products. This is important to licensors because its goodwill and company reputation are tied to the IP it is licensing to the licensee, so if a licensee is tied to a scandal or hires a celebrity to endorse the product that is tied to a scandal, there could be damage to licensor as a result of its relationship with licensee or such celebrity and so licensor would want to distance itself from the licensee. This can be particularly important if licensee is a nonprofit, where funds limit the ability to run a public relations campaign to repair a damaged reputation and could ruin the organization's ability to fund-raise for its cause.

If licensee is manufacturing the licensed products or providing the licensed services, licensor should seek a right to terminate the license agreement for product defects or service failures that remain uncured by licensee. Again, licensor is tying its brand and reputation to its products, and if licensee fails to provide the level of products or services that licensor has become known for, it would damage licensor's reputation, and so licensor will want the right to terminate its relationship with licensee.

If the license agreement is terminated, the parties should be clear on what payments are still due. For example, if licensor terminates without cause, licensee may want the right to a refund of fees paid on a pro-rata basis. Conversely, if licensee terminates without cause, licensor may seek to have unpaid guarantees and royalties paid within a short time period thereafter.

At the end of a license agreement, whether terminated prior to the specified termination date or not, it frequently is not sufficient to end the relationship immediately on such date because the parties will need time to wind down sales of the licensed products and advertising related thereto. Frequently, at the end of a license agreement term, licensor will require licensee to provide it with a list of unsold licensed products in its inventory, and licensee will seek a "sell-off" provision allowing it a certain amount of time post-termination to sell off the remaining inventory it has and use up its remaining marketing materials. In exchange for licensor's granting such sell-off right to licensee, and provided that licensee is in full compliance with all of its obligations under the license, licensor should seek to limit licensee's manufacturing extraordinary quantities of product immediately prior to termination or nonrenewal by prohibiting licensee from manufacturing the licensed products during the last several months of the term in excess of the amount licensee reasonably anticipates will be sold prior to the conclusion of the agreement. Upon expiration of the sell-off period, licensor should require licensee to destroy and show evidence of the destruction of all licensed products and material relating thereto, or alternatively to send the licensed products back to licensor (at licensor's cost).

At the end of the license agreement, licensor should also seek to place an obligation on its licensees to advise its distributors that the license has ended so that the distributors are not continuing to put products into the market bearing your company's IP. This is particularly important with licensed products that have a limited shelf life, because consumers buying such products in the discount market may be buying an inferior product that the licensor originally put into the market, and therefore licensor's goodwill would be diminished.

Confidentiality

As previously noted, a confidentiality agreement (or a nondisclosure agreement) should be signed before the parties enter into discussions that may lead to a written agreement. Licensor will typically be the party requiring this, as they are the party with the IP and will want to protect confidential information about its products and marketing strategies.

In addition, as with all contracts, the license agreement should include a confidentiality provision. Licensor should seek a strong confidentiality provision protecting its IP (as defined in the license agreement), "know-how," and any other IP that may be created during the parties' relationship.

Managing Costs: Insurance, Indemnifications, Reps, and Warranties

Allocating risk and the cost of risk are heavily negotiated in all contracts, and licensing agreements are no exception. This is a key area to seek the advice of legal counsel.

Standard contract representations and warranties should be included in the license agreement, such as that each of the companies are in good standing, and that the execution and performance of the agreement by each of the parties will not violate the law or a contract with a third party. Other standard warranties that a licensor may seek include merchantability and fitness for a particular purpose, and these should be considered in an IP context as to whether they make sense for the specific products/services covered by the license agreement.

Licensee should absolutely always require the licensor to provide representations, warranties, and indemnifications that it owns the IP.[22] If the licensor will not agree, this should raise a red flag to the licensee that there may be a question as to ownership and that the licensee is taking on the additional risk that a third party may assert ownership claims to the IP.

Licensors may also seek a representation from a licensee that it has manufacturing expertise, and that it will use its best efforts to promote and sell the products it manufactures. An additional representation sought by licensors may be that licensee has adequate staffing to fulfill its obligations under the license agreement.

All licensors will have issues that are specific to their industry, and they should consider these when drafting the license agreement. For instance, an organization operating in the animal welfare industry may want licensee to represent and warrant that it will not conduct animal testing or include fur in any of the licensed products.

As with all contracts, a license agreement should specify which party will cover which costs in the event of a claim by a third party related to the license agreement. These are known as "indemnification" provisions where one party pays the costs of the other party in certain circumstances, typically related to claims of damages related to the products/services. For instance, licensor may seek a broad indemnification from licensee for lawsuits arising out of injury caused by a product licensee manufactures or a more narrowly tailored indemnification for lawsuits brought by purchasers injured by licensed products negligently manufactured by licensee. Licensee may also seek an indemnification from licensor for lawsuits arising out of third party claims that licensor does not own the IP.

A poorly drafted indemnification provision can cost dearly if it allows for broad payments in many circumstances. Several examples are defense of claims, types of costs and claims arising out of or in connection with (described in further detail below).

It is important for the parties to be clear as to whether the indemnification includes defense of claims, since claims can be baseless yet costly to defend. The typical language used in a contract is "indemnify and hold harmless" or "indemnify, defend, and hold harmless."

The parties should also be mindful as to what type of costs they are indemnifying for, if any. Damages can be excluded completely, limited, or capped at a certain dollar amount, such as the amount of insurance being provided. For example, even if indemnification is for "damages," this should be specified further because damages can be direct, indirect, consequential, special, incidental, exemplary, and/or punitive. In addition, other costs may include claims, fees, liabilities, settlement payments, fines, diminution in value, expenses, attorney fees, and court filing costs, so these should be specified as well. Both parties should watch for broad indemnification language for claims "arising out of or in connection with the agreement" or the like, as these can be extremely costly. Instead, the parties should explicitly state which claims are covered by the indemnification. In a license agreement, these may include breach of any representations and warranties, any actual or alleged infringement of IP rights of any party in connection with the licensed products/services, and/or any damages for injury arising out of any person's use of the licensed products (including product liability claims).

The licensee should hold insurance, at its cost, during the term and for a certain number of years after the termination of expiration of the agreement, depending on the statute of limitation for likely claims, and licensor should require licensee to provide it annually with a copy of its certification of insurance. Further, licensor should require licensee to provide it with notice of insurance cancellation, termination, lapse, material modification, or expiration of the policy 30 days in advance and if a lapse occurs the licensor should carve out the right for itself to secure new insurance for licensee at licensee's cost. Each party should check with its insurance broker as to the coverage it has, and should consider carefully agreeing to claims on a per occurrence basis, waiving its right of subrogation against additional insureds, advertiser's liability, personal injury coverage, product liability coverage, and naming a third party as an additional insured. Licensor should also require a manufacturer licensee to name licensor as an additional insured in the event of a lawsuit arising out of injury caused by the product licensee manufactured.

Conclusion

License agreements can provide companies with a lucrative revenue stream and be an effective method for promoting brand awareness around the globe. However, to protect licensors and licensees, a written agreement should be put into place. The agreement should address the considerations noted above, and should be drafted with the assistance of legal counsel with IP licensing experience. A well-drafted agreement that is clearly written and addresses the concerns of both parties will set expectations appropriately and lay the groundwork for a productive relationship between the parties, while also protecting the parties (and the IP) should the relationship end.

Notes

[1] Because contract law applies, this section will not address basic contract law principles but rather will address contract provisions specific to licensing agreements.

[2] See Lorelei Ritchie, "Reconciling Contract Doctrine with Intellectual Property Law: An Interdisciplinary Solution," 25 *Santa Clara Computer & High Tech. L.J.* 105, November 2008; and Elizabeth I. Winston, "Why Sell What You Can License? Contracting Around Statutory Protection of Intellectual Property," 14 *Geo. Mason L. Rev.* 93, Fall 2006.

[3]See "Blackberry Patent Dispute Settled," *Washington Post,* March 4, 2006; available at www.washingtonpost.com/wp-dyn/content/article/2006/03/03/AR2006030301489.html.

[4]See "Retired NFL Players Win $28 Million in Royalties From Union," *Bloomberg,* November 11, 2008; available at www.washingtonpost.com/wp-dyn/content/article/2006/03/03/AR2006030301489.html.

[5]See "What's 'Even Worse' About Buying Fake Handbags?," *New York Times,* May 16, 2008; available at http://cityroom.blogs.nytimes.com/2008/05/16/whats-even-worse-about-buying-fake-handbags/, citing press release from New York City Law Department at www.nyc.gov/html/law/downloads/pdf/pr041404.pdf.

[6]See "Judge Lets Foreign Bazooka Maker Use Bubblegum Recipe," *Wave3,* 2006; available at www.wave3.com/story/5363027/judge-lets-foreign-bazooka-maker-use-bubble-gum-recipe?redirected=true.; see also Footnote 18 *supra.*

[7]See "Martha Graham Center Wins Another Round in Legal Fight," *New York Times,* June 29, 2005; available at www.nytimes.com/2005/06/29/arts/dance/29grah.html?scp=3&sq=Martha%20graham%20center%20wins%20rights%20to%20the%20dances&st=cse.

[8]For an excellent explanation of fashion law, written for businesspeople as well as attorneys, see Guillermo C. Jimenez and Barbara Kolsun, *Fashion Law,* New York: Fairchild Books, 2010.

[9]See, for example, Furine Blaise, "Game Over: Issues Arising When Copyrighted Work Is Licensed to Video Game Manufacturers," 15 *Alb. L.J. Sci. & Tech.* 517, 2005.

[10]See, for example, Michael P. Widmer, "Application Service Providing, Copyright, and Licensing," 25 *J. Marshall J. Computer & Info. L.* 79, Winter 2007.

[11]See, for example, John W. Schlicher, "Patent Licensing, What to Do after *Medimmune v. Genentech,*" 89 *J. Pat. & Trademark Off. Soc'y* 364, May 2007; and Jennifer L. Collins and Michael A. Cicero, "The Impact of *Medimmune* upon Licensing and Litigation," 89 *J. Pat. & Trademark Off. Soc'y* 748, September 2007.

[12]Kelly M. Slavitt, "U.S Appeals Court Provides Guidelines for Enforceable Online Contracts," *World E-Commerce and IP Report* (BNA), October 2002.

[13]See, for example, Alan J. Tracey, "The Contract in the Trade Secret Ballroom—A Forgotten Dance Partner?," 16 *Tex. Intell. Prop. L.J.* 47, Fall 2007.

[14]See Kelly M. Slavitt, "Licensing Your Intellectual Property: Benefits and Risks of Granting Exclusivity," Thelen Reid & Priest LLP, *Intellectual Property and Trade Regulation Journal* Fall 2004, at www.thelen.com/resources/documents/IP_TradeReg_Journal_Fall2004[1].pdf and reprinted in *Global Intellectual Property Asset Management Report,* at www.mhmlaw.com/article/GIPAMR1004.pdf; for a discussion in the context of bankruptcy, see Karen Turner and Craig S. Blumsack, "The Licensing of Intellectual Property in Bankruptcy," 24-8 *ABIJ* 2, October 2005.

[15]See *Nano-Proprietary Inc. v. Canon Inc.,* 537 F.3d 394 (5th Cir. 2008) regarding irrevocable perpetual clause.

[16]Id.

[17]See *Jacobsen v. Katzer,* 535 F.3d 1373 (Fed. Cir. 2008) (under contract law, "provided that" language creates a condition, and not just a covenant, that limits a license grant); see also Robert W. Gomulkiewicz, "Conditions and Covenants in License Contracts: Tales from a Test of the Artistic License," 17 *Tex. Intell. Prop. L.J.* 335, Spring 2009; and Hersh R. Reddy, "*Jacobsen v. Katzer:* The Federal Circuit Weighs In on the Enforceability of Free and Open Source Software Licenses," 24 *Berkeley Tech. L.J.* 299, 2009.

[18]For a good example of a famous case where this was at issue, see *Topps Co. v. Cadbury Stani,* 526 F.3d 63 (2d Cir. 2008).

[19]This is sometimes seen as a way to incentivize a licensee to be efficient in its manufacturing and/or diligent in its marketing efforts.

[20]Terms frequently defined in software license agreements are *improvements, upgrades,* and *updates.*

[21]See Kelly M. Slavitt, "U.S. Ninth Circuit Sets Naked License Standard for 'Simple Products,'" *World Licensing Law Rep.* (BNA), August 2002; see also Irene Calboli, "The Sunset of 'Quality Control' in Modern Trademark Licensing," 57 *Am. U. L. Rev.* 341 (December 2007) (arguing that courts focus more on product quality than on what is adequate control of the mark and consistent quality).

[22]The use of open source software raises some interesting issues that will not be discussed here.

CHAPTER 9

Working with Government

David J. Rikkers
Raytheon Company

As a purchaser of goods and services and as a source of funding for innovative efforts, the U.S. government offers many opportunities for companies.[1] The government is a large consumer of many of the same commercial goods and services purchased by other companies. In order to maximize the return when spending the taxpayer dollar, the government typically purchases according to the generally commercially available terms of each good or service. This allows the government to benefit from commercially available products and leverage commercial market competition that sets prices and terms. When the existing, commercial-off-the-shelf (COTS) alternatives are unable to meet the government's needs, the government may solicit proposals in order to determine one or more sources to develop a custom solution. In some cases, the development efforts funded by the government have not only established a solution to the government need, but also led to technology successfully adopted for nongovernment applications.

Examples of commercial successes based on earlier government-funded development efforts include the microwave oven, semiconductors, and the global positioning system (GPS). While radar research in the 1940s was directed to finding enemy aircraft, the ability to use a component of a radar system to cook food was discovered by Percy Spencer of Raytheon, resulting in Raytheon Company's successful product launch of the first microwave oven, the Amana Radarange. Technology in semiconductors, a foundational aspect of electronics today, were developed by AT&T Bell Labs, Fairchild Semiconductor and others. The GPS is another example of a government-funded effort that has resulted in much commercial success.

This chapter addresses some major themes of intellectual property (IP) aspects of working with the government. It is important to note that this discussion should be viewed as an illustrative guide only, as the legal issues with any specific interaction with the government are driven by a variety of factors. As with any transaction, the contract between the parties is important. However, when working with the government, many regulations, including government branch or agency-specific clauses, as well as various statutory provisions, often impose additional requirements. The content and manner in which some of these regulatory provisions are enforced can and have changed over time. Advice of counsel to ensure an appropriate understanding of the specific situation is always recommended.

The Big Picture

IP rights of interest to the government can be driven in part by factors not prevalent among most commercial consumers. This can lead to the government's desiring access to more IP than a typical commercial customer. These factors can include relatively short commercial product cycles compared to anticipated government use of the item; multiyear procurements of the same products, or large time gaps, even multiple years, between such purchases; need for interoperability among products purchased by different parts of the government; unusual uses such as for hostile military environments or space exploration. Other aspects of the government's interests include long-term maintenance of the items it procures, the training of operators and maintainers, the option to improve the item or change it to work with different items.

Turning now to the contractor, in addition to being selected by the government to be a supplier, the contractor's interests include a sustainable business model. This usually includes maximizing its return on investments, producing innovations that distinguish its products and solutions in the marketplace. Importantly, this can require avoiding a loss of effective control of its IP, such as by the government's having such extensive licenses or ownership rights that would enable the government to make more of the contractor's product, or an improvement of the product, with no involvement by the contractor.

The government's acquisition policies have varied over the decades, with significant variations in the scope of IP rights sought by the government. The trend has swung from the government's owning the rights to the government's obtaining a license to only the rights it needs, enabling the contractor to better commercialize and benefit from the technology. Currently, the emphasis is again swinging back in the direction of increasing government rights in the IP at the expense of a contractor's ability to protect its ideas and innovations from being freely used and modified by competitors.

The government's regulatory approach has traditionally provided a reward for private investment by allowing the contractors to prevent the corresponding technical data and software from being disclosed and used by other competitors. However, if the government had funded the development, the government had the option to freely share the resulting technical data or software of which it had taken delivery.

However, with many development projects, the government is now commonly seeking very broad rights, including rights sufficient to enable any government contractor to compete directly against the company that privately funded the development, using any or all of the technical data and software for free. This is likely to both reduce willingness to work with the government and reduce private investment in areas of unique interest to the government, to the detriment of the government. The government is additionally now dividing procurement programs requiring development into smaller portions, to provide additional opportunities for sharing of technical data and software among competitors, further diminishing the value of private investment in development. For example, the Department of Defense (DoD) is more frequently dividing large development programs into at least three portions, each having a separate competitive phase and contract, with fewer winners in each successive phase, resulting in a single competitor's winning the final stage. As is becoming more common, the solicitation at each phase establishes an evaluation criterion to downgrade "proprietary" solutions, indicating that the government desires rights to freely share all technical data and software with any contractor working on any government program for any purpose, and in some cases, to disclose to the general public at large.

Common government uses of such technical data and software include operation of the items or systems delivered, support and maintenance, modifications and future enhancements, as well as procurement of additional items or systems. All of these uses of interest to the government may be undertaken by competitors of the original supplier, without involvement by the original supplier, if the government is provided with sufficient rights. Therefore, it is critically important when considering an opportunity to accept government funding for development, to obtain counsel skilled in government contracting to ensure that proposals and any resulting contract properly address the interests of the contractor. In performing any government contract, a solid understanding of the procedural requirements of the contract is vitally important, as many are very different than typical commercial development contracts.

COTS products, which are unmodified products available to the general commercial market, purchased on their own, are likely to be acquired by the government under Federal Acquisition Regulation (FAR) Part 12. Under this approach, the government would not seek IP rights beyond those offered with product sales to the commercial market. However, substantial modifications to commercial items and commercial items purchased in combination with noncommercial items under FAR Part 27, will often result in the government's desiring extensive access and rights to IP that are critical to the competitive commercial position of the product and its manufacturer.

Changes in technology have broadened the impacts of the policy shifts, making it easier to replicate and transmit technical data and software. With electronic storage, transmission, copying, access, and sharing of technical data, it is much easier now to distribute and use information. For example, historically, government access to detailed technical data and software was largely limited to insight gained by viewing a copy at various design review meetings, followed by possession of an official, final delivery paper copy at the conclusion of the contract. It is much more common now for the government to have a contractual requirement to use a shared electronic workspace or shared server arrangement to enable government access to the full electronic copies of interim drafts and final versions of the technical data and software, including underlying design models.

Determining how to address these challenges and shifting environment, while enabling a company to execute a long-term, survivable business model, requires a familiarity with the significant aspects of the regulatory environment. The impact of any particular transaction with the government will depend heavily on the underlying circumstances of both the government's need and the specifics of the item or process.

Commercial or Noncommercial

When planning to work with the government, it is important to understand whether the item or service to be provided to the government qualifies as a commercial item according to FAR § 2.101 (48 CFR 2.101). IP applicable to commercial items or services, when sold to the government, is subject to the same commercial terms that the contractor has chosen to offer to all commercial customers, enabling the contractor much greater control over the terms. The government is treated much the same as every other customer purchasing the item or service.

Typically, if an item is available to the general public for nongovernmental purposes, or will soon be offered to the public, the item qualifies as a commercial item.[2] Somewhat similarly, a service offered and sold competitively in substantial quantities in the commercial marketplace can qualify. The service will qualify if it is based on established catalog or market prices for specific tasks performed or specific outcomes to be achieved and provided to the government under standard commercial terms and conditions.[3] If an item or service does not qualify as commercial, it is treated as a noncommercial item or service under the regulations.

Commercial Item

There are typically significant differences in the rights provided to the government pertaining to a commercial item versus a noncommercial item. If the item or service qualifies as a commercial item or service, the government will typically act as a participant in the commercial marketplace and acquire the item or service according to its generally available terms, unless a provision is prohibited by law. For example, provisions in a commercial software license obligating the government to indemnify the software provider will not be enforceable. In general, the activities required of the contactor in selling a commercial item or service to the government are not unlike those for any other customer. The license rights and activities often required of a contractor providing a noncommercial item are discussed later in this chapter.

Changes to COTS Using Government Funding

A commercial item to be provided to the government need not be identical to the COTS product. Two types of modifications to the commercial product are permissible while maintaining commercial status.[4] First, modifications that are generally available in the commercial marketplace are permitted. For example, there is a commercial market for computers sold to aircraft manufacturers and other customers that mount and operate the computers in less than ideal conditions. In each case, the computers may be supplied with custom mounting arrangements, custom cooling hookups, and specific power supply interfaces. Various degrees of ruggedization are also available to typical commercial customers, so as to avoid interruptions in the computers' operation, such as during a turbulent flight or a hard landing. Because these types of custom configurations are available to the general public, the government can also participate in the market as a typical commercial customer and procure the customized computer as a commercial item.

A second type of permitted modification to a commercial product, while retaining commercial status, is a minor modification not customarily available in the commercial marketplace but made to meet federal government requirements. Examples include, but are not limited to, adding an extra handle to aid in lifting or securing the item on a military cargo aircraft or painting a product with a special military-grade paint. Such modifications must not significantly alter the nongovernmental function or essential physical characteristics of the item or component, or change the purpose of a process. Factors to be considered in determining whether a modification is minor include the value and size of the modification and the comparative value and size of the final product.[5]

Noncommercial Item

A government-funded effort will be subject to noncommercial item regulations if modifications to a commercial item are beyond the scope previously noted, if the effort is for the initial development of an item, or if the effort is for further development to an already-existing noncommercial item. Some important differences between typical commercial development projects and government contracts for noncommercial item development include the determination of license rights for technical data, software, and inventions, and restrictions on treatment of subcontractors, as well as requirements for specific internal procedures and processes.

For many branches of the government, noncommercial item regulations address the source or sources of funding used for development of each subcomponent or part of items, components, processes or software in order to determine what restrictions, if any, will apply to associated technical data or software later supplied to the government. There are significant regulatory differences within the U.S. government agencies, with many agencies using the provisions of the FAR without modification. The DoD uses their own supplement, the DoD FAR Supplement (DFARS), at 48 CFR 2, as do many other agencies, including the Department of Energy, at 48 CFR 9, and the National Aeronautics and Space Administration (NASA), at 48 CFR 18.

It is important to understand that the specific contract provisions and regulations applicable to a particular contract must always be consulted in determining license rights that the government will obtain in technical data and software supplied to the government.[6] The following discussion assumes a DoD contract subject to the DFARS.[7]

Because of the nature of the government's long-term product use, support requirements, and modification needs, there is often significant interest by the government in obtaining rights to technical data and software, including source code, that is not typically provided in commercial market transactions. Because of the high frequency of acquiring and managing such technical data and software, regulations typically specify the details of the default rights in technical data and software, using standardized terms like *unlimited rights, government purpose rights, limited rights, and restricted rights.*[8] In the case of the DoD, the DFARS also provide for *specifically negotiated license rights.*[9] These various license rights are explained in more detail below. In that rights in technical data and software govern the government's ability to use, disclose, and authorize others to do so, they are, in many ways, analogous to the concept of trade secrets and licenses thereto in the commercial marketplace.

With the exception of specifically negotiated rights, the default level of license rights provided to the government hinge on determinations of funding of development of the underlying item, component, process, or software. *Developed* is a term that is used somewhat differently in the DoD regulations than its common commercial industry meaning.

Noncommercial Item Development

The term *developed* is defined in DFARS at 252.227-7013 and 252.227-7014.[10] In the case of technical data, it is important to note that the analysis does not turn on development of the technical data, but instead looks to the development and status of the underlying item, component, or process as existing and being workable. Workability is established when analysis or testing is sufficient to demonstrate to reasonable people skilled in the applicable art that there is a high probability that it will operate as intended. Curiously, the regulatory definition explicitly notes that the item, component, or process need not be actually reduced to practice within the meaning of the patent laws.[11]

In an illustrative court decision demonstrating how an item can be considered as developed on private funding, a manufacturer of holdback bars used in launching fighter planes from aircraft carrier decks had a privately funded design prior to contract award.[12] The contractor then used government funds to change the design to withstand 2,000 successful launches, rather than the 700-cycle capability of the precontract design. The court summarized that the government funds were used to increase performance, not achieve workability. Workability was established by the precontract design.[13]

For software, the definition of *developed* has two parts, each directed to different types of software. First, a "computer program," that is, something capable of causing a computer to perform specific operation(s), is developed when it has been successfully operated in a computer and tested to the extent sufficient to demonstrate to reasonable persons skilled in the art that the program can reasonably be expected to perform its intended purpose.[14] The second part addresses "computer software," that is, "computer programs, source code, source code listings, object code listings, design details, algorithms, processes, flow charts, formulae, and related material that would enable the software to be reproduced, recreated, or recompiled. . . ."[15] Computer software is developed when it "has been tested or analyzed to the extent sufficient to demonstrate to reasonable persons skilled in the art that the software can reasonably be expected to perform its intended purpose."[16] This second part is broader and allows for an argument that design details, flowcharts, or other related material could be analyzed to demonstrate that it can reasonably be expected to perform its intended purpose. This may provide a viable approach for a contractor seeking to establish completion of Development in the absence of code executing on a computer, as would typically be required under the first part of the definition.[17]

Because of the significance of determining when an item, component, process, or software is developed, it is important to retain documentation that may be valuable later in establishing that the item, component, process, or software (to include "computer program" or "computer software") was developed as of a certain date. This documentation should include information that specifies the intended operation/purpose and satisfies the demonstration requirements in the "developed" tests set forth above. As discussed in more detail later in this chapter, the source of the funding for development activities is also important and should be correlated with the records establishing completion of development. Because the corresponding technical data or software may be applicable to another contract years later, a need to reference or produce documentation on this issue can arise a decade or more after development.

Noncommercial Item Development Funding

In short, while the specific level of license rights to the government can be negotiated to provide other than what the regulations specify, the regulations provide a default in the absence of negotiation. As explained elsewhere herein, additional procedural requirements need to be met by the contractor to avoid the regulatory default presumption of development by government funding. In the case of an item, component, process, or software that is developed exclusively at government expense, the government is entitled to unlimited rights in any corresponding technical data or software. Alternatively, when an item, component, process, or software is developed exclusively at private expense, the government is entitled to limited rights in any corresponding technical data or restricted rights in any corresponding software.[18] Finally, in the case of an item, component, process, or software developed with a combination of private funds and government funds, the government is entitled to government purpose rights in any corresponding technical data or software.[19] Note that government purpose rights automatically broaden to unlimited rights five years after delivery, absent negotiation of a different time period.[20]

Noncommercial Item License Rights to the Government

While the DFARS provides the details,[21] generally speaking, unlimited rights means that the government can use, modify, disclose the technical data or software for any purpose, and authorize others to do so. Government purpose rights provide similar rights for such activities within the government, but limit the authorized purposes for nongovernment parties to be some activity in which the government is involved. This includes any U.S. government action or contracted activity. Note that foreign military sales contracts involving the U.S. government's selling products to foreign governments qualify as a U.S. government action. By requiring some U.S. government involvement, non-government-related commercial markets are protected. However, the default is that after five years, government purpose rights automatically expire and the applicable technical data or software automatically becomes subject to an unlimited rights license.

Limited rights and restricted rights are somewhat similar, but limited rights are used only in connection with technical data, and restricted rights are used only in connection with software. In short, limited rights enable use, modification, and release within the government. The government cannot disclose the technical data outside the government, except under specific purposes, such as emergency repair, subject to restrictions on further disclosure and with notification to the originator or to a covered government support contractor.[22] Restricted rights limit the government to use of the software on only one computer at a time, the one copy transferable to another government agency, with backup copies permitted. Modifications are permitted, but the modifications remain subject to the same terms. Other contractors performing service contracts may be permitted access to the restricted rights software to respond to urgent tactical situations under certain circumstances. The government may also permit covered government support contractors to use and modify the software.[23]

An important license right alternative found in the DFARS is the category of Specifically Negotiated License Rights.[24] These are, as the title indicates, negotiated rights and do not require a specific funding type. They can be used to tailor rights to meet a government procurement need while seeking to preserve additional competitive advantage for the contractor. For example, a contractor may benefit by limiting government use of technical data to use only on a specific program or for use with a specific product, instead of for any government purpose. An additional benefit of this type of license right is avoiding later disputes as to the nature of the funding used to develop the corresponding item, component, process, or software to which specifically negotiated rights have been negotiated by the parties in advance. Creativity is the license scope is not required. For example, the rights granted in a specifically negotiated rights license could be, but are not required to be, identical to those set forth as the scope of rights granted as limited rights or restricted rights. Use of the Specifically Negotiated License category removes the (exclusively private) funding requirement inherent in limited rights or restricted rights.

Noncommercial Item Doctrine of Segregability

The analysis and corresponding license rights are applied at the lowest segregable level. This means that seldom would the analysis focus on a particular overall contract deliverable item or software program. Instead, the lowest level of segregation, such as a subcomponent or part, can be used to determine when completion of development for that subcomponent or part has occurred, as well as the applicable funding. This means that the rights granted to the government in the corresponding technical data may vary across all the parts of an overall assembled end item. This can be used strategically by a contractor to prevent the government from having sufficient rights in a complete package of technical data to share the full package with competitors of the contractor. For example, the government may have unlimited rights or government purpose rights in technical data of many components for which it funded development. However, for those components that were exclusively privately funded, the government would typically not receive more than limited rights in corresponding technical data, which prevents the government from distributing the technical data in most situations.[25]

Likewise with software, for example, in source code form, development of a subroutine may have been exclusively funded at private expense. If such a subroutine were delivered under contract to the government, it would typically be provided to the government with restricted rights. If the government funded the entire development of another subroutine, the government would typically receive unlimited rights in any such delivered subroutine. Other subroutines developed by a combination of private and government funding are typically provided to the government with a government purpose rights license. Therefore, one or more of the subroutines that collectively make up a functioning software computer program may be provided to the government with a different level of rights. The government is typically prohibited from providing to others outside the government, software to which it only has restricted rights.[26]

In some cases, instead of the subroutine level, each line of source code may be segregable, particularly where the intended purposes of the lines of code are known, facilitating the analysis at the source line of code level.

Different types of software, such as source code, object code, design details, algorithms, processes, flowcharts, formulae, etc., are typically applicable to the same intended purpose. This can make the segregability analysis more complex and provide opportunities to a contractor not having finished development of object code. Since there is not substantial case law in this area and the regulation can be viewed from different perspectives, it is best to be aware of the issue of segregability at every step of the software process.

For example, at an executable software level, it is a good idea to maintain segregability of compiled code having different license rights if it is important to avoid a determination of mixed funding. Not doing so and compiling a subroutine developed by exclusively private funding with a subroutine developed at least in part by government funds may result in a determination that development of the compiled code is considered to have been mixed funded, which would typically result in a determination of a government purpose rights license in such a deliverable. As previously discussed, government purpose rights enable the government to freely use internally and share the executable code with any outside party acting on the government's behalf. Conversely, compiling code separately to avoid mixing exclusively privately funded code with other code types, even in executable form, better protects the contractor's investment. Practically speaking, this can be done by use of a strategy relying on use of an installation program delivered to the government to enable a combination of the restricted rights code with other code types after delivery, but the resulting combined code at that time would be subject to the most restrictive limitations, that is, the restricted rights license detailed earlier. In short, the contractor's not doing the combining for the purposes of delivery avoids the mixed funding status. That the government later combines the code, such as via an installation program, does not trigger the mixed funding status; hence, the more restrictive license applies to the government-combined code.

Noncommercial Item Assertions Table

Procedurally, when the government will receive other than unlimited rights in noncommercial technical data or noncommercial software specified for delivery under the contract, the contractor must specify such technical data or software in an assertions table,[27] specifying the rights to be provided and the basis for such rights (e.g., funding source). This assertions table is subject to agreement by the government and should first be presented in a proposal, with its becoming an official part of the contract at contract award. In response to any contract modifications or anticipated changes in the technical approach that may trigger changes to the assertions table, any assertions table changes should be negotiated with the government before adopting the different technical approach or agreement to the contract modification. The prime contractor and higher-tier contractors are responsible for presenting to the government any assertions of their own and any assertions identified by their subcontractors. Documentation of the completion of development and funding source are important records to retain for many years. The government, in recent years, has shown greater interests in challenging the content of the assertions table, likely necessitating access to such records.

Marking

Marking is another critical procedural activity. Absent a restrictive marking on items delivered to the government, the government is entitled to assume that it has unlimited rights in the technical data or software. DFARS at 252.227-7013 and 252.227-7014 specify the markings in DoD contracts that should be used in connection with the relevant noncommercial technical data and software rights granted to the government.

Also important is that the government is, in some cases, taking the position that inadvertent access by the government to technical data or software is sufficient to qualify as delivery, allegedly enabling the government to act as though it may proceed according to the marked license rights, with unlimited rights allegedly having been granted to the government in unmarked technical data or software. It has not been established that the government is entitled to such rights absent an official contract delivery. However, government requests to access e-rooms, and other collaborative efforts giving government access to nondelivered technical data, software, or any type of documents, need to be carefully considered and established only with procedures and monitoring to ensure that excessive rights are not inadvertently granted to the government. A similar problem can occur with others, like a subcontractor or prime contractor, having access to such collaborative tools and unmarked data, as nondisclosure agreements typically require marking of data to avoid a determination that the document is not freely disclosable or useable.

Deferred Ordering

An increasingly common provision in government contracts is DFARS 252.227-7027, also known as the deferred ordering clause. In short, deferred ordering with the DoD involves a potential obligation to supply *any* technical data or software generated in the performance of the contract to the government.[28] The government may request this up to three years after acceptance of all items to be delivered under the contract. The contractor may be compensated for converting the technical data or software into the prescribed form, for reproduction and for delivery. However, the government is entitled to receipt of these items under the default license level as determined by funding of development of the underlying items, components, processes or software, subject to the segregability concepts discussed above.

Due to the unilateral ability of the government to vastly increase the required deliverables under a contract subject to deferred ordering, several additional precautions are often warranted. Negotiating the deferred ordering clause out or limiting its scope is the first and most desirable option. Pricing for the risk and loss of proprietary nature of many internal tools and processes should a deferred ordering clause require delivery of associated technical data or software needs to be considered and can be an effective method of negotiating the applicability of the clause. To the extent the clause remains in, planning to understand what existing intellectual property could be compromised by anticipated technical data or software generation under the contract, and monitoring adherence to the plan, can help mitigate the risk. Should a deferred ordering request be received, an update to the assertions table is likely in order. Upon mutual agreement to the table, ensuring any technical data or software to be delivered in response to the deferred ordering request are properly marked is critical to avoid unnecessary rights being granted to the government.

Beware the Prototype

Even when a contractor has taken all precautions and negotiated a favorable position regarding technical data and rights in software, it is important to be mindful of other ways in which the government can induce technology disclosure and sharing among competitors. Notably, absent a contractual provision, there are no restrictions on the government's use of hardware. In one case, the Air Force did not have sufficient rights to share technical data among competitors participating in a multiphase competitive procurement, but was able to share delivered prototypes from each contractor among all the contractors. A winning bidder of a later phase of the competition was able to freely reverse engineer and incorporate features of another's prototype.[29]

Inventions and Patents in Noncommercial Contract Effort

Quite apart from license determinations for noncommercial technical data and noncommercial software is the determination of rights in inventions. As previously discussed, rights to delivered technical data and software rights are typically governed by the type of funding source for development of the underlying item, component, process, or software. In contrast, the government's license rights to inventions and corresponding patent applications do not depend on delivery and are usually governed by the funding source of two distinct events. If the government funds either (1) the conception of the invention or (2) the first physical reduction to practice of the invention, the invention is considered a subject invention.[30] A subject invention is one in which the government obtains specific rights, as will be explained more below. Importantly, the patent law concept of constructive reduction to practice, such as by filing a patent application, does not apply in this analysis.

For any subject invention, the government typically receives a worldwide, paid-up, royalty-free license.[31] Provisions granting some rights in an invention to a party that funds an engineering effort resulting in conception of the invention are not particularly unusual in the commercial marketplace. However, what is unusual is the additional aspect of the DFARS that stipulates that government funding of the first physical reduction to practice of the invention also provides the government such a worldwide paid-up, royalty-free license, even if the government did not fund the conception. For example, a company can privately fund the conception of an invention, file a patent application and even obtain an issued patent. However, if the company did not actually, physically practice the invention, such as by building a prototype, or writing some software code in the case of software inventions, prior to doing so while on a government contract, the invention is likely considered a subject invention at the time of the government funding of the first physical reduction to practice of the invention.

Not appreciating the significance of the reach of the subject invention applicability to first physical reduction to practice is very unfortunate for those who believe that simply filing a patent application before accepting government funding is sufficient in order to fully protect their rights in the invention. Filing a patent application is considered a constructive reduction to practice for purposes of patent law, but this satisfaction of the patent law reduction to practice requirement is not be considered a first reduction to practice for purposes of the DFARS.

Conversely, should a contractor privately fund conception and first physical reduction to practice events apart from government contract efforts, subsequent government funding can be used to conduct extensive engineering efforts, with the government receiving no rights in the invention.

Regardless of the government agency, timely and proper notifications[32] by the contractor to the government of any event triggering a subject invention are critical. In one case, a contractor made the government aware of the invention via briefings and reporting, but failed to complete and submit the proper form. In that case, the court sided with the government in its claim that the government was entitled to title to the invention, with no license or other rights in the invention remaining with the contractor.[33]

Rights in inventions are treated separately from rights in any corresponding technical data or software. The government's having rights in a subject invention does not provide the government rights in any associated technical data or software. Likewise, the government's having rights in technical data or software does not give the government a license or ownership to any inventions reflected or inherent in the technical data or software or any underlying item, component, or process.

Noncommercial Item Effort Impact

In order to sell a noncommercial item or service to the government, the provider of the item or service will likely be subject to many obligations not normally performed by many companies, such as specific accounting, disclosure, and license grant obligations. As an example of such obligations, FAR 12.504[34] provides a list of many statutory provisions exempted from commercial item procurements.[35]

Private Funding and Government Funding

As an example of restrictions on a contractor performing noncommercial item development work for the government, the contractor's cost accounting principles are subject to additional regulation. The cost accounting principles are relevant to IP rights in that designation of funding as private funding can relate to license rights provided to the government, as discussed above.

As of 2011, the government appears to be changing some long-held provisions of some agencies regarding designation of various funds as private funding. Specifically, in 10 U.S.C. 2320, an amendment enacted in January 2011 sought to designate funds for independent research and development and bid and proposal costs as federal funds in some circumstances. Implementing regulations appear to have been delayed, with further legislative changes expected. Importantly, any contractor interacting with the government should understand the nature in which any government funds or reimbursements may impact the contractor's IP rights, even when not on a contract.

Furthermore, once on a government contract, it is noteworthy that use of private funding for purposes of influencing rights while performing work on the contract may be prohibited, if pertaining to a task specifically called for by the contract. Case law in this area has been evolving, but a recent decision by the Court of Appeals for the Federal Circuit[36] addressed an area that previously had involved substantially different standards between outcomes of the preceding decision at a lower court and a different case addressing a similar issue.[37] In short, advice of counsel is likely required should a contractor be using noncontract funds while on a government contract, as a determination of correct cost designation may be dependent on several factors, including a contractor's disclosed or established cost accounting practices. However, general guidance provided by the recent court decision is that the current standard is one in which a privately funded effort may be conducted simultaneously with a government funded contract if the government contract does not "specifically require" the development activity.[38]

Reuse Prohibitions

In view of the many benefits and advancements that can occur on government programs, contractors will often want to reuse, in whole or in part, technical data, software or inventions associated with a government program. The most common impediment to doing so is the contractor not having sufficient rights to the intellectual property corresponding to the complete product. For example, work done by a different contractor (whether a prime or subcontractor) does not automatically result in rights for use on other programs. By way of illustration, a prime contractor on a government effort may receive software and technical data from a subcontractor. While the prime contractor typically will have sufficient rights to use the software and technical data for purposes of performing on the contract under which it was received, those rights seldom extend to any other activity, absent a separately negotiated license or assignment.

Contractors should be aware that some government programs require that information about the program not be publicly disclosed. Should the government solicitation include the DFARS 252.204-7000 clause titled "Disclosure of Information," the contractor should be aware of potentially broad restrictions applicable to activity associated with the program. It is advisable to negotiate the applicability of this clause to either specific topics or deliverables, so as to limit its impact on the contractor's ability to elsewhere utilize information or lessons learned on the government effort. Distribution statements will often be a required legend on technical materials generated on such a program, providing a limited preapproved scope of distribution with a point of contact listed for requests for permission to distribute more broadly.

Contracts that involve classified subject matter involve many specialized issues. *Classified* in this case refers to programs having information designated by commonly known terms, such as *top secret, secret,* or *confidential.* IP rights issues on classified programs require consultation with counsel.

Other potential factors to be aware of that may impact a contractor's ability to reuse IP created or associated with government programs can include restrictions previously negotiated in earlier contracts involving the IP. Also, depending on the desired reuse, export control prohibitions and, in some cases, restrictions under the International Traffic in Arms Regulations (ITAR), may also apply.

Treatment of Subcontractors

When the government funds development of noncommercial items, prime contractors and any higher-tier subcontractors or suppliers are prohibited from using their power to award contracts as economic leverage to obtain rights in technical data or software from their subcontractors or suppliers. This is very different from commercial market practices, but recognizes the use of taxpayer dollars and helps smaller companies retain rights to IP associated with their product.

Because rights to IP funded by the government can be important to later projects, including projects not involving the government, retention of IP rights by subcontractors is an important consideration as a contractor considers what work it wants to perform and what work, if any, it wants to subcontract out. If other uses for the technology outside of the specific contract opportunity with the government are known well in advance of the specific government contract solicitation, various teaming agreements and license agreements can be put in place, as the prime contractor is not then in a position of power to award the government-funded subcontract.

Outsourcing of Government Work

A relatively recent trend is the use of nongovernment employees to do the work of government. This has been accomplished by the government's hiring companies, known as covered government support contractors, having skilled employees to aid in everything from competitive proposal evaluation, to acquisition program management, and creation and administration of test programs.[39] Until recently, the law did not provide for the level of sharing outside the government required to enable these activities by nongovernment personnel, so in government programs requiring such staffing, the government was usually seeking to negotiate while contracting with sellers, an ability to provide these nongovernment workers/companies with access to the necessary, seller-owned IP to do their jobs. Recently, Congress passed a law that essentially provides the government with an ability to share this information with nongovernment workers and support contractors, provided a nondisclosure agreement is used.[40] The risks and additional parties that may obtain possession of technical data or software should be weighed by a contractor in exploring potential points of negotiation in any such contract with the government nondisclosure agreement to mitigate risks inherent with broad distribution.

IP Owner's Rights Relative to Government Activity

The discussion above primarily focuses on various IP issues when doing work for the government.[41] However, IP rights holders, whether working with the government or not, may at some point believe their IP rights are infringed by the actions of others interacting with the government or by the government directly. Briefly, the type of IP right at issue is important.

While the government does not have an ability to authorize itself or others acting on its behalf to infringe rights in technical data or software, it often does have such authority relative to patents and copyrights. This doctrine, known as Authorization and Consent,[42] often comes as a surprise to patent holders. In short, a patent is often ineffective in preventing anyone else from practicing your invention for the benefit of the government. Although the invention may be practiced, a patent holder is entitled to compensation. However, the patent holder is typically unable to use litigation against any commercial company infringing the patent on behalf of the government. Where Authorization and Consent applies, the patent holder must pursue compensation against the government, either through the government agency benefiting from the infringement or through the U.S. Court of Federal Claims.[43]

Conclusion

In summary, planning early, knowing what assets are at stake, and being aware of the various IP provisions can pay huge dividends in having a successful interaction with the government and sustainable, long-term business model. Knowledge of the specific regulatory provisions and proposed or current contractual provisions is essential and often may require advice of counsel.

Notes

[1] As one example of a way to locate and learn about government needs, the government has established the www.fbo.gov web site to enable searching for opportunities to work with the government.

[2] FAR 2.101 (2010)

[3] Id.

[4]Id.

[5]Id.

[6]While not addressed explicitly herein, copyright law also applies in working with the government, as it does in any nongovernment, commercial transaction. Consultation of the applicable contract and regulations is advisable regarding any required copyright license or ownership grants to the government. Typically, the copyright license grant will parallel the scope of activities permitted under the technical data rights or rights in software granted to the government.

[7]Because regulations are updated periodically, it is important to verify the applicable regulation in both number and date. A contract typically includes specific reference to both. Note that in late 2010, the DoD proposed a draft update of many of the DFARS Part 227 clauses cited herein. This draft was not implemented as of mid-2011.

[8]DFARS 252.227-7013 and 252.227-7014 (MAR 2011) (48 CFR 252.227-7013 and 48 CFR 252.227-7014) Some programs at some agencies are designated for Small Business Innovative Research (SBIR) status. SBIR programs typically have three phases, during which the SBIR data rights may apply. DFARS 252.227-7018 details the DoD approach to rights in noncommercial technical data and software when implementing the SBIR program.

[9]DFARS 252.227-7013 and 252.227-7014 (MAR 2011).

[10]The basis of the current definition of *developed* in connection with rights in technical data was first set forth in *In re Bell Helicopter Textron,* 85-3 B.C.A (CCH) para. 18,415 (1985).

[11]DFARS 252.227-7013(a)(7) (MAR 2011). Also, the patent laws are found at 35 USC.

[12]*Dowty Decoto v. Dept. of Navy,* 883 F.2d 774 (1989).

[13]The court opinion includes mention of receipts from the contractor at the time of performance of the contract that were stating "a completely new design was developed." However, the court did not find this determinative, looking instead to the definition of *developed.* 883 F.2d at 780. While outside the scope of this article, the definition of *developed* at the time of this case was in a precursor of the regulatory structure that now includes the FAR and DFARS discussed herein.

[14]DFARS 252.227-7014(a)(3) and (7) (MAR 2011).

[15]DFARS 252.227-7014(a)(4) (MAR 2011).

[16]DFARS 252.227-7014(a)(7)(ii) (MAR 2011).

[17]Ralph C. Nash, Jr. & Leonard Rawicz, *Intellectual Property in Government Contracts,* 6th ed. (Chicago: CCH Inc., 2008), 768.

[18]It is noteworthy that computer software documentation required to be delivered is provided with unlimited rights to the government, regardless of funding source. Computer software documentation means owner's manuals, user's manuals, installation instructions, operating instructions, and other similar items, regardless of storage medium, that explain the capabilities of the computer software or provide instructions for using the software. DFARS 252.227-7014 (a)(5) and (b)(1)(ii) (MAR 2011).

[19]DFARS 252.227-7013 and 252.227-7014 (MAR 2011).

[20]DFARS 252.227-7013(b)(2) and DFARS 252.227-7014(b)(2) (MAR 2011). Note that the five-year period is negotiable up until time of delivery of the technical data or software. In some cases, the period has been negotiated to be permanent, meaning the government purpose rights do not later change to unlimited rights.

[21]DFARS 252.227-7013 and 252.227-7014 (MAR 2011).

[22]DFARS 252.227-7013(a)(5) and (a)(14)(i)(B)(1) (MAR 2011).

[23]DFARS 252.227-7014(a)(6) and (a)(15)(vii) (MAR 2011).

[24]DFARS 252.227-7013(b)(4) and DFARS 252.227-7014(b)(4) (MAR 2011).

[25]See DFARS 252.227-7013(a)(14) (MAR 2011) for details on the scope of limited rights to the DoD.

[26]See DFARS 252.227-7014(a)(15) (MAR 2011) for details on the scope of restricted rights to the DoD.

[27]See DFARS 252.227-7017 (JAN 2011).

[28]FAR 52.227-16 (1987).

[29]*Night Vision Corp. v. U.S.*, 469 F.3d 1369 (Fed. Cir. 2006).

[30]DFARS 252.227-7038(a) (DEC 2007).

[31]DFARS 252.227-7038(d)(2) (DEC 2007). When contracting with the DoD, the DFARS typically provides that the contractor retains title and grants a license to the government. Non-DoD contracts with other government agencies typically use FAR 52.227-11 regarding patent rights. However, if the contract is with the Department of Energy or NASA, the default in their regulatory supplements to the FAR is that the contractor does not retain title of the invention, but instead receives a license to the subject invention. In such a case, the government takes title to the subject invention.

[32]See, for example, DFARS 252.227-7038 (DEC 2007) and DFARS 252.227-7039 (APR 1990).

[33]*Campbell Plastics Eng. & Mfg. v. Brownlee*, 389 F.3d 1243 (Fed. Cir. 2004).

[34]Also known as 48 CFR 12.504 (2010).

[35]10 U.S.C. 2631, Transportation of Supplies by Sea (except for the types of subcontracts listed at 47.504(d)); 15 U.S.C. 644(d), Requirements Relative to Labor Surplus Areas under the Small Business Act (see Subpart 19.2); 41 U.S.C. 43, Walsh-Healey Act (see Subpart 22.6); 41 U.S.C. 253d, Validation of Proprietary Data Restrictions (see Subpart 27.4); 41 U.S.C. 254(a) and 10 U.S.C. 2306(b), Contingent Fees (see Subpart 3.4); 41 U.S.C. 254d(c) and 10 U.S.C. 2313(c), Examination of Records of Contractor, when a subcontractor is not required to provide cost or pricing data (see 15.209(b)), unless using funds appropriated or otherwise made available by the American Recovery and Reinvestment Act of 2009 (Pub. L. 111-5); 41 U.S.C. 416(a)(6), Minimum Response Time for Offers under Office of Federal Procurement Policy Act (see Subpart 5.2); 41 U.S.C. 418a, Rights in Technical Data (see Subpart 27.4); 41 U.S.C. 701, et seq., Drug-Free Workplace Act of 1988 (see Subpart 23.5); 46 U.S.C. App. 1241 (b), Transportation in American Vessels of Government Personnel and Certain Cargo (see Subpart 47.5) (except for the types of subcontracts listed at 47.504(d)); 49 U.S.C. 40118, Fly American provisions (see Subpart 47.4); Section 806(a)(3) of Pub. L. 102-190, as amended by Sections 2091 and 8105 of Pub. L. 103-355, Payment Protections for Subcontractors and Suppliers (see 28.106-6).

[36]*ATK Thiokol v. U.S.*, 598 F.3d 1329 (Fed. Cir. 2010).

[37]*U.S. v. Newport News Shipbuilding*, 276 F. Supp. 2d 539 (E.D. Va. 2003).

[38]598 F.3d at 1332.

[39]While not the subject of this book, companies exploring pursuit of this type of work should weigh, with advice of counsel, the impact on an ability to sell other goods and services to the government, as companies having access to proprietary information of others are typically prohibited from offering similar products or services. See, for example, 10 USC 2320(f)(1) (JAN 2011). This area of the law is often known as organizational conflict of interest (OCI).

[40]10 USC 2320(f) (2010). See implementing regulations including DFARS 252.227-7013 (MAR 2011) and DFARS 252.227-7014 (MAR 2011)

[41]Using the DoD as the illustrative agency.

[42]28 USC 1498 (1998).

[43]Ibid.

CHAPTER 10

Valuation, Monetization, and Disposition in Bankruptcy

Fernando Torres, MSc

IPmetrics® LLC

After lengthy and intense negotiations, the bankruptcy auction proceedings drew to a close around 3 o'clock in the morning. The representatives of the winning bidder were satisfied that they had acquired a valuable asset for close to $4 million. Their hard-fought purchase consisted of intangible rights to two simple words, supported by trademark registrations, a handful of contracts, and the associated domain name and e-commerce site. These intangible assets embodied enough goodwill to justify what amounts to the $2 million-per-word price paid although, after 40 years in business, the last of 90 U.S. stores bearing the brand had closed months before and the entire inventory had been liquidated.

The "Tower Records" intellectual property (IP) was thus the last asset converted into cash to satisfy the claims of a multitude of creditors, but those two words were the foundation upon which an electronic retail business would, in a matter of weeks, continue to generate value for the new, overseas-based, owners.

IP and the Bankruptcy Context

The notion that intangible assets (IAs) and IP in particular are an increasing proportion of total corporate assets is relatively undisputed by now. Industries such as pharmaceuticals, communications, and media are the clearest examples of this phenomenon. Pharmaceutical products depend on patent protection to establish a degree of niche monopoly to raise prices and recoup extraordinary investment costs, and patent offices across many jurisdictions routinely restore to patent owners the term lost to slow approval processes. Compatibility across diverse communication devices produced by otherwise competing manufacturers relies on standards and the pooling of patents embodying them. Media companies increasingly depend on controlling content—copyrights—rather than specific communication media, such as newspapers or television stations, for example.

At appropriate stages in the economic cycle, stock analysts justify apparently excessive price-to-earnings ratios by attributing the incremental valuation to the unreported value of internally generated trademarks, patents, and intangible assets in general.[1] This is a widely shared notion, but it is not the best way to measure the value of a corporation's IP, as evidenced by the consequence that it leads to an apparent evaporation of IP values in the subsequent and unavoidable bear markets as the book value of tangible assets is assumed to remain constant.[2]

Despite these difficulties, it is clear that most businesses find value in the characteristic adaptability and flexibility of trademarks, which can be extended or licensed; patents, which can also be licensed and traded; and intangibles in general. By contrast, tangible business assets can quickly be in the wrong location, the wrong scale, using obsolete or uncompetitive production processes, and specialized in making outmoded products with few or very expensive ways to relocate, retool, or sell.

Correspondingly, in corporate bankruptcy processes (restructuring and liquidation), IP assets have been gaining in recognition as some of the most flexible, salvageable, and consequently most valuable assets the debtor possesses.

From an economic perspective, the bankruptcy process can be thought of as a set of laws providing for the regulated transfer of debtor's assets to creditors in order to settle claims. Consequently, the debtor's assets and liabilities must be valued, in a mutually and legally satisfactory way, to arrive at the appropriate transfer ratio between the parties. This is an eminently administrative process, not a freely negotiated transaction in a competitive market. Intangibles, furthermore, are typically unique and have few, if any, organized secondary markets that can provide arm's-length prices to establish values as they do for financial assets.[3]

Therefore, the bankruptcy valuation process must be carried out in a context of competing interests, under a necessity or compulsion to sell or buy, while ensuring all available, relevant, and valuable assets are taken into consideration. In the 21st century, IP has thus emerged as a significant, relevant, viable, and valuable asset class that can settle an increasing proportion of the claims and supporting, in some cases, the possibility of restructuring the original business retaining a substantial proportion of its value.

In the general area of IP and intangible assets, in the face of the increasing need noted earlier, the fact that generally accepted accounting principles (GAAP) do not reflect internally generated assets such as trademarks, patents, and other IP is an obstacle. At the outset, therefore, it is difficult to determine with certainty what IP and intangible assets the debtor actually owns and, moreover, what their book values were on the eve of filing. Nevertheless, acquired IP and certain types of intangibles have been recognized in GAAP financials as a result of the implementation over the last few years of the Financial Accounting Standards Board's (FASB) Statements 141 and 142, as well as the International Accounting Standards Board's guidelines for business combinations (the IFRS-3 standard).[4]

In practice, simple ratios and arbitrary "rules of thumb" have been used to fill this information gap, and closure, liquidation, financing, and restructuring decisions have been made on this incomplete basis. In the current environment, these practices are no longer acceptable, and the prevailing standard tends to include a specific audit of the IP and intangible assets, with appropriately wide variations among industries and the size and length of corporate history of the debtor.

Quality, Hierarchy, and Value

The intangibles that a business entity undergoing the bankruptcy process possesses must be closely examined to determine realistic prospects for their monetization. The first consideration in this process is the performance of an IP inventory, whereby the basic questions as to the status of all registrations and applications are answered and licensees, licensors, as well as all other relevant intangible assets are clearly identified.

Business executives and their advisers must then refer to this inventory list and segregate core and peripheral assets. Core intangibles are those that are truly necessary for the continued operation of the line, or lines, of business that make up the core competency of the debtor. Over time and through merger-and-acquisition (M&A) activities, the intangible inventory of most major companies gathers unused, obsolete, and redundant assets, which must be identified as such. All noncore assets have a supporting role to play for the restructuring or liquidation of the bankrupt company and, as peripheral assets, their main characteristic is their separability from the core activities.

A clear example of this classification came up in the bankruptcy of a major innovator that had been developing chemical compounds for many years, prosecuting patents diligently, but advancing only some of these compounds into their core product.[5] Some of the patents that did not make it into the company's core product were also bundled with brand names, which had trademark registrations, and extensive scientific documentation, which would inform their best uses in other applications. From management's perspective, at the outset, the monetization of any IP seemed doomed because their core product and technology had suddenly become obsolete in the context of rapidly advancing technology and due to a major breakthrough in the company's main line of business. After a comprehensive IP audit, however, the patents, trademarks, and trade secrets classified as peripheral assets not only had a higher fair market value than the core IP, but were enough to satisfy the majority of creditors' claims in the case. Years after, the core trademark assets remain a valuable and active asset in the global economy, and several applications in disparate chemical industry segments have benefited from the technology identified and monetized as peripheral assets of the original company.

In general, therefore, there are two dimensions to the IP inventory process: a qualitative audit and a strategic review. The qualitative audit aspect of the IP inventory deals with the comprehensive examination of the intangibles the company owns, the classification of the assets in the basic core/periphery framework, while the strategic review is concerned with identifying alternative users, industries, processes, and exploitation methods for the assets, particularly those in the periphery.

Significant value can be uncovered by this process, whereby IP specialists work closely with the appropriate members of the management team at the debtor company, and perhaps other analysts from the appropriate advisers in the process.

The Valuation Process

Although not every professional involved in the restructuring process needs to perform an IP valuation, they all require an understanding of the process in order to make informed decisions and provide the best advice. The valuation of intangibles is partly an application of the financial and economic valuation techniques used in assessing business valuations, and partly a specialized analysis of the drivers of value and the potential application of these assets. As in any valuation, clarity as to the definition of what is being measured is central to the interpretation of the numerical results. This is the first element of the valuation standards, to which we now turn.

Valuation Standards

Typically, the concept of value applied in bankruptcy analyses is the familiar notion established by the Internal Revenue Service (IRS) with reference the more general concepts of fairness and arm's-length negotiations; the concept of *fair market value.* The notion of *fair value,* as utilized in financial reporting under the guidance of the FASB, is often used as well. These confusingly similar notions can differ significantly in their quantification and, consequently, awareness of their distinctions is very important for sound decision making.

Fair market value is defined as "the price that (the subject intellectual) property would sell for on the open market. It is the price that would be agreed on between a willing buyer and a willing seller, with neither being required to act, and both having reasonable knowledge of the relevant facts."[6] The key concept in this definition is the hypothetical nature of the market participants that would be selling/buying the subject asset. No specific information or advantages about the parties is part of this definition.

By contrast, for financial reporting purposes, the notion of fair value is "the amount at which an asset could be bought or sold in a current transaction between willing parties, that is, other than in a forced or liquidation sale."[7] In this case, as the rest of the FASB indicates, the specifics of the parties are important. In capitalizing the cost of acquiring a patent, for example, it does matter for its value that the buyer can bolster its competitive position by adding otherwise partial coverage of a key technology to an existing portfolio. The same patent in the hands of a new entrant to the industry will not be as valuable if this new owner cannot enforce a licensing strategy due to insufficient cost effectiveness or must accept lower royalties due to a weak negotiating position with respect to existing competitors. Thus, the fair market value of the intellectual property will be the same in either case, but the fair value will be higher if the property is acquired by the established licensor.

The bankruptcy context creates a significant challenge to the underlying assumptions of fair market value. Obviously, the seller is actually "required to act," and the buyer seldom has a "reasonable knowledge of the relevant facts." As far as fair value, the standard explicitly excludes " . . . a forced or liquidation sale."

In the practical application of these principles in bankruptcy and reorganization scenarios, a key process is the analysis and specification of the concrete and relevant ways in which the situation, the assets, and the market participants differ from the standards. To derive the range between the maximum amount a buyer would be willing to pay for an asset and the minimum amount a solvent (hypothetical) seller would rationally accept for it, analysts must compensate for the circumstances that, in each materially significant case, create valuation distortions. The court administered process strives to determine fair values, but this is only possible is those distortions are explicitly considered by all parties.

Therefore, early in the valuation process, it will be critical for all professionals involved in using the information to be clear as to the applicable standard of value and any necessary adjustments.

Methods

Given the standard, the next decision point is how the valuation is actually performed. Among the various financial valuation approaches, the cost, market, and income approaches are the most commonly applied. Differences among these approaches are important not simply because each measures economic value from diverse perspectives, but because the concept and time frame being considered is different as well.

The cost approach adopts the notion that an asset is worth today what it actually cost to develop in the past, or what in the current environment it would cost to reproduce the existing asset with a new one of equivalent utility. This notion is relevant for specific items of IP that are relatively straightforward to reproduce, such as software with specified functionality, but the actual cost to develop a creative or breakthrough idea, or to create and maintain a trademark registration are logically unrelated to the economic value these assets can capture for a business enterprise. Generally, this approach should only be used when the underlying assumptions are reasonably valid because, for the most part, IP seldom can be attributed with intrinsic value, unlike tangible commodities such as gold.

The market approach, however, strives to measure value by the range of prices actually observed in a relevant market, assuming informed market participants exist in sufficient numbers and execute a sufficient number of publicly disclosed transactions. This, of course, has been a persistent problem for intangible assets in general, and intellectual property in particular; IP tends to be unique[8] and secondary markets for IP are developing only gradually. As an indication of a range of reasonable values, however, it has been applied often enough so that suitable databases of IP licensing and sale transactions are being accumulated and can be used, in the most active industries like electronics, pharmaceuticals, and telecommunications, as reference points for ranges of value. Its application, nevertheless, is far from being generally accepted as it is in real estate transactions and the familiar price-to-earnings ratios of Wall Street finance.

Finally, the income approach takes a more specific look at the realities that can be expected to determine the economic value creation made possible by the use of the intellectual property at issue. In this approach, value is measured by estimating the potential net revenue (or gross profit) streams of income that can be generated through licensing a property, the incremental price premium of a unique patented technology, or the exclusive exploitation of a copyright, and adjusting these forecasts to reflect the applicable degree of risk implicit in the projections and the time value of money.[9] If the entity under consideration does not earn royalties on the IP because it makes internal use of its own assets, then the relief from having to pay an opportunity cost of the royalties that a typical competitor would have to pay in the market for an equivalent property is considered the measure of value, in what is appropriately known as the *relief from royalty* method.

New Approaches

The established methods outlined so far all rely on the assimilation of IP and IAs to tangible and monetary assets. Nevertheless, in considering patents in particular, IP is essentially a bundle of rights, namely, the right to exclude others from practicing an invention. This characteristic is not reflected in the generally accepted approaches; it requires additional valuation tools.

One such approach is the assimilation of patents to financial options, whereby additional components of value are measured, such as the value due to the volatility of the value of the underlying asset (the patent) and/or industry. Thus, patent assets are valuable as a function of:

- The incremental profit available to the patent owner form practicing the invention with protection with respect to practicing it without protection.[10]
- The incremental profit that may be available from licensing or exploiting other embodiments or fields of use for the invention.
- The volatility of the industry, which increases the value of the right to exclude the competition and waiting to implement until there is less uncertainty about the profit potential of the invention (for example).
- The point in time at which the decision to implement must be made, given the statutory life span of the patent.[11]

This valuation framework, referred to as the *real options* approach, clearly enriches the analysis of value, which traditionally values patents as a conventional financial asset investment project.

Empirical Lessons

In our practice, the considerations of standards of value and the specifics of the valuation of a patent portfolio came to the fore in the analysis and negotiation of the sale of the European factories and intellectual property assets of a once-prominent auto parts manufacturer, which was one of the first casualties of the decline of the U.S. auto industry in the aftermath of the sharp rise in oil prices and intensified competition beginning in 2003.[12]

The European subsidiary's debt and assets stood approximately in balance, and the U.K.-based administration[13] case focused on the fact that, after the creditors took over the tangible assets, the only cash flow available for the debtor's estate, itself in Chapter 11 in the United States, was the value of the IP: the marketing and technology intangibles. The marketing intangibles of an auto industry supplier are usually considered minimal, as contracts are awarded on a technical and price basis more than any branding leverage. Consequently, the remaining value of the patent portfolio was of keen interest to the administrator and the debtor. The valuation consultants for the latter party argued for a very low value given the limited remaining life of the production programs under contract, the imperfect implementation of the issued patents in the production process, and a high-risk premium that minimized the value of the patent portfolio under the income approach. One significant obstacle in the valuation was the expiration of several patents in some European jurisdictions, a consequence of "cost-cutting" measures taken in the year leading up to the bankruptcy, which included the suspension of patent maintenance fees. As a result, the claimed value of the patent portfolio according to the administrator's consultants was approximately US$1 million.[14] Engaged by the debtor, in our examination we determined that, in addition to the patent portfolio itself, the operation of the factories relied on a series of indispensable and documented (but not patented) adaptations, improvements, and innovations, as well as systematic knowledge bases, which were systematically protectable as trade secrets. These intangibles formed a valuable complement to the patent portfolio, enough to justify nearly a 10-fold difference in the value of the intangibles, once the value of a transitional license for the marketing assets was considered, thus increasing the total value of the IP/IA portfolio by another approximately $1 million.

As the remaining potential acquirer of the manufacturing facilities negotiated the final price, the additional intangibles brought forth in our analysis provided solid support for the debtor's position that the value of the technology and marketing intangibles attached to the factories went far above the discounted value of a few patents. The negotiated outcome represented a substantial infusion of cash to the U.S.-based debtor, and its unsecured creditors, as it was closer to the $10 million upper bound than the $1 million initial assessment.

Once again, a central lesson to be drawn from the practical valuation and disposition of intangibles in bankruptcy is the importance of a thorough due diligence process, during which the complete IP/IA portfolio can be identified and prioritized, and a clear understanding of the valuation process, specific assets, and techniques applicable in a situation. A conventional approach to the patent-related revenue, and the dismissal of trade secrets, technical know-how, and marketing assets as immaterial, would have seriously affected the settlement amount for the estate.

Impact of Bankruptcy on Value

The fact that an item of IP is acquired under bankruptcy conditions obviously has an adverse effect on its realized value. However, the question often asked in the process leading up to the negotiation of an asset sale, liquidation, or reorganization is exactly by how much will it affect the value of a specific IP, such as the debtor's trademark?

In our practice, we have had occasion to gather and research enough empirical evidence to respond to such questions statistically. To begin with, based on the relief from royalty method, and using data for trademark sales disclosed in and out of bankruptcy due to the current financial reporting standards, we have been able to develop and test a framework to analyze the statistical value of trademarks in different industries and conditions.[15]

The statistical value of a trademark, normalized per $1 of sales, is higher in growth industries but is lower in high-risk situations. This is not a surprising result in the abstract, but it is important when considering a specific firm. For example,

TABLE 10.1 Trademark Value per Dollar of Sales Risk and Growth Scenarios

$\dfrac{V^{TM}}{S}$	Slow Growth (2%)	Fast Growth (5%)
High Risk (30%)	$0.15	$0.18
Low Risk (12%)	$0.48	$0.69

operating in low-volatility conditions, say in the medical services sector (12 percent volatility), a slow-growing firm's trademark may be valued at $0.48 per dollar of annual sales, whereas a fast-growing competitor's trademark may be valued at $0.69 per dollar of annual sales (see Table 10.1). Correspondingly slow and faster-growing market participants in a high-risk sector such as consumer electronics (30 percent volatility), would have trademark values of $0.15 and $0.18, respectively (see Table 10.1). The effect of higher risk is two-pronged: it increases the required rates of return and, by extension, the scope for average trademark royalty rates in each industry, while lowering the value of future cash flows by increasing the applicable discount rate for the industry. Growth directly increases trademark values via higher sales throughout the forecast period considered in valuation models.

Based on data for transactions in and out of bankruptcy, this empirical model also allows for the calculation of the impact a sale in bankruptcy has on the average trademark fair value. In business-to-consumer industries, two-thirds of all trademarks acquired in bankruptcy are sold at discounts ranging between 8.8 percent and 18.5 percent of total fair value.[16] On average, our research indicates trademark values are only 13.6 percent of the going concern value (see Table 10.2).[17] This is a significant loss of value, and it reflects the inevitable fact that trademarks typically bear the brunt of the loss of goodwill and negative consumer perceptions as a result of publicized bankruptcies, and trademark buyer interest reflects this phenomenon. Technology assets, however, typically withstand the loss of leverage in restructuring and liquidation negotiations with greater success.

Value Extraction: Monetization and Disposition

As a consequence of the high rate of value destruction that is attached to IP values in bankruptcy, value extraction becomes a process with a potentially high rate of return. The key, in our experience, is to begin with a due diligence process that not only identifies the registered IP the company owns, but identifies the full

TABLE 10.2 Trademark Value upon Restructuring Risk and Growth Scenarios

$\dfrac{V^{TM}}{S}$	Slow Growth (2%)	Fast Growth (5%)
High Risk (30%)	$0.02	$0.02
Low Risk (12%)	$0.06	$0.09

spectrum of ancillary intangibles that are created in the operation of any organization. Second, the IP/IA portfolio thus identified has to be reexamined with new and extended applications of the assets in mind. There is usually a good reason a company ends up in bankruptcy, and looking at the assets in the same way the company has "always done it" is a sure way to miss potentially valuable applications.

Retail Case Study

A case in point is the 2009 bankruptcy and liquidation of a prominent New York–based retailer of home, jewelry, and furniture stores, its second round under Chapter 11 since the start of the recession at the end of 2007.[18]

After the real estate, both owned and leased, was relatively quickly liquidated, the merchandise inventory was sold to specialized liquidators. However, as the IP monetization consulting team was brought in at an early stage, at least some of the liquidation sales were conducted under a trademark license. The liquidators had to recognize, and pay for, the market power of the mark "Fortunoff Diamonds" vis-à-vis a generic "diamond liquidation." This licensable use of the estate's intangible assets has been, more often than not, overlooked and a monetization opportunity lost. The use of the trademark as part of domain names and online liquidations should also be closely monitored.

Another category of ancillary intangibles identified in the due diligence process was customer databases, in particular the bridal registry information asset. Given a suitable privacy policy, and respecting third-party rights during the process, the long history of the stores had created a valuable asset, not necessarily for a new and similar store, but for new and valuable uses. To identify suitable buyers of the information, and to make them aware of the value of the opportunity, the IP monetization team engaged in a nationwide campaign, with public relations, online promotions, and directly contacting investors that, in the past, had indicated interest in leveraging intangible assets. The two main ways in which the database information was monetized were: (a) segmenting the information by product category, to appeal to specialized buyers as opposed to the same type of department stores; and (b) identifying new uses for the information. For example, the bridal registry database contained detailed information regarding dinnerware sets selected by, and gifted to, a multitude of couples during the past 20 years. A specialty company dealing in discontinued dinnerware pieces saw the value of knowing with surprising precision which consumers could benefit from maintaining or completing their sets with the specific dinnerware pieces in their own inventory. In the disposition process, this company obviously bid to acquire a nonexclusive license to that database. Other nonexclusive uses were also made available for information from different departments and product categories. In a way, as long as the data acquisition process has been properly conducted, and the appropriate privacy policies are followed, the same core information intangible asset can be monetized by different buyers, thus greatly enhancing the total value of the company's assets.

Finally, with several competitors, specialty buyers, and former owners of the retailer expressing interest, the bidding for the core IP asset, the trademark, easily exceeded the expectations of the unsecured creditors committee. A few months after the final auction, the brand has been recast into a new, smaller, and more focused store, under new ownership.

Banking Case Study

In a completely different context, the seizure, bankruptcy, and sale of a prominent bank in the wake of the 2008 financial crisis provides additional lessons regarding the preservation and monetization of intangibles.[19]

One of the purposes of a thorough due diligence process at the outset of a corporate reorganization must be the identification of the ownership structure of the IP and other intangible assets. In this banking case from our experience, the acquiring bank and the regulators overlooked, in our opinion, the fact that the entity that was seized and sold did not own the trademarks under which the bank operated and, most importantly, the acquirer continued to operate. Thus, simply put, the acquirer had control of the deposits and the branch system, but not title to the bank's trademark, copyrights, and patents. By continuing to operate the bank seamlessly, the acquirer was thus infringing on the IP of an entity that was not under the regulators' control.

The bank's holding company filed for Chapter 11 protection after the seizure of the retail branches and the aftermath of this unanticipated situation. In this context, our team was engaged to identify and value the IP the holding company was arguably entitled to sell or license to the acquiring bank. The value of such license to continue the use of the IP to retain the original bank's customers and facilitate the expansion of the acquiring bank into new regions was substantial, even taking the impact of bankruptcy on trademark values into account. For the next 30 months, this value was an important leverage element for the holding company in its litigation efforts and the negotiations to settle with creditors.

Lessons: Due Diligence and Marketing

The single most important lesson the practice of valuation and monetization in bankruptcy has to teach is that the due diligence process is key. The intangibles a business entity undergoing bankruptcy possesses must be closely examined to determine:

- The complete inventory of IP and IAs.
- The ownership structure of the identified IP/IA.
- The potential new applications of the existing IP/IA.
- The full universe of potential buyers of elements of the IP/IA inventory.
- The realistic prospects for value beyond the continued use in exclusivity in the same scope, segment, or industry.

If this complete process is not followed, the outlook for monetizing the IP in the same use is likely limited to a fraction of the value, not too far off the historical norm of recapturing less than 14 percent of the pre-petition trademark value.

Finally, as the thorough due diligence process is completed, a comprehensive and imaginative marketing process is necessary to fully extract above-normal value from the assets identified—from licensing the merchandise liquidation to structuring multiple nonexclusive licenses for trademarks or patents, to working closely with potential bidders to identify the full scope of the potential value of repurposing the assets at hand.

IP Monetization in the 21st Century

As in all processes in the 21st-century economy, time is of the essence in IP due diligence and marketing efforts. Consequently, an early start to the due diligence process is more than likely to yield higher returns. A major obstacle to overcome in the near future is, thus, the inefficiency of traditional information gathering and, particularly, patent quality assessment tools.

In the modern global economy, large patent portfolios are not uncommon, and managing the multitude of patent families across jurisdictions and technology segments requires the use of computerized databases. Yet, beyond calendaring, patent annuity, and maintenance tracking, the information about the precise economic significance of the underlying individual patents is absent. Patent tracking systems still lack, for the most part, a reliable and clear patent valuation field. Given the complexity of the valuation process of any asset that is yet to be commercialized, this type of information can only be derived indirectly in IP database management systems. The near future is pointing to the application of econometric analysis techniques to eventually provide estimated ranges of value for patents. Several models have been proposed in the literature, but most base the estimation of patent bibliographic data and only a few proprietary models use additional data, such as economic value-added by segment (or industry "GDP"). A systematic, up-to-date analysis of large portfolios will add significant value to the valuation and monetization process in M&A transactions, and will definitely reduce due diligence costs.

Trademarks are also increasingly managed through software applications, and some of these have begun to implement simple algorithmic valuations based on sales/revenue information attributed to the trademarks. Problems that will have to be resolved as these techniques are diffused among trademark owners are the valuation of umbrella brands and the attribution of value in licensing situations or when distribution networks or the selling process are a distinct and separable intangible asset.

The situation for copyrights, trade secrets, and other intangible assets is much further behind with regard to becoming systematized to the point where the due diligence process can be fast-tracked.

In the near future, we should see the fruits of research and development in automated valuation indicators, but not the obsolescence of the imaginative analysis that interdisciplinary teams of professionals reviewing specific business cases will continue to provide.

Conclusion

The bankruptcy process essentially provides for the transfer of a debtor's assets to settle creditors' claims. Valuation is a way to establish a fair transfer ratio between assets and liabilities. The identification, valuation, and eventual transfer of intellectual property are not straightforward processes. They require thoughtful contracts, procedures, and conscientious follow-through of established best practices in prosecuting, monitoring, and enforcing IP rights.

As this chapter has shown, IP valuation can frequently be a defining factor in the transition from bankruptcy to a restructured business and a significant amount of value can be lost if the monetization and disposition process cannot proceed smoothly to leverage the intangibles created in the 21st-century corporation.

Notes

[1] Since U.S. and international GAAP do not allow for the reporting of internally generated intangible asset values, it is only through acquisitions that the market value of IP is recognized in the balance sheets of publicly traded companies.

[2] It also assumes that market participants value stocks based on their (assumed) accurate value assessment of the (unobservable) intangible assets used in publicly traded companies.

[3] In the aftermath of the real estate bubble, however, so-called financial "toxic assets" had no easily discernible prices, contrary to the assumptions at their creation and issue.

[4] The new accounting framework for business combinations requires acquiring entities to perform a detailed purchase price allocation that segregates the values attributable to trademarks and other IP from general *goodwill,* which has long been the catch-all term reflecting the excess of total consideration paid over book value.

[5] The debtor in this case is a well-known brand that has undergone several restructuring processes and is now a pure trademark licensing organization, no longer manufacturing products.

[6] The typical source reference for this definition is IRS publication no. 561 in the context of valuing donations.

[7] FASB SFAS 157, issued in September 2006.

[8] This characteristic is, of course, at odds with the necessary step of identifying "comparables" in this valuation approach.

[9] The specific financial technique is the discounted cash flow method based on the concept of the net present value.

[10] In other words, given the competitive characteristics of the market and the technology in use, what is the first-mover advantage likely to be?

[11] The value of right to postpone implementation, for example, declines as the expiration date approaches.

[12] The company in this case was Collins & Aikman, Inc. and subsidiaries, which had acquired manufacturing operations in North and South America, as well as several countries in Europe.

[13] The administration regime in the United Kingdom is governed by the Insolvency Act 1986, as amended by the Enterprise Act of 2002. On the whole, it is somewhat analogous to Chapter 11 Bankruptcy proceedings in the United States.

[14] The monetary values in this case have been rounded.

[15]This method has been applied in several bankruptcy valuation reports, including our work for the reorganization of Interstate Bakeries, Inc. and was presented by the author at the 2007 Conference of the Western Economics Association International (available online as "Trademark Values in Corporate Restructuring" (July 1, 2007) at the Social Science Research Network web site, http://ssrn.com/abstract=1014741).

[16]Technically, this is the 95 percent confidence interval for the statistical parameter measuring the discount.

[17]The calculations shown in the tables simplify, for the sake of generality, a slight sensitivity of the value loss to the overall pre-restructuring sales level; trademarks associated with significantly larger volumes are more resilient.

[18]The originally family-owned company, Fortunoff, was founded in 1922.

[19]The identity of this bank is not disclosed due to continuing litigation.

CHAPTER 11

Outsourcing of Branding and Marketing

Terry Heckler

Heckler & Associates

S ince the mid-1990s we have witnessed a dramatic reduction of outsourcing branding and marketing based on the onset of desktop publishing and the growing sophistication and broad access to computer-driven communication design and marketing tools. Previously, it was larger companies that had internal marketing groups where outsourcing was reserved for highly specialized talents and top-level execution of mass communication campaigns. Small and midsized companies usually relied on outsourcing most of their ongoing marketing and branding assignments until it was realized much of the more routine work could be handled by employees interested or trained in communication design and armed with their new computer capabilities. Today, our industry has adjusted to offer more specialized services, that are much more strategic, creative, and intensive, in order to compliment in-house capabilities even in the smallest companies. No matter what size company, branding and marketing has been caught up in a changing landscape of communication media. Broadcasting has to deal with narrowcasting. Cable diced up the networks, and now the Internet along with growing mobile network access has provided history, news reporting, advertising, public relations, entertainment, shopping, education, and public opinion instantaneously created and edited to a large degree by the digital-savvy public. How best to migrate and merge on the media front has become a major challenge and new area for outsourcing.

Another area of evolving outsourcing requirements has been consumer research. Never before has there been the speed and ease of technology to create and mine data on consumer behavior. Twenty years ago, brand managers relied more on intuition than metrics. I have sensed greater hesitations and a lack of confidence in marketers today when a respectable amount of research hasn't been executed and smartly interpreted. There is a marked shift in the marketing mind-set from the right to left side of the brain.

Technology has also given the information and tools for marketing managers to become dangerously seduced by the action of the day-to-day tactical management compromising valuable strategic attentions. Also, most brand managers we work with today expect things to happen incredibly faster than just a few years ago.[1] There is a prevailing assumption that everyone is working 24/7. Outsourcing today, more than ever, requires scheduling expectations to be clear to all parties. As successful brands expanded globally, diversified more, and broadened licensing, brand oversight became more important. Graduating MBAs with brand stewardship and specialized brand growth tools started to become more evident. Practitioners from various areas of business, academics, advertising, market research, and design will present themselves as "branding professionals" with multidisciplinary capabilities. It's basic but more important than ever to have a clear definition of the branding project objective and deliverables to help ensure the best fit with the essential disciplines.

Brand Naming Project Dynamics

One of the most important, if not the most important, brand-building tools to have is an effective brand name and it's wise to outsource expert advice on the subject. Outsourcing of brand naming projects in larger companies can originate from many different areas, people, and circumstances. Project dynamics are rarely consistent. Protocol, procedures, and terminology can vary widely. Consequently, there isn't much agreement on the best way to do this.

Legal oversight can occur at different points in the development process sometimes with unpredictable and unintended consequences. Name options presented early to managers without legal protection can create emotional attachments to alternatives that are unprotectable yet can progress into costly final evaluation stages. Name options closed down too early in the process by overprotective legal scrutiny can short circuit the creative efforts, limit options, and frustrate the decision process.

Outsourcing branding managers must understand the degree of protection confidence ultimately required in the project and the degree of legal scrutiny applied to name alternatives at any given point in the naming process. Within our own brand naming development process, we try our best to present alternatives that have passed several online searches.

We make it clear within our brand name development process that any of the alternatives we present have been through national and international online trademark searches. There are several search sites, but we primarily use USPTO, Dialog Trademarkscan from Thomson and Thomson, and RIC International for translation interpretations. During the Dialog™ search, we first make sure that the names do not exist as an exact trademark in all international class codes. We then narrow the search to the industry relevant class codes to search spelling variations of the names. Since the advent of the Internet, we have presented only cleared domain name alternatives as well as search engine first-page contexts for names and a review of possible incumbents from code names in the social media sites. We never have presented this as a legal search and refer to it as a "cursory search." We recommend a full legal search on any of the alternatives, to be managed directly by our client's attorneys. We offer referrals when necessary.

It's refreshing to have learned that good brand marketers, designers, and trademark attorneys all agree that distinctive brand names and distinctive graphic realizations of the names are the best for building and protecting vessels for brand equity. While such important overriding agreements are refreshing, there has always been an interesting distinction between the legal and communication design perspective. Distinctions between legal and design-based terminology is a simple but rich example as follows:

Legal	Design
Standard character/wordmark	Brand name
Stylized mark	Logotype
Composite mark	Mark plus logotype
Design/devicemark	Mark

The reference used most by the general public for any brand name in its graphic trade dress, formal or informal, is *logo*. Most people seem to know what that means, but it doesn't help when there is a need to refer to specific elements that make up a logo. That's why it's common in the design world to hear references to the total brand name configuration, which is often designed to incorporate multiple visual and verbal elements like ad slogans, address copy, and Web addresses as the "brand signature." It's how the brand signs its name. Many people and even marketing professionals have a tendency to refer to a brand name as the brand, and *branding* meaning the process of brand naming. This leads to some serious confusion about what a brand and brand equity is. We try and avoid this by making sure people understand that a brand name is a brand signal, not the brand itself or brand equity.

Without a doubt, the most important brand signal is the brand name. It is what offers the durable brand building powers and legal protection of brand equity. For this reason, it's important to share some common misconceptions about brand naming we often encounter.

Brand Naming Compared to Reference Naming

Brand naming is often confused with reference naming. Brand naming is a separate class of naming from what we call reference naming. Brand names are names that need to perform brand roles and facilitate long-term brand equity building. These are names that will outgrow launch and start-up business plans and sometimes traverse many market positions. These names need legal ownership and legal protection and strive for being first in the minds of consumers, sometimes in vast numbers of people.

Reference names do not have a brand role intention. They are names given to something to more specifically refer to it rather than using a generic category name referring to a group of similar things. These names are often, but need not necessarily be literally descriptive words and word phrases using words straight from dictionaries.

There is an ongoing extensive need for straightforward reference naming far more compared to brand names. Everything needs a name to distinguish it from the generic category in order to facilitate communication or distinction. For instance, in a resort development, neighborhoods, buildings, rooms, roads, parks, trails, ponds, streams, horses, beverages, entrees, events, and so forth need reference names.

We have done several resort reference naming systems where hundreds of names were required, for instance, the non-descriptive names of lodges at Beaver Creek resort:

- The Bordes Lodge
- Centennial Lodge
- Creekside Lodge
- Park Plaza Lodge
- Townsend Lodge
- Poste Montane Lodge

The overwhelming dominance of reference descriptive names is one major reason why many people erroneously believe a brand name must literally describe what is being named.

We frequently develop nonbrand names for our clients. These names are often descriptive, and sometimes rendered with brand signals to convey distinctions. We are careful when working with descriptive names with brand signals because they will automatically mimic brand roles and be subjected to brand competition, no matter how devoid of brand intention. Sometimes these names get attached to things that prove to be brand worthy and cause serious protection concerns. An example of this is "Procare," a name we did for a client. It was developed as an internal program that slipped out into the consumer world and is encumbered with ongoing legal protection issues. Part of our job in brand naming is to clear up the confusion between true brand intentions versus straight descriptive intention.

The Descriptive Brand Name Problem

One of the most damaging misconceptions about brand names is that they must be descriptive, that is, literally describing what the brand is or does. Conveying what a brand is or does is a fundamental step in grasping its relevance. Many marketers see the literally descriptive name as the quickest route to relevancy.

We explain there are three serious liabilities in descriptive brand names. First, they are oversaturated vessels of preexisting meaning. They offer little potential for exclusivity in people's minds. Second, anyone can use them at any time, making a descriptive name difficult and costly to protect, particularly if the brand becomes successful. Third, descriptive brand names lack endurance.

We have done many name changes, and one of the most common reasons for undertaking a name change is the crippling limitation a descriptive name places on a dynamic brand. Most often, the descriptive name either encounters protection problems or restricts growth.

We have never worked with a client that did not want their brand building to be successful. Brand building stimulates expansion and extensions beyond start-up. Descriptive names invariably fail to convey evolving brand positions; this is one reason we often see the phrase "and much more" stuck on to a descriptive name. All that does is create more confusion and even a longer name for space management. Descriptive brand names are names without legs.

The Unique Brand Name Value

We stress the utility of a unique brand name, but point out that the unique name must have a certain level of credibility and relevant associations to be effective. Herein is our rebuttal to competitors that deride our "empty vessel" philosophy: we know there is no true empty vessel for any invented word. The vessel always comes in degrees of being filled and we strive to find vessels that have enough room for effective additional meaning.

People learn almost immediately a one-to-one reference relationship between a word and what it means, as in learning vocabulary words. This is no less true with learning brand names. In fact, brand names are easier to learn than vocabulary words because they're usually presented within a rich multicued sensory context. So when people explain that unique names will take a lot of time and money to build meaning awareness, they're flat out confusing a word-learning process with a brand equity–building process. Building brand equity does take time and money. But we have learned, through hundreds of naming project results, that unique names are actually more efficient for building brand equity. Less time and money are spent on capturing a more precise brand signal to fight noise and significantly less money is required for ownership protection. Over the years we've tried to explain this with a quick example of throwing a fictitious brand name at the client and asking them what it means, lie, "Have you ever heard of the Twoyet Company?" They say, "no," and we say, "They make these incredibly designed eyeglass frames. They're out of Vancouver." We then proceed with something else, and after a bit of time has passed, we reask the question, "You ever hear of the Twoyet Company?" Most clients can immediately demonstrate they learned the meaning. They learned the meaning of a unique brand name, and there was not a penny spent.

We sometimes run into the insistence that a certain brand name doesn't need to be legally owned, so a unique name is not required. This may be true of pure reference naming, like street names in a development, but for business brand names, ownership is always an issue and always hoped for in some degree; if not legally, at least in people's minds. You can risk taking a brand name into the public market without legal registration, but it's always wise to know who might object to your using it.

Other businesses might be protecting the same name or similar names. Usually, it's no problem until your brand becomes successful and others fear the confusion or see deep pockets. But this can happen at start-up as well. Also, we can get tricked into thinking we're working on a tightly controlled brand name for a segmented business-to-business (B2B) market and later find it sliding out into the broader consumer market through unintended circumstances and by people misunderstanding its original intention.

A Memorable Brand Name?

Often, it is requested that the name bc memorable. Give us the key to understanding human memory, please. My mind is wired to remember things differently than yours. Time and time again, we have experienced our name teams review six name alternatives and each of the team members remembers them differently. Our clients show this to us constantly. They will review our short list and pick out names that are "memorable" to them that do not correlate to the ones others seem to remember.

Common Misguided Brand Name Criteria

Often, the name is requested to be short. No more than four or five letters, please. This is sometimes expressed as a memory key. Names using initials are all short. Many people seem to have a difficult time with remembering initial names. The world is filled to the brim with them. Short character names are called for at times by brand purpose and restrictions like tiny presentation space for key applications. Lately, we have found four-letter name variations extensively explored as uniform resource locators (URLs).[2] This expectation has been so common, they overpopulate that conventional standard practice. Given the option, we prefer to go with the shorter words for purposes of application flexibility and gestalt value. However, we do not consider this an effective name criterion and try to discourage our clients from expecting ultra-short names.

The request for a catchy name comes up often. What does catchy mean? It probably means a name that is easy to remember and easy to roll off the tongue. Some clients have defined catchy as "creative" or as a name people just "love to say." Generally, we like to have the client realize that catchy really implies that the name catches on and works well. This is what effective names do, but "catchy" is not a functional criterion for guiding our naming work.

Occasionally, there is the request that the name should be real, not made up, contrived, or abstract. This is another way of requesting literal or descriptive names straight from the dictionary. Unique protectable names are usually contrived and made up. In other words, effective names are created. Sometimes we'll get a client that will qualify alternatives as being "too contrived." It's not productive to split hairs over this. What's contrived to one person is inventive to another.

One request that is particularly difficult to disengage is the name must be easily explained with a story or have a real development story—"where it came from." This is another argument leading to a descriptive name. The reason for the name must be seen as something immediately logically connected to brand purpose or, if not, to be easily and quickly rationalized in a meaningful way. This naming necessity is intensified when we're working with a client that must represent the names to higher authority. This is a tip-off we're not working with the real decision makers (although we're always told we are) and our procedure will be more complicated. Also, this story or explanation necessity is increased in all name change situations.

When it's a name change situation, we'll hear this: "A name change transition is so much easier if the name can be quickly explained or almost inherently understood." This adds another level of complication, forcing the name to function as an explanation about the brand rather than just signal the brand. There are really two story requirements involved, but usually they are wrapped up together. There is the "what does the name mean?" explanation story, and there is the answer story to "how did you come up with that name?"

One reoccurring question seems to always emerge somewhere along the process. "What does the name mean?" We try our best to reduce our clients' concerns over this by carefully explaining our criteria for effective names, none of which suggest utility in descriptive or literal names. (Note again, we're talking about naming situations involving brands). We try and explain that they need their name to identify, refer to, and to stand for the thing we are naming as clearly away from other associations as possible. If the name is a word that stands for other things, shared primary meaning compromises it.

When people ask what the name means, it's an opportunity to tell them about the brand itself. Sometimes a client will say, "We don't want people asking about this all the time." We counter by asking, "You don't want people interested in your brand?" Of course, clients have an immediate need to explain the name development process to other important decision makers, as well as partners outside the naming process, and they assume this to be a key aspect of name credibility. They want something more interesting than, "We worked with Heckler Associates on coming up with what we thought would be an effective name." They want a "real story connection," to know the name was developed out of an association to other things. They need to see this story fairly clearly in order to appreciate the name itself. We explain that their desire for a romantic story around the name is not required for its inherent effectiveness and that it has been our experience that name development stories are mostly corporate mythology that naturally can be and sometimes need to be messaged into various cultural agendas. A name development story can be developed after a name is selected to address immediate needs. Most of the time this seems to settle them down. Sometimes it doesn't, and the naming process becomes seriously flawed. The story part becomes a primary requirement in generating or evaluating alternatives.

Six Criteria for Effective Brand Names

Every smart marketing person can roll out criteria for brand naming. Sometimes it's carefully spelled out, covering a wide range of objectives. "The name must describe" is usually at the top of the list, and we've covered that ad nauseam.

Early on, we struggled through many naming projects playing ping-pong with people on criteria until we realized that no matter how the project was framed, the intuitive sense that guides us adheres to six basic criteria for effective results:

1. *Unique.* A unique name will minimize existing associations, which leaves more ownership potential for mind share. It will take a lower budget to protect legally and offer an immediate and constant point of distinction in the marketplace. A truly unique name will always be able to absorb and signal the ever-widening definitions and changing distinctions of a growing business. This is our empty vessel concept. Yet we clearly understand that no name will exist without some level of associations and particularly when there is an international audience involved. We just strive to invent names as empty as possible with the greatest feeling of relevant association.
2. *Credible.* A brand name must meet a satisfying level of appropriateness and believability in reference to the sustaining fundamental purpose of the brand.

The type and degree of associations in the name must feel credible and be compatible with what the brand is or does. These associations should be sensed to some degree, no matter how unique the name is.

3. *Reproducible.* The name must be easily and correctly spoken, written, spelled, read, and heard. Except for an international requirement, this is the clearest criterion to judge, particularly if you're a poor speller and you have a slight problem pronouncing words. However, most every name can be pronounced in various ways if only by emphasizing the syllables differently. Our test for multiple pronunciations is to determine if the different ways take you to different places. For instance, we avoid or watch carefully any word with a "'tique" morph at the end, like mystique or antique. A name like "Montique" could be pronounced. Montie-Q or Mon-teak. When there is a reproducible glitch with a name, it creates friction that can wear the name down to the point where a name change situation is necessary. We have done many name changes for this reason.

4. *Legible.* An extension of the reproducibility criterion, legibility should be considered carefully in instances where a name will depend critically on a certain medium (as on a phone or small screen). Ideally, a name should have an ease of reproducibility in all communication media with immunity to noise factors. Legibility is the criterion of correct presence and impact, no matter how or where the name is encountered.

5. *Durable.* The name needs to have the ability to meet the test of time. It must withstand not only the ups and downs and growth of the business but the modulation of the market and culture. Here again, the name with a minimum of associations and frictional issues provides legs for the long run.

6. *Compatible.* The name must anticipate the workaday words, phrases, and brands that might immediately precede or follow. For example, how does a company brand name work for phone reception or someone saying I'm working with X? When we develop a name for Microsoft, we must always anticipate the Microsoft brand name as a preface. This requires compatibility for preexisting brand architecture.

No name will meet these six criteria to everyone's satisfaction. Everyone will have a different opinion about how a name measures up and emotionally resonates. It's a judgment on how problematic certain glitches might become. Here is where our intuition and experience apply. We do know that names that stand up to these criteria will be effective brand names.

There are many effective brand names out there for successful companies without legal trademark protections. But it just isn't smart business practice to skip over the protection of intellectual property (IP) assets, particularly equity-rich brand names. As we noted earlier, we make sure all our brand name alternatives are as clear of legal issues as possible with the limited tools and judgment we have. But as we explain to our clients, professional legal judgments are necessary to determine how protectable certain names are, even if they can be registered. As we understand it, legal protection is not a static state. A registered name entering the market can soon be compromised, depending on the business success, extent of exposure, and the emergence of copycat competitors. Also, U.S.

trademark laws do not universally apply, and it is a common assumption that a small local or regional U.S. brand need not be concerned with international exposure, yet some of these brands have a component of offshore production that provides exposure and easy adoption in certain countries that do not have protection of use beforehand. China is a good example where a brand is protected by first-use. The best protection for any growth brands requires ongoing legal stewardship.

The Supporting Role of a Descriptive Phrase

A unique, protectable brand name is far more possible and effective particularly in its early development phases, when it is accompanied, in direct proximity, with a descriptive copy line of seven words or less. This phrase takes care of the need for the name to literally describe or define itself. This is essential for unlocking the potential of the name to grow and adjust with the developing and often unanticipated potentials of the brand. A descriptive phrase can easily be adjusted for refocusing a brand rather than facing the risk of a name change.

We classify brand name descriptive copy into four groups.

1. *Single generic descriptive words.* Generally, the single generic word designates the product category the brand is primarily involved with.
   - Starbucks—coffee.
   - Panera—bread.
   - Pagliacci—pizza.
2. *Generic description phrases:*
   - Lowe's—home improvement warehouse.
   - Doubletree—hotels, suites, resorts, clubs.
   - Qpoint—home mortgage loans.
3. *Differential descriptive phrases.* This is a phrase that not only describes what the brand is involved with but also includes a distinguishing aspect that serves to separate it from competitors or ad specialness:
   - Cinnabon—world-famous cinnamon rolls.
   - Beaver Creek—Colorado's Alpine resort hideaway.
   - Courtyard—the hotel designed by business travelers.
4. *Slogans.* A slogan is usually a word or phrase used to reinforce a specific marketing or brand change-up objective. It's most often developed through ad campaigns and fused with emotional associations to stimulate imagination, aspiration, brands or calls to action for short promotions. A notice is required here. Slogans have created an expectation in many marketers' minds that a descriptive phrase must be cool, clever, or catchy in some way. This is particularly true when they feel the brand name itself fails a bit on these counts. We have no problem with slogans but engage with them selectively and mostly for brands that have attained significant brand awareness. But for brands starting up or struggling to build equity, we try to make sure the client understands the value of a good descriptive copy line and steer them away from a slogan.

Slogans can be used more effectively by brands with extensive existing equity:

- Vail—There's No Comparison.
- Nike—Just Do It.
- Marlboro—Come to Where the Flavor Is.

The Graphic Realization of a Brand Name

When we determined the inherent brand builders, early in our work, inclusion of the brand name graphic was passed over because there have been many successful brands built without this element. Think of all those successful business-to-business service brands and many professional service consumer brands that present their brand names in straight generic type without any distinguishing treatment or additional marks.

Brand signature graphics are not inherent brand builders, but they can be enormously important and effective brand-building tools. We have never approached a brand-building effort without trying to have distinctive brand graphics in place. Good brand builders are sensitive to the visual nonverbal powers of brand name graphics to attract attention, convey rich message content, and evoke emotional connections. It is putting the value of art to work.

Going about our daily lives, we confront a wide range of brand signature graphic constructions. Figures 11.1 through 11.6 show some common examples. (The brand graphic signature examples shown are original designs by Heckler Associates, except Kovacs and Poliform).

FIGURE 11.1 Generic Logotype (Standard Character Word)

FIGURE 11.2 Logotypes (stylized marks)

FIGURE 11.3 Mark with Logotype (Composite Marks)

FIGURE 11.4 Logotype Mark Integration

FIGURE 11.5 Fused Logotype and Mark

FIGURE 11.6 Cobranded Construction

Information necessities often complicate brand signatures. The more complex these constructions become, the more challenging is the graphic realization. The entire structure needs to be presented as a comfortable unit, yet must be a clear reinforcement of the brand name. In addition, certain elements within the total signature need to show properly placed legal protection signals. This is another area where legal insight is important.

The Value of Graphic Realizations

There are several reasons to apply graphics to a brand name, but the main value historically has been to quickly signal distinctiveness and ownership as in branding animals. Over the years, this recurring effort contained within the boundaries of a brand name signature has set up conventional graphic practices that almost universally signal "brand presence." An example of this would be to take any word out of the dictionary, such as *mast,* present it in generic type to 100 people, and ask them for the meaning. Then repeat the same survey with *mast* in a graphic realization emulating brand signature conventions and note the expanded range of responses the graphics stimulate (see Figure 11.7).

FIGURE 11.7 Mast Graphic

We think the primary value of the graphics applied to brand names is to signal "brand presence operating here," this name is trying to be distinctive and owned." This graphic function becomes particularly important when the brand name itself lacks distinctiveness. Smart marketers know this and will apply brand signals to products (or anything) to signal branded specialness without any true brand building intent. Sometimes these signals basically represent an entire marketing program. Knowing and respecting the value of these signals becomes important in big companies where a wide range of brand building efforts exist with many different kinds of brands. Understanding where brand building intent is most important and supporting it with the right tools can be a challenge.

Another key value of a graphic realization is the inherent *summum bonum* positions they provide communication practitioners. This has been confirmed over and over in our work for clients where we have implemented private label or proprietary branded programs. As an example, when we were doing ski-top cosmetic designs for K2 and putting together private-label skis designed for certain ski retailers, we found ourselves doing ski cosmetics to extend or complement the retailer's brand graphic signature, which was the key brand signal on the ski. The more sophisticated, hip, or attractive the retailer's brand signature, the more sophisticated, hip, or attractive the overall ski cosmetic options were. This practice emerged with private-label communications we've exercised over the years with a wide range of clients from banks to beers. The brand graphic signature sets a "tone and tune" for designers to design by. The better the brand signature is, the better the follow-through communication harmonies.

Comparing "Logotypes" and "Mark Plus Logotypes" for Brand Development Powers

The weakest graphic realization for a brand name is a generic typographic logotype. It has a minimum of visual signals for distinguishing itself from any generic piece of typography. Sometimes this strategy is rationalized to represent simple, no frills, no overcommercialized hype, straightforward, reserved, subtle, rational business approach. We do not recommend this graphic realization even for the least aggressive roles brands play. It is simply too generic.

The strongest signature graphic formats for brand building power are logotypes with marks, integrated with marks, or fused as marks. These three approaches provide the fullest orchestration and richest palette to engage the senses and mind of a viewer.

Here is where the attorneys take issue. As we understand it, the widest breadth of protection comes from the distinctive brand name itself. If you engage the name with other visual elements, each additional element or particular setup may need to be protected seperately. Those modulations actually open up a wider range of information to be potentially similar to other marks and are therefore more challenging to protect the brand name itself. Also, multiple variations of a particular style or rendering of a mark can weaken the protection of the primary trademarked version. With all due respect to the value of trademark protection, which is so important for maintaining brand equity value, I'll attempt to explain further why we favor mark with logotype formats for building brands.[3]

There's a greater message potential compared to working with a generic logotype. Simple type-style variations, accents, and extensions are fairly limited in their capacity to convey nonverbal associations. Extremely exaggerated type styles often begin to deteriorate legibility. With the addition of a visual mark to the logotype, there is a wide world of image content and rendering styles to create a brand signal that taps into nonverbal feelings that can attract and engage a viewer far more effectively than a word alone.

Nonverbal recognition is heightened by a visual mark. In many application instances, a flash of exposure may be all there is for recognition. The cues for mark recognition do not require verbal cognition. We understand that words themselves are gestalt visual recognition events, but they require verbal learning first and depending on the degree of distinctive letterforms, partial exposures to logotype may not provide enough cues for recognition. Good brand marks have a high degree of resistance to environmental noise and can be recognized with a minimum of exposure.

Broader presentation flexibilities are offered by a brand mark. It can be presented by itself in understated ways for application circumstances where stylized marks are too overt and commercial. The design device comes off more like a piece of art or a suggestion of the brand rather than the exact name of the brand. The mark offers ways to suggest brand presence in a broad universe of media. We use the example of United Airlines using their brand mark as a decorative motif on fabric used in their Red Carpet Rooms. We are aware of the overuse of brand marks in this way as well.

A brand mark can transcend language barriers. Most people living in industrialized countries can quickly recognize and learn visual mark designations. Generic type and logotypes alone present literacy challenges.[4]

While we favor the logotype plus mark formats, we learned early on the strategic issues involved and that not everyone agrees that marks enhance the brand-building process. We recall a highly respected designer suggesting that marks or symbols actually distract from name recognition. They should be used only when brand names achieve household word status and never used when communication funds are limited. Clearly, we do not agree with this. How many successful brands in the world actually achieve "household word" status, and since when do the majority of brands in their early phases enjoy unlimited funds? As stated earlier, we believe marks offer valuable enhancements to independent growth brands, but there are certain situations when we do consider a logotype by itself without a mark. Keep in mind we are not referring to a logotype using generic type but to a distinctively enhanced word graphic.

Logotype treatments are often given to products that do not have brand growth intentions but need distinction within a competitive market. They are usually products scheduled for obsolescence, program names for limited promotions, and specialized services for specific product cycles.

For example, look at the trunk of a Nissan car. In the center is a Nissan master brand signature. On the far left side is the name "Sentra" presented as a logotype. In the same type style as Sentra, "GXE" appears on the far right side. I'm not a car buff. I'm not sure if Sentra is a Nissan subbrand or a name for a product line or model. I'm not sure if GXE is part of the Sentra name or a model variation of the Sentra. It doesn't matter much because the master brand, Nissan, is made clear to me through its brand mark signature realization. If a mark appeared with Sentra or GXE, I'd find myself wondering about the master brand reference.

Logotypes are sometimes preferred for the immediate credibility they suggest in certain categories where for years they have become a conventional signal for serious competition in the category. Names of movies, and most names used to appeal to children, such as confectionery product names, are examples. There are credibility trends always in evolution for just logotypes in certain niche markets where simplicity, anticommercialism, ego-driven arrogance, no-frills technicality, or minimalism dominates. Running counter to the convention is sometimes judged too risky. Finally, there are always those primary decision makers who superimpose their own personal bias for just a logotype, no matter what level of diligence supports the contrary.

The Criteria for Graphic Signature Effectiveness

The criteria we recommend to judge effective graphic work follows closely the same criteria for effective brand names. However, there are some fascinating differences that stem from the differences between verbal and visual information.

As we pointed out with brand naming criteria, every smart marketing person can roll out criteria for brand names no matter how oddball some of it is. In contrast, very few can articulate or use words to spell out their criteria for graphic realization of the names. It is nonverbal communication, and it is difficult to imagine visual decisions without seeing them. Some clients, however, have prepped us with their criteria, and often it mirrors the common naming request for literal descriptive aspects. One client I remember gave us a whiteboard lecture on "good logos." I remember his first criterion, "A quick sense of meaning that feels good." I guess you can't beat that. He also insisted on a "natural reference instead of an abstract one." Sometimes highly motivated clients prepare an elaborate visual lifestyle montage, with which our logo needs to be compatible. Most recently, we worked with a high-level marketing vice president with a major quick-service restaurant chain who insisted that our brand graphic "must engage." A common request over the years has been "it must be cool." At best, clients will study the competitive landscape and make comments about what graphics they like and dislike, then turn it over to us. This is good.

Our five criteria are:

1. *Unique.* As with brand names, the graphic employment must have the degree of distinctiveness to effectively contrast it from competitors and be reasonably able to legally protect it within the broader marketplace. It's interesting to note a recurring aspect here: most graphic designers have a higher degree of sensitivity to visual details than people untrained or inexperienced with visual communications. They are more aware of the subtle distinction between graphics and see them quicker and more clearly than the general public. This has been confirmed in our work over and over. You can see where this leads. What might appear unique to the designer can look very familiar to the client. Many times, when we have presented graphic signatures employing elements reversed out of a circle-based format, clients will immediately reject it based on it being too similar to Starbucks. The overall graphic can be completely different, yet the circle is seen as the primary graphic signal and it's the same as Starbucks. To some degree this is attributed to clients knowing we did the Starbucks signature, but not always.

   It is difficult to determine how unique a graphic is or will be interpreted. We try to keep an extensive reference library of brand graphics at hand and review the web sites such as TinEye, PicScout, Ginipic, and Eyealike.[5] It's only in the legal registration process that visibility on graphics per category can be judged similar to other protected graphics. However, even if a registration procedure is successfully exercised, it doesn't mean that others will not protest it. We remember the broadly publicized legal battle over a new NBC brand graphic that was forced to be retracted due to a conflict with a small Nebraska TV station. Millions of dollars were spent to deal with the resolution. This involved big companies with enough resources to protect themselves but it confirmed for us at the time that it isn't a simple matter to assess how unique a graphic realization is or to anticipate the degree of legal inspection it might receive. A great complication of this is the fact that there are many more unregistered brand graphics in the world than registered. A brand graphic registration helps in legal battle but does not guarantee legal or mind-share ownership in the United States and some other countries.

2. *Credible.* The brand graphic must have an appropriate and believable compatibility with the fundamental purpose of the brand. This not only applies to the graphic content but also to the form and stylistic rendering. Credibility is usually judged by the predominance of graphic conventions within segments of business. The question is how much to tap into those conventions and yet still meet the criteria of being unique. This is similar to the trade-off between these two important criteria in brand naming.

3. *Legible.* The graphic content, form, and style all play a part in assuring that a graphic realization will be easily recognized in its primary and secondary applications. All media needs to be considered as well as scale. Form revisions are usually necessary if there are important small or large applications. Effective graphics within the normal application sizes do not necessarily hold up to extreme sizes in either direction.

The integrity or gestalt of the graphic components composing a signature is important to protect itself from the surrounding environmental noise. Without this internal gravity, signatures can easily link up, and fragment into the bordering context, lose their impact and cease to be legible. However, tightening up the gestalt too much can pinch the graphics and lead to a merging of the information and loss of legibility. A good designer can judge the thresholds for optimum gestalt on any signature.

It's interesting to note that graphics normally do not address the criteria of reproducibility that names do, although they can be a good feature. The general public does not need to draw the brand graphic like speaking a brand name. The necessity of hand-drawing graphics has been eliminated by technology for even the sign painters today.

4. *Durable.* The graphic needs to meet the test of time. Stay away from trends as well as highly realistic associations. Recently, we reluctantly did a real estate brand graphic that related to the form of a house. The brand will grow naturally into commercial real estate and find the specific residential association a piece of friction. They will probably face the need for a new mark. We strive for more classical aspects in graphics and carefully use specific associations metaphorically rather than descriptively.

5. *Likeable.* Not only must the graphic be appreciated for the feelings it expresses, it must be liked for the way it looks. We never directly ask a client reviewing graphic options which one looks best. We frame our presentation discussion around which option we think works best based on the first four criteria. There is little doubt however that aesthetic appeal must be satisfying enough for an option to even be considered. Though the aesthetic appeal is difficult to articulate, it is definitely a strong factor in the decision process.

We have often employed baseball hat mock-ups to evaluate and present brand graphics to determine how visually appealing they can be. We want them to become instant "gimme" hats.

Meeting these five criteria takes experienced judgment. In designing a brand signature we try our best to provide at least six to eight options that we think effectively address these criteria yet provide significant variations in content strategy.

Evolving Influence of the Internet on Brand Naming and Graphics

In the early 1990s during the online business gold rush, there was a sharp dividing line between the "virtual" and "real" business world. Younger entrepreneurs who clearly saw the potential and how to implement the technology drove online businesses. Many of them thought big and overinvested in the strength of the first-to-market differential. They targeted entire categories and opted for generic brand names like Drugstore, Hotels, Shoes, and Encyclopedia. Our criteria bias for unique brand names was often scoffed at. Within a decade, the real-world brands adapted to the online medium and established their traditional brand equity competition. Today, domain names have proliferated at a blistering pace and have placed an enormous challenge on creating and protecting unique brand names.[6] Coming up with a brand name that can obtain a multiple top-level domain position is difficult. Even if a name acquires dot-com clearance, it sometimes shares the exact name within other dot-com name phrases, names within other domain designators, and names used to designate entries on social and business network sites, all of which can lead to protection issues. In addition, a domain name ownership must be renewed regularly, and without proper attention, a name can be lost to any number of rogue "name squatters" that grab and resell names as a daily business. These firms even have insight on domain research and will obtain names based on signals of interest.

Because of the domain clearance issues, reviewing search page contexts is wise when looking at brand name alternatives. For example, your name might not send the right signals sitting in the middle of dog trainers and belly dancers. Also, precise spelling may not always occur, particularly with names that can easily be spelled differently (e.g., "Seastar," "Seestar," and "Sister"). This is not so easily forgiven in some cases. Earlier in our brand naming projects, we asked if dot-com clearance was a requirement. Now it's a given. Where this will lead to in the next decade is an interesting question for namesmiths and trademark attorneys.[7]

Digital Facilitation of Content

The control of brand names and brand graphic signals was a carefully crafted business before the advent of a digital populace. Graphic designers, in concert with corporate legal, set strict brand signal standards under various titles, such as "Corporate Identity Programs" or "Trademark Guidelines," which were regularly conveyed to marketing functions throughout companies. The caveat was for proper and consistent presentation of the brand signals and trademark registration indicators. There were usually many examples of proper and improper variations of use shown. Relatively few people were in a position to significantly manipulate those standards. Things have changed dramatically now that many different people within the company and the public at large have the tools to present and manipulate content as they please, with or without any concerns for consistent or proper guidelines. Guidelines are still issued, but with different expectations. The digital revolution has opened the floodgates on all forms of content for easy proliferation, variation, sampling, bootlegging, and retouching by anyone. There are obviously two sides to this: the prospects for increased creative content versus unprotected and abused authorship. It's going to take a bit more time to appreciate this. So until then, let's enjoy the ride.

Conclusion

The expansion of technology and manipulation of information will assist big brands to consolidate more, grow globally, and interact more with world governments. Mid-sized brands will become smaller and small brands will become tiny. It is hoped that the big global brand loyalties will also grow and foster better value of mutual co-existence even without political endorsements. The smaller and tiny brands will revert to more face-to-face interactions so vital for sustaining healthy emotions. But within this scenario, my guess is we'll need to deal with the unintended consequences of a cyberinfo implosion within the next decade. This in part based on the rising intensity and effects of the social media and identity theft. Identity theft jumped 12 percent to 11.1 million in 2009.[8] Also, Internet fraud cases reported to the Internet Crime Complaint Center climbed 23 percent to 336,655 in 2009. As the cyberworld becomes more personally invasive, people will find ways to opt out or seek higher ground. Potentially, we will effectively adopt three identifications: secure, public, and cyber. Consumer-generated opinion on any brand will be "wordshopped" by brand-driven overriders. A neutralized zone of speculative facts will challenge business, science, and academic study more than ever before. There will be a growing search for more secure information and the willingness to pay for degrees of veracity, protection, and transparency.[9]

Some interesting brand marketing opportunities will be offered. Brands will probably strive to develop and perfect their own media systems adjusted to stimulate and reward many diverse target audiences. I seriously believe certain consumer brands will, out of necessity, develop their own languages. Specific brand loyalists will be assigned marketing missions creating new forms of outsourcing. Expertise for in-house brand management and marketing will become highly skilled and absolutely secure.

Where might all this lead branding and marketing? As long as there remains the human desire for individuality and the recognition of certain forces in the world that conspire to make us the same, brand distinctions will always be defined, communicated, and protected in some way. We can be sure of that.

Notes

[1]The use of *we* throughout refers to myself and associates in our firm unless otherwise qualified in the text.

[2]See also Dennis S. Prahl and Elliot Lipins, "Domain Names," in Chap. 5.

[3]Note from the Editors: As trademark attorneys, we do not question the value of accompanying a brand name with distinctive graphics, and in fact, we frequently recommend that such graphics be created and utilized. However, when a brandowner presents a composite graphic and word mark for us to help protect, we often advise clients to seek registration of the name independently in addition to registering the composite or the graphic itself. By doing so, brandowners are ensured that they can change the graphics in the future if necessary or desired while still preserving the registration for their name no matter how it changes in appearance over time.

[4]Note from the Editors: Where names may need to be different in different countries, for instance, when another party owns prior rights in one jurisdiction, the use of graphics to tie brands of different names together can help, particularly where consumers travel internationally. See, e.g., www.unilever.com/brands/foodbrands/heartbrand/index.aspx, where the Heartbrand logo for ice cream is accompanied by different names in different countries.

[5]www.tineye.com; www.picscout.com; www.ginipic.com; www.eyealike.com.

[6]See also Dennis S. Prahl and Elliot Lipins, "Domain Names," in Chap. 5.

[7]Note from the Editors: We typically recommend that trademark applications be filed before registering domain names, since owning a registered trademark can assist in later obtaining

the domain name rights, if necessary, while mere ownership of a domain name with a corresponding trademark can sometimes result in other parties eventually owning the rights.

[8]Javelin Strategy and Research, "Hackers Aren't the Only Threat to Privacy," *Wall Street Journal,* June 23, 2010. *But see* JavelinStrategy.com, News & Events, *Identity Fraud Fell by 28 Percent in 2010 According to New Javelin Strategy & Research Report,* Feb. 8, 2011, www .javelinstrategy.com/news/1170/92/1, reporting results of 2011 Identity Fraud Survey Report, which found a 28 percent decrease from 2009 to 8.1 million cases in the United States in 2010; Internet Crime Complaint Center's 2010 Internet Crime Report, http://ic3report.nw3c.org/ national_report.cfm, reporting 303,809 complaints received, while fewer than 2009, it is the second highest number reported since data has been collected.

[9]See, e.g., www.quora.com.

CHAPTER 12

Trademark Searches

Joshua Braunstein
Corsearch (a Wolters Kluwer Business)

Once a trademark name has been selected, a trademark search is a necessary and fundamental step in the clearance process. Trademark searching is one of the easiest and most cost-effective steps you can take to identify potential problems, get a closer look at the "commercial landscape" where the mark will be used, and manage the risk of bringing a new trademarked product or service to the marketplace. As trademarks and brands become increasingly global, attention to the equity that they create and foster has grown.

The act of conducting a trademark search allows you to better understand the challenges the mark will face, in effect, the ever-important ability to "look before you leap." Other reasons exist for conducting a trademark search (audits, policing, litigation), but trademark search reports are primarily used at the clearance level. From a simple cost perspective, the cost of conducting a search almost always outweighs the risks of not conducting a search. Of course, the level and scope of searching must be weighed in consideration of the potential risk, but some level of searching is always advised.

Trademark searching can act as a "good-faith" gesture in the event a conflict does arise, an indication that you made the effort and that the consideration of potentially confusingly similar trademarks was important in your decision. However, proceeding with use after being made aware of a close reference could be used as a basis for a claim of willful infringement. While there is no legal obligation to search before using or filing a trademark in the United States (some jurisdictions outside the United States such as Venezuela do require a search prior to filing), there is some case law that indicates that the act of conducting (or not conducting) a search may have an impact when the court assesses damages (*International Star Class Yacht Racing v. Tommy Hilfiger U.S.A.,* 2d Circuit, 1992), and in determining bad faith (*Sands Taylor & Woods v. Quaker Oats,* 7th Circuit, 1992). Besides the legal and monetary risk of not searching, the inherent value you wish to get from the trademark is put at severe risk if you do not search. The act of conducting a search is absolutely in the best interest of anyone launching a new trademark, and there should almost never be a consideration of whether to search or not, but more a decision of how and where that search will be conducted.

In this chapter, we look to explore the overall search process and the balance of objective "science" and subjective "art" that goes into every trademark search. This chapter also explores the use of a professional trademark search firm, along with the varying levels of searching that can be employed. A survey of available search types, tools, and products also is discussed in context of brand clearance challenges.

The Trademark Search Process

The prospect of searching for "confusingly similar" trademarks is an inherently subjective process. In most cases, a trademark search is used to determine whether trademarks or brands already exist that may prove to be similar enough to the mark you want to use to cause confusion in the marketplace. To search for trademarks that may or may not elicit a mental response in the mind of a consumer requires a unique organic process that evolves over time and can change from day to day, based on the unique parameters of the name selected. The relationship of the trademark and the user of that trademarked product or service can be thought of as a mental contract. The mark and its owner define themselves through their brand—in regard to origin, quality, and overall identification of the product or service they represent. In turn, the buyer or user must accept that definition and agree that those attributes (origin, quality, and purpose) are associated with that mark. A trademark search helps you to identify where that contract may break down—where another mark is already in use or whether trademarks exist that may confuse the consumer and weaken or invalidate the implied mental contract. In most jurisdictions, it is not only an exact match, but a similar one that can cause problems to a potential new trademark. Similarly, in most jurisdictions, the channels of commerce where the trademark or brand will interact with consumers are incredibly important in determining whether that confusion may occur.

In an elemental sense, the heart of searching revolves around the interaction of the trademark and the goods or services it will be associated with. The two may be thought of as having an inverse relationship to each other. The closer a mark is to a preexisting one, the further apart the areas of commerce may be and still cause potential confusion. The further apart a mark is to an existing name, the closer the areas of commerce must be before there is a likelihood of confusion. Two trademarked names that are somewhat close may be weighted differently in regard to risk based on their areas of commerce. If you conduct a search for the term *MOO* to be used on nondairy creamer, an existing trademark of MU for yogurt products may be more important than MOO for software products or NOO for coffee. There is not always a right answer.

Of course, other considerations come into play when weighing the relevance and impact of marks found. The status of the potentially conflicting mark is obviously of large importance. Is it filed, registered, canceled, or abandoned with the Patent and Trademark Office (PTO)? Is it actually in use, only used historically, or filed to be used in the future? The "global footprint," along with the potential fame or marketing around a trademark can also play a role. Is the mark you've found used in only one country or in 20? Is there a major marketing campaign associated with it? Is it your competitor or a major player in a particular space who is likely to defend their trademark? All these questions will play a role in the search process as records are returned and evaluated.

Science and Art

The search process is a balance between science and art. The science of trademark searching centers on definable and repeatable steps to bring back potential results that involve crafting queries to capture variations and roots of words, and classification and restriction steps to make sure the marks retrieved are in related areas of commerce.

In regard to classification and restriction of trademark search results based on the areas of commerce they are used, global standards exist. An international class system organizes and classifies goods and services into 45 distinct classes.[1] These classes are relatively stable and accepted by most major industrial nations. These classes are most often accompanied by a written description of how the mark will be used in commerce. The act of identifying and utilizing proper classes is certainly part of the science. While normalized across most countries, the use of Nice Classification of Goods/Services and their impact on searching does vary. This impact occurs in three primary areas.

First, countries differ on how they require applicants to file based on class. In some jurisdictions (such as the United States) you can file for multiple classes of goods in one application. In other jurisdictions (such as Brazil), it is necessary to file a separate application for each class requested. To the searcher, this means that if searching in a jurisdiction such as Brazil, they must ensure they've retrieved and reviewed all the relevant filings for each mark reported, because different areas of commerce may be covered in different applications.

Second, while standardization of classes does occur, rules for the corresponding written description of the goods/services (the "list") vary between jurisdictions. In the United States, detailed and specific descriptions are required by the PTO, detailing the exact goods and services to be used with the trademark. In other jurisdictions, the list of goods may be much broader, or even simply a blanket description of the entire class of goods/service. As an example, a U.S. registration for a financial software package may contain a highly specific description of the software, what it does, and what customers are served (as required by the USPTO). A similar application for that software in another country may just list a broad designation of "computer software" where another country may allow the applicant to file the mark for protection in all of Class 9 (using the broad identification of all goods in Class 9, which includes software, but also includes goods ranging from cameras to fire engines). In other jurisdictions, such as China, class is the primary restriction, but official subclasses are used to normalize and codify specific goods within those classes. These variances have an impact on how queries are constructed, how classes are checked, and how the researcher will structure their strategy for reviewing classes and descriptions.

Third, how each respective PTO clears trademarks based on that classification will have an impact on how the search is conducted. In most jurisdictions, the international class is the primary means of determining whether two marks are considered to be in a related area of commerce. However, in jurisdictions such as the United States (and Canada), the actual description of the mark itself is of much more importance than the actual class designated. A restaurant selling coffee (Class 43) is much more likely to be an issue for a company selling an electric coffeemaker (Class 11) in the United States, than in a country where the actual class is used to determine if the marks are in related areas of commerce. Because of this, searching criterion will fundamentally change based on where you are searching. A search in the United States will necessarily focus on the written description of the goods, whereas a search in Europe will more likely focus on the actual classes. These are considerations that researchers must keep in mind when setting up the "science" of their search.

The art of trademark searching focuses on the subjective process of culling through results to identify those records that are most likely to cause confusion, while ignoring or managing the hundreds or thousands of hits that may be retrieved and offer nothing other than "noise" (hits that either are not close enough to be confusingly similar or do not help the user determine whether or not a particular mark would be available or not). The art of searching centers on the meaning of words, the phonetic or orthographic similarity between them, and the relative strength of each term. Could a cellular plan Quickconnect be confused with Fastlink? Could Xanopheks be pronounced like Zenafix? Could V Vi-iile be confused with While? As before, there is no black-and-white answer. The science of searching helps one define how they will get to a limited universe of potential hits. The art of searching is the thought process to determine which of those, if any, must be considered and reported before the mark is used.

Trademark Search and Risk

The act of conducting a search and reviewing the commercial landscape imparts a degree of risk mitigation. Of course, the biggest risk that a new trademark faces is that an existing trademark owner will claim infringement and send the dreaded "cease and desist" letter or oppose the application with the trademark office. This can come with substantial monetary impact, if marketing or actual product has been produced, and will absolutely slow time to market of your product or service. Negative connotation is another risk of not performing a search. Your new software tool to speed up computer processes may not be opposed by any current trademark owner, but sales may be affected by a negative connotation (i.e., the same name was a much maligned automobile from the 1970s that had slow acceleration). Future uses and expansion of the trademark are also a risk consideration and a factor when considering how broadly to search. The trademark you choose may be clear for sunglasses, but may not be clear for handbags or cosmetics, markets you may wish to enter in the future. Similarly, the mark may be wide and clear in the United States, but a direct conflict may exist in the United Kingdom, a market you wish to enter in the next three years. The degree of risk you are willing to take will help dictate how extensively and where you will conduct your search. This delicate balance should help you in creating your budget, instructing your internal staff, outside counsel and partner search firm, and managing expectations.

The explosion of available data and services on the Internet and the rapid globalization of commerce have made it increasingly difficult to conduct a "comprehensive" search. There is no foolproof way to guarantee that any relevant mark or name will be retrieved in any search. PTO registers have gotten larger, while the act of searching common law, including domain names and Web content has grown increasingly precarious. Time gaps also exist that may affect the comprehensiveness of a search (your search may not include recently launched or in-process trademarks) and must be factored into a risk strategy. Search reports are arguably more voluminous than they used to be, and less inclusive of the total commercial landscape. This is, to a degree, a risk in itself.

Taking this into consideration, it is the duty of every trademark owner and potential owner to balance the specific situation with the risk that something may be missed. Trademark owners should consider the size and reputation of their company (are they a large target for lawsuits), the scope of the launch (local, national, global), the jurisdictions they would like to use the mark in, and their tolerance for lawsuits. The owner must also assess the current or future emotional and financial attachment to the trademark; will they be willing to change the mark if a problem arises, and what will the financial impact of that change be to their business and their reputation?

Options exist across the spectrum (low to high risk tolerance), and these will be discussed in turn.

Use of a Professional Search Firm

For anything more than a quick screen for identical or near-identical records in a jurisdiction, it is in the best interest of a concerned party to secure the services of a trademark search firm for a number of reasons. Search firms often provide more advanced screening tools up front, with advanced query capabilities, and allow their customers to search multiple registers at once. This offers a higher level of comprehensiveness and quality, even before a decision is made to order a comprehensive search. A reputable search firm possesses expertise in the structure of search strategies, review and selection of relevant records in both trademark registers and common-law sources, and in the nuances of trademark searching. The professional search firm is likely better able to effectively execute, format, and deliver a reliable and objective (as much as it can be) trademark search. Most search companies employ teams of expert researchers that are trained extensively in the process of searching, and are tasked to remain up-to-date in changes to data sources, trademark law, and the industries and markets they are searching. Expert searchers who hone their skills continually can complete a search with greater efficiency and objectivity than an in-house staff member may. They usually have access to proprietary tools and databases that allow them to work fast and smart, in order to locate exact, phonetically equivalent, and confusing similar marks within PTO registers and common-law databases. By employing a search firm, one gains access to all this expertise.

Some search firms manage an exhaustive collection of data sources, both official trademark records registered with the PTO, and common-law sources that will almost always eclipse the resources available to searchers outside of a professional firm. Economy of scale plays a great role here. Because search firms search all day, they necessarily need their data to be as comprehensive and accurate as possible, employing teams of analysts to update, correct, and correspond with data providers to make sure the information is as current, complete and searchable as possible. They can also manage common-law source lists effectively, securing better volume discounts and managing a much larger stable of common-law sources than others. As an example, the current U.S. comprehensive search offered by our company includes a search of trade directories, publications, catalogs, business name directories and other information sources numbering in the tens, if not hundreds, of thousands. These sources are accessed online, on CD-ROM, and in actual hardbound sources, through a trained team of experts. Analysts, both search and technology based, also constantly work with incoming data to confirm relevant names are retrieved by adding search cross-references (an incoming record for XLR8 would and should be cross-referenced to Accelerate) and honing algorithms that automatically look for phonetic and orthographic similarities specifically tuned to trademark searching. These are exercises that any enterprise not focused on trademark law will not be able to handle as effectively, or quite frankly, have any interest in matching. In this sense, the search firm acts as a valuable and trusted legal process outsourcer, and provides efficiency, accuracy, and expertise.

When a business, law firm, or individual turns to a search firm to execute a trademark search or provide services to help them search on their own, they take an important first step in enjoining that search firm in their own success. Due to the subjective nature of the work, the relationship that ensues is primarily based on trust and mutual success. The search firm relies on its thoroughness, strong reputation in the marketplace, and responsiveness to changing needs to preserve and grow its business. The client of the search firm has best success when they can rely on a thorough and focused search process that paints a clear picture of the commercial landscape facing a potential mark. The search firm should be thought of as a collaborative partner in the trademark clearance process.

In many ways, the selection of a search partner relies on trust. Past history and quality reputation, word of mouth, and client testimonial, along with service and relationships are the factors by which search companies grow or disappear. Another consideration in choosing the search firm you partner with is the presentation of information. With trademark records, more information is definitely beneficial. However, it is critical that the information be provided in a meaningful manner that allows efficient and thorough yet quick review of potentially large reports. Personal preference plays a role, as does the availability of robust online platforms, tools, and contents. This conception will be discussed later in this chapter.

Working with the Search Firm In-House or through Outside Counsel

In addition to deciding whether to use a professional search firm, a decision must also be made as to how the search process will be managed: will the trademark owner interact directly with the search firm or use a law firm or agent to act as "buffer" and professional aid in the process. This decision is multifaceted. Factors to consider include cost/budget, anonymity, and arm's-length objectivity in search review and the issuance of an opinion.

In considering whether to use outside counsel, the corporate staff will want to objectively (as possible) consider whether:

- They possess the appropriate human resources internally to interface with the search firm and provide all the information and feedback that is often needed to establish the best search.
- They have the skilled personnel available to establish and conduct targeted and effective knock-out screening (more on this later).
- They have the human resources with the time and skill to fully and objectively review the search.
- They are not emotionally compromised and/or unduly influenced by other individuals or departments that may alter their judgment or decision-making process; they must be able to maintain arm's-length objectivity; it is much harder to say no to a chief executive officer or vice president of marketing who is totally sold and committed to a new trademark when you work for (or even with) them.
- Sufficient specialized legal expertise exists to review and opine on trademark matters.

If these criteria can be met, there are often benefits to managing the search process in-house. Individuals within the corporation will have the best handle on their own products, their competition, and their industry. They may be best equipped to describe the goods or services for which the trademark will be used, have insight into the history of the mark or product, and may have better skill at determining whether two products would be sold in related areas of commerce. An in-house representative can also serve as a valuable liaison to the search firm, informing them of their preferences, and letting them know about industry or market conditions that may affect the search. As an example, the in-house representative can give a "heads up" to a search firm if a term is generic, descriptive, or even famous within their industry.[2] Arguably, an outside law firm may not be able to offer the same level of industry expertise during the search process. In many cases, large and medium corporations will have specialized trademark divisions as part of their legal team, and these groups interface and work with search firms on a regular basis.

The use of outside counsel is the other option. While potentially carrying the additional cost of outside review and management, use of outside counsel may very well save time and money in the long run and offer the best chance for qualitative review of a new mark. First and foremost, outside counsel can provide the objectivity so needed when reviewing a new trademark. Someone outside the reporting chain of the corporation, other than the obvious desire to satisfy their clients, has no vested emotional or political attachment to the potential new trademark. It is easier for them to say no, and to offer objective reasons why they are doing so. It is not uncommon for a corporation to begin work on a product and to become desirous of a particular name or slogan that seems a "perfect fit." The marketing department may have begun investing in marketing campaigns, packaging, and messaging before the legal department even becomes aware of the potential new trademark.[3] In this case, the outside counsel may pose a good choice to reestablish objectivity and should be consulted as early as possible to look at the full risk and reward of moving forward with the use of the trademark.

An outside firm also can offer specialized trademark expertise that is leveraged across all its clients. In effect, this is the same "economy of scale" that allows search firms to do their work so effectively. Due to a high volume of clients, law firms hire trademark and intellectual property (IP) specialists that focus all their attention on trademark matters. Particularly in smaller and midsize corporations where inside counsel, if it exists at all, is more general in approach, this aspect can be very appealing. On top of this, use of an outside approach may help provide a more holistic view of the opportunity and challenges the mark may face in commerce. Additionally, many corporations are very concerned with providing transparency to investors and auditors concerning their expenses and investments. When outside counsel is hired, the outside firm will carefully track the work they perform on each project along with associated fees and expenses, and provide detailed invoicing to the corporation. In these situations, tracking of legal expenses related to the trademark clearance may be clearer and more readily documented, due to this invoicing process, than when tracked as time spent by employees of the corporation.

Budget must play a role in deciding whether or not to use outside counsel. It goes without saying that this counsel will want to be paid for services rendered (pro bono work excluded). If a budget does not exist, it will be next to impossible to outsource, unless the need for services is sporadic and limited. In such cases, every corporation must make their own decision on how to balance internal versus external spending to ensure their trademark and intellectual property needs will be covered. In recent years, some firms have started moving away from "hourly rate" billing to a "flat-fee" model for review of a clearance search and opinion. While hourly billing has historically been the norm, flat-fee billing has been finding favor in recent years. A flat-fee model allows the corporation who is hiring outside counsel to more reliably track spending and manage their budget; it gives the corporation a sense of comfort in planning their IP spending. The flat-fee billing option may make the use of outside legal representation even more appealing for some corporations and for certain projects. Outside counsel, through their ongoing relationships and high volume of requests may often be able to obtain searches at a discount compared to the fees paid by in-house counsel with lower volume.

If the choice is made to use outside counsel, a further decision must be made as to which outside counsel to use. Luckily, as awareness of trademark rights and the need to promote and protect trademarks and brands globally have grown, several options exist. One can choose to use the firm they conduct the majority of their business with, if this firm has trademark specialists or a trademark department. Many general practice firms have trademark departments offering specialized services. IP boutiques (law firms engaged almost exclusively in IP matters) are another choice. Whether to use a "name brand" law firm is a decision that also must be made and may depend on how you plan on using and protecting your mark. Locality, cost, and personal preference all play a part in firm selection. Additionally, the reach of a particular firm, whether through its multinational offices or its extensive network of established relationships with local counsel throughout the world, may be a relevant deciding factor. In many cases, inside and outside counsel will work hand-in-hand on trademark clearance. Collaboration and coordination of the effort is the norm for many corporations. Search firms routinely send two copies of reports—one to the corporation and one to outside counsel, and some online review platforms allow inside and outside counsel to collaborate interactively on review. This may affect a "best of both worlds" scenario, with the objectivity and expertise of the outside firm married to the industry expertise of the in-house specialist.

Questions to Ask before a Search Is Conducted

One of the most important things to do before conducting a search is to determine where and how you will be using the trademark, and what level of search you need. Too often, the process of searching is done in "cookie-cutter" mode, where the same search is ordered for every situation. That inevitably leads to under- and oversearching. Asking yourself a few simple, key questions will help you define your search needs up front:

- Do you wish to just use the mark, or file and register it with the PTO?
- Do you care if others have a similar mark or name? Will you actively protect the trademark?

As simple as these questions sound, how the mark will be used can have an impact on how and where you search. While a trademark filing is undoubtedly a helpful and sometimes necessary step in distinguishing and protecting your mark, the very act of filing it can actually increase the risk of conflict. The act of filing your trademark serves as constructive notice to the business community that you plan to use and protect that mark. As part of that process, your trademark becomes part of the PTO database, meaning your mark will come up when others conduct searches, PTO examiners may cite your mark as a block to others, and your name may appear in watch reports ordered by owners of other similar marks. This may affect the level and type of search you order.

You must also decide if you can "play nice with others" and allow other companies to use a similar mark. If you are unwilling to do so, and wish to actively protect your mark, a greater level of comprehensiveness may be needed up front to determine that no potentially confusing trademarks are preexisting. As previously mentioned, within the United States, rights are granted by use, and not necessarily by filing. Someone with prior use may have superior rights to a later filed or used name. With this in mind, a trademark owner who wishes to actively protect and defend its mark should conduct a comprehensive search as soon as possible prior to launch to identify any common-law uses of the name and mark. These decisions must be weighed against the relative "strength" of the terms you have selected for use, a concept we will discuss later in this chapter. Choosing a strong term (term with higher recognition and less likelihood of being confused once it is accepted by the market; in the broadest sense, the less generic or descriptive a term is for what it is being used for, the stronger it is) is somewhat of a double-edged sword in regard to searching. It is absolutely the smartest and most reliable way to pick a trademark that will not be confused in the marketplace. However, prior to adoption, strong terms may have even greater likelihood of being confused with another strong mark already in use. This necessitates a vigilant and comprehensive approach to searching to confirm that you will not introduce the trademark against another strong trademark already out there.

- Where will the trademark be used? What are the core markets?
- Where do I plan to expand?

The jurisdictions in which the product will be used have an obvious impact on the search. Increasingly, as data becomes more readily available, it is easier to search in more places. However, one must balance realistic expectations, budget, and future potential to expand the mark. If a mark will clearly be used only in a local jurisdiction, a global search is probably not needed. If a mark will be used nationally or regionally, a regional level of coverage may suffice. If the mark will be used primarily in one jurisdiction, and lightly or potentially later in others, it may make sense to conduct a comprehensive search in core jurisdictions, and a lighter screening type search in others. Future expansion of the use of the mark must also be weighed, with an eye toward where the mark's use may expand in the next few years.

- What are the areas of commerce for the trademark searched?
- How broadly should the goods/services be searched?
- Who are my customers?

The areas of commerce in which a trademark will be used have tremendous impact on the search reports and should be well thought out and organized prior to launch. It should be noted that in jurisdictions such as the United States, you need to be able to prove you are actually using the trademark on *all* the goods you claim in your application. In this sense, it does not always make sense to search based on an extremely broad description of goods/services that may or may not be actually used with the name, or that may not be used for several years. There is often the natural desire to go as broadly as possible in describing the goods, but the broader you go, the harder it will be for the search report to focus on those names that may matter most. This also applies to "all class" searches, or searches conducted without a product's description. These searches tend to yield the least focused results, and may not provide a reliable picture of the commercial landscape.

It sometimes helps to prioritize the goods and services during the search to allow for more dynamic and customized searching. This is especially important when the overall desire is to use the trademark on a very broad range of goods and services. As an example, if your trademarked product is primarily a book but you are interested in producing T-shirts, lunch boxes, and key chains as well, it may be helpful during the search to identify whether the mark is clear for a book, and second, clear for those other goods. The wider you cast your net in regard to goods, the more "fish" will be returned in the search report; prioritizing your goods will help you sort out those "fish" that are most important. A prioritized goods description is often an excellent tool to help the researcher structure and focus the search results.

Based on the earlier conception of the inverse relationship of mark and goods, it is usually the case that a close mark will appear in a search report even if it is not exactly the same or closely related to the goods you used in your search. A general principle in searching is to start as broadly as possible, which often means not adding international class or goods and services descriptions up front. The searcher can often manually browse the universe of hits that are extremely close and select those records in related areas of commerce. The use of class and goods descriptions usually comes later in the search, when the marks are arguably further from your own proposed product or service. As an example, if you are searching Red Rocket for a computer, Red Rocket for stereo equipment would likely be included in the search report, because the marks were identical and the goods were broadly related. (Remember the inverse relationship—the closer the marks, the farther the goods can be and still be potentially relevant.) However, in reviewing records that were less close (Red Ship or Blue Rocket, perhaps), the search may focus in closer on the goods description provided. The focus and reach of the search report at any level will usually rely on how many hits are retrieved.

If struggling to determine how to define or classify a product or service, it is often an excellent tool to view other trademark records in similar industries. A check of the USPTO database of registered trademarks is an excellent way to view how others have described a similar product. As an example, if the product you are searching is semiconductors, a search of the USPTO database can help you identify that when other trademark names mentioned semiconductors in their goods, they frequently also mentioned chips, processors, integrated circuits, and capacitors. This is an excellent tool in identifying goods used in the search process, and may also help down the road if you choose to file the name with the relevant PTO. (It should be noted here that despite the existence of a commonly adopted treaty (i.e., the Nice Agreement), classification standards vary widely from country and country, and an acceptable goods description in the United States may be completely unacceptable at the United Kingdom Patent Office, or vice versa). Searching in this manner can also help you identify proper terminology and avoid infringement at the descriptive level. Rollerblades are a brand, not a description of a type of product (in-line skates).[4] PTOs also vary in how specific you need to be in describing your product. As previously discussed the United States PTO is generally more strict in definition, and asks for detailed and focused descriptions of the goods/services (where in some countries mentioning computer software or even the general class would be acceptable (i.e., Class 9 for electronic goods), the USPTO will almost always ask you to define what the software is used for and whether it can be downloaded or offered on a physical medium).

The goods/services involved will also have an impact on the marks retrieved. Records are retrieved based on their relative strength and that relative strength is absolutely affected by the goods that the product is used on. Apple may be considered an arbitrary name for computer products (strong), suggestive for teaching services (weaker), and generic for food products (weaker still).

While weighing and determining the goods to search, a parallel analysis of the customers who will use and interact with the trademarked product should also occur. Are the customers sophisticated or impulse buyers? Do they understand the market and competing products? How long does it take to make a buying decision? The level of sophistication of the users can have an impact on searching and analysis. A consumer could possibly confuse two products if they were sold in the same aisle (i.e., Red Rocket for frozen pizza and Blue Rocket for packaged ice cubes), even if they weren't for highly similar items. Because the channel of commerce is the same (the freezer) the buyer may automatically assume an affiliation or similar origin. Conversely, a buyer of software servers for a corporation may have no problem differentiating two servers (the same Red Rocket and Blue Rocket) if they are for different operating systems. She would have ostensibly done considerable research on these servers before making a purchase, and would not confuse them based on their name. Channels of trade (in-person sales, retail, and Internet) also have an impact in this regard. Consideration of the customers will help frame the search process and request, and help provide a focused and relevant result.

- How long will the name be in use?
- How extensively or aggressively will the name be used? (How big of a launch is it?)
- How painful would it be if you needed to abandon the name after it was already in use or filed?

The type of use you envision can help you frame and scale your search request. If a trademark will be used for only a short period, such as a promotional slogan, your search strategy may be different than if the mark is slated for long-term use. Similarly, if a trademark is being used in a national launch, the risk may be higher. As an example, if a large telecommunications company rolled out a new service plan with a celebrity spokesman during a major sporting event, the risk associated may be substantially different than if the launch was localized or less aggressive.

You must also assess how difficult it will be to pull back the mark if it runs into trouble. This can be particularly problematic after a trademarked product or service has gone to market. Besides the already discussed monetary implications of rolling back, overall trademark and brand equity may become threatened. Think of the national telecommunications company changing the name of their service plan after launching it during that major sporting event. Not only would this company lose the money they had already invested in marketing and launching the service plan, their overall reputation could take a hit as news outlets reported and commented on the story. If nothing else, it would be extremely embarrassing to the overall brand. Again, it comes back to risk tolerance and how much risk you are willing to take on as part of the search and clearance process.

- What is the budget?

Always the simplest and hardest question to ask, the budget available must always be weighed when determining how far to go with a trademark search. As previously mentioned, the budget associated must be balanced by the potential risk if no search or a lesser search is conducted. In terms of the scope of the search, the mark owner or its representative will want to assess whether a broad but less deep screening (or knockout) search will suffice for a certain mark or slogan or a more comprehensive search is advisable. A decision must be made whether to conduct the search in-house, have outside counsel perform a search, or have analysts from a professional firm conduct a comprehensive level search. Jurisdictions must be selected, and as discussed, the global needs of the search must be balanced with the cost of searching. Budget will also determine how quickly you receive your comprehensive search, a decision that is usually dictated by the specific needs of each new mark. A rush search (one performed in generally less than three days, sometimes as quickly as a few hours) offers the benefit of speed, but at a much higher price tag.

■ When should I conduct my search?

There are several options in this regard, but by and large, U.S. practitioners choose to search before the mark is used or filed. This is the most reliable way to manage the risk and the only way to truly "look before you leap."

Searches can also be conducted in coordination with a filing; meaning search and file at the same time. This can allow you to get a "jump" on the filing date and prevent other companies from filing the same or similar name before you, while still having your search completed before the name is actually in use in the market. This is a more effective strategy in jurisdictions where rights are conferred by filing and not by use. In the United States, where a first-use date can trump a filing date, the benefits of this method are less. It may be an effective method in any jurisdiction where the decision is rushed, and the stakeholders want to get moving on the filing immediately. By filing and searching at the same time (but not launching the trademark to the market) you mitigate your risk to some degree; you provide constructive notice to the trademark community that you have filed (the PTO will publish the mark in the Official Gazette assuming it passes examination), which may increase the risk of an opposition, but you limit your monetary risk to the cost of the filing. The worst thing that can happen is your mark is rejected by the USPTO or opposed, and you potentially lose the fees you paid to the USPTO and any processing or legal fees you incurred to date. It should be noted that in jurisdictions such as the United States, the act of filing will automatically get you a level of "free searching"; the USPTO will examine the mark themselves, and determine if they believe another confusingly similar mark exists on the trademark register.

Searching after use has already been established in the market is not generally advised, as this carries with it the least risk mitigation. It is certainly better than nothing and may provide guidance and insight to the future risk to the trademark, but it is by nature an "after the fact" approach. These types of searches may happen with a change of legal counsel, with an acquisition or merger where one party is more vigilant than the other, or when the mark actually encounters an opposition or gets a "cease and desist." Ordering a search at that stage will allow the trademark owner to get a more accurate view of whether the opposition or conflict is valid, whether other similar marks peacefully coexist, or whether the best risk mitigation is to accept the opposition and stop using the mark. Searching after use has been established (or the mark has been filed) is also helpful when the brand holder is looking to expand the use of the brand, either to new geographies or to new industries.

Information to Keep in Mind

The more information the searcher or search firm has, the better the potential result. Regardless of whether you conduct a search on your own or use a search firm to conduct a search, several pieces of information should be available. This information will help the searcher present focused results that will present the best picture of name clearance. First, an accurate and plain English explanation of the goods/services associated with the trademark will be the primary tool to help the searcher find other trademarks in related areas of commerce. As previously mentioned, while there can be an inclination to search in all classes, or provide a very broad goods description, this can often actually hurt the focus of the search report and raise the risk of missed references that could be important to the clearance. If the trademark is a foreign language term, provide the translation as you understand it (as it may be different from what the searcher thinks, or the searcher may not realize it is a foreign term). Let the searcher know if the mark has a history, or a specific thought process went into the selection of the mark (i.e., our marketing group came up with it by combining two of our company strengths, integrity and trust—TRUSGRITY). If you know of marks your competitor has that may be somewhat similar or if there are identical or similar famous marks in the industry it may be advisable to share these as well. Providing the searcher with as much information as you have and feel comfortable with sharing will lead to a better search result.[5]

A thorough trademark researcher may contact the end client to describe the scope of their findings and narrow the results provided according to preference and needs (this often happens when the scope of results is large, and the end report could become over-inclusive, or under-inclusive if the searcher focuses in a particular way or chooses not to include records from all search criteria.) Alternatively, the search firm may have a client profile on hand that specifies the client's preferences for search strategies and results delivery. As an example, a client may specify they always like to see more rather than less, or vice-versa. This customized service furthers the bond between the search firm and trademark professional and heightens the client's faith in the reliability of results provided by the search firm.

Strength of Mark and Its Effect on the Search

When choosing a trademark, "distinctiveness" is the accepted standard to indicate the strength of the mark and an important goal for IP professionals and their marketing teams. A stronger mark will help distinguish the owner's product or service from others but may face stiffer opposition if a similar name already exists. A weaker mark may be harder to defend and offer less distinction to the brand, but may benefit from "strength in numbers," meaning that no one company or brand will be able to claim exclusive rights to the name.

Trademarks are classified into several categories that can be used to gauge the relative strength of a mark. Each different type of term poses its own unique challenges and must be handled differently in regard to searching.

- *Fanciful.* Fanciful marks are created for the purpose of representing a product or service. They have no individual definition or meaning outside of acting as a name or trademark for that precise product or service. Fanciful marks are considered to be the strongest type of mark. An example is Kodak for photographic film. By their nature, most pharmaceutical companies tend to pick fanciful marks. Although done for a host of legal and regulatory reasons, one chief reason is that a fanciful mark for a drug offers the least risk in regard to confusion. While trademark or name confusion in any industry is an issue, within the pharmaceutical industry, confusing two drugs can lead to physical harm and even death. For that reason, pharmaceutical name clearance is governed by both the PTO and health regulatory bodies (the Food and Drug Administration in the United States), and names are formulated and adopted that offer the most strength and least risk of being confused with others. Fanciful marks are used for this reason. In some cases, the lines between fanciful and suggestive may blur, where a word is ostensibly a new or contrived term, but a root in that word offers an inference that borders or crosses the line to suggestive. Claritin for allergy medication and Acura for cars are examples of fanciful marks that may also seek to plant a suggestive seed in the buyer's head.

The main challenge in searching for fanciful terms is that queries must be robust and inclusive enough to capture all relevant marks. This usually involves some level of phonetic checker and assisted query logic. Most search firms utilize that intelligence in both their online screening tools and comprehensive search reports. Using a free online PTO database may not offer the same sophistication or yield the same level of comprehensiveness.

- *Arbitrary.* An arbitrary mark is a common word whose definition is in no way related to the product or service being sold. Examples include Shell for gasoline and Apple for computers. By their nature, these marks tend to be inherently strong, as long as no one has already made a claim to the name in a similar industry. The challenge for the search process is that due to the strength of these marks, the areas of commerce that may be considered similar tend to be broader than on weaker marks. Would two uses of Pilgrim for paints and fans be confusing? Because there is no direct link or association between the word *Pilgrim* and paints or fans, and a consumer might make an assumption that the same company may make both as they are often sold in the same stores, goods/services restrictions may be considered differently than for other types of marks.

- *Suggestive.* A suggestive trademark is one that indicates a quality or feature of the product or service. They are intended to invoke a consumer's imagination and infer certain product or service attributes without hitting you over the head with it. Examples include Mustang for an automobile and Arrid for a deodorant. Mustang conjures the quality of speed and strength, while Arrid infers that the product will keep you dry. Less strong than an arbitrary or fanciful mark, but much stronger than a descriptive or generic one, a search of a suggestive mark should uncover other uses of that or similar-meaning "suggestions" that may be confused. The use of synonymous term searching factors heavily in searching for suggestive marks. A search of Cherry Boom! for soda pop may uncover other suggestive terms such as Cherry Pow! that may have a similar connotation.

- *Descriptive* (includes surnames): A descriptive mark is one that would actually describe qualities of the product or service. These marks require less active thought on the part of the consumer to conjure product attributes. As an example, Quickdry for paints or fans would be searched differently than our earlier Pilgrim example. Descriptive marks often are made up of multiple descriptive or generic terms, and tend to be less strong than suggestive, arbitrary, or fanciful names. These names also pose a challenge in searching because of the large number of hits they can retrieve in both related and unrelated industries, for both identical and similar records. For this reason, focus and size often become issues when dealing with descriptive marks, and search results can be either extremely tight or overly comprehensive. Simply put, if a term is truly descriptive of the product it describes, unless the product concept itself is entirely new, someone has probably already thought of it, or something close to it.

A fair amount of subjectivity can necessarily be part of record selection in this regard. As an example, over 65 active records are currently found in the USPTO database for variations of "Quick and Easy"; over 200 active records exist for Quick in food-related categories; and over 400 records exist for Easy in food-related categories. For arguments sake, if searching "Quick and Easy" for frozen prepared entrees, would a "Quick and Easy" for retail convenience stores be more or less important than Quick-Convenience for prepared sandwiches? Where would Fresh 'N Easy for refrigerated meals fall? While it is possible, most practitioners do not have the time or inclination to view every possible descriptive trademark that may or may not be confused with theirs. As you can see, the task of choosing and prioritizing records when dealing with descriptive marks can be inherently challenging. Obviously, the act of clearing and defending a descriptive mark can also be more difficult. While it may not be possible to stop marketing departments from creating and requesting clearance of descriptive trademarks, it is the role of the trademark professional to educate and manage expectations in regard to the challenges and limitations of the searches such names will generate.

- *Generic.* A generic mark is one where the term (mark) actually and clearly describes the type of product or service. A hypothetical example of this is calling a product that vacuums floors "Vacuum." It would not be permissible to register the term (as a trademark) that generically describes a large category of products, as that term would not allow the product or service to be distinguished from others in the market. At its heart, a generic mark violates the contract between seller and consumer discussed earlier. There is no way for the consumer to actively associate the trademark with only one provider. Attempts have been made to create more identifiable versions of generic names, to grow distinctiveness from more descriptive or generic terms. Examples of this include recent trends to add an "e" or an "I" to generic terms for use in web site domain names (e-toys, I-trade, e-furniturestore, etc.). The success of such names in creating distinctive and identifiable trademarks varies widely, as do national laws regarding the legality of trademarking such terms. From a search perspective, generic terms can be challenging or impossible to search based on the potential mark and the jurisdiction searched. Generally speaking, it is extremely difficult to perform any sort of "common-law" or Internet search of a generic mark because too many hits are retrieved for any sort of reliable review. (Imagine typing the word *computer* into a commercial search engine and hoping to review the results for potential trademark names). Conversely, a trademark search can potentially help prove that a mark is generic and nonprotected by retrieving a "sampling" of records showing how the term is used in a purely generic sense. Examiners at the USPTO will actually reject trademark applications if they find the mark to be a generic description of a product or service that they can verify in a dictionary or information sources.

In addition to the preceding considerations, the relative strength of a prefix or suffix, or a term within the mark can help the researcher to focus search results. A trademark search should always begin with an analysis of the entire name, and then each term within the mark to help identify and prioritize what similar marks may be most important. The strength of the mark and the component terms will also help the researcher frame their goods and services restrictions, and decide how broadly or narrowly to search for each term. It may not be the case that the same goods/services restriction set is used or needed for each component term within a mark. The researcher must keep the relative strength of the term in mind, and tighten or expand their selection criterion in regard to goods. If searching for Sweet Zebra for candy, the researcher may be using much broader categories of goods when searching for Zebra than when searching for Sweet. Similarly, the reviewer of the search report will likely expect to see more focus on Zebra than Sweet, because Zebra is an arbitrary term for candy and any name in a broadly related area of commerce may be a concern, while Sweet is descriptive or generic for candy and is less likely to cause problems unless coupled with a similar term, such as Sweet Giraffe.

What a Clearance Search Can Provide

First and foremost, a search should uncover any obvious blocks to use in the jurisdictions checked. Blocks to use can include the preexistence of a "confusingly similar" mark in the same location and in the same or relatively similar categories of goods and services (also dissimilar industries in the case of fanciful or famous trademarks). By and large, the role of a clearance report is to look for marks that would be confusingly similar to other marks in the market in which the trademarked product will be launched. It should be noted that other blocks to filing and use exist in most jurisdictions that may or may not be covered in a search clearance. Using profanity or discriminatory terms, being overly descriptive or misdescriptive (i.e., calling your company New York City Bagel Factory when the bagels are made in Ohio), and using an individual's likeness or name without consent are examples of other ways your mark may be blocked. While the clearance report may retrieve records that help you formulate opinions in these matters, this is not its primary role.

A trademark search can also help you determine the commercial landscape in which the mark will interact with consumers. Having an understanding of the commercial landscape will help you determine whether or not your mark may coexist with others, whether the terms you are using may be descriptive or generic, if families of marks exist, or even if a famous mark exists in the space. The commercial landscape may also include the types of trademarks and services that others in your industry, namely, your competitors, are using. The scope and quality of this commercial view obviously depend on how broadly you choose to search, and should be determined by your specific need.

If you do not need or wish to actively defend and protect the mark or components of the mark, but simply want to peacefully coexist with others, a trademark search will help clarify that prospect during the clearance process. In many cases, a search of registered trademarks can suffice. A search of U.S. trademarks finds over a thousand active records for the term *link* that mention some form of software in their goods and services. This may be sufficient to allow you to make the judgment that you can also use Link in your trademark with little risk of opposition, as long as the overall name is not overly similar or the goods and services identical and distinctive to a preexisting mark. A comprehensive search, including Internet and common-law content, can also be extremely valuable in helping gauge the prospect of co-existence. Based on a search of registered trademarks, it may appear that only one company is using a specific name or word for a product, but a common-law search can reveal additional nonfiled uses that may allow you leverage in using the name as well. (The more companies use a name for a specific service, the harder it is for any one of them to claim exclusive rights therein).

A trademark search can also help you determine if the term you are searching is generic or descriptive in the industry. Use of a common-law search, including a search of Internet page content, is often extremely valuable in this regard. A trademark may seem completely clear in a search of USPTO records, but a common-law search may reveal that hundreds of companies already use that term to describe their own products or services. The proposed mark "Optical Medical Imaging" may appear clear after a search of the U.S. trademarks, but a common-law and Internet search will reveal that the term is used pervasively and descriptively throughout the medical community. USPTO examiners will conduct a similar search on their own when they examine a proposed name, and reject a trademark that appears to be used in a descriptive sense by others in the field.

A search may also help you identify families of marks, the same term used on a host of products or services by the same company. An example of this may be a cosmetics company with 10 different registrations for Purpose (Bold Purpose, Clean Purpose, Fresh Purpose, Pure Purpose, etc). The company would arguably have a strong attachment and claim to Purpose and would be more likely to object to you launching your own cosmetics product with Purpose in the name. The experienced searcher will always be on the lookout for such families, and will attempt to identify such families in the report. A less careful search or review may misinterpret a family as proof of coexistence. If the searcher or reviewer did not realize that each of those Purpose records were owned by the same entity, they may make the incorrect assumption that those multiple uses of Purpose for cosmetics show that coexistence is possible.

Similarly, a search may help reveal if a "famous" mark exists within the industry. Many countries, including the United States, have adopted famous mark doctrines that provide additional protection to existing "famous" marks, including broader protection across industries. (Computer maker Dell could make the argument that their name is famous, and that consumers would assume any product with a plug and the name Dell on it, even if completely unrelated to computers, came from them.) The purpose of these doctrines is to protect the equity inherent in these famous marks from being stolen or hijacked by others. Unfortunately, no corresponding doctrine exists to help you identify or search for famous marks. A trademark search can help in two regards. First, a search can show you if a particular mark is widely used or filed; a search for Farmer in the Dell for computer products would very quickly reveal that Dell Inc. has over 35 active registrations for Dell in the United States. A common-law search would "light up" with references to Dell computers from official sites around the globe, resellers and retailers, news articles, blogs, and multimedia. This would be a fair indication that the mark may be considered famous in the United States. Second, the global scope of a name revealed in a search can have a bearing on any fame analysis. A global screening search (described later) reveals that hundreds of registrations exist around the world for Dell, all owned by the same entity. This is a strong indication that this mark plays on a global stage and has high exposure worldwide, making it more likely to qualify as a famous name. Most likely, the existence of Dell would have already been known before the search was conducted due to the inherent fame of that particular mark, but a search report can absolutely help prove or disprove claims of fame, and identify famous marks within industries that may not have been previously known.

Importance of Online Platform and Tools in Clearance

An integrated, online platform is increasingly becoming a crucial part of the trademark search clearance process. A true evolution and revolution in trademark clearance has occurred, driven by the globalization of trademark work and the need to review and tie information together more effectively. Driving this change has been the growing complexity of the work, coupled with an increasing need for efficiency; a robust online platform can greatly boost efficiency and quality by providing a wealth of information, functionality, and tools to make the trademark clearance process better. Search firms know that each search recipient is tasked with doing more with less on a continual basis. The main reason why companies pioneered online tools (other than the obvious environmental impact of not printing everything on paper) was to benefit the reviewer. Firms like Corsearch worked hand-in-hand with trademark professionals to build these tools and grow and expand them as workflows changed and became increasingly more sophisticated. It was not so long ago that those doing trademark clearance would order a comprehensive search that would arrive in print format sometimes totaling more than 400 pages. The reviewer would page through, adding removable notes and flagging records that seemed particularly interesting or potentially harmful to their mark's clearance with color-coded tags. Any additional investigations that seemed of value would have to be conducted separately and potentially added later to the docket. Charts and work product were manually typed in from the flagged references, and opinions and correspondence to the end client followed.

An online trademark platform should allow the user to mirror the work they used to do in print, but use technology to improve that work. In some systems, the reviewer can employ notes and colored tags similarly to the method used in the previous era of print search review. Advanced filtering and sorting options allow the reviewer to view the report in the organization that works best for them, and quickly hone those records that are most important. Charts and work product that used to take hours now take seconds, and client correspondences can now be generated and saved directly from the platform. Online collaboration is a must. The platform should allow practitioners to review a report together online, and share thoughts and comments during the course of the review. Online review tools can also quantify and report data in new ways, such as automatically sorting and reporting families of marks, or linking records with a common owner across jurisdictions.

Integration of workflows within a platform can improve review and offer additional insights. As an example, a platform that can integrate data from screening and comprehensive results in one review can quickly identify differences in focus and strategy, and save the reviewer time by eliminating redundant review of records already encountered at the screening level.

Trademark review platforms can also harness the power of the Internet to bring additional content in context to the reviewer. Using data from the search report itself, some platforms call out to the Internet and specialized databases to retrieve additional information on the marks cited in the report. This is especially relevant in common-law jurisdictions such as the United States where a determination of whether the mark is actually in use is paramount. Reviewing a trademark record abandoned several months ago, a reviewer can now easily pull back (and include in their analysis) web sites showing current or past usage of the name to prove or disprove that the mark is actually in use. Reviewing a record of potential concern, the reviewer can now instantly call out to company name databases to find out how large the applicant is, where they do business, and even whether or not they are in good financial standing. Online tools can also help illustrate or prove nonuse of a mark that has been canceled or abandoned by showing that use cannot be found on the Internet, or that the filing company no longer appears to be in business.

As a cautionary note, online platforms are clearly a matter of personal preference. First and foremost, no matter how sophisticated and fancy the platform is, it still relies on the quality of the data and research work done. This should be the primary consideration in selecting a search firm and the platform should be an extension of that quality. You should find that those firms that spend the most time understanding why trademark professionals do what they do, who see themselves as collaborative partners in your success, will naturally have better research services and platforms to support that research.

Online Screening Uses and Options

It is often advisable to perform an up-front screening before proceeding to a more advanced comprehensive search. The most common type is a "knockout" search, a quick search that looks for marks that are identical and nearly identical to the one you wish to use and that are either already registered or pending at the PTO. The reasons are simple. Mainly, it is dollars and sense. A comprehensive search can cost several hundred dollars, and takes substantial time to review and opine on. The use of a screening tool up front will help you to identify obvious blocks to use (i.e., whether the same mark already exists in a similar industry, or whether your competitor is using a similar mark) that will save you the cost of the full search, and the time it would have taken to review. There may not be a point in ordering the larger search when a known, obvious block exists. This will also save time and allow the branding and trademark team to regroup and select a new mark faster. Some search firms offer online screening tools that can precede the comprehensive search step in the clearance process. A "knockout" search will provide a preliminary report that gives a picture of the general landscape facing a potential new trademark. It is not usually advisable to use a screening search as your only clearance tool, but it provides a sound and reasonable first step in the process. If you are comfortable in your query skills and ability to review larger result sets, screening tools can also be used to cast wider nets, and create trademark searches of similar marks, as opposed to identical and near-identical knockout searches. At the screening level, use of a professional firm's system can greatly enhance and facilitate searching and review. Many PTOs, including the USPTO, offer free and often robust online tools with access to their trademark database. There are many uses for these databases, particularly in checking on particular records and doing quick look-ups; however, the utility and limitations of these systems should be understood before a decision is made to use a free resource. For one, search functionality is far more robust in the pay systems. Most systems, including free PTO resources, allow limited searchability that includes basic tools such as prefix and suffix searching; however, a pay system will provide a far more advanced set of functionalities and intelligence. Advanced cross-indexing, phonetic engines, and intelligent query technology are used to provide reasonable assurances that relevant marks are retrieved, regardless of how simple or complex your query is. Search companies often back up their database indexing with manual editor review of trademarks. They look for spelling permutations, will add informal translations to the index if the applicant or PTO has not applied them and they can reasonably confirm the translation, and pay special attention to plays on words that a phonetic engine may not catch (i.e., potentially adding a cross-reference from Pig Chore to Picture). The system may also apply a proprietary phonetic dictionary, an index of spelling variations for commonly used words. As an example, if you type in Quick, the system may automatically check dozens of spelling variations such as Kwik, Quyx, or Cwic. A phonetic engine also applies automatic phonetic rules to each query for common permutations, such as replacing F with PH (Fone or Phone) and X with KS (Kix would retrieve Kicks). To illustrate this power, a search in the free USPTO database for Lion King retrieves approximately 30 hits at the time this chapter was written. The identical query in Corsearch®: Advantage™: Screening retrieves over 40 records, including records such as The Lien King and Line King that are not included in the USPTO query results. Whether you prefer using advanced or simple query options, the systems provided by search firms can help you retrieve a more relevant and comprehensive result.

In addition to more advanced query options, the use of a professional search service allows you to search and report on multiple jurisdictions at once, rather than searching individual sites. Beside convenience and speed, this also allows you to see families of marks (that the search system may be able to identify) and obtain a more global view of the commercial landscape. The authorities covered include the specialized Pharma In-Use selection as well as domain names collections that will cover both the most common domain extensions: gTLDs (generic top-level domains like .com and .edu) and ccTLDs (country code top-level domains like .de for Germany and .uk for the United Kingdom). Screening search pricing is usually available by subscription and transactionally by record (or in some cases, query). Hybrid models are also available, where subscription is used for core databases and transactional pricing is used for databases and jurisdictions you may use less often.

"Knockout" searches can be conducted in-house, through outside counsel, or even by the search firms themselves. (Some firms will deduct the price of the knockout search if you proceed to order a full search.)

Comprehensive Search (United States and Canada)

If a mark passes the "knockout," it will often move to the comprehensive stage, where a broader search of trademark records will be analyzed and reviewed by an experienced and specialized trademark researcher. Many search firms, such as Corsearch, actually provide specialization at the industry level, with research analysts specifically trained and educated in certain industries (such as pharmaceutical or telecommunications). A U.S. state trademark search and a common-law search will be conducted of general and industry-specific product databases, business names, news sources, press releases, and a host of other data sources, all with the aim of retrieving potentially relevant names that may not have been registered with the PTO. A common-law search from most search providers in the United States will also include coverage of Internet domain names and Internet web site content. The scope of results provided in a comprehensive search will include newly filed trademark applications, active registrations, canceled and abandoned trademarks, and all current and comprehensive state data from secretary of state offices. It should be noted that U.S. results should also include a search of the World Intellectual Property Organization (WIPO) for international registrations that are filed through the Madrid Protocol and have designated protection in the United States. While these marks will eventually become part of the USPTO database, substantial delays can exist as the mark is processed and forwarded by WIPO, and a search of the WIPO database mitigates the risk of that delay. (It is also advisable to follow this step during the knockout process.)

Specialized Search Services

Within the realm of trademark clearance, certain areas demand special treatment, such as trade-dress (e.g., the three stripes that are synonymous with Adidas). Whether by industry or specialized search need, a wealth of products and services exist to ensure that the clearance is tailored and suited to the specific needs of the relevant product or service.

Images and logos can also be searched at the clearance stage. Design searching and clearance require specialized expertise. Each category of design carries a design code and design phrase that can be searched by the professional search firm or in an online screening tool. The searcher should be clear about the jurisdictions being searched because the codes vary according to jurisdiction. In the United States, the USPTO issues USPTO design codes; the search firm will reference these in their U.S. federal trademark database. Non-U.S. trademark databases may reference different classification systems. While most design codes are organized in similar fashion and are based on commonly agreed global standards within Vienna Classification Codes, variations and material differences exist in the codes between jurisdictions. The searcher must be comfortable with the different national and regional standards, depending on which geographic area is being searched. The researcher can also look at "design phrases" or "description of mark" fields within trademark records. Design searches can be used to clear logos, images stylized letters in combination with graphics, and color claims. Specialized searches can also be done in regard to trade dress, although these searches clearly trend toward the art as opposed to science of searching as they rely heavily on written descriptions entered by the applicant. Design search review can be even more subjective than word review; the research analyst is tasked with determining whether two images, logos, or pictures are close enough to be confused. Another challenge inherent in design searching is the lack of true reliability in design code indexing. Many search firms edit or reindex designs due to the lack of consistent and reliable coding by various PTO offices. While recent technology, developed initially to assist copyright owners in identifying unauthorized uses of their image, allows pixel patterns to be compared by computers, the prospect of design searching is still a challenge to searchers of any experience level.

U.S. pharmaceutical searching presents another unique challenge to the trademark professional as well as the researcher. Pharmaceutical trademarks are unique in that brands and product names must be cleared with the U.S. Food and Drug Administration (FDA) along with the USPTO. Each year, the FDA rejects about one-third of the approximately 400 brand names it reviews. A trademarked name must be dissimilar to other existing names that could cause confusion, which is standard for trademark clearance, and also avoid consumer confusion by ensuring it is not similar to the name of a preexisting drug or device in the look, sound when spoken, and appearance when written. Corsearch offers a pharmaceutical search that combines trademark name safety databases as specified by the FDA in one integrated report.

The alcohol and beverage industry also has searching nuances and special requirements. Alcohol and beverage searches are specialized in that they consider beverage labels along with trademarks associated with beverages. This targeted search will provide complete records from trademark registers along with common law and other sources referenced in discussing comprehensive trademark clearance. It goes further to search the complete database of alcoholic beverage labels managed by the Alcohol and Tobacco Tax and Trade Bureau (TTB), formerly known as the Bureau of Alcohol, Tobacco, and Firearms (BATF).

Searches for the entertainment industry also require additional attention and sources. The client considering the availability of a name to be trademarked for use in motion pictures, television, books, licensing, or software in the United States will want to assess titles registered with the U.S. Library of Congress along with trademark registers, books in print, entertainment data sources, and the full range of sources provided in a comprehensive trademark search. Copyright records will be searched and reported as part of this type of industry-specific specialized search, requiring a manual search of in-process and pre-1978 (before the database became available in electronic format) as part of the search process.

These searches represent a small sample of the specialized search types offered by the professional search firm.

Global Search Options (non–United States and Canada)

The expansion of the Internet and dissolution of geographic barriers to trade have spurred the globalization of many trademarks—not just those associated with multinational companies. Trademarks and brands are often among a company's most valuable assets. Their creation, from conception to development and implementation of packaging, marketing, and messaging materials can represent a significant investment for any company. Proper trademark clearance is critical in ensuring that no investment is made in a potential new trademark until the client has certainty that it is clear for registration and use. Global trademarks are on the rise, and searches are needed to help navigate their growth. More and more, companies choose to rapidly expand from their core, or even launch a new brand in multiple jurisdictions at once. This is fueled by the globalization of commerce, and also by the growing ease to file through regional and global filing mechanisms (such as the Madrid Protocol and Community Trade Mark [CTM] filings for clearance in Europe). The task of searching on a global basis can be daunting. The sources required for search will vary based on whether the country or region in question is a first-to-file or first-to-use jurisdiction. In the case of first-to-file, the trademark search firm may recommend limiting the search to trademark registers because the trademark filing/registration will determine the holder of trademark rights. In jurisdictions where a first-to-use doctrine is in force, a full common-law search may be recommended. This common law search is a critical part of the process in these jurisdictions, identifying potential marks that are in use, but potentially not filed with the relevant PTO. Even in jurisdictions where common-law rights are minimal, a light common-law or business name search may be recommended. In general, however, the scope of search reports outside of North America tends to be focused more on the actual trademark registers. It is also important when ordering and reviewing non-U.S. trademark reports to not infuse too much of a U.S.-law-centric view on the results and subsequent opinion on use and filing. Search reports will be relevant to the laws of the jurisdiction in which they are searched, and the philosophy and record selection may be very different from a U.S. search. As a case in point, in most jurisdictions outside of the United States, searches are focused on international class, not on goods. This may result, in the opinion of a U.S. practitioner, in a less focused search result. But, in reality, that result may be properly tuned to the needs and filing and clearance requirements of the country in which the mark is searched for.

In some areas, local PTOs make their records available via an electronic database to search firms and the general public. While this is increasingly the case, some data is still only available "on the ground" at the PTO of that particular country, sometimes in print or card catalog form. The professional trademark search firm will have access to local agents who are able to visit any local PTOs where electronic information is not available. Apart from availability of data, there are benefits to performing searches locally. Local agents with native language skills and knowledge of local trademark law, culture, and custom are the best equipped to perform searches. Apart from understanding the language of the marks they are searching, they will have a better handle on pronunciation and goods descriptions, and may have a better chance of identifying famous marks in the space. This is relevant in all jurisdictions, but increasingly important in countries with language and character sets totally different from Western language (such as China).

Once the search is conducted, a decision will need to be made on whether a local agent (who is sometimes the same agent who conducted the search) should also write an opinion on use and filing. While there is always an inclination to review a search personally, a local agent can be better at providing an objective view, based on local law and not affected by the mark's clearance (or failure to clear) in other jurisdictions. A local agent will also perform a connotation analysis, letting you know if the name you have selected, or something close to it, may have a negative or un-wanted connotation. They can also opine on other considerations (such as whether your mark may clear the PTO of a Middle Eastern country, but may be blocked at Customs due to morality regulations). As data becomes increasingly available and economy and culture become more globalized, the role and need of local agents in the search process may change; however, the benefit, value, and insight they bring to the clearance process are clear. As always, choices will need to be made as global searches are conducted; for instance, does the value the agent brings outweigh the risk of conducting the search personally or remotely via an electronic database. The choice may vary by mark searched, by company, and by country. (You may feel reasonably confident in conducting your own search in Australia, but less confident in Russia.)

Many practitioners follow what may be termed a tiered approach to global clearance. This involves prioritizing search jurisdictions to manage budget and expectations. First, a search would be conducted in core jurisdictions (with a possi-ble global screen to identify roadblocks outside of the core jurisdiction). This would be considered the first tier. For a U.S. company, this could possibly be the United States, or both the United States and Canada. Assuming the name clears this tier, additional searches may be ordered in Tier 2 jurisdictions (jurisdictions that the mark would likely expand to first). For argument's sake, for a U.S. practitioner, this might be the United Kingdom, Australia, and Japan. As the mark continues to clear, additional tiers may be added to provide a more global view of the trademark's prospects. For instance, Tier 3 might be continental Europe, China, and India, while Tier 4 might be Latin America and the Middle East. At any step in this process, the trademark holder can "cut bait" and stop searching if a block is found in a critical jurisdiction.

Searching everywhere at one time, while tempting, may turn out to be under-inclusive or cost prohibitive. Certainly, options exist to conduct screening searches at the regional and global level, and these will be discussed in turn. However, by their nature, these searches are screens, and are only meant to uncover obvious blocks. They cannot and do not claim to provide full insight into the mark's pros-pects in any one jurisdiction, and will often fail to uncover close but not identical hits that may be considered confusingly similar. However, performing comprehensive searches in 200 jurisdictions worldwide can be extremely expensive (potentially costing hundreds of thousands of dollars), and time consuming.

Conducting the search in a tiered fashion allows you to follow a metered logical process that will effectively identify areas of concern in your most important jurisdic-tions, manage budget and provide the end-client with an effective clearance strategy for the brand. Of course, how many tiers you have and how deep you go depends on budget and risk tolerance. Suffice to say, unless the mark is absolutely global, and will be a household name in 200 countries worldwide, trademark holders can priori-tize those jurisdictions that matter most (maybe 20 to 50), tier them for effective clear-ance, and devise a global strategy. Coupled with this, the trademark owner must decide whether it needs the same mark in each jurisdiction, or is willing to use a slightly or completely different version in different jurisdictions. A tiered approach to global clearance may identify if a mark is clear in the United States, Canada, United Kingdom, and France, but not in Australia and Germany. In this case, the owner must decide if this is a showstopper or not, and whether they still wish to use the mark in the jurisdictions where it is clear.

In addition to comprehensive searches, regional and global search packages are available at varying levels of comprehensiveness (from identical screens to similarity (full) searching). These searches combine several countries into one search, allowing the reviewer to get a better idea of the regional or global challenges the brand may face (the searches can be done by local agents on a country-by-country basis). For example, Corsearch offers the CMKO (cross-market knockout), a search of approximately 60 major economies. This type of global screening product provides a wide breadth of coverage at a very reasonable price point and can lessen the risk of launching a global brand; partnering with a professional search firm for assistance in non-U.S. or global clearance can help alleviate the challenges of global searching. The search firm will not only provide local expertise through their network of agents, they will also act as consolidator in a number of ways. It will ensure that a consistent search strategy is employed across all sources/geographies; it will provide a single report that covers all relevant countries, regions, and authorities, and will deliver a single invoice in a single currency to facilitate budgeting and accounting. Through economy of scale, the search firm can also pass on discounted pricing options through its volume with local agents that most companies could not get on their own. Finally, a search firm will stand behind their result, and perform their own quality checks before you receive the search.

Global clearance can be challenging, but working in a coordinated and metered manner can help reduce risk, control cost, and provide a reasonable and accurate view of the trademark's prospects outside of the United States.

Conclusion

"Look before you leap." In naming and branding a product or service, conducting a trademark search is one of the most efficient, cost-effective means to evaluate the commercial landscape facing your potential new mark. The fact that in today's economy a company's trademarks and brands represent some of its most valuable assets means that entities that currently own trademarks are more likely to protect them strongly. So those considering the establishment of new trademarks should clear their marks carefully. The questions around the trademark search should focus on how and where to conduct the search, rather than whether to conduct a search. The cost of conducting a search is quite small when compared with the risks of not searching.

Consider those involved in the trademark selection and clearance process your partners in this endeavor. All parties have a shared interest in a successful outcome, from the marketing team that selects potential trademarks to the trademark search firm that provides valuable arm's-length objectivity in the process to the internal trademark team and external law firm. Each will play an integral role in ensuring that your final trademark will be strong enough to withstand the test of not being confusingly similar within your marketplace or in the locations in which you will make it available, as well as those into which you may expand. Important considerations for the team will include:

- Risk tolerance.
- Deciding to use a professional search firm and identifying one.

- Using in-house or outside counsel, or a combination of the two.
- Determining the most efficient scope for your trademark search in terms of search strategy.
- Determining the most efficient geographic scope for your search process, including the possibility of a tiered approach.

Effective trademark clearance is a combination of art and science and enlisting the proper team to best protect your trademark from conception to implementation will yield tremendous benefits as your mark is introduced and matures in the market, and gains in value and recognition along the way.

Notes

[1] *International Classification of Goods and Services under the Nice Agreement,* 9th ed., WIPO, www.wipo.int/classifications/nivilo/nice/index.htm?lang=EN#, accessed on August 20, 2010.

[2] Absence of confidentiality/privilege: is what in-house/outside counsel advises a search firm privileged? If not, probably better to keep concerns about genericness or a citation of concern in the privileged sphere.

[3] See also Robert Doerfler & Matthew D. Asbell, "Trademark Costs," in Chap. 4.

[4] US Registration No. 1326171.

[5] See note 2.

CHAPTER 13

Investigations

Considerations for Selecting and Directing Outside Investigators

Jeremiah A. Pastrick, Esq.
Continental Enterprises

Acquiring accurate information is essential to the creation of new intellectual property (IP), for example, an invention that already exists; a book, song, or poem that has already been written; or a logo or product design that has already been taken. All of these things can transform a business plan, a work of art, or a new brand from your ticket to an early retirement, at best, to a failed venture or, at worst, an infringement lawsuit and heavy financial penalties. Private investigators can provide a reliable and efficient means of collecting the information necessary to keep you, your ideas, and your brand protected.

In addition to assisting in the creation of IP and protecting you from infringement, private investigators also have a valuable role to play in the protection of your IP. Collecting information on potential infringements, assisting in the examination of that information and the creation of an enforcement strategy, and acquiring top-quality evidence are all functions that you should be able to rely on a seasoned IP investigator to perform. Furthermore, some of the traditional and modern skills of a private investigator also come into play in the world of IP, including tracking and locating individuals, surveilling individuals, connecting online identities and aliases to real persons, and uncovering anonymous or concealed domain name owners.

Like many other professions in the 21st century, private investigation has become increasingly more specialized. The person you hire to find out if your spouse is cheating is not the same person that you hire to uncover fraudulent claims by an insured party. And neither are the same person that you hire to assist in the creation and protection of your intellectual property. Investigators who specialize in IP are increasingly more common. But even among their growing ranks, the quality of the work product that you receive from them can vary greatly. As such, it is important to exercise discretion when selecting an investigator to assist you in creating and/or protecting your IP.

This chapter will provide you with guidance on the issues that should be given consideration when deciding whether and when you need a private investigation and how to select and manage an investigator.

Why Hire Outside Investigators

The first issue that you are likely to confront when deciding whether to hire a private investigator is, "Do I really need to hire someone to do this?" In this author's opinion, the answer is "yes." You may be thinking, "Why don't I just have my intern/paralegal/least favorite child do this?" The answers to those questions include:

- The quality of the investigation and the information that you receive is largely a function of the investigator's experience.
- Investigations can be dangerous, especially as they delve deeper into the sources of counterfeit goods.[1]
- The manner in which the evidence is collected, handled, and maintained will have a significant impact on its use, especially if there's a trial.[2]
- Conducting private investigations often requires a license.[3]
- The person who collected the evidence may have to act as a witness, especially if there's a trial, and investigators typically serve as better witnesses than an employee or an acquaintance or a family member.[4]

Experience

As with all service industries and skilled professions, experience varies greatly and matters significantly with private investigators. Good investigators may make it look easy, but collecting information and evidence can be a difficult task, especially if undertaken haphazardly or done by someone with little experience.

In my years working with private investigators, I have certainly come to learn that there is both an art and a science to the field of investigations. Uncovering facts, checking and verifying them, examining the conclusions that can be drawn from them, and reexamining and retesting those conclusions is a process that certainly has features akin to the scientific method. However, some of the best information that comes out of any investigation is the information that comes directly from people's mouths. And, while modern technology, databases, and the increasing (and at times irresponsible) inclination of people to publicize endless information about themselves and their activities on the Internet has made some of the science of investigations easier, the age-old art of getting someone with key information to spill the beans has not been furthered that much by technology. For this, you need someone with skill and experience. You need someone who knows how to elicit information in a conversational style so that the person they are talking to does not feel like they are being interviewed or interrogated. This type of person will be able to get you information that no database will uncover. This type of person is a good private investigator. As an attorney, I can tell you that I am not able to do it; I always come off sounding like I'm cross-examining someone. That is one of the many reasons why I rely on professional investigators.

In addition to general investigation experience, it is also essential to employ an investigator with experience in and knowledge about your field. No matter whether you are a software manufacturer, a clothing company, or a heavy equipment maker, you need an investigator who knows your industry.

Finally, you need and should expect your investigator to be well versed in IP. As mentioned earlier, the investigator who catches your spouse cheating is not the same investigator who catches your competitor infringing. Since most investigations are either undertaken to determine whether someone is infringing on your IP or whether you are (or will be) infringing on someone else's IP, a firm knowledge of the bases of an infringement claim is essential if you expect your investigator to deliver evidence and information that is valuable to you.[5]

Danger/Training

Despite a certain level of ambivalence that exists in today's culture about this, it is worth remembering that counterfeiting is often considered a crime.[6] This ambivalence about the criminal nature of counterfeiting may come from the manner in which most people encounter counterfeiting and/or their experience with counterfeiting. The neighborhood housewife selling counterfeit handbags in her living room at a "purse party" or even the guy trying to sell you a $20 Rolex outside the subway station hardly seem like dangerous, hardened criminals. And, in all likelihood, with the exception of the crime they're committing by selling you fake goods, they may not be. However, if you investigate and follow both of their supply chains far enough up the line, you will likely encounter a more organized and dangerous criminal element.

For both liability reasons and employee morale reasons, putting your employees in situations where they are likely to encounter these types is not recommended. Mitigating and dealing with this danger when it arises is part of what an investigator's training and experience provide. Moreover, part of what you are paying for when you pay an investigator is his insurance to cover operating in these situations.

Because the investigations that will ultimately lead you to a large source or manufacturer of the counterfeit goods (i.e., the type of investigation you want) will likely cause the person undertaking the investigation to come into contact with a criminal element of some variety and, very likely, some level of danger, it is best to leave this work to professionals who have experience in dealing with these situations and have taken the financial risk associated with these dangers into account by way of insurance policies.

Evidence Handling

The manner in which evidence is collected and maintained will greatly affect its value. This is especially true if the investigation involves a suspected infringement on your IP. In situations where you may end up being the plaintiff in an infringement lawsuit, the quality of your evidence will have a significant impact on your success.

Any investigator with whom you work should collect and handle evidence in accordance with law enforcement standards. In general, this means that the evidence should be kept with an unbroken chain of custody that begins where the investigator acquired it. Anyone who handles the evidence should be documented on the chain of custody. If the evidence is transferred, both the method of transfer and the date of the transfer should be documented along with signatures by both the sender and the recipient. When the evidence is not being examined or transferred (by individuals who have signed the chain of custody) it should be kept secured under lock and key. All of this may seem a bit excessive. However, infringement disputes can simmer for a long time before a lawsuit is filed. And even after the suit is filed, it can still be years before the evidence comes into play. Being able to confidently recreate the exact circumstances in which the evidence was obtained and document all of the evidence's "movements" and handlers protects the integrity of the evidence.

This is especially important when there is a long time between when the evidence is collected and when it is needed. Perhaps the defendant is not even infringing anymore, but you are still seeking damages and a prospective injunction. Without a valid, unbroken chain of custody, your alleged counterfeiter can easily make the argument that the alleged counterfeit was not made by or did not originate from him. The chain of custody and an evidence control procedure that is consistently applied to all pieces of evidence are your best tools to refute claims like these. Creating this process and ensuring that it is *always* applied to every piece of evidence is the essential element of the evidence control process. When long periods of time elapse between when the evidence is acquired and when it is used at trial, you must be able to say with certainty that no one other than those listed on the chain of custody has handled the evidence. This will insulate you from evidence mishandling/tampering claims. Would you create and monitor this process on your own? It is possible, but it is not efficient. Instead, you should seek out an investigator who already has an evidence control process in place, appreciates the importance of this process, and rigorously applies it to all pieces of evidence that he acquires. Providing and strictly managing an evidence control process is two of the essential functions of the private investigator.

Licensing

Most U.S. states, including Washington, D.C., require private investigators to be licensed by a state regulatory agency. As of the date of this writing, the states that do *not* have licensing requirements for private investigators are:

- Alabama[7]
- Colorado
- Idaho
- Mississippi
- South Dakota
- Wyoming

All other states, including Washington, D.C., require private investigators to be licensed. If you are hiring a private investigator in a state requiring a license, it is advisable that you do a bit of investigating yourself in order to ensure that your investigator is licensed.[8]

The agencies responsible for licensing private investigators vary by state. Some states have specific agencies responsible solely for licensing private investigators. In other states, licenses are issued by secretaries of state, the state police, departments of public safety, or other state agencies. However, finding the agency responsible for licensing private investigators in your state or the state where an investigation is needed can be accomplished with a simple Internet search. Additionally, *PI Magazine* maintains a database of state licensing requirements and the agencies that oversee private investigation licensing.[9]

Finally, if you would like to verify whether the investigator that you are considering hiring is licensed, most state agencies maintain online search tools that allow you to check the status of an investigator's license. It is worth noting that many states issue licenses to the investigation firm, which cover all investigators employed by the firm. As a result, searches for individuals by name may not generate a result, and it is advisable to search by both firm name and individual name when verifying whether your investigator is licensed.

The types of services or activities that require a private investigation license also vary by state and can be gleaned from the state's licensing agency. However, in general, the following activities, which may be performed as part of an IP-related investigation, typically require a private investigation license:

- Determining identity, habits, conduct, movements, whereabouts, affiliations, associations, transactions, or reputation of character of any society, person, or group of persons. This may be required in identifying and/or tracking infringers and counterfeiters.
- Determining the credibility of a witness or other person that may be required in an infringement trial.
- Locating and/or recovering lost or stolen property. While IP is intangible it often has tangible manifestations. For example, the author has been involved in investigations to locate equipment that had been stolen from a factory. A number of patents covered this equipment and various trademarks were affixed to the equipment. Moreover, the equipment was used to make other patented products to which further trademarks were affixed. Locating and recovering this equipment was essential to stopping the production of counterfeit goods that were nearly indistinguishable from the IP owner's legitimate goods (in large part because the counterfeits were being made with the IP owner's own equipment).
- Securing evidence to be used before investigating committees, boards of arbitration, or civil or criminal trials.[10]

It is also worth noting that the following are often excluded from state licensing requirements:

- Activities of "in-house" investigators who are solely, exclusively, and regularly employed as an investigator in connection with the business of the employer. The investigator cannot advertise himself as an investigator or provide investigative services for anyone other than his employer. This typically only applies if the employee-investigator does not carry a firearm.

- Investigations by law enforcement officers during the course of their work.
- Insurance investigators or adjusters licensed by their state insurance agency.
- Investigations into insurance applicants' financial standing or habitual activities.
- Attorney conduct within the regular course of their profession and within the ethical boundaries of their profession.[11]
- Banks, credit unions, loan providers, and credit reporting agencies.
- Persons holding professional licenses and providing expert advice within the bounds of their professional license.
- Individuals providing investigative services solely and exclusively for a U.S. agency.
- Activities of licensed certified public accountants (CPAs) acting within the scope of their practice.

It is important to point out that the information contained in this section should be used as a guide in your search for a private investigator but should not be considered a definitive resource on the licensing of private investigators. The purpose of this section is to inform the reader of the idea that most states require private investigators to be licensed, to provide guidance on how to determine whether an investigator is licensed, and to introduce the activities that must typically be performed by licensed private investigators, as well as common exemptions to those requirements. Ultimately, you should consult with state licensing agencies in order to determine what specific activities require a license in that state and, more importantly, develop strong relationships with private investigators who are reputable and whom you trust. These investigators can and should be expected to guide you in understanding the nature of their profession and the effective use of their services.

Acting as Witness—The Advantages of an Investigator on the Stand

As discussed throughout this section, collecting information and evidence is one of the main tasks of a private investigator. However, as more and more information is increasingly available through public and easy-to-find resources on the Internet, the question of "Why don't I just do the investigating myself?" often comes up. Hopefully, this chapter answers that question. But this section in particular is intended to focus your thinking on testimony at trial, on whether you want to testify or avoid testifying, whether you want your employees to testify or avoid testifying, and whose evidence collection and maintenance you want subjected to scrutiny and cross-examination. This type of forward thinking will guide you in parsing out tasks to your investigator.

In general, the role of the private investigator often does not end once the evidence and information is collected. If the information and evidence that you are pursuing ends up being used to support a criminal prosecution or civil litigation, then the person who collected it is likely to end up on the witness stand. It is important to be prepared for this circumstance right from the beginning. That means having someone who you would want to be a witness conducting your investigation and information gathering.

In the adversarial cauldron of the courtroom, the evidence that is presented on your behalf, the manner in which it was collected, and the person who collected it are all going to come under fire. If you, your law clerk, your summer intern, or your least favorite child have haphazardly, or perhaps even with the best of intentions, taken on the tasks of the private investigator, you are likely to end up with evidence that is substandard and a witness who is ill prepared. In other words, you have liked your desired outcome.[12]

In contrast, an experienced private investigator should also serve as an excellent witness. The manner in which the investigator obtained his information should be well documented and within the bounds of the law.[13] His evidence and its provenance should be unimpeachable.[14] His ability to articulate his methods for gathering information and evidence and the conclusions that he has drawn from them should be unflappable. He should be a poised witness, which is a result of experience on the stand. Additionally, private investigators are beneficial as witnesses because their testimony does not create the productivity loss associated with pulling people out of your organization to testify. Finally, the evidence and testimony proffered by someone who is not a party to the litigation or a victim of the criminal act will be more objective and therefore better received by a jury.

Ultimately, the value of a private investigator does not stop once the evidence and information that you are seeking has been accurately collected. An experienced private investigator combined with sound investigation techniques and results are essential to successfully and efficiently advancing your objectives in the courtroom.

What to Expect from Your Investigators

A good private investigator should be more than just "another set of hands." A good private investigator should be able to play an active role in helping you develop, capitalize upon and protect your IP. Good decision making and long-term strategic planning is predicated on good information. As gatherers of information, private investigators are therefore essential to your growth and success. A good private investigator should be viewed as an ongoing team member rather than an outsider. The more you are willing to include them and share information with them, the more they will be able to assist you efficiently and effectively.

As with anyone that you would bring on to your team and with whom you would share sensitive information, you need to invest the time to vet potential investigators to ensure that they are able to make high-level contributions that will make them truly valuable to you. So what should you be looking for to know whether you have a good private investigator? Here are some essential criteria:

- *Experience.* As with any profession, performance improves with experience. Good investigative firms should have a mix of seasoned investigators as well as "apprentice-level" investigators, who will be developed into that firm's next group of experienced investigators. This is the hallmark of an investigative firm that is focused on longevity and one with whom you can develop a long-term relationship. The explosion of information available on the Internet over the past decade has, in some ways, lowered the barriers to entry for the investigative profession. As a result, the numbers of retired police officers and unemployed criminal justice majors starting one-man investigative firms are increasing. However, good online investigating requires skills beyond advanced Google searching; thorough investigations require interaction with human beings to obtain information that cannot be found (or cannot be found efficiently) on the Internet; and IP investigations, in particular, are of the highest quality when the investigator has a wealth of experience in the IP field.

- *Knowledge of IP.* As mentioned earlier, investigators who focus specifically on IP are more and more common. While these investigators may not have an attorney's depth of knowledge on IP, you should expect them to be well versed in the laws relating to the field of IP and to be competent in discussing issues related to the development and protection of IP. Some of the best private investigation firms also have attorneys on staff, and this close working relationship between investigators and attorneys provides the investigators with a much more thorough and intimate knowledge of IP, how it is created and protected and an intuitive knowledge of how to conduct investigations to support the objectives and necessities of IP development and protection.

- *Critical thinking.* Much of investigating revolves around problem solving— figuring out how to get information that is often hidden. There is no manual for how to conduct an IP investigation, and each investigation will entail some obstacles that will have to be overcome. An investigator who can analyze, on an ongoing basis, the challenges that he is facing and the resources that he has at his disposal to overcome those challenges will, more often than not, be able to meet the desired goals of the investigation. This requires the investigator to be analytical, creative, and resourceful. You should be able to tell early on whether you are dealing with this type of an investigator. If you are not, continue your search.

- *Good written and verbal communication skills.* This is critical in almost every profession, and investigations are no different. However, good communications skills are particularly desirable in an investigator for a few reasons. First, as mentioned earlier, investigations do not always go as planned; obstacles arise and must be overcome. IP owners must understand this. However, in order to develop and maintain a strong investigator/client relationship, it is also incumbent upon an investigator to be able to articulate the obstacles that he is facing, his plan for overcoming them and the resources needed to achieve that goal. He must not only possess the critical thinking skills necessary to formulate and carry out his plans, but he must also possess the communication skills required to keep his client apprised of his progress. Second, your investigator's reports, and perhaps even his in-person testimony, may become critical pieces of evidence, especially in an infringement or counterfeiting context. A poorly written report or an inarticulate witness could therefore imperil your chances of success. In general, knowledge about your organization and your specific IP issues are things that you should allow an investigator to develop over time. However, good written and verbal communication skills are something that your investigator should bring to the table on day 1.

■ *Ability to match personnel to tasks.* Your investigative firm should not assign tasks to investigators in the same way that hostesses assign tables to waiters, that is, to whoever is next or not busy. Instead, your investigative tasks should be assigned to investigators based on which investigator will be able to best perform the tasks that are required for the job. The investigator's knowledge and experience as well as factors like their extracurricular interests and, yes, even their sex will have a role to play in matching the best investigator to the job. For example, if your investigation involves counterfeit golf clubs, it makes sense to give the investigation to an avid golfer.[15] With this being said, I would not recommend getting into the business of micromanaging which investigators are assigned to certain tasks. Instead, I suggest developing a trusting relationship with an investigator or firm who you know has investigators that are interested in and knowledgeable about your industry and let the results speak for themselves.

If you have an investigator with strong marks in these criteria, you are on your way to having the type of desired team member that you are seeking. Now the question is, how do you use the investigator to maximize his contribution to your IP development and protection objectives? As previously mentioned, your investigator should not just be an "extra set of hands." He should be someone that you more deeply and broadly involve in the management and protection of your IP. In order to get the most out of your private investigator, he should be someone with whom you can engage in a Socratic dialog as part of your planning and problem-solving processes. For this dynamic to work, *he* must have that ability and *you* must have the willingness to engage in those types of discussion with him.

For example, here are samples of varying levels of instructions for investigators:

■ "Buy a sample of product A from company X so that I can determine whether it's infringing on my/my client's patent, trademark, copyright, etc."
■ "I think company X is infringing on my trademark; please confirm or refute this. Find and collect information that supports your conclusion and provide me with a detailed report supported by evidence."
■ "Please help me develop and deploy a strategy to prevent counterfeiting on my brand and uncover and address it when it arises."

You should view investigators as being able to undertake the types of higher-level projects embodied in the second and third set of instructions. You should seek out investigators who can perform work at this level. And, once you have found those investigators, you should involve their skills more deeply in the process of achieving the goal(s) that you have for your IP.

The manner in which private investigators can play a more active role in helping you to develop strategies to prevent counterfeiting and infringement is highly dependent upon your business. However, as a general rule, I recommend consulting with an investigator as part of any expansion that involves intellectual property. For example:

- Are you considering opening a new factory that will manufacture branded goods or use proprietary materials or technology? Consulting with an investigator at the outset can reduce the chances that you enter into a relationship with a factory where your IP is loosely guarded.
- Are you launching a new product? Consulting with an investigator can provide insight into how vulnerable your product may be to counterfeiting, where counterfeiting is likely to occur, and what steps you can take to reduce your exposure.
- Are you entering a new geographic market or expanding your distribution? Consulting with an investigator can provide you with insight on how to reduce theft from your distribution channel, thereby reducing the prevalence of gray market goods.

Additionally, full-service investigative firms can perform audits on your processes (if you have them) for identifying and responding to infringement and counterfeiting activity. This can improve your sensitivity to IP-related issues and improve your response time, which, in turn, reduces the vulnerability of IP issues and the number of IP-related issues that you must deal with. Finally, I would recommend periodic (quarterly or biannually) surveys of the market for counterfeit and infringing goods. Commissioning these types of surveys can help you stay ahead of burgeoning IP issues and address them before they become a more serious and more costly threat to your IP.

In conclusion, a good investigator is more than someone with whom you have a one-sided dialog and from whom you expect the performance of simple tasks. Good investigators can be so much more than that. The key is that they must possess the attributes listed earlier, and you must foster a relationship with them in which they are able to contribute to the fullest extent possible.

Special Considerations for Attorneys

As the heading implies, this section addresses some issues that are unique to attorneys that can arise and should be considered when hiring investigators. For the attorney, it is worth noting that the author's comments in this section are based upon the current (2010) ABA Model Rules of Professional Conduct (the "Model Rules").[16] As with any issue of professional responsibility, you should consult with your state's rules of professional conduct and seek counsel from an attorney licensed in your state and specializing in issues of professional conduct for specific guidance on how those issues should be addressed. This section is simply meant to call your attention to issues of professional conduct that may arise when hiring an investigator and guide your inquiry on these issues.

For the nonattorney, it is still worth reviewing this section, as it will provide insight into the issues that your attorney may face when hiring an investigator and may also reveal circumstances in which it would be advantageous for you to hire and instruct an investigator directly. It is also worth noting that some activities that attorneys are prevented from undertaking by the rules that govern their profession (the Model Rules of Professional Conduct) are *not* illegal for others. The Model Rules are standards of conduct to which attorneys and nonattorneys under their direction are held; they are not generally applicable to the public at large. Therefore, the activities discussed below are, by and large, not illegal *per se*. Problems with many of these activities arise only when a lawyer involves himself in these activities. For example, an attorney is prevented from contacting a party whom he knows is represented by another attorney.[17] The purpose of this rule is to support the protection that is afforded by being represented by an attorney and to prevent attorney harassment of parties.[18] However, the sanctions and penalties that could be imposed on an attorney if he or someone directed by him contacted a represented party would not be imposed on a nonattorney for contacting a represented party. Only an attorney could be penalized if he or someone under his direction contacts a represented party or commits any violation of the rules. Those penalties are handed down by state bar associations and can come in the form of warnings, sanctions, and even disbarment. More examples of these types of conundrums are discussed next.

Ethical Issues[19]

Model Rule 8.4(a) states that it is professional misconduct for an attorney to "knowingly assist or induce another to [violate or attempt to violate the Rules of Professional Conduct]."[20] Additionally, Model Rule 5.3 regarding nonlawyers employed or retained by or associated with a lawyer states that:

a. A partner, and a lawyer who individually or together with other lawyers possesses **comparable managerial authority in a law firm shall make reasonable efforts to ensure** that the firm has in effect measures giving reasonable assurance that the person's conduct is compatible with the professional obligations of the lawyer;
b. A lawyer having direct supervisory authority over the nonlawyer shall make reasonable efforts to ensure that the person's conduct is compatible with the professional obligations of the lawyer; and
c. A lawyer shall be responsible for conduct of such a person that would be a violation of the Rules of Professional Conduct if engaged in by a lawyer if:
   1. The lawyer orders or, with the knowledge of the specific conduct, ratifies the conduct involved; or
   2. The lawyer is a partner or has comparable managerial authority in the law firm in which the person is employed, or has direct supervisory authority over the person, and knows of the conduct at a time when its consequences can be avoided or mitigated but fails to take reasonable remedial action.[21]

Model Rule 5.3 is typically considered in the context of nonattorney employees in a firm such as paralegals, legal secretaries, etc. However, it is almost certain that both Model Rule 8.4 and Model Rule 5.3 expand the ethical obligations of an attorney onto the investigators that they hire, especially when the attorney directs their conduct, ratifies their conduct or has knowledge of illegal or unethical conduct. As a result, actions of a private investigator that are assisted or directed by an attorney and which violate the Model Rules could give rise to attorney misconduct. Jonathan G. Polak, an IP attorney with Cincinnati-based Taft, Stettinious & Hollister,[22] who frequently works closely with IP investigators, suggests[23] considering the following model rules that could be implicated if the attorney/investigator relationship is mishandled:

Rule 4.1 Truthfulness in Statements to Others

- Rule: "In the course of representing a client a lawyer shall not knowingly:
  - (a) Make a false statement of material fact or law to a third person.
  - Consider: An essential element of an investigator's job is masking his identity in order to obtain information and conduct surreptitious inquiries. Does it matter if the investigator is or is not directly asked about his identity and therefore must or must not provide an alias? Is his identity material? What other types of facts, besides his identity, might an investigator need to hide in order to perform his job? Are these facts material?[24]

Rule 4.2 Communication with Person Represented by Counsel

- Rule: "In representing a client, a lawyer shall not communicate *about the subject of the representation* with a person the lawyer knows to be represented by another lawyer in the matter, unless the lawyer has the consent of the other lawyer or is authorized to do so by law or a court order."
  - Consider: Is the party that you are seeking to investigate represented by counsel? If so, directing your investigator to contact that represented party could be imputed on you. In this regard it is advisable to give your investigator investigative objectives and avoid dictating the manner in which he pursues these objectives.

Rule 4.4 Respect for Rights of Third Persons

- Rule: "In representing a client, a lawyer shall not . . . use methods of obtaining evidence that violate the legal rights of such a [third person]."
  - Consider: Is your investigator using illegal methods of obtaining evidence? If so, not only may your investigator be subject to criminal liability, you may be subject to sanction.

Moreover, Mr. Polak encourages attorneys to consider whether an attorney's duty to preserve evidence can extend to investigators in his employ, whether an investigator's documents and files can be subject to discovery, and whether the attorney/investigator relationship can be recast as a "consulting expert" relationship in order to avoid disclosure of activities.[25] However, these issues remain unresolved at this time.

Attorney as Witness

Above we addressed some of the practical considerations for why it may be more advantageous to use an investigator, and have that investigator serve as a witness, rather than attempting to undertake an investigation on your own and, as a result, having to act as a witness yourself. However, in addition to these considerations, Model Rule 3.7 provides restrictions on when a lawyer must recuse himself as counsel due to his potential role as a witness. More specifically, Model Rule 3.7 states that:

a. A lawyer shall not act as advocate at a trial in which the lawyer is likely to be a necessary witness unless:
   1. The testimony relates to an uncontested issue;
   2. The testimony relates to the nature and value of legal services rendered in the case; or
   3. Disqualification of the lawyer would work substantial hardship on the client.
b. A lawyer may act as advocate in a trial in which another lawyer in the lawyer's firm is likely to be called as a witness unless precluded from doing so by Rule 1.7[26] or Rule 1.9.[27]

Taking into consideration the prohibitions contained in Model Rule 3.7, an attorney may imperil his ability to represent his client if he seeks to undertake the evidence-gathering functions on his own and, as a result, avails himself to becoming a witness. This is yet another reason why it is recommended that attorneys outsource the evidence and information gathering tasks, and the related duties as a witness that accompany those tasks, rather than perform these tasks on his own and jeopardize his opportunity to advocate on behalf of his client.

How to Find IP Investigators

As mentioned in other parts of this section, an investigator is someone with whom you should seek to develop a long-term relationship. The investigator should be skilled, trustworthy, and knowledgeable about his industry and yours and, ultimately, should be someone with whom you can work closely. Although hiring an investigator into your organization full time is rarely done,[28] the process of finding an investigator is not unlike searching for and selecting any new hire. However, you're not going to put an ad in the paper or on Monster.com for an IP investigator and there are no IP investigator headhunters. So, here are some reliable resources, where you can begin your search:

■ *International Trademark Association* (INTA, www.inta.org). Members include IP owners, attorneys, investigators and other trademark-related service providers. This is a global organization with members from over 190 countries. Investigators who are serious about IP work will be members. A directory of members, including investigators, is available to members. INTA will confirm whether an investigator is a member on a case-by-case basis but will not give a list of its members to nonmembers. With that being said, if intellectual property plays a significant role in your business, becoming a member of INTA is definitely worth your consideration.

- *International Anti-Counterfeiting Coalition* (IACC, www.iacc.org). Similar to INTA in that members include brand owners, attorneys and investigators. However, IACC's focus is more narrowly tailored to counterfeiting rather than the broad scope of INTA's focus on trademarks.
- *Intellectual Property Owners Association* (IPO, www.ipo.org). Members include IPO owners, attorneys, and investigators. This organization caters to both patent and trademark owners. Information on members is available only to other members.
- *Thompson Delphion* (www.delphion.com). A significant resource for conducting patent searches prior to a patent filing.
- *References.* As always, your peers and the experiences that they have had with investigators good and bad may provide good direction.

IP owners directly seeking out and employing investigators rather than relying upon their IP counsel to manage investigative tasks appears to be a trend that is gaining momentum. For example, over 90 percent of Continental Enterprises' clients are the IP owners themselves. Continental Enterprises primarily takes instruction from and works directly with the IP owners rather than their outside counsel. This arrangement seems to foster more open and direct communication and also reduces transaction costs. Moreover, some of the considerations related to attorneys' ethical obligations[29] are mitigated with this arrangement. Using these resources plus the information from the "What to Expect from Your Investigators" section and your own instincts about who you will be able to trust and work closely with will enable to you select an investigator with whom you will be able to develop an effective long-term relationship.

Other Services that Investigators Can and Should Be Able to Provide

In addition to investigative tasks, private investigators can also be a helpful resource in a number of areas related to the protection of your intellectual property. These include:

- *Process servers.* Investigators can also be deployed for service of process, that is, hand-delivering court documents on a party to a lawsuit. Ultimately, the manner in which service of process must be undertaken is a function of state law, and your attorney managing the action(s) that require service of process should oversee the service of process. Most law firms have process servers that they typically use. However, if, due to your direct relationships with your own investigators, you would prefer that your investigator be used for service of process, you should discuss this option with your attorney. At time of publication, eight states require process servers to be licensed: Alaska, Arizona, California, Illinois, Montana, Nevada, Oklahoma, and Texas.
- *Serving cease-and-desist (C&D) letters.* This is somewhat similar to service of process in that it usually requires hand-delivery of documents to a party. However, C&D letters are not issued by a court so they are therefore not governed by state laws regarding service of process. Other state laws, such

as those related to trespassing, may apply to C&D service but the manner in which C&Ds are served is dictated as much by personal style as by law. The important thing to remember is that the investigator serving the C&D letter will be publicly representing you and your company. So, as with so many aspects of the client/investigator relationship, having an investigator that you trust and who takes seriously the responsibility of representing you and your company is essential.

■ *Overseeing product surrenders.* Most C&D letters do (or should) include a demand that the infringer/counterfeiter surrender his inventory of infringing/counterfeit product to you for destruction. Many infringers/counterfeiters comply with this demand, if only because they hope that a surrender will keep them from facing harsher civil or criminal penalties. If you are going to accept a voluntary surrender from a counterfeiter/infringer, you must *always* inventory the goods and obtain the surrendering party's signature that the goods were *voluntarily* surrendered to you. To circumvent this step could open you up to allegations that you (or your investigator) stole the goods, turning you from a plaintiff into a defendant. This happens; the author has seen it happen. So, before accepting a voluntary surrender, be sure that the goods are inventoried and the surrendering party has signed a statement authorizing you to take the goods. If you (or your investigator) take(s) "surrendered" goods without a signed statement, you (or your investigator) do so at your own risk.

When it comes to inventorying surrendered goods, the process is easy when the quantities are small. However, when you are dealing with large quantities of goods, the good news is their removal from the market. The bad news is someone is going to have to inventory it all in order to take possession of it in a way that reduces your exposure to counterclaims by the infringer/counterfeiter. Having your investigator oversee and manage this process is typically the most efficient and cost-effective way to properly accept large quantities of surrendered goods.

■ *Coordinating with law enforcement and assisting in criminal investigations.* In the United States, a majority of IP disputes and counterfeiting issues are resolved in the civil arena, either informally through C&D letters and negotiations or through the formal process of litigation. However, counterfeiting is also a crime[30] and, like any citizen who is the victim of a crime, you have a right to seek assistance from police and prosecutors to redress this transgression.[31] With that being said, the more information and evidence collection that you are able to do on your own in order to assist law enforcement, the more likely it is that you will receive their assistance. In this context, collecting evidence in a controlled manner becomes even more important. As discussed earlier in the Evidence Handling section, your investigator's evidence control practices should be in accordance with law enforcement standards. If your goal is to turn your evidence over to police to be used in the prosecution of a criminal counterfeiting case, then the issue of proper evidence handling becomes an all or nothing proposition. If a prosecutor does not feel that your evidence could withstand the scrutiny of defense counsel in a criminal setting, it will be useless to them. Private investigators, especially since many come from law enforcement backgrounds, understand this and should be well versed in ensuring that their evidence collection practices are in keeping with law enforcement standards.

- *Due diligence investigations.* In addition to investigations that help you put a stop to counterfeiting and infringement, investigators can also play a role in helping you prevent these issues in the first place. One way that they can do this is by conducting due diligence and background investigations on potential partners. For example, if you are considering outsourcing your manufacturing to a factory overseas, and that process will entail a transfer of sensitive information or materials, investigators can and should be used to conduct investigations into the factories that you are considering in order to help further mitigate your risk that your trade secrets or proprietary materials will not be secure. These investigations can take place before a contract is signed as well as on an ongoing basis to ensure compliance with contract terms. Preventing or shoring up "leaks" in factories is a critical step to preventing the proliferation of counterfeit and gray market goods, and investigations are key to that prevention.

All of these services are specific examples of how reliable and trustworthy investigators are a critical asset to your efforts to develop and protect your IP, and an investigator who is actively involved in your IP development and protection should be able to identify additional ways that he can assist you in achieving your goals.

International Investigations

An April 15, 2010, article in *The Economist* on innovation in emerging markets discussed the Chinese concept of *guanxi* as a contributing factor to Chinese firms' ability to nimbly adapt to market and demand fluctuations. *Guanxi* is, in essence, "personal connections" and, according to *The Economist*, it has served as one catalyst to the Chinese economy's rapid growth in the 21st century. These personal connections are the underpinnings of flexible networks that allow practitioners of *guanxi* to call on individuals or organizations with specialized skills, knowledge, equipment, and the like, and to utilize those attributes on demand. When the demand subsides, so, too, does the immediate need for that individual or organization; however, they remain within your *guanxi*, available to be deployed again when called upon.

Perhaps unbeknownst to many U.S. business owners and service providers, especially the most capable investigative firms, they too often practice *guanxi*. They simply had not reduced this concept to an ethos of business management and attached a cool, Zen-sounding name to it.

Those who do business in China are probably familiar with the ways in which this concept manifests itself. This is why the guy that you buy ball bearings from can also provide you with spark plugs. This is why a T-shirt factory can also start making ice skates in 24 hours. Your ball bearings dealer and your T-shirt factory are not just blowing smoke; they can deliver the spark plugs and the ice skates, probably faster, more cheaply, and of similar quality to what you would get if you went in search of a spark plug dealer or an ice skate factory on your own. This is because their *guanxi* allows them to meet your demands more efficiently. This same concept applies to private investigations and should be embraced as an asset to any capable investigative firm.

Private investigation firms are typically small. More than 20 full-time employees would constitute a pretty sizable firm. The fact of the matter is most cannot support the expense of having full-time staff in Missoula, Montana; Valdosta, Georgia; and Utica, New York simultaneously, and if they can, you're subsidizing those employees with the rates you are paying. Similarly, even firms focused exclusively on IP may not have a full-time employee with vast knowledge of your particular issue. In this author's opinion, that's OK. To expect your investigative firm to have full-time employees ready to deploy in any location and with expertise on any IP-related issue is to expect your investigator to have a firm the size of a small army and this just does not make economic sense.

However, it is not too much to expect, and in fact you should expect, that your investigator has deep caches of personal connections to draw upon in order to provide you with the best outcomes. Need someone in Valdosta? Your investigator should have a guy. Need someone who speaks Farsi? Your investigator should have a guy. Need an expert on developing and investigating e-commerce networks? Your investigator should have a guy. Tapping into your investigator's *guanxi*, rather than developing your own from scratch, is the most efficient way to achieve your investigative goals.

With that being said, you should spend the time to seek out and develop a long-term relationship with an investigator or investigation firm to serve as the hub of your investigative network. You should be able to have an honest conversation with this investigator about what your needs and objectives are. You should expect your investigator to deliver when he says he can and honestly tell you when what you are asking for is outside of his, and his *guangxi's*, knowledge and abilities. However, once you have set upon your hub, efficiency would demand that you utilize your investigator's resources to their fullest extent before undertaking the task of creating your own investigative network.

In this author's opinion, this concept and its value extends into the realm of international investigations. In truth, relying on a trusted investigator to properly match personnel with investigative tasks becomes even more important as your needs arise further and further from home. Having an investigation in China, or Brazil, or India managed by an investigator in the United States may seem counterintuitive. However, for other IP-related tasks, patent and trademark registrations, for example, this system of domestic-based management and oversight of offshore service providers is *de rigueur*. The legal industry may still be a bit ahead of the investigative industry in terms of providing services overseas through partnerships and other less formal forms of cooperation, and this may be based, in part, on the fact that foundational IP-related services like registrations often precede the need for investigations and anti-counterfeiting. But investigation firms are catching up quickly, and having a centralized hub close to home from which investigations are managed around the world is becoming increasingly more available to IP owners. This trend is likely to continue and, in this author's opinion, offers an efficient framework for conducting investigations on a global scale.

Conclusion—The Future

As with every industry I can think of, technology and the Internet are changing and often improving the way that investigations are done. It seems a foregone conclusion that the use of and reliance upon technological tools will continue to increase. My advice to the reader, though, is "be leery of the investigator who believes that there is a technological answer to every problem." While the Internet is a blessing in terms of the information that it makes available to the investigator, those vast quantities of information can also slow the investigation process, distract the investigator and hide as much as they reveal. In other words, the haystack in which the needle is lost has become a whole lot bigger, so digging for that needle can often be that much more difficult. There may also be five needles in that haystack where before there was only one.

To counterbalance the glut of information that is now available on the Internet, software tools have been developed to cull through that information and separate seemingly important pieces of information from the rest of the white noise. However, at this point, these tools still have limitations. In my opinion, they should play a role in the investigative process but cannot yet supplant the human factor completely. Is it more efficient to have a software tool isolate the web sites that include "Nike" and variants thereof from the billions of other sites in the world? Absolutely. But, at this point, further analysis is still required in order to distinguish what is threatening from what is benign within that pool of search results, to establish the priority levels of those threats, to create a strategy for putting a stop to those threats and to bring the resources together to successfully implement that strategy. That is still the task of the investigator and for every advance that technology has afforded him it has also bestowed a counterbalancing advantage on infringers, counterfeiters and criminals.

Ultimately, there are two essential elements to being a good investigator: (1) thoroughly and properly collecting evidence; and (2) analyzing it in order to determine its value to achieving the ultimate objectives of the client. Technology is improving this first task and will likely continue to do so. However, this second function is much more humanistic. It relies on training, intelligence, experience, astuteness, and inquisitiveness, all of which are the hallmarks of a first-rate private investigator.

Notes

[1] Jayne O'Donnell, "Raids Crack Down on Counterfeit Goods," *USA Today* (McLean, VA), December 18, 2009, available at www.usatoday.com/money/industrie s/retail/2009-12-18-counterfeit_CV_N.htm.

[2] See section on "Evidence Handling," p. 233.

[3] See section on "Licensing," p. 234.

[4] See "Acting as Witness" on p. 236 which will further discuss some of the complications that can arise when serving as a witness as well as some specific issues related to attorneys serving as witnesses.

[5]More on this topic is included in the "What to Expect from Your Investigators" section on p. 237.

[6]For example: U.S. federal code states that "whoever; intentionally traffics or attempts to traffic in goods or services and knowingly uses a counterfeit mark on or in connection with such goods or services . . . shall, if an individual, be fined not more than $2,000,000 or imprisoned not more than 10 years, or both. . . . " 18 USCA §2320. Canada's copyright law imposes penalties for infringement of up to $1 million and 5 years in prison. See, Copyright Act (R.S., 1985, c. C-42), http://laws-lois.justice.gc.ca/eng/C-42/page-3.html#anchorbo-ga:l_IV-gb:s_42. Canada also has federal statutes that impose criminal penalties of up to two years in prison for forgery and passing off. See Criminal Code (R.S., 1985, c. C-46), http://laws-lois.justice.gc.ca/eng/C-46/page-7.html. Brazil punishes those who buy, sell, rent, receive, import and/or copy intellectual property without authorization with up to four years in prison plus restitution. See, Federal Laws n° 10.695, de 1°.7.2003 § 2° and n° 9.426, de 1996 - Art 180.

[7]Although Alabama does not have any statewide licensing requirements, some municipalities in Alabama require licensure.

[8]It is also worth noting that variations in licensing requirements extend beyond the United States. For example, private investigators are also required to be licensed in Canada, and licenses are issued at the provincial level. In Taiwan and Malaysia, investigation firms must be licensed by individual investigators need not be. Conversely, Brazil, India, Thailand, and Hong Kong has no licensing requirement for private investigators. The issue of investigator licensing is even more complicated in China, where investigators operate with tacit approval from State and provincial governments but must take precautions not to engage in activities that could be construed as spying for foreign companies. Navigating the intricacies of this system is best left to experienced and reputable Chinese investigators who can guide you in what activities they can and cannot undertake.

[9]See at www.pimagazine.com/private_investigator_license_requirements.html.

[10]The following activities also typically require a private investigation license but have been relegated to a footnote as they come up much less frequently in IP investigations:

> Subcontracting with the government to investigate crimes against the United States
> Finding the whereabouts of a missing person, the owners of escheated property or the heirs to an estate.
> Uncovering the causes or origins of fire, libel, slander, loess, accident, damages, or injuries to real or personal property.

[11]See section on "Special Considerations for Attorneys" on p. 240.

[12]And, to the attorney, you may also be imperiling your ability to represent your client. See "Acting as Witness—The Advantages of an Investigator on the Stand" regarding attorneys acting as witnesses for their clients, on p. 236.

[13]Examples of laws that could be broken by an investigator attempting to collect evidence include: trespass; theft; invasion of privacy (England has invasion of privacy laws that are particularly easy to break); and forgery. The legality of pretexting has also received some attention in recent years, especially as it relates to obtaining personal information about an individual by using false pretenses. The following two are articles are instructive on this issue:

> www.faegre.com/showarticle.aspx?Show=2721
> www.law.com/jsp/article.jsp?id=900005478366

[14]See Evidence Handling section above.

[15]More about the networks that allow your investigator to successfully match personnel to tasks is included in the section on "International Investigations" on p. 246.

[16]www.abanet.org/cpr/mrpc/mrpc_toc.html.

[17]Model Rule 4.2, Communication with Persons Represented by Counsel, www.abanet.org/cpr/mrpc/rule_4_2.html.

[18]Comment to Model Rule 4.2, www.abanet.org/cpr/mrpc/rule_4_2_comm.html.

[19]As any lawyer who has sought guidance on issues of professional responsibility knows, case law on ethical issues can be scant. However, the following cases do directly address issues related to the attorney/investigator relationship and are therefore worth consulting as they are likely to be either precedent or persuasive authority on these issues depending on your jurisdiction:

> *Gidatex v. Campaniello Imports*, 82 F. Supp. 2d 119 (S.D. N.Y. 1999).
> *Apple Corps v. International Collectors Society*, 15 F. Supp. 2d 456 (DNJ 1998).
> *A.V. by Versace Inc. v. Gianni Versace*, 2002 WL 2012618 (S.D. N.Y. 2002).
> *Midwest Motor Sports Inc. v. Arctic Cat Sales, Inc.*, 144 F. Supp. 2d 1147 (D.S.D. 2001).

[20]www.abanet.org/cpr/mrpc/rule_8_4.html.

[21]www.abanet.org/cpr/mrpc/rule_5_3.html.

[22]www.taftlaw.com/attorneys/413-jonathan-g-polak.

[23]In a July 7, 2010, interview with the author.

[24]Here again, the issue of pretexting is relevant and the following articles should be consulted for further instruction on this issue:

> www.faegre.com/showarticle.aspx?Show=2721.
> www.law.com/jsp/article.jsp?id=900005478366.

[25]In a July 7, 2010, interview with the author.

[26]www.abanet.org/cpr/mrpc/rule_1_7.html.

[27]www.abanet.org/cpr/mrpc/rule_1_9.html.

[28]When done in-house, investigation work typically falls to brand protection managers, corporate security, loss prevention managers, and even members of a corporation's legal department, which, as noted in this section, the author does not advise. It is also worth noting that some general business liability insurance policies cover trademark infringement. As a result, in-house investigators with insurance companies may also find themselves in the unfamiliar position of investigating trademark infringement claims from a defense standpoint.

[29]See "What to Expect from your Investigators" on p. 237.

[30]"Whoever; intentionally traffics or attempts to traffic in goods or services and knowingly uses a counterfeit mark on or in connection with such goods or services . . . shall, if an individual, be fined not more than $2,000,000 or imprisoned not more than 10 years, or both. . . ." 18 USCA §2320.

[31]As an analogy, pretend that your neighbor is growing and selling marijuana, that you ask the police to do something about it and they say they have no proof and are too swamped with other cases to assign an officer to stake out your neighbor's house. So, you collect the proof yourself, perhaps taking photos and videos of your neighbor growing and selling the marijuana. You turn this proof over to the police and encourage them to make an arrest based on the proof that you collected. And maybe they do arrest your neighbor based on the evidence that you collected and he gets convicted. The relationship between IP owners, investigators, and law enforcement is not unlike this situation. IP owners have an interest that a particular crime (the counterfeiting of their goods) is redressed. So IP owners, through their investigators, collect evidence that could be helpful in putting a stop to this crime, turn that evidence over to law enforcement, and advocate that the evidence be used to prosecute the crime.

CHAPTER 14

Model Intellectual Property Internship Programs

Internship Programs within the Scope of Employment Law

Barbara Kolsun
Stuart Weitzman Holdings, LLC

L egal internship programs exist to help train lawyers-to-be in the subjects relevant to their company's field of business. For example, fashion companies, whose work is largely comprised of intellectual property (IP) matters, have slowly appreciated the value of these programs to train future lawyers about fashion-specific areas, such as counterfeiting. When I started the internship program at Kate Spade, a fashion company specializing in luxury handbags, to help the company deal with the enormous number of counterfeit handbags for sale on the Internet, few fashion companies used interns. Fashion companies often have small legal departments, and interns may perform many projects while learning the workings of the industry. The press has recently addressed the labor issues specifically related to unpaid legal internships that have proliferated in the downward economy. However, as long as companies give interns challenging work that utilizes and develops their legal skills and have programs that are academically oriented, the company most likely will not face any labor issues.

In this chapter, we discuss the issues that surround hiring legal interns, including: the benefits and drawbacks, employment law issues, where to find interns, how to utilize interns, how to maintain relationships with interns, and how to develop an intern program at your company.

Benefits and Drawbacks of Using Legal IP Interns

There are numerous benefits to hiring a legal IP intern, but, simultaneously, there are drawbacks as well. It is important to be aware of both the benefits and drawbacks in order to tailor the best internship program for your company. Starting with the benefits, legal interns are eager to learn about the practical workings of the legal field, particularly in a specialized field such as IP. As a result, legal interns take their work seriously and are prepared to embrace new tasks. This translates into diligent and well-prepared work. Secondly, legal interns are willing to work for a nominal fee, and often for no fee at all. Legal interns can increase company savings by performing time-consuming tasks, such as researching discrete questions, updating policy, reviewing template contracts, preparing drafts of agreements, and organizing and creating summaries of client files. The increased productivity and the money saved allow IP in-house counsel to reduce their reliance on outside counsel and can also enable a company to liaise more efficiently with outside counsel.[1]

The drawbacks of hiring a legal intern include the time commitment involved with training an intern, and the fact that interns, who are customarily law students, are only dedicated to working for a limited time. As a result, you must balance the amount of time invested in training an intern with the amount of time an intern intends to stay and the type of work the intern will be doing. Training an intern is a vital step to an internship program because most interns are students who need guidance, unlike attorneys who have passed the bar examination. Therefore, it is imperative to revise and approve all work that an intern performs. This practice can be time consuming, and you must therefore allocate intern assignments based on time sensitivity and importance. Internships have an underlying goal of creating an educational experience for interns. As a result, there is a substantial time commitment that comes with training, teaching, and reviewing work that an intern submits. Additionally, when establishing an unpaid internship program, there is an even greater commitment, both in time and resources, to ensure that your program is not taking advantage of an intern, but rather is providing the intern with a unique and educational experience.[2]

Employment Law Issues

When considering hiring a legal intern for the first time, it is imperative to check the regulations of the Labor, Wage, and Hour Division of the United States Department of Labor before determining whether the proposed internship program requires you to pay the interns.[3]

The key determination in this query is whether an intern would be classified as an employee, as determined by the scope of his or her work. Over 50 years ago, the Supreme Court narrowed the definition of an "employee" through its interpretation of the Fair Labor Standards Act of 1938, in the landmark case *Walling, Adm'r, Wage & Hour Div., U.S. Department of Labor, v. Portland Terminal Co.*, 330 U.S. 148 (1927). The Supreme Court in *Walling* established that the definition of "employee" under the Fair Labor Standards Act "was not intended to stamp all persons as employees who, without any express or implied compensation agreement, might work for their own advantage on premises of another.[4]" Therefore, *Walling* established that there is a category of "trainees" that are not legally mandated to be paid as long as they are receiving "great benefit" from their work.[5]

Generally, the preceding rule of law implies that if a program provides the intern with experience that furthers his or her legal education and is academically oriented for the intern's benefit, then an intern will not be considered an "employee," subject to wages.[6] Specifically, most states' departments of labor follow six criteria set out by the U.S. Department of Labor, which were derived from the opinion in *Walling*.[7] Notably, New York and California are more stringent than federal laws because both states require that "the training be an essential part of an established course of an accredited school or of an institution approved by a public agency to provide training for licensure or to qualify for a skilled vocation or profession."[8] When analyzing whether a student's contribution entitles him or her to "employee" status, within the meaning of the Fair Labor Standards Act, ideally all the following six criteria must be met in order to exempt students from monetary requirements:

1. The training is similar to that which would be given in a vocational school.
2. The training is for the benefit of the trainees or students.
3. The trainees or students do not displace regular employees, but work under their close observation.
4. The employer that provides the training derives no immediate advantage from the activities of the trainees or students, and on occasion the employer's operations may actually be impeded.
5. The trainees or students are not necessarily entitled to a job at the conclusion of the training period.
6. The employer and the trainees or students understand that the trainees or students are not entitled to wages for the time spent in training.[9]

In order to have an unpaid internship program, many companies take structural precautions to avoid legal confusion with regard to the above factors. For example, companies and firms often instate a policy requiring student interns to obtain academic credit for their work.[10]

This practice helps establish that the company is committed to providing training similar to that of a vocational school. In addition, to establish that the program is educational and for the benefit of the student, employers can set up weekly seminars with other attorneys to discuss the students' experiences as well as issues that arise in their daily work.

Likewise, employers can set up meetings to discuss current events and any subsequent ramifications on the law. Additionally, companies can require their interns to sign statements acknowledging that they were informed and understand that they will not be paid and that they are not entitled to a job at the conclusion of the internship. Finally, companies should develop a policy that sets out the objective of the internship program, including: an intern's duties and responsibilities, supervisory employees, and specific assignments that the intern is required to complete. This would help to avoid any legal issues that may arise when the benefit to a student is questioned, or when the student's contribution to the company is questioned. Furthermore, if working at an international company, it is also possible to hire interns outside of the United States. When hiring foreign interns, a company should consider the same six "employee" criteria set forth above. In addition, an employer must submit an application under the Fair Labor Standards Act regarding the sponsorship of exchange visitors.[11]

Sources and Screening of Potential Interns

First and foremost, when considering hiring an IP law intern, it is important to limit your scope to law students. Law students are exposed to contracts, property agreements, and other legal issues that arise in IP law. In general, college students do not possess the experience, understanding, or interest in a specialized field of law, such as IP, that law students possess. For example, law students come into an internship familiar with the components of a contract, they understand the legal issues that arise from contractual relationships, and, as a result, they can interpret contracts and even help prevent common contractual problems from arising. For reasons such as this, hiring a law student as a legal intern will help you get the most out of an IP internship program.

There are many resources that can be utilized to find an appropriate legal intern for your company. Contact local law schools through either their career services departments, IP professors, or the alumni office. The career services department can publish your internship program on its web site or in materials that are distributed to the students. A law school professor can announce your internship to his or her students and often prescreen students that fit your qualifications. Additionally, you can post the internship on networking web sites such as Doostang, LinkedIn, and Facebook. Although this method does not focus exclusively on law students, the internship description on the networking site can lead to someone who can recommend an intern that meets your needs. Finally, word-of-mouth is often the best way to solicit intern recommendations. For example, in-house lawyers in fashion companies routinely recommend law student interns to each other.

Once a relationship with local law schools has been established and students begin to send out their resumes, the next step is to interview the best candidates. A good rule of thumb is to choose candidates with business backgrounds in similar industries. For example, at an in-house legal department for a fashion company, a candidate with a retail or business, fashion-related background would be ideal, as he or she would likely understand the types of transactions that are regularly conducted within the company (e.g., licensing agreements, purchase orders).

In addition to having relevant industry experience, it is advantageous to have a cross-section of interns with different skill sets, particularly if there is a high volume of work that needs to be completed.[12] A diverse class of interns enables the interns to learn from each other and assist each other throughout their experience. For example, an intern who speaks fluent French can translate contracts or leases for his or her fellow interns, or an intern with an engineering background can perform and assist his or her fellow interns with complex math to draft royalty provisions in licensing agreements.

When hiring law students, it is important to keep in mind the time of year during which you wish to employ the student's help and the duration of his or her internship. Law students typically attend class during the fall and the spring; therefore, hiring a summer intern can be a different experience than hiring an intern during the school year. For example, when hiring summer law interns, assuming they are not taking any classes, you can reasonably expect them to work full days for the duration of their summer break. However, an intern hired during the school year is only allowed to work 20 hours per week when enrolled as a full-time student at an American Bar Association (ABA)-approved law school.[13] In addition, if a student is attaining credit for his or her internship work, many law schools only require students to work for a set amount of weeks (e.g., 10 to 12 weeks in a typical semester).[14] Due to this limitation, you need to coordinate the interns' schedules with each other and with your needs so that you have interns present every day, but not all interns on the same days. Therefore, be strategic about the number of interns you accept by taking into consideration the volume of work expected and the time of year the interns are accepted. For a year-round internship program, it would be advantageous to accept more interns during the school year than in the summer, thereby enabling your department to maintain the same level of support year-round.

Structure of the Internship Program

It is important to consider a variety of details before implementing an internship program, to ensure that both your company and interns will benefit from the program. An internship program has various components, including: Setting up an Internship Program, Structuring Assignments, Mentorship and Training, and Oversight of Interns.

Setting Up an Internship Program

In structuring an internship program, the company should first discuss with the operations team whether it has space available for interns who need computers and desks. At the fashion companies I have worked for, including Kate Spade, 7 for All Mankind, and Stuart Weitzman, we generally have space for three interns, who may sit in the legal department or in any area where there is free space, including in the middle of the design floor, with sales or marketing employees, or even in production, depending on space. With that in mind, interns must understand, if they are sharing an area with other business units, that legal department information is confidential and must be carefully handled and returned to the legal department at the end of each work period. Interns will also need an individual e-mail address, which involves coordination with your technology department. It is important to create shared legal databases and to teach interns to delete old drafts, when appropriate, in order to keep the database up-to-date. This creates a space for documents that may be edited by more than one intern and may be augmented, updated, and edited over a period of time (e.g., summary of leases, adding new leases). Most important, the legal department must be able to locate documents when the intern who worked on such document is not in the office.

Structuring Assignments

The most important thing for an intern is to have a well-structured and organized program in place, so that the intern is able to receive the unique training and knowledge expected of the internship. A good internship program starts with creating a syllabus of the work the intern will encounter—in other words, structured assignments. In order to provide an accurate description of the work, the attorney must have a good sense of the company's needs at the time the internship occurs. Specifically, the attorney should know the type and amount of work that will be coming in, and what portion of that work the intern can assist with and learn from. When developing structured assignments, it is also important to keep in mind the goal of your company and the goal of benefiting the intern. Giving an intern irrelevant or low-importance work does not help you reach your company's goal, nor does it give the intern true work experience. Therefore, whenever possible, give your interns challenging assignments that require them to effectively integrate their legal studies.

One method of creating a syllabus is to list the different types of assignments you, as an attorney, encounter on a daily or weekly basis (e.g., real estate agreements, licensing agreements, anti-counterfeiting work). From that list, discern what tasks a legal intern could competently handle and adequately learn from (e.g., review documents, research forms, investigate counterfeit retailers). Finally, ensure that every intern gets exposure to the various different assignments. Having structured work assignments enables the intern to have a steady work flow, learn how to work efficiently, gain exposure to different types of work, and, ultimately, learn as much as possible from each assignment.[15]

Mentorship and Training

The challenges that come with hiring temporary interns are that interns usually do not have sufficient experience in a specialized field of law; after all, students take internship positions precisely to gain such experience. In order to overcome this challenge, it is essential to train your interns and also to provide mentorship.

You can use several methods to train your interns: you may personally train them, provide former interns to train them, or provide instructional memos. Personally training the interns is the most effective way of teaching them the material that you intend for them to learn. Interns benefit from superficial exposure to IP work, but an additional way to enhance an intern's experience is to walk him or her through your thought process or analysis of a problem. Breaking down thoughts that come automatically to a practicing lawyer helps to teach interns how to think like a lawyer. In addition, you can instruct an intern to research a common IP problem and then discuss his or her analysis of the problem and the possible solutions.

Another source of training for new interns is former interns. A former intern provides a good source of training in an informal setting by warning interns of common mistakes and also imparting wisdom from their own experiences. Finally, generating a memo for new interns can be useful as well. A memo should contain an introduction, basic instructions on how to use the technology in the office, sample documents, and, most important, step-by-step instructions on how to complete common intern tasks. Although providing a written document that reminds interns of important steps can be helpful, it is nevertheless essential to advise interns that they should approach you with any questions or comments regarding relevant issues, in order to enrich their experience.

In general, some of the most important information and advice an intern can receive is from a mentor. As an employer, it is crucial to mentor your interns. Providing career advice and guidance can prove to be extremely valuable to student interns. Helping interns tailor resumes, assisting with job searches, and using your own resources and contacts to help interns secure summer positions and/or permanent jobs after graduation are all ways you can be a mentor to your interns. Mentorship is especially important during trying economic times such as these.

Oversight of Interns

As a result of an intern's lack of experience, it is essential to carefully review an intern's work and give the intern feedback. This ensures that the work being done satisfies the standards of your company and simultaneously gives an intern the opportunity to improve and learn not only from the intern's own work but from the employer's input as well.

Real-Life Case Studies

At Kate Spade and 7 for All Mankind, a luxury denim fashion company, interns were charged with assisting in the "takedown" of web sites and eBay postings that sold counterfeit goods. The interns wrote cease-and-desist letters and assisted in training law enforcement members in connection with anti-counterfeiting enforcement. They participated in trademark prosecutions, for example, filing and attending to applications for trademarks worldwide and responding to discovery requests in IP lawsuits.

At Stuart Weitzman, interns have assisted in drafting distribution and license agreements; filing trademark, copyright, and design patent applications; and have even drafted responses to office actions in the U.S. Patent and Trademark Office (USPTO), communicating directly with examiners. They have been integral in building and maintaining our IP database, including trademarks, copyrights, design patents, European design registrations, and domain names. Further, the interns have assisted in resolving domain name disputes, preparing cease-and-desist letters and drafting settlement agreements. At both 7 for All Mankind and Stuart Weitzman, interns have helped prepare disclosures in connection with corporate transactions. Also, they have assisted in drafting design services agreements for designers and consultants, considering the many IP issues related to such agreements.

Since I speak extensively at various conferences and panels throughout the country, and have coedited a book on fashion law,[16] I am constantly working on updating the educational materials I author. Interns have assisted in preparing outlines and continuing legal education materials for my presentations, and have aided me in writing and editing my book and various other articles. My very first intern created drafts of a law review article on contributory and vicarious infringement, as well as a chapter in the book *Trademark Counterfeiting in the United States*.[17]

Retaining and Maximizing the Benefits of Postinternship Relationships

Despite the temporary nature of internships, it is important to maintain a relationship with an intern long after he or she completes an internship with your company. At the completion of an internship, a good way to maintain contact is to keep a record of the intern's contact information; specifically, develop an intern database. An intern database is an open file that should be updated with an intern's mailing and e-mail address, phone numbers, and employment history. In fact, an intern can develop the database and communicate with current and former interns from the mailing list. One can also maintain communication with interns through an appropriate social networking site, such as LinkedIn or Facebook. For example, there is a "Barbara Kolsun Interns" group on LinkedIn, giving current interns a forum to communicate with former interns, allowing them to share experiences, inquire about employment opportunities, or seek any type of related advice.

On a separate but related topic, it is important to discuss social media and e-mail etiquette with your interns, particularly as this relates to confidentiality. Further, in that regard, all interns should sign confidentiality agreements before commencing their internships. The benefit of maintaining a relationship with interns is that you can assist a former intern throughout his or her career, and, ultimately, an intern may be able to assist you in the future as well. After all, your legal interns will likely be attorneys one day; therefore, having a postinternship relationship helps you expand your personal network and increase the contacts you have in the industry.

A Model IP Law Internship Program

The most effective way to assist a legal intern's learning process is to have a well-structured and developed internship program. The seven steps below will guide you to create your own successful IP legal internship program:

1. Use law students for legal internship positions.
2. Create formal assignments before an internship begins.
3. Provide a method of training for all interns.
4. Give interns meaningful work, for example:
   a. Prosecution of trademarks globally:
      i. Draft communications with foreign associates.
      ii. Compile databases of trademarks, copyrights, design patents, and domain names.
      iii. Conduct, review, and analyze trademark searches. Specifically, interns can search "style names" on the USPTO database and perform a global Internet search to eliminate unavailable names.
      iv. Prepare copyright and trademark applications.
   b. Trademark enforcement:
      i. Draft cease-and-desist letters and settlement agreements.
      ii. Conduct counterfeiting investigations, including web sites, such as eBay.com, and retail stores.
      iii. Assist in preparation of training materials on detection of counterfeit merchandise for law enforcement.
      iv. Train law enforcement in detecting counterfeits.
      v. Document and update database of all steps taken in trademark enforcement.
   c. Organize evidence and other documents related to the matter.
   d. Create redline drafts of trademark licenses, franchise, and distribution agreements.
   e. Perform legal research, including research latest issues in IP law.

    f. Review of contracts:
       i. Review commercial agreements.
      ii. Review license agreements.
     iii. Review work for hire and other employment agreements.
     iv. Review and summarize retail store leases.
    g. Maintain financial documents:
       i. Review and update Uniform Commercial Code (UCC) filings.
      ii. Review and update annual tax filings.
     iii. Maintain board minutes and approvals.
5. Give interns feedback on their work.
6. After an internship is over, help interns find other internships and permanent jobs.
7. Maintain a relationship with former interns.

The Current Trend in Internship Programs

Based on a 2010 study conducted by the National Association of Colleges and Employers,[18] 52 percent of graduating students from the Class of 2010 had held internships during their college years, an increase from 50 percent in 2008.[19] Experts estimated that of these thousands of internships, one-fourth to one-half of them were unpaid interns, and, for the most part, many students expected that.[20] Particularly within certain industries, such as the entertainment and fashion industries, students recognize that an unpaid internship is the clear first step to getting your foot in the door.

Conclusion

An internship program that is well structured and organized can provide many benefits to both the company's legal department and to the interns participating in the program. The program can increase the company's productivity significantly, while still being cost effective. Furthermore, the internship program will provide its interns with real-life experience that cannot be taught in the classroom. This will help interns develop a skill set that they will be able to utilize and build upon throughout their careers.

Notes

[1] The Department of Labor has established criteria that must be met in order to withhold compensation when hiring unpaid legal interns. These criteria are discussed in this chapter in the section entitled Employment Law Issues.

[2] Bernadette Feeley, "Examining the Use of For-Profit Placements in Law School Externship Programs," 14 *Clinical L. Rev.* 37 (2007).

[3] Fair Labor Standard Act, 29 USCA § 203(e).

[4] Fair Labor Standard Act. 29 USCA § 203(e); and *Walling, Adm'r, Wage & Hour Div., U.S. Department of Labor, v. Portland Terminal Co.,* 330 U.S. 148, 152 (1927).

[5]Id. at 152. Note this law is federal regulation. See below for state specific requirements.

[6]Id. at 152.

[7]Id. at 152.

[8]See CA Dept. of Labor. Opinion Letter 1996. Available at www.dir.ca.gov/dlse/opinions/1996-12-30.pdf.

[9]Administrative Letter Rulings: Department of Labor, Wage and Hour Division, May 19, 2004.

RULE: It is our position that where education or training programs are designed to provide students with professional experience in the furtherance of their education and training and are academically oriented for their benefit, the students will not be considered employees of the institutions to which they are assigned, provided the criteria noted above are met. However, where an individual is serving in an after-graduation internship, an employment relationship would exist between the graduated intern and the employing institution.

[10]See www.californiawagelaw.com/wage_law/2006/07/most-unpaid-internships-are-unlawful.html. R. K. Kaplan, Legal Counsel, National Association of Colleges and Employers, list of additional questions to ask when contemplating an unpaid internship programs:

1. Will the student receive credit for the work or is the internship required for graduation?
2. Does the student have to prepare a report of his/her experience and submit it to a faculty supervisor?
3. Have you received a letter or some other form of written documentation from the school stating that the internship is approved/sponsored by the school as educationally relevant?
4. Will the student perform work that other employees also perform, with the student doing the work for the purpose of learning and not necessarily performing a task for the employer?
5. Is the student working and providing benefit to you less than 50 percent of the time and/or is the student in a shadowing/learning mode?
6. Will you provide an opportunity for the individual to learn a skill, process, or other business function, or operate equipment?
7. Is there educational value to the work performed, that is, is it related to the courses the person is taking in school?
8. Is the individual supervised by one of your staff members?
9. Is it clear that a job is not guaranteed upon completion of the training or completion of the person's schooling?

[11]See 72 Fed. Reg. 33669 (June 19, 2007); Fair Labor Standards Act and the Migrant and Seasonal Agricultural Worker Protection Act. IMLB § 2:31. Sponsorship of exchange visitors programs—application process.

[12]Keep in mind the issue of obtaining a "benefit" deriving from the fourth criteria of the *Walling v. Portland Terminal Co.* set of factors. Having a relevant cross section of skills also enables applicants that wouldn't ordinarily get chosen for a particular position to be chosen because of their diverse skill set.

[13]Section 304 (f), "Standards for Approval of Law Schools"; the American Bar Association mandates that law students enrolled in more than 12 class hours may not work more than 20 hours per week.

[14]The internship duration requirements are different at all institutions. Check with your local law schools for their policy.

[15]See Model IP Law Internship Program for a list of sample assignments.

[16]Guillermo C. Jimenez and Barbara Kolsun, *Fashion Law: A Guide for Designers, Fashion Executives and Attorneys* (New York: Fairchild Books, 2010).

[17]Barbara Kolsun, "Building a Comprehensive Anti-Counterfeiting Program," *Trademark Counterfeiting* (New York: Aspen Law & Business, 1999), Chapter 7; *Trademark Counterfeiting in the United States,* International Anticounterfeiting Coalition, 2008.

[18]"Moving On: Students' Approaches and Attitudes towards the Job Market for the College Class of 2010," National Association of Colleges and Employers, September 2010.

[19]Steven Greenhouse, "The Unpaid Intern, Legal or Not," *New York Times,* April 2, 2010.

[20]Id.

CHAPTER 15

Maximizing "Green" Brand Exposure and Minimizing Perceptions of Greenwashing

Maureen Beacom Gorman, Esq.
Marshall, Gerstein & Borun LLP

The United States is going green and companies that do not "go green" are lagging behind consumer demand,[1] behind governmental policy,[2] and, perhaps, behind the times.[3] However, many companies claiming to have already "gone green," including some reputable mainstream companies, have been accused of overstating or misstating their "greenness."[4] In fact, TerraChoice Environmental Marketing Inc.,[5] in its now famous survey of green marketing claims, after analyzing 1,753 environmental claims on 1,018 products and testing the claims against current best practices in environmental marketing,[6] found that all but one of the 1,018 products surveyed in 2007 made false or potentially misleading claims to the targeted consumer.[7] In 2009, TerraChoice's survey in the United States and Canada found of the 4,996 green claims on 2,219 products, 98 percent of them were false or misleading.[8] The act of "misleading consumers regarding the environmental practices of a company or the environmental benefits of a product or service" has come to be known as *greenwashing*.[9]

This chapter serves as a guide to the trademark practitioner in the "green" issues arising in the current market. Specifically, it attempts to address some of the most pertinent legal issues in green branding and the legal pitfalls of greenwashing by discussing issues in green branding, competitor-initiated allegations (litigation) of greenwashing, and identifying some of the various government policies and agency rules that affect environmental marketing.

Green Branding

In 2008, the United States Patent and Trademark Office (USPTO) received more than 3,200 filings for marks containing the word *green,* an increase of 32 percent over 2007 filings.[10] *Eco*-prefix and *enviro*-prefix marks increased 86 percent (to more than 1,700 filings) and 22 percent (to more than 500), respectively.[11] Filings containing the word *clean* "to suggest environmental friendliness" increased 30 percent (to more than 1,000 filings).[12] The evidence suggests that green marketing is not simply a fad, "but rather a strategic initiative."[13] However, as the TerraChoice report suggests,[14] applying a "green sheen" without greenwashing is challenging.

The Federal Trade Commission's Restrictions on Green Brand Selection

The trademark practitioner's first resource when analyzing green branding issues is somewhat surprisingly not the USPTO's "go-to" source, the Trademark Manual of Examining Procedure (TMEP), but rather the Federal Trade Commission (FTC) policy manuals.[15] The FTC, along with the Environmental Protection Agency (EPA), issued in 1992, 1996, and most recently in 1998 its policy statements regarding environmental marketing claims, commonly referred to as the "Green Guides."[16] The Green Guides cover:

> . . . *environmental claims included in labeling, advertising, promotional materials and all other forms of marketing, whether asserted directly or by implication, through words, symbols, emblems, logos, depictions, product brand names, or through any other means, including marketing through digital or electronic means, such as the Internet or electronic mail. The guides apply to any claim about the environmental attributes of a product, package, or service in connection with the sale, offering for sale, or marketing of such product, package, or service for personal, family, or household use, or for commercial, institutional, or industrial use.*[17]

The Green Guides are not "enforceable regulations" in and of themselves, and they do not "preempt regulation of other federal agencies or of state and local bodies governing the use of environmental marketing claims."[18] In this regard, the Green Guides note that compliance is "voluntary."[19] However, it is voluntary only in the sense that "they are intended to aid compliance with Section 5(a) of the FTC Act as that Act applies to environmental marketing claims," rather than being law themselves.[20] Therefore, a voluntary disregard for the Green Guides could nonetheless lead to an FTC investigation and enforcement under Section 5 of the FTC Act for noncompliance with federal, state, or local law and environmental claim regulations.[21]

Section 5 of the FTC Act, of course, prohibits unfair or deceptive practices, and provides in pertinent part:

> *The Commission is hereby empowered and directed to prevent persons, partnerships, or corporations . . . from using unfair methods of competition in or affecting commerce and unfair or deceptive acts or practices in or affecting commerce.*[22]

Section 5 makes "deceptive acts and practices in or affecting commerce" un-lawful,[23] and the Green Guides set forth the "general principles and specific guid-ance on the use of environmental claims"[24] to avoid making environmentally deceptive acts and practices. In this regard, it is clear that green marketers without a reasonable basis at the time of making claims must avoid:

> . . . *An express or implied claim that presents an objective assertion about the environmental attribute of a product, package, or service.*[25]

> *   *   *

> *A reasonable basis consists of competent and reliable evidence. In the context of environmental marketing claims, such substantiation will often require competent and reliable scientific evidence, defined as tests, analyses, research, studies or other evidence based on the expertise of professionals in the relevant area, conducted and evaluated in an objective manner by persons qualified to do so, using procedures generally accepted in the profession to yield accurate and reliable results.*[26]

Generally, environmental marketing claims should: "be sufficiently clear, promi-nent and understandable to prevent deception"[27]; clearly indicate "whether the environmental attribute or benefit being asserted refers to the product, the product's packaging, a service or to a portion or component of the product, package or service"[28]; not overstate "the environmental attribute or benefit, expressly or by im-plication"[29]; and substantiate and clearly state comparisons so that consumer decep-tion does not occur.[30] The Green Guides specifically discuss deceptive acts and practices as they pertain to environmental claims including the following specific ter-minology: *degradable/biodegradable/photodegradable,*[31] *compostable,*[32] *recyclable,*[33] and *recycled content.*[34] The Green Guides also specifically address environmental claims regarding source reduction (claims that a product or package has been re-duced or is lower in weight, volume or toxicity),[35] *refillable,*[36] and ozone safe and ozone friendly.[37] The brand owner should cautiously consider use of the aforemen-tioned terms as part of a proposed brand name, logo, or on labels or product packag-ing before introduction into the marketplace.

The Green Guides also give many examples of proper and improper use of envi-ronmental terms incorporated in brands and logos. Some examples are:

> *A brand name like "Eco-Safe" would be deceptive if, in the context of the product so named, it leads consumers to believe that the product has environmental ben-efits which cannot be substantiated by the manufacturer. The claim would not be deceptive if "Eco-Safe" were followed by clear and prominent qualifying lan-guage limiting the safety representation to a particular product attribute for which it could be substantiated, and provided that no other deceptive implica-tions were created by the context.*[38]

As mentioned in the Introduction, more than 1,700 applications for marks with the *eco* prefix were filed with the United States Patent and Trademark Office

(USPTO) in 2008.[39] In light of the TerraChoice survey finding that 98 percent of products included false or misleading statements,[40] one cannot help but consider whether at least some of the 1,700 applications for marks with the *eco* prefix seek to protect deceptive brands and logos.

One can successfully implement new green brands and logos by substantiating the environmental claim contained within the brand logo. An example of "best practices" in that regard is one found in the brand name Pendleton® Eco-Wise Wool.

According to the EPA,

> *McDonough Braungart Design Chemistry (MBDC) is a recognized authority on sustainable design of products and the materials used to create them. Utilizing a scientific assessment process known as the Cradle-to-Cradle Design Protocol,[41] manufacturers submit products to be evaluated and, if necessary, redesigned. Successful products that pass rigorous audit by MBDC are granted Cradle to Cradle certification.[42]*

Beginning in 2002, Pendleton, a wool products manufacturer claiming roots in the wool mill industry from 1863[43] "created a classic wool flannel" using the cradle-to-cradle protocol.[44] The products are sold under the Pendleton Eco-Wise Wool brand name.[45] By utilizing the EPA-recognized Cradle-to-Cradle certification process to substantiate the environmental claim incorporated in the brand name—that the product is "Eco-Wise"—Pendleton appears to have complied with the FTC Green Guides.

Another Green Guides example discussing a potentially problematic type of logo is:

> *A product label contains an environmental seal, either in the form of a globe icon, or a globe icon with only the text "Earth Smart" around it. Either label is likely to convey to consumers that the product is environmentally superior to other products. If the manufacturer cannot substantiate this broad claim, the claim would be deceptive. The claims would not be deceptive if they were accompanied by clear and prominent qualifying language limiting the environmental superiority representation to the particular product attribute or attributes for which they could be substantiated, provided that no other deceptive implications were created by the context.[46]*

As of April 18, 2010, twenty live USPTO registrations contained the words *Earth Smart*.[47] If an advertiser used an Earth Smart mark with biodegradable products, for example, the label should indicate the extent of degradation as well as the rate of degradation.[48] The Green Guides caution that "claims of degradability, biodegradability, or photo degradability should be qualified to the extent necessary to avoid consumer deception about: (1) the product or package's ability to degrade in the environment where it is customarily disposed; and (2) the rate and extent of degradation."[49] Moreover, "An unqualified claim that a product or package is degradable, biodegradable, or photodegradable should be substantiated by competent and reliable scientific evidence that the entire product or package will completely break down and return to nature, that is, decompose into elements found in nature within a reasonably short period of time after customary disposal."[50] Since most products are disposed of in a landfill, a biodegradable claim would be false if the products did not biodegrade in a landfill within a reasonably short period.[51] If an advertiser cannot substantiate the biodegradable claims, then the government might consider the mark Earth Smart, for example, a deceptive environmental marketing claim under the Green Guides.[52]

In fact, Kmart Corporation in 2009 advertised to the U.S. public that its American Fare paper plates were "biodegradable" without defining, describing, or qualifying such biodegradability.[53]

Such advertisement caused the FTC to bring an enforcement action against Kmart alleging that: (1) the American Fare brand paper products did not "bio-degrade," that is "decompose into elements found in nature, within a reasonably short period of time after customary disposal"; and (2) Kmart did not possess and rely upon a reasonable basis that substantiated the biodegradability claim in its advertisement. [54] The enforcement action settled with Kmart's agreeing not to advertise any product as degradable, biodegradable, or photodegradable, unless Kmart possessed and relied upon competent and reliable scientific evidence that substantiated the biodegradability claim.[55] However, Kmart might well have avoided the FTC enforcement action if it had sought third-party certification of its advertising environmental claims, as Pendleton did.

The Clorox Company is another entity that has successfully implemented a green brand in the potentially green-challenged industry of hazardous chemicals. The Clorox Company developed the brand, Green Works, now used with ten "natural cleaners" made using plant-based, biodegradable ingredients, packaged in recyclable materials, and not tested on animals.[56] The EPA has recognized the Green Works products for using safer chemistry and has certified the products under the EPA's "Design for Environment" certification logo.[57] Again, by securing reputable third-party certification from the EPA itself, The Clorox Company is another example of a company apparently able to implement a new green brand without greenwashing.

Another example from the Green Guides mentions use of the symbol commonly referred to as the "three chasing arrows":

A nationally marketed 8 oz. plastic cottage-cheese container displays the Society of the Plastics Industry (SPI) code (which consists of a design of arrows in a triangular shape containing a number and abbreviation identifying the component plastic resin) on the front label of the container, in close proximity to the product name and logo. The manufacturer's conspicuous use of the SPI code in this manner constitutes a recyclability claim. Unless recycling facilities for this container are available to a substantial majority of consumers or communities, the claim should be qualified to disclose the limited availability of recycling programs for the container. If the SPI code, without more, had been placed in an inconspicuous location on the container (e.g., embedded in the bottom of the container) it would not constitute a claim of recyclability.[58]

The USPTO Design Search Code Manual lists the recycling symbol under the design code 24.17.19.[59] As of April 18, 2010, the USPTO database lists 350 live applications or registrations for marks with the recycling symbol design code indicated.[60] Whether the product is recyclable to a substantial majority of consumers or communities must be clear.[61] One must consider whether the nature of the product itself raises the question of how it can be disposed of.[62] Perhaps advertising the recyclability of the product to a certain type of consumer is useful, but, if the product is not recyclable for the majority of the product's consumers, the Green Guides specify that the advertiser should qualify the recycling symbol to disclose how and where the products might be recycled, or should not label the product "recyclable" at all.[63]

As previously mentioned, the FTC last updated the Green Guides in 1998.[64] In 2008, the FTC conducted three workshops to determine whether the Green Guides were still useful and relevant or whether they needed to be updated.[65] The content of the three workshops were topic specific, addressing (1) carbon offsets and renewable energy certificates, (2) green packaging claims, and (3) green building and textiles.[66] Because of the workshops, we expect that the amended Green Guides will likely address environmental claims related to the above categories. It is also likely that the FTC will define the terms *sustainable* and *carbon neutral* as "environmental marketing claims" when it publishes the amended Green Guides.[67] The trademark practitioner should be mindful of both the current Green Guides and the publication of the anticipated amended Green Guides when considering new green brands and logos, designing product labels, and implementing green advertisement.

USPTO Restrictions on Green Brand Registration

In the same manner that the trademark dot-com boom busted in 2002 with the Trademark Trial and Appeal Board's (TTAB or Board) decisions that top-level domain name indicators could not indicate source[68] except in rare cases,[69] the Board's 2009 and 2010 decisions make it equally clear that *green* cannot function as a source indicator for environmentally friendly products and services. Attempts to register green marks have been rejected for being either "merely descriptive" or "generic." Avoiding merely descriptive refusals should be one key consideration when implementing green brands. However, avoiding §2(a) deceptiveness issues is paramount.

With regard to USPTO refusals based on the mere descriptiveness of a mark for the identified goods or services, the Lanham Act provides in pertinent part:

> *No trademark by which the goods of the applicant may be distinguished from the goods of others shall be refused registration on the principal register on account of its nature unless it—*
>
> *   *   *
>
> *Consists of a mark which (1) when used on or in connection with the goods of the applicant is merely descriptive or deceptively misdescriptive of them.*[70]

The TMEP states:

*To be refused registration on the Principal Register under §2(e)(1) of the Trade-
mark Act, 15 U.S.C. §1052(e)(1), a mark must be merely descriptive or deceptively misdescriptive of the goods or services to which it relates. A mark is
considered merely descriptive if it describes an ingredient, quality, characteristic, function, feature, purpose, or use of the specified goods or services.[71]*

According to USPTO policy, when an examiner issues a refusal on the grounds
of "mere descriptiveness," or any other substantive refusal, "the examining attorney
must always support his or her action with relevant evidence and ensure that proper
citations to the evidence are made in the Office Action."[72] The examiner bears the
burden of proving that a term is merely descriptive in relation to the goods or
services.[73]

Similarly, the USPTO initially refuses registration of generic terms under §2(e)(1)
of the Trademark Act, 15 U.S.C. §1052(e)(1), upon applying the *Marvin Ginn* two-
part test.[74] The USPTO first considers the class or genus of goods or services at issue.[75] Then, it considers whether the relevant public understands the designation
primarily to refer to that class or genus of goods or services.[76] The TMEP states, "The
examining attorney has the burden of proving that a term is generic by clear evidence."[77] To establish genericness, then, examiners, and the Board on appeal, typically consider "evidence of the public's understanding of a term" that "can be
obtained from any competent source, including dictionary definitions, research databases, newspapers, and other publications."[78]

In 2009, the TTAB had the opportunity to consider the registrability of three[79]
"green" marks: Green Indigo,[80] AllergyGreen,[81] and Green Key Stylized.[82] A review
of these cases demonstrates the Board's increasing reluctance to allow green marks
on the USPTO Principal or Supplemental registers due to increasing evidence available via the internet that third parties commonly use such terms to describe environmentally friendly brands and products.

In the beginning of 2009, the Board reversed the examiner's merely descriptive
refusal of the standard character mark Green Indigo for "bottoms; [and] tops," finding the combination word mark *suggestive* for environmentally friendly clothing,
rather than merely descriptive.[83] Even though the examiner presented evidence to
establish that the terms *green* and *indigo* are merely descriptive for clothing, the
Board found that the combination word mark did not retain the descriptive meaning
of the individual words.[84]

Later, in May 2009, the Board upheld the examiner's merely descriptive refusal of
AllergyGreen for "protective bedding, namely zippered and fitted covers for mattresses, comforters; bed sheets and waterproof mattress pads; reusable bed pads,"
finding the combination word mark merely descriptive for the goods.[85] The examiner presented dictionary definitions for the individual terms, and prevalent Internet
use showing that third parties used the individual terms *allergy* and *green* to describe
a desirable attribute of bedding.[86] The Board found the examiner's evidence persuasive.[87] Over the applicant's arguments, the Board ruled, "although 'green' bedding
may have various meanings, all of these meanings describe a characteristic of the
products as being environmentally friendly."[88] Accordingly, the Board found that

the two descriptive terms, *allergy* and *green,* when combined as the term *Allergy-Green,* remain merely descriptive when used with bedding.[89]

Still later, in September 2009, in the *Cenveo* decision, the Board went further.[90] Based on a finding of genericness, the USPTO refused the mark Green Key Stylized for use with "paperboard keycards made of environmentally friendly materials." In determining genericness, the Board first applied the test set forth in *Marvin Ginn.*[91] In analyzing the first prong, the class or genus of the goods, the Board determined that the class or genus was "keycards made of environmentally friendly materials."[92] Then, in analyzing the second prong—whether the relevant public understood the mark primarily to refer to that class or genus—the Board applied additional "subtests."[93] The Board said that the mark must be classified as either a compound word mark or a phrase.[94] If a compound word mark, then *In re Gould* applied.[95] If a phrase, then *In re American Fertility Society* applied.[96] If *Gould* applied, the examiner had to establish by clear evidence that: (1) that each word is generic and (2) that the meaning of the joined compound word mark is identical to the meaning of the words separately.[97] If *American Fertility Society* applied, then the examiner had to establish by clear evidence that the meaning of the phrase as a whole is generic.[98]

In *Cenveo*, the Board decided that the mark was a compound word mark, not a phrase, taking judicial notice of the dictionary definition of "compound word mark."[99] The Board determined that each word *green* and *key* was generic for the goods, "environmentally friendly key cards."[100] The Board also found that the meaning of the compound word mark was the same as the meaning of the separate terms, concluding that the mark was generic for the intended goods.

The Board went further, determining under the *American Fertility Society* standard that Green Key Stylized, even as a phrase, was generic. The Board based its determination on merely three internet uses of the mark as a phrase,[101] even though, historically, an examiner would have a difficult time supporting a generic refusal with so few uses of the phrase.[102]

The Board also considered another green mark, Green Cement.[103] The Board observed, "The issue before us is whether the term Green Cement is merely descriptive of applicant's cement and cement-related goods."[104] The Board found Green Cement merely descriptive of the applicant's cement and cement-related goods without considering whether the term *green cement* was generic.[105] In making such determination, the Board considered the evidence of record, namely dictionary definitions, Web pages, and third-party registrations disclaiming[106] the term *green* or claiming acquired distinctiveness[107] under Section 2(f) of the Trademark Act.[108]

If the Green Guides do not directly address the green term in a proposed mark, the trademark practitioner should analyze the applicability of the types of evidence considered by the TTAB in these four opinions before prosecuting a trademark application for a green brand. For example, even though the Green Guides do not currently define the term *sustainable,* a search of the USPTO records, dictionary definitions, the Internet, and U.S. news articles would suggest that the term *sustainable* for household goods in International Class 20 (as an example) is merely descriptive or teetering toward mere descriptiveness.[109]

Combining a design element with a nondescriptive slogan might avoid a merely descriptive finding. Sam's Club, for example, adopted the logo Simple Steps to Saving Green and Design in 2008 to indicate that a product bearing the logo "has taken a step toward being more environmentally responsible in the way it was created, processed, and/or distributed."[110]

According to Sam's Club,

> *Some of our products displaying the eco symbol have been certified by one of the following third-party organizations that set standards for protecting the environment. Other products that display the symbol have been recognized as being better for the environment than their alternatives. Recognizing products, such as compacted laundry detergent, that take steps in the right direction helps highlight choices we can all make to support sustainability.*[111]

The Simple Steps to Saving Green and Design logo would not likely face a merely descriptive refusal.

In 2001, S. C. Johnson similarly developed the "Greenlist[TM] process" "to classify ingredients considered for use in our products by their impact on the environment and human health."[112] S.C. Johnson states, "For example, by reformulating Windex[®] brand glass cleaner, we cut 1.8 million pounds of volatile organic compounds (VOCs) from it while giving it 30 percent more cleaning power."[113] In 2008, S. C. Johnson used the Greenlist and Design logo on Windex products that met the internally set environmental standards.

Combining elements that are possibly suggestive or merely descriptive with a distinctive design element, S. C. Johnson's Greenlist and Design logo did not receive a merely descriptive refusal from the USPTO during its first examination of the mark.[114]

Yet, although environmentally friendly logos, like those discussed here, might initially avoid a merely descriptive refusal, brand owners must still be careful when selecting a mark as to how they intend to use it to avoid subsequent cancellation based upon deceptive or unfair competition claims. For example, S. C. Johnson, which avoided the USPTO's merely descriptive refusal, is now the defendant in a class action lawsuit brought by an individual in California, alleging that S. C. Johnson's Greenlist and Design label is "deceptively designed to look like a third party seal of approval, which it is not, and it falsely represents that the products are environmentally friendly."[115] The complaint has survived S. C. Johnson's motion to dismiss.[116]

Deceptive marks are absolutely barred from registration under § 2(a) because a deceptive mark is one where "the misdescription or falsity is 'material' in that it is likely to significantly induce a purchaser's decision to buy."[117] The TTAB's three-part test of § 2(a) deceptiveness is: "(1) Is the term misdescriptive of the character, quality, function, composition or use of the goods? (2) If so, are prospective purchasers likely to believe that the misdescription actually describes the goods? (3) If so, is the misdescription likely to affect the decision to purchase?"[118] The "deception" that occurs at the time of the consumer's purchase cannot be erased even "if the consumer later finds out that the designation is not deceptive."[119]

Whether adopting a new eco-friendly brand or rebranding an old logo with a new environmentally friendly message, the risk is that the new message leaves the government, competitor, or consumer with the impression that the product has been greenwashed. To avoid claims of greenwashing or worse deceptiveness, the best practice is to know how consumers perceive the intended green mark.

To this end, brand owners might participate in brand studies that rate consumer perception of the brand in the context of sustainability concerns. One such brand study is MapChange 2010, which "tracks both climate change actions of more than 90 leading U.S. corporations and consumer perceptions of these actions."[120] The goal of MapChange 2011, to be published in fall 2010, is to provide the brand owner with information about the "brand's 'green' revenue opportunities" within its industry.[121] To know how consumers perceive one's mark before greening it may help the brand owner in its green image evolution.

To succeed in "sustainability branding," Maddock Douglas—Agency of Innovation®, a brand and business consulting firm and the publisher of the MapChange studies, identifies "The 5 'C's of Sustainability Branding." One's green and sustainable brands should be:

1. *Competitive.* The product associated with the sustainable brand should have a tangible competitive advantage.
2. *Consumer facing.* The consumer should be able to experience the sustainable initiatives.
3. *Core.* Sustainability changes should be tied to the brand's core business.
4. *Conversational.* Brand owners should be honest and transparent about what they are doing well and what still needs to be done in the area of sustainability.
5. *Credible.* Sustainability efforts should be in "place, functioning and measurable" before the brand owner advertises the sustainability initiatives to its consumers.[122]

A catastrophe in one's industry might give rise to a new "conversation" with the consumer regarding its understanding and the brand's intended message.

Government and Competitor Restrictions on Green Brands

Trademarks used on products that do not comply with green laws, overstate their environmental impact, or disregard continually evolving trade and labeling regulations are vulnerable to attack by government agencies, competitors or, as shown above, even the brand owners, consumers. With regard to greenwashing litigation, we are "going to see a potential tidal wave of this litigation—it's just a matter of time,"[123] and we already have begun to see such actions initiated by all three entities—government agencies, competitors, and consumers.

GOVERNMENT RESTRICTIONS ON GREEN BRANDS   In 2009, the FTC investigated the use of the term *bamboo* in advertisements[124] by four different companies claiming that their rayon clothing products were bamboo fiber.[125] The respondents used the brand names ecoKashmere, Pure Bamboo, Bamboo Comfort, and BambooBaby to advertise their products.[126] The associated advertisements made claims that the rayon products had antimicrobial properties, were environmentally friendly, or were biodegradable.[127] One of the parties involved advertised the rayon product as follows:

> *PURE BAMBOO PURE QUALITY. PURE INGENUITY. PURE CLOTHING. We are dedicated to providing high performance wear that brings together comfort, simplicity, and our own unique pure style to create an eco-friendly bamboo clothing line committed to fitting your one of a kind environmentally conscious life style.*[128]

The FTC filed its complaints against the respondents (the Bamboo Respondents), alleging in each matter violations of Section 5(a) of the FTC Act[129] as well as the Textile Fiber Products Identification Act[130] and the textile fiber related rules and regulations.[131] The Textile Fiber Products Identification Act provides in pertinent part:

> *(b) The sale, offering for sale, advertising, delivery, transportation, or causing to be transported, of any textile fiber product which has been advertised or offered for sale in commerce, and which is misbranded or falsely or deceptively advertised, within the meaning of this subchapter or the rules and regulations promulgated thereunder, is unlawful, and shall be an unfair method of competition and an unfair and deceptive act or practice in commerce under the Federal Trade Commission Act (15 U.S.C. § 41 (2006))*[132]

With regard to textile products, the Code of Federal Regulation further clarifies:

> *Words, coined words, symbols or depictions, (a) which constitute or imply the name or designation of a fiber which is not present in the product, (b) which are phonetically similar to the name or designation of such a fiber, or (c) which are only a slight variation of spelling from the name or designation of such a fiber shall not be used in such a manner as to represent or imply that such fiber is present in the product.*[133]

*   *   *

> *Any term used in advertising, including internet advertising, that constitutes or connotes the name or presence of a textile fiber is deemed to be an implication of fiber content.*[134]

The FTC stated in the complaints against the Bamboo Respondents:

> *The process used to manufacture rayon from cellulose involves hazardous chemicals. See 40 C.F.R. Part 63 ("National Emissions Standards for Hazardous Air Pollutants: Cellulose Products Manufacturing"). [H]azardous air pollutants (HAP) emitted from cellulose products manufacturing operations" include carbon disulfide, carbonyl sulfide, ethylene oxide, methanol, methyl chloride, propylene oxide, and toluene. 40 C.F.R. § 63.5480. Many plant*

sources may be used as cellulose precursors for rayon fabric, including cotton linters (short cotton fibers), wood pulp, and bamboo. Regardless of the source of the cellulose used, however, the manufacturing process involves the use of hazardous chemicals and the resulting fiber is rayon and not cotton, wood, or bamboo fiber.[135]

Accordingly, the FTC alleged, among other claims, that the Bamboo Respondents had: (1) labeled their textile fiber products bamboo and advertised the fiber content using the terms *bamboo* and *bamboo fiber* when in fact the respondents' textile fiber products were not bamboo fiber but rather rayon; and 2) manufactured misbranded textile fiber products or falsely and deceptively advertised them.[136] Therefore, the FTC complained, the Bamboo Respondents violated the Textile Act and the Textile Rules and Regulations and such violations constituted deceptive acts or practices in violation of Section 5(a) of the Federal Trade Commission Act.[137] The Bamboo Respondents settled their disputes with the FTC and agreed to advertisement modifications.[138]

However, the FTC later alleged that the Bamboo Respondents were not the only ones falsely advertising bamboo products.[139] In January 2010, the FTC issued a letter to 78 retailers notifying them of the problem and advising them that mislabeling of rayon clothing products as bamboo violated the FTC Act.[140] The FTC warned that it would assess financial penalties against those parties who advertise rayon clothing products as bamboo fiber products.[141] The FTC listed the 78 retailers receiving letters on its "Bamboo Textiles: Issues Cases & Education" web site.[142]

The Bamboo Respondents might have avoided an enforcement action by reviewing trade specific labeling requirements before describing their products as "bamboo." Accordingly, brand owners' best practice includes analyzing and complying with trade specific labeling requirements. In addition to the Textile Fiber Products Identification Act, numerous other trade-specific laws exist that address proper labeling and branding requirements. The USPTO lists some of these applicable laws in the TMEP, Appendix C.[143] Other such product-specific laws that impact branding and might be ripe for green rebranding concern fur, wool, seeds, hazardous substances, meat, poultry, foods, drugs, cosmetics, and alcohol, to name but a few.[144] It is good practice when adopting a green brand to consider the product-specific labeling requirements and relevant legislation.

COMPETITORS AND THE RESURGENCE OF "LAWFUL USE"   Just as the FTC used the Textile Identification Act as the basis for its deceptive practices and unfair competition claims, competitors too may claim that violations of trade-specific labeling requirements, like the Textile Identification Act, prevent the senior user from claiming "lawful use."

Background   The lawful use principle grew out of an interpretation of the Trademark Act by the Commissioner of Patents in a decision written over half a century ago.[145] The 1957 case *Coahoma Chemical Co. v. Smith* introduced the notion that the USPTO should refuse to register marks on the basis that their use had violated other federal statutes.[146] In *Coahoma*, the Commissioner considered as a matter of first impression whether the trademark use on goods incapable of lawful shipment in interstate commerce could acquire rights superior to those of a later user whose goods lawfully shipped.[147] He concluded that unlawful shipments of goods in commerce could not be the basis of trademark rights, relying on the general principle drawn from the law of real and personal property that an alleged owner may not obtain property rights via illegal means, commenting that, "the principle is so well-established that citation of authorities is unnecessary."[148] The Court of Custom and Patent Appeals affirmed the Commissioner's decision on other grounds, explicitly declining to rule on the lawful use basis for the cancellation.[149]

Trademark Rule 2.69 codified the *Coahoma* lawful use doctrine as follows[150]:

Compliance with other laws. When the sale or transportation of any product for which registration of a trademark is sought is regulated under an Act of Congress, the Patent and Trademark Office may make appropriate inquiry as to compliance with such Act for the sole purpose of determining lawfulness of the commerce recited in the application. 37 C.F.R. § 2.69.

The rule leaves to the examining attorney what an "appropriate inquiry" might be, and therefore gives the USPTO considerable discretion to evaluate whether owners used their marks in violation of federal law.[151]

The Office applied the lawful use principle aggressively at first in denying trademark rights to sellers whose proof of use or priority hinged on sale of products not in compliance with FDA regulations.[152] However, in the years following *Coahoma*, numerous new federal statutes and regulations applicable to all types of trademark-owning businesses became law, and the Board expressed dismay over the magnitude of the task of making reasoned judgments about lawful use.[153] "The rule has long been interpreted as *not* giving the Patent Office authority to undertake to police all of the different regulatory statutes to insure compliance therewith."[154]

Modern Application of Lawful Use Doctrine   In 1992, the Board, critical of the lawful use doctrine,[155] set forth in *General Mills Inc. v. Health Valley Foods*[156] what has become the accepted standard for modern "lawful use" claims:

[T]he better practice in trying to determine whether use of a mark is lawful under one or more of the myriad regulatory acts is to hold a use in commerce unlawful only when the issue of compliance has previously been determined (with a finding of noncompliance) by a court or government agency having competent jurisdiction under the statute involved, or where there has been a per se violation of a statute regulating the sale of a party's goods.[157]

The Board's standard places a high burden of proof on the one seeking to invalidate a registration or application based on the doctrine of lawful use and a relatively low burden on the party claiming lawful use.[158]

Perhaps because of the Board's standard and its high burden of proof, the authors of at least one treatise suggest that the lawful use issue has somewhat fallen out of favor except for cases of extreme wrongdoing.[159] It is true that a relatively small number of reported inter partes proceedings have recognized the doctrine;

parties have used the doctrine as an affirmative defense to attack the validity of an opponent's registration,[160] to challenge claimed priority dates,[161] as the basis of an allegation of abandonment on the grounds that illegal use is equivalent to nonuse,[162] and to deny a cancellation petitioner standing because the use on which petitioner based its claim of priority was illegal under the Federal Clean Air Act and various state statutes[163] or the Food, Drug, and Cosmetic Act.[164] Courts have extended the rule to services in a case holding that use of a mark in violation of the federal banking laws failed the lawful use standard.[165]

Lawful Use Applied to Green Brands   Although courts narrowly apply it, the doctrine may be sufficiently viable in the context of green labeling and advertising regulations, particularly in light of the FTC's recent reliance on the Textile Identification Act as the basis for its deceptive practices and unfair competition investigatory action.[166] One federal district court declined to apply the lawful use doctrine in another FDA labeling violation because, "although Plaintiffs may not have complied with the requirements for labeling fragrances, their transgressions are not of such a material nature and do not raise serious consumer protection concerns such that their mark should be invalidated."[167] However, the question that arises is whether consumer protection concerns in the arena of green branding have risen to the level where the lawful use doctrine should apply. Although we do not want to turn "every federal judge hearing a trademark infringement suit into a potential collateral enforcer of hundreds of labeling and licensing laws,"[168] we neither want to extend "the benefits of trademark protection to a seller based upon actions the seller took in violation of that government's own laws" nor reward the "hasty at the expense of the diligent."[169]

The 9th Circuit Court of Appeals expressly adopted the lawful use doctrine in 2007 in *CreAgri, Inc. v. USANA Health Sciences, Inc.*, where the manufacturer of Olivenol dietary supplements sued a competitor for trademark infringement, unfair competition, and unjust enrichment action.[170] Finding that "only lawful use in commerce can give rise to trademark priority,"[171] the Court granted the competitor's counterclaim, canceling the trademark registration for Olivenol because the Plaintiff could not establish lawful first use.[172]

Not long thereafter, the Northern District of California handed the Target Corporation a defeat in its effort to fend off an infringement claim by proving priority of use over the plaintiff's registered mark in its cancellation counterclaim.[173] There, Target based its claim of priority on sales of a product that did not meet the labeling requirements under the Food, Drug, and Cosmetic Act.[174]

Under current decisional law, a party opposing a green mark used on a noncompliant product under labeling laws and regulations must prove by clear and convincing evidence that (1) a court or relevant administrative agency determined the product's noncompliance, or (2) the noncompliant use was a per se violation of a statute and that the noncompliance was material.[175]

Materiality was described in *General Mills* as meaning that the use was so "tainted that, as a matter of law, it could create no trademark rights—warranting cancellation of the registration of the mark involved."[176] In *CreAgri*, the court held that the defendant met the materiality requirement showing that but for the unlawful use, the defendant would have had priority over the registrant.[177]

A party wishing to challenge an opponent's registration as based on an unlawful use should also be prepared to plead and prove that there is a close relationship between the unlawful use and the trademark.[178] The 9th Circuit in *CreAgri* neither adopted nor rejected this "nexus" requirement, which grew out of TTAB decisions,[179] because the court held that the relationship between the trademark and a mislabeled product for human consumption would readily meet any such requirement.[180] Subsequently, however, the 9th Circuit affirmed a district court's refusal to apply the lawful use rule in a case where the trademark owner illegally acquired the business to which the mark pertained and committed crimes while it owned the business on the ground that an insufficient nexus between the trademark and the illegal acts existed.[181]

Green litigation could likely link deceptiveness and lawful use claims. In 2009, an individual purchaser and consumer of FIJI water brought a class-action lawsuit in California state court against FIJI's owner, Roll International Corp., alleging that use of the mark FIJI green, a green water drop, and the slogan "Every Drop Is Green" was unlawful greenwashing in violation of numerous general California consumer protection and advertising laws.[182] Although she did not allege unlawful use under the *Coahoma* doctrine, the plaintiff's allegations had a familiar sound. According to the plaintiff, FIJI's use of such advertisement was unlawful in a broad and general sense because the product's distribution allegedly required enormous expenditures of energy harmful to the environment.[183] The Court ultimately dismissed the complaint with prejudice in 2010 for failure to state a claim.[184] However, such claims of "unlawful use" brought on the auspices of consumer protection should be the concern of brand owners in the current environmental climate. A finding that a brand owner has violated general consumer protection laws might be the "back door" to infringement and unfair competition claims seeking remedies such as trademark registration cancellation, as well as the government's method for enforcing its policies.

To avoid an unlawful use claim, one should consider what TerraChoice calls the "Seven Sins of Greenwashing," which is really a road map to consumer protection concerns and green advertisement:

1. *Sin of the Hidden Trade-off,* committed by suggesting a product is green based on an unreasonably narrow set of attributes without attention to other important environmental issues. Paper, for example, is not necessarily environmentally preferable just because it comes from a sustainably harvested forest. Other important environmental issues in the paper-making process, including energy, greenhouse gas emissions, and water and air pollution, may be equally or more significant.

2. *Sin of No Proof,* committed by an environmental claim that cannot be substantiated by easily accessible supporting information or by a reliable third-party certification. Common examples are facial or toilet tissue products that claim various percentages of postconsumer recycled content without providing any evidence.

3. *Sin of Vagueness,* committed by every claim that is so poorly defined or broad that its real meaning is likely to be misunderstood by the consumer. "All natural" is an example. Arsenic, uranium, mercury, and formaldehyde are all naturally occurring, and poisonous. "All natural" isn't necessarily green.

4. *Sin of Irrelevance,* committed by making an environmental claim that may be truthful but is unimportant or unhelpful for consumers seeking environmentally preferable products. "CFC free" is a common example, since it is a frequent claim despite the fact that chlorofluorocarbons (CFCs) are banned by law.

5. *Sin of Lesser of Two Evils,* committed by claims that may be true within the product category, but that risk distracting the consumer from the greater environmental impacts of the category as a whole. Organic cigarettes are an example of this category, as are fuel-efficient sport-utility vehicles.

6. *Sin of Fibbing,* the least frequent Sin, committed by making environmental claims that are simply false. The most common examples were products falsely claiming to be Energy Star certified or registered.

7. *Sin of Worshiping False Labels,* committed by a product that, through either words or images, gives the impression of third-party endorsement where no such endorsement actually exists—fake labels, in other words.[185]

Avoiding TerraChoice's Seven Sins may help a company to avoid claims of unlawful use. Considering the "Sins" in the context of the Green Guides, trade-specific legislation and regulations, and the current marketplace may go a long way toward avoiding government enforcement actions, consumer protection claims, or unfair competition and infringement claims by competitors. It may also give the brand owner a leg up in establishing "lawful" priority of use and establishing its claim of ownership.

Conclusion

Under the current green climate, using green branding not compliant with the Green Guides, trade-specific labeling laws, and USPTO decisional law exposes the owner to multiple risks: the inability to secure registration rights, potential government investigation and/or penalties, or the inability to enforce one's registrations against third parties, even if such registrations actually issue. For these reasons, the trademark practitioner should look beyond trademark law and policy to evaluate whether "green" brands are vulnerable to a collateral attack on their validity.

Summary of Green Branding Practice Considerations

Green Guides
1. Do the current Green Guides or in the anticipated amended Green Guides directly address the proposed mark?
   If yes, consider:
2. Should a third-party certifier substantiate the perceived environmental benefits of products or services offered under the proposed mark?
3. If yes, ensure that the certifier is legitimate.

USPTO
4. Does the dictionary definition of the words contained in the proposed mark have anything to do with the environment?
5. Have news articles discussed the environmental attributes of the product with terms found in the proposed mark?

6. Have third parties on the web discussed the environmental attributes of the product type by using terms found in the proposed mark?
7. Have numerous third parties previously sought registration of marks containing the term in the proposed mark?
8. Does the proposed mark sound "environmental"?

FTC Enforcement
  If yes to any of the foregoing questions:
  9. Review FTC guidelines, trade-specific legislations, and the Code of Federal Regulations for product-specific labeling requirements/prohibitions. For example, if the product is rayon, then check the Textile Fiber Products Identification Act. If the product is lipstick, then check the Federal Food, Drug, and Cosmetic Act.
  10. Review specimens of use/product packaging for any inadvertent or unintended environmental claims.
  11. Analyze new brands and rebrands in light of "The 5 'C's of Sustainability Branding."

Avoiding Consumer- and Competitor-Initiated Litigation
  12. Regularly review FTC guidelines, trade-specific legislation, and the Code of Federal Regulations for product-specific labeling requirements/prohibitions. Know the current marketplace and consumer mind-set for your client's products.
  13. Advise retailers to consider implementing policies for environmentally friendly products that require the manufacturers: (a) to identify relevant trade-specific legislation governing their product; (b) to secure an attorney's opinion that the products comply with relevant labeling requirements/brand selection; or (c) to secure third-party certification that product meets environmental standards in place at the time the advertiser makes the environmental marketing claims.
  14. Avoid TerraChoice's Seven Sins of Greenwashing.

Notes

[1] K. C. Jones, "Consumers Demand Greener Products, and Tech Companies Are Responding," *InformationWeek*, May 3, 2007; www.informationweek.com/news/global-cio/showArticle.jhtml?articleID=199203597 (last visited May 8, 2010).

[2] Press Release, White House, "President Obama Signs an Executive Order Focused on Federal Leadership in Environmental, Energy, and Economic Performance" (Oct. 5, 2009); available at www.whitehouse.gov/the_press_office/President-Obama-signs-an-Executive-Order-Focused-on-Federal-Leadership-in-Environmental-Energy-and-Economic-Performance (last visited May 8, 2010); Exec. Order No. 13,514, 74 Fed. Reg. 52,117 (October 8, 2009).

[3] Julie Morrison, "Students Looking for Green Practices When Choosing Local College Campuses," *Flint Journal*, January 28, 2009; available at www.mlive.com/news/flint/index.ssf/2009/01/students_looking_for_green_pra.html (last visited May 8, 2010); Barbara Mahany, "A Greener Teen," *Chicago Tribune*, April 15, 2010; available at www.chicagotribune.com/features/family/sc-fam-0415-green-teen-20100415,0,5077330,full.story (last visited May 8, 2010).

[4] For example, *In re Kmart Corp.*, No. C-4263, 2009 WL 2189691, Compl. (FTC July 15, 2009); available at www.ftc.gov/os/caselist/0823186/090717kmartcmpt.pdf; see Eric L. Lane,

"Consumer Protection in the Eco-mark Era: A Preliminary Survey and Assessment of Anti-Greenwashing Activity and Eco-mark Enforcement," 9 *J. Marshall Rev. Intell. Prop. L.* 742 (2010) (citing *Koh v. S.C. Johnson & Son, Inc.,* No. 09-cv-00927-HRL, Compl. paragraphs 5–9 (N.D. Cal. Mar. 2, 2009) [hereinafter Koh] (alleging that defendant engaged in greenwashing in marketing its Windex cleaner)).

[5]TerraChoice Environmental Marketing, Inc. is an environmental marketing and communications firm.

[6]According to TerraChoice, they tested the claims under the International Organization for Standardization (ISO), the U.S Federal Trade Commission, U.S Environmental Protection Agency, Consumers Union, and the Canadian Consumer Affairs Branch. TerraChoice Environmental Marketing Inc., "The Six Sins of Greenwashing™": A Study of Environmental Claims in North American Consumer Markets," November 2007; available at www.terrachoice.com/files/6_sins.pdf (last visited May 8, 2010) [hereinafter TerraChoice 2007].

[7]Id.

[8]TerraChoice Environmental Marketing Inc., "The Seven Sins of Greenwashing™": Environmental Claims in Consumer Markets Summary Report: North America," April 2009; available at http://sinsofgreenwashing.org/findings/greenwashing-report-2009 (last visited May 8, 2010) [hereinafter TerraChoice 2009].

[9]TerraChoice 2007, *supra* note 6.

[10]Glen A. Gunderson, "2009 Dechert LLP Annual Report on Trends in Trademarks," April 2009; www.dechert.com/library/Trends_in_Trademarks_2009.pdf (discussing the continued increase in 2008 of "green-themed marks" that Mr. Gunderson first noted in 2007).

[11]Id.

[12]Id.

[13]Brandweek, "Green Strategies Not a Fad in Retail," July 23, 2009; www.brandweek.com/bw/content_display/news-and-features/green-marketing/e3ide42830a4943f36c223a559cdbab326b (last visited May 8, 2010).

[14]TerraChoice 2009, *supra* note 8.

[15]The FTC's published resources for environmental marketing claims are available online at www.ftc.gov/bcp/menus/consumer/energy/environment.shtm (last visited May 8, 2010).

[16]Guides for the Use of Environmental Marketing Claims, 16 C.F.R. §§ 260.1–260.8 (2009) [hereinafter Green Guides].

[17]Id., § 260.2(a).

[18]Id., § 260.2(b).

[19]Id., § 260.8.

[20]Id., § 260.8.

[21]Id., § 260.2(b).

[22]15 U.S.C. § 45(a)(2) (2006).

[23]15 U.S.C. § 45(a)(1) (2006); see also Green Guides, *supra* note 16, § 260.5.

[24]Green Guides, *supra* note 16, § 260.3.

[25]Id., § 260.5.

[26]Id.

[27]Id., § 260.6(a).

[28]Id., § 260.6(b).

[29]Id., § 260.6(c).

[30]Id., § 260.6(d).

[31]Id., § 260.6(b).

[32]Id., § 260.7(c).

[33]Id., § 260.7(d).

[34]Id., § 260.7(e).

[35]Id., § 260.7(f).

[36]Id., § 260.7(g).

[37]Id., § 260.7(h).

[38]Id., § 260.7(a), Example 1.

[39]Gunderson, *supra* note 9.

[40]TerraChoice 2007, *supra* note 5; TerraChoice 2009, *supra* note 7.

[41]EPA.gov, Environmentally Preferable Purchasing (EPP), http://yosemite1.epa.gov/oppt/eppstand2.nsf/Pages/Standards.html?Open (last visited May 10, 2010) [hereinafter EPP] (stating "The criteria utilized to evaluate products as well as those that have attained certification are listed on their Web site.").

[42]Id.

[43]Pendleton Woolen Mills: Company History, www.pendleton-usa.com/custserv/custserv.jsp?pageName=CompanyHistory&parentName=Heritage (last visited May 10, 2010).

[44]EPP, *supra* note 41.

[45]Id.

[46]Green Guides, *supra* note 16, § 260.7(a), Example 5.

[47]On April 18, 2010, the author conducted the following base search: *earth*[bi,ti] and *smart* [bi,ti] and registrant[on] and live[ld] on publicly available USPTO TESS trademark database and retrieved 20 results. Trademark Search—TESS, http://tess2.uspto.gov (search results on file with author).

[48]Green Guides, *supra* note 16, § 260.7(b)(1)-(2).

[49]Green Guides, *supra* note 15, § 260.7(b).

[50]Id.

[51]Id., § 260.7(b).

[52]See *Kmart Corp.*, supra note 4; *In re Tender Corp.*, No. C-4261, 2009 WL 2189692, Compl. (FTC, July 13, 2009), available at www.ftc.gov/os/caselist/0823188/090717tendercmpt.pdf; *In re Dyna-E Int'l Inc.*, No. C-9336, 2009 WL 2810351, Compl. (FTC, May 20, 2009), available at www.ftc.gov/os/adjpro/d9336/index.shtm.

[53]*Kmart Corp.*, *supra* note 4.

[54]Id.

[55]Id.

[56]Press Release, The Clorox Company, "Green Works Natural Cleaners and Sierra Club Celebrate Two-Year Anniversary; Doubling of Natural Cleaning Category" (March 1, 2010); available at http://investors.thecloroxcompany.com/releasedetail.cfm?releaseid=448538 (last visited May 10, 2010).

[57]Id.

[58]Green Guides, *supra* note 16, § 260.7(d), Example 2.

[59]USPTO Design Search Code Manual is available at http://tess2.uspto.gov/tmdb/dscm/index. htm (last visited May 8, 2010).

[60]On April 18, 2010, the author conducted the following base search: 241719[dc] and live[ld] on publicly available USPTO TESS trademark database. Trademark Search—TESS, http://tess2. uspto.gov (search results on file with author).

[61]See Green Guides, *supra* note 16, § 260.7(d) (stating "Unqualified claims of recyclability for a product or package may be made if the entire product or package, excluding minor incidental components, is recyclable. For products or packages that are made of both recyclable and non-recyclable components, the recyclable claim should be adequately qualified to avoid consumer deception about which portions or components of the product or package are recyclable.").

[62]Id., § 260.7(d) n.4 (discussing special issues arising from recyclable batteries).

[63]Id., § 260.7(d).

[64]Green Guides, *supra* note 16.

[65]FTC.gov, Reporter Resources: The FTC's Green Guides, www.ftc.gov/opa/reporter/ greengds.shtm (last visited May 8, 2010).

[66]*It's Too Easy Being Green: Defining Fair Green Marketing Principles: Hearing Before the Subcomm. on Commerce, Trade, and Consumer Protection of the H. Comm. on Energy and Commerce*, 111th Cong. (2009) (statement of James A. Kohm, Associate Director of the Enforcement Division in the Bureau of Consumer Protection at the Federal Trade Commission); available at www.ftc.gov/os/2009/06/P954501greenmarketing.pdf (last visited May 8, 2010). The FTC planned to amend the Green Guides in early 2009, but it determined in May 2009 that it needed further input from consumers regarding their understanding of additional environmental claims, specifically their understanding of such terms as *green eco-friendly, sustainable, renewable,* and *carbon neutral.* As of publication, the FTC still has not issued the anticipated revised Green Guides.

[67]*It's Too Easy Being Green, supra* note 66.

[68]See U.S. Pat. & Trademark Office, U.S. Department of Commerce, Trademark Manual of Examining Procedure § 1209.03(m) (6th ed. 1st rev. 2009) [hereinafter TMEP] (citing *In re CyberFinancial.Net, Inc.*, 65 U.S.P.Q.2d 1789, 1792 (TTAB 2002) (stating "Applicant seeks to register the generic term 'bonds,' which has no source-identifying significance in connection with applicant's services, in combination with the top level domain indicator '.com,' which also has no source-identifying significance. And combining the two terms does not create a term capable of identifying and distinguishing applicant's services."); *In re Martin Container, Inc.*, 65 U.S.P.Q.2d 1058, 1061 (TTAB 2002) (holding "[N]either the generic term nor the domain indicator has the capability of functioning as an indication of source, and combining the two does not result in a compound term that has somehow acquired this capability.")).

[69]Id., § 1209.03(m) (citing *In re Steelbuilding.com*, 415 F.3d 1293, 1297 (Fed. Cir. 2005) (reversing the TTAB's generic refusal of the term Steelbuilding.Com, noting that in "rare instances, a term that is not distinctive by itself may acquire some additional meaning from the addition of a TLD, such as '.com,' '.net,' etc. In those unusual circumstances, the addition of the TLD can show Internet-related distinctiveness, intimating some 'Internet feature' of the item." (internal citation omitted); *but see Advertise.com, Inc. v. AOL Adver., Inc.*, 616 F.3d 974, 979 (9th Cir. 2010) wherein the Court, distinguishing *Steelbuilding.com*, found that the addition of ".com" to "advertise" for online advertising services did not change the generic significance of the term advertise.

[70]15 U.S.C. § 1052(e)(1) (2006).

[71]TMEP, *supra* note 68 § 1209.01(b).

[72]Id., § 710.01.

[73]See *In re ObjectStyle, LLC*, 2008 WL 1741887 (TTAB, April 8, 2008) (holding mark not merely descriptive for software consulting services because examiner's burden not met where the examiner offered "several" internet cites showing use of the mark OBJECTSYLE with "object-oriented system engineering tools"); *In re Jones Investment Co. Inc.*, 2009 WL 273242 (TTAB, January 21, 2009) (nonprecedential) (stating the "examining attorney bears the burden of showing that a mark is merely descriptive of the relevant goods and/or services.") (citing *In re Merrill Lynch, Pierce, Fenner, and Smith, Inc.*, 828 F.2d 1567, 1571 (Fed. Cir. 1987) (stating "It is incumbent on the Board to balance the evidence of public understanding of the mark against the degree of descriptiveness encumbering the mark, and to resolve reasonable doubt in favor of the applicant, in accordance with practice and precedent.")).

[74]See *H. Marvin Ginn Corp. v. International Ass'n of Fire Chiefs, Inc.*, 782 F.2d 987, 990 (Fed. Cir. 1986) [hereinafter *Marvin Ginn*].

[75]Id.

[76]See TMEP, *supra* note 68, § 1209.01(c)(i) (citing *Marvin Ginn*, *supra* note 74).

[77]Id., § 1209.01(c)(i) (citing *Marvin Ginn*, *supra* note 74).

[78]Id., § 1209.01(c)(i). The USPTO finally refuses a mark as generic either for failure to show acquired distinctiveness under 15 U.S.C.A. § 1052(f) (2006) or for being "incapable" of registration on the Supplemental Register under 15 USC § 1091 (2006).

[79]*In re Cenveo Corp.*, 2009 WL 4086560 (TTAB, September 30, 2009); *In re Bargoose Home Textiles Inc.*, 2009 WL 1719383 (TTAB, May 27, 2009); *Jones Investment*, *supra* note 73.

[80]*Jones Investment*, *supra* note 73.

[81]*Bargoose*, *supra* note 79.

[82]*Cenveo*, *supra* note 79.

[83]*Jones Investment*, *supra* note 73, at *3.

[84]Id., at *3 (stating "The individual words comprising applicant's mark have commonly understood meanings that are merely descriptive for clothing. We do not believe, however, that the specific combination of the words Green Indigo results in a designation which, when considered in its entirety, is merely descriptive of applicant's goods.").

[85]*Bargoose*, *supra* note 79, at 5.

[86]Id., at 4.

[87]Id., at 4.

[88]Id., at 4.

[89]Id., at 5.

[90]*Cenveo*, *supra* note 79.

[91]*Marvin Ginn*, *supra* note 74.

[92]*Cenveo*, *supra* note 79, at 4.

[93]Id., at 4–5.

[94]Id., at 5.

[95]Id.

[96]Id.

[97]Id.

[98]Id.

[99]Id., at 6 (finding that a compound word mark is "a word composed of two or more base morphemes, whether hyphenated or not: English compounds are usually distinguished from phrases by reduced stress on one of the elements and by changes in meaning,") (citing "compound word mark," Merriam-Webster New World College Dictionary (2009), www .yourdictionary.com/compound (September 18, 2009). The Board also stated, "The Board may take judicial notice of dictionary definitions including online dictionaries which exist in printed format." See *In re CyberFinancial.Net Inc.*, 65 U.S.P.Q.2d 1789) (TTAB, 2002); *University of Notre Dame du Lac v. J. C. Gourmet Food Imports Co., Inc.*, 213 U.S.P.Q. 594 (TTAB, 1982), *aff'd*, 703 F.2d 1372 (Fed. Cir. 1983).

[100]Id., at 3. The Board considered the evidence that the examiner made of record "to demonstrate that the relevant public understands that 'green-key' primarily refers to keycards made of environmentally friendly materials." A review of the evidence considered by the Board is useful to acquire a sense of what evidence is considered relevant in a genericness determination. A detailed discussion of the evidence can be found in the case decision, in particular the type of definitions and web site excerpts showing third-party use and applicant's own use.

[101]Id., at 6.

[102]See *In re Merrill Lynch, Pierce, Fenner, & Smith, Inc.*, 828 F.2d 1567, 1570–71 (Fed. Cir. 1987) (reversing the Board's decision that Cash Management Account was generic for stock brokerage services and related financial services finding that seven generic uses was insufficient to establish genericness).

[103]*In re Calera Corporation*, 2010 WL 1233877 (TTAB, March 24, 2010).

[104]Id.

[105]Id., at 5.

[106]See TMEP, *supra* note 68, § 1212.02(e) (citing Section 6(a) of the Trademark Act, 15 U.S.C. §1056(a) (2006), that states, in part, "The Director may require the applicant to disclaim an unregistrable component of a mark otherwise registrable.").

[107]See 15 U.S.C. § 1052 (f) (2006) (stating "Except as expressly excluded in subsections (a), (b), (c), (d), (e)(3), and (e)(5) of this section, nothing herein shall prevent the registration of a mark used by the applicant which has become distinctive of the applicant's goods in commerce. The Director may accept as prima facie evidence that the mark has become distinctive, as used on or in connection with the applicant's goods in commerce, proof of substantially exclusive and continuous use thereof as a mark by the applicant in commerce for the five years before the date on which the claim of distinctiveness is made. Nothing in this section shall prevent the registration of a mark which, when used on or in connection with the goods of the applicant, is primarily geographically deceptively misdescriptive of them, and which became distinctive of the applicant's goods in commerce before the date of the enactment of the North American Free Trade Agreement Implementation Act. A mark which would be likely to cause dilution by blurring or dilution by tarnishment under section 43(c), may be refused registration only pursuant to a proceeding brought under section 13. A registration for a mark which would be likely to cause dilution by blurring or dilution by tarnishment under section 43(c), may be canceled pursuant to a proceeding brought under either section 14 or section 24.").

[108]*Calera, supra* note 103, at 5.

[109]On April 25, 2010, the author conducted the following base search: *sustainable*[bi,ti] and "020"[cc] and live[ld] and retrieved 221 results on publicly available USPTO TESS trademark database. Trademark Search—TESS, http://tess2.uspto.gov (search results on file with author). On April 25, 2010, the author searched Google for (sustainable and household goods) and

retrieved 345,000 results. On April 25, 2010, the author searched Westlaw's NEWSUS-PRO database for the terms *sustainable* and *household goods* and retrieved 205 results. On April 25, 2010, the author searched Onelook.com for the term *sustainable* and retrieved 24 dictionary definitions, one under the heading "Science" from http://oregonstate.edu/instruct/anth370/gloss.html that read: "sustainable—using natural and human resources in a way that does not jeopardize the opportunities of future generations."

[110]SamsClub.com, "Sustainability Simple Steps to Saving Green," www.samsclub.com/sams/pagedetails/content.jsp?pageName=sustainability-symbol (last visited May 11, 2010).

[111]Id.

[112]SCJohnson.com, "Our Greenlist Process," www.scjohnson.com/en/commitment/focus-on/greener-products/greenlist.aspx (last visited May 10, 2010).

[113]Id.

[114]U.S. Trademark Registration No. 3522370 (filed March 23, 2007) (registered October 21, 2008).

[115]*Koh v. S. C. Johnson & Son, Inc.,* No. C-09–00927 (N.D. Cal. Jan. 6, 2010) (Order denying Def.'s Motion); *but see Hinjos v. Kohl's Corp.,* CV 10-07590 ODW AGRX, 2010 WL 4916647 (C.D. Cal. Dec. 1, 2010) wherein the Court, distinguishing *Koh,* found that the claim of lost money or property did not involve a price discount; *Hill v. Roll Int'l Corp.,* A128698, 2011 WL 2041574 (Cal. Ct. App. May 26, 2011) wherein the Court, distinguishing *Koh,* found significant differences between the *Koh* labels and those at issue in *Hill.*

[116]Id.

[117]2 J. Thomas McCarthy, *McCarthy on Trademarks and Unfair Competition* § 11:55 (4th ed., 2004) [hereinafter McCarthy].

[118]Id.

[119]Id.

[120]Maddock Douglas—Agency of Innovation®, "Mapping the Future of Green Innovation MD's Sustainability Leadership Perspective, Sustainability Leadership Perspective 2010," www.maddockdouglas.com/sustainability-leadership-perspective-2010 (then follow "Download a PDF version of this report").

[121]Id.

[122]Maddock Douglas—Agency of Innovation®, *supra* note 120.

[123]Fiona Smith, "Wave of Litigation Over 'Greenwashing' Poised to Break," *Daily Journal,* February 10, 2010; available at http://wflc.org/inthenews/forestcertnews/2.10.10 (quoting Neal Marder, Chair of Winston & Strawn's Litigation Group in Los Angeles).

[124]*In the Matter of SAMI DESIGNS, LLC,* No. C-4279, Compl. (FTC Aug. 11, 2009), available at www.ftc.gov/os/caselist/0823194/090811samicmpt.pdf; *In the Matter of CSE, INC.,* No. C-4280, Compl. (FTC Aug.11, 2009), available at www.ftc.gov/os/caselist/0823181/090811madmod cmpt.pdf; *In the Matter of Pure Bamboo, LLC,* No. C-4278, Compl. (FTC Aug. 11, 2009), available at www.ftc.gov/os/caselist/0823193/090811purebamboocmpt.pdf; *In the Matter of The M Group, Inc.,* No. 9340, Compl. (FTC Aug. 11, 2009), available at www.ftc.gov/os/adjpro/d9340/090811bamboosacmpt.pdf.

[125]Id.

[126]Id.

[127]Id.

[128]See *Pure Bamboo, supra* note 124.

[129]Id., Part A.

[130]15 U.S.C. § 70 (2006).

[131]16 C.F.R. § 303 (2009).

[132]15 U.S.C. § 70a(b) (2006).

[133]16 C.F.R. § 303.18 (2009).

[134]16 C.F.R. § 303.40 (2009).

[135]*SAMI DESIGNS, supra* note 124.

[136]Id.

[137]Id.

[138]See, generally, FTC.gov, "Bamboo" Textiles Issues, Cases, & Education, www.ftc.gov/
bamboo (last visited May 9, 2010).

[139]Press Release, Federal Trade Commission, "FTC Warns 78 Retailers, Including Wal-Mart,
Target, and Kmart, to Stop Labeling and Advertising Rayon Textile Products as 'Bamboo'"
(February 23, 2010); *available at*www.ftc.gov/opa/2010/02/bamboo.shtm (last visited May 9,
2010).

[140]FTC.gov, Model Letter, www.ftc.gov/os/2010/02/100203model-bamboo-letter.pdf (last visited May 9, 2010).

[141]Id.

[142]FTC.gov, List of Companies, www.ftc.gov/os/2010/02/100203company-letter-recipients.pdf
(last visited May 9, 2010); see also *supra* note 138.

[143]TMEP, *supra* note 68, app. C.

[144]Id.

[145]*Coahoma Chemical Co., Inc. v. Smith v. Howerton Gowen Company, Inc.,* 113 U.S.P.Q. 413
(Comm'r Pat. & Trademarks 1957) [hereinafter *Coahoma I*], *aff'd,* 264 F.2d 916 (1959) [herein-
after *Coahoma II*].

[146]Id., *Coahoma I.*

[147]Id., at 417.

[148]Id., at 418.

[149]Id., *Coahoma II,* at 920.

[150]*Western Worldwide Enterprises Group, Inc. v. Quiqdao Brewery.* 17 U.S.P.Q. 1137, 1990 WL
354566 (TTAB, 1990).

[151]However, the USPTO formalized the shift away from frequent issuance of Rule 2.69 inquiries during ex parte examination of applications, discussed below, in Examination Guide No.
1–91, issued March 28, 1991, of the Office's position that it would cease making routine inquiries regarding compliance with federal labeling requirements. This Guide was incorporated
into the latest edition of the TMEP, *supra* note 68, § 907.

[152]For example, an examining attorney in one case, dissatisfied with the applicant's response
to a Rule 2.69 inquiry, went so far as to secure the opinion of the General Counsel of the Food
and Drug Division of the Department of Health and Human Services that the submitted label
did not comply with the requirements of the Food, Drug, and Cosmetic Act. *In re Garden of
Eatin' Inc.,* 216 U.S.P.Q. 355 (TTAB 1982) *In re Taylor,* 133 U.S.P.Q. 490 (TTAB, 1962) (sandwiches); see also *In re Pepcom Industries, Inc.,* 192 U.S.P.Q. 4100 (TTAB, 1976)(soft drinks).
The Board refused an applicant whose specimens for packaged food items did not list the
ingredients as required by the food labeling regulations for want of proof of lawful use in

commerce. In another case, *In re Cook*, 188 U.S.P.Q. 284 (TTAB, 1975), sales of meat in Ohio to out-of-state customers did not meet the "in commerce" requirement where interstate sales would not be legal due to noncompliance with FDA regulations. The USPTO used the "lawful use" doctrine to construe lack of compliance with federal regulations as a *de facto* admission that the applicant did not meet the "in commerce" requirement.

[153]The Board articulated the reasons for its reticence in *Satinine v. P.A.B.*: "During the years since the *Coahoma* decision, the Board has had cases involving the lawfulness of use under such statutes as the Federal Food, Drug, and Cosmetic Act, the Federal Meat Inspection Act, the Federal Insecticide, Fungicide, and Rodenticide Act, and the Federal Clean Air Act. Due to a proliferation of federal regulatory acts in recent years, there is (sic) now an almost endless number of such acts which the Board might in the future be compelled to interpret in order to determine whether a particular use in commerce is lawful. Inasmuch as we have little or no familiarity with most of these acts, there is a serious question as to the advisability of our attempting to adjudicate whether a party's use in commerce is in compliance with the particular regulatory act or acts which may be applicable thereto." *Satinine Societa in Nome Collettivo di S.A. e M. Usellini v. P.A.B. Produits et Appareils de Beaute*, 209 U.S.P.Q. 958 (TTAB 1981).

[154]*Pennwalt Corporation v. Sentry Chemical Company*, 219 U.S.P.Q. 542, 553 (TTAB, 1982) (citing cancellation of a registration, no matter how minor or harmless the violation may be . . . serves the interests of neither justice nor common sense.").

[155]See *General Mills Inc. v. Health Valley Foods*, 24 U.S.P.Q.2d 1270 (TTAB 1992) (stating "A blanket policy of finding every possible technical violation to result in *Foods, Inc.*, 6 U.S.P.Q.2d. 2045 (TTAB 1988).

[156]Id. (finding the opponent failed to demonstrate to the Board's satisfaction that the lack of nutritional labeling on token shipments of the Opponent's Fiber One cereal was a material violation of the FDA requirements).

[157]Id., at 1273–1274 (citing *Satinine, supra* note 153; *Kellogg Co. v. New Generation In re Stellar International, Inc.*, 159 U.S.P.Q. 48, 51 (TTAB 1968); *Armour & Co.*, 180 U.S.P.Q. 351 (TTAB 1973); *In re Garden of Eatin' Inc.*, 216 USPQ 355 (TTAB 1982)).

[158]*General Mills, supra* note 155 (stating "It is clear from even a cursory review of the relevant labeling regulatory statutes that many requirements are purely technical in nature and that violations of such requirements may be relatively harmless and may be subsequently corrected.").

[159]Louis Altman and Malla Pollack, 3 *Callmann on Unfair Comp.*, Tr. & Mono. § 20:15 (Thomson Reuters/ West 4th ed., 2011).

[160]*Dessert Beauty, Inc. v. Fox*, 617 F.Supp.2d 185, 190 (S.D. N.Y. 2007), *aff'd*, 329 F. App'x. 333 (2d Cir. 2009) (cancellation petition failed where a reasonable jury could find that the registrant's labeling did not violate the Food Drug and Cosmetic Act, or that such violation was immaterial); *The Clorox Company v. Armour-Dial, Inc.* 214 U.S.P.Q. 850 (TTAB, 1983) (applicant alleged opposer did not comply with labeling requirements, but failed to carry the burden of proof for its affirmative defense).

[161]*Lane Capital Mgmt., Inc. v. Lane Capital Mgmt., Inc.*, 15 F.Supp.2d 389 (S.D. N.Y. 1998), *aff'd.*, 192 F.3d 337, (2d Cir. 1999) ("lawful use" waived because not properly raised as an affirmative defense); *but see Dessert Beauty, Inc. v. Mara Fox*, 617 F.Supp.2d 185 (S.D. N.Y. 2007), *aff'd*, 329 F. App'x. 333 (2d Cir. 2009) wherein the *Dessert* court declined to follow *Lane*, finding that the failure to raise the "lawful use" defense was not due to bad faith and that the defendants could assert the defense without undue prejudice to the plaintiff.

[162] *Satinine, supra* note 153.

[163] *Geraghty Dyno-Tuned Products, Inc. v. Clayton Manufacturing Company*, 190 U.S.P.Q. 508 (TTAB, 1976).

[164] *Erva Pharmaceuticals, Inc. v. American Cyanamid Co.*, 755 F.Supp. 36 (D.P.R. 1991) (infringement plaintiff failed to establish priority of use of drug name due to violation of drug labeling law and regulations); Relatively minor labeling infractions, such as failure to list the quantity of an ingredient, have been the basis of refusal of registration. See *In re Stellar International, Inc.*, 159 U.S.P.Q. 48, 1968 WL 8159 (TTAB 1968) (failure of applicant to list quantity of contents of mouth freshener on label violated FDCA labeling rules and therefore was an "unlawful use"). But see *Dessert Beauty, Inc. v. Mara Fox*, 617 F. Supp. 2d 185 (S.D. N.Y. 2007), aff'd, 329 F. App'x. 333 (2d Cir. 2009) (summary judgment based on unlawful use denied where a reasonable finder of fact could conclude that non-compliance with requirement to list perfume contents in fluid measurements was non-material).

[165] *Intrawest Financial Corp. v. Western National Bank of Denver*, 610 F. Supp. 950 (D. Colo. 1985).

[166] Id., Part C-1.

[167] *Advertising to Women, Inc. v. Gianni Versace S.P.A.*, 2000 WL 1230461 (N.D. Ill. Aug. 24, 2000).

[168] 3 McCarthy, *supra* note 117, at § 19:124.

[169] *CreAgri, Inc. v. USANA Health Sciences, Inc.*, 474 F.3d 626, 630 (9th Cir. 2007); *but see Dessert Beauty, Inc. v. Mara Fox*, 617 F.Supp.2d 185 (S.D.N.Y. 2007), aff'd, 329 F. App'x. 333 (2d Cir. 2009) wherein the Second Circuit found that, unlike *CreAgri*, defendants in *Dessert* failed to offer compelling evidence to demonstrate significant non-compliance.

[170] Id.

[171] Id. (registrant could not rely on sale of dietary supplement that was inaccurately labeled).

[172] Id., at 633–634.

[173] *GoClear LLC v. Target Corporation*, 2009 WL 160624 (N.D. Cal. 2009).

[174] *GoClear*, supra note 172, at *2. (The Court agreed with Plaintiff GoClear that Target did not have "lawful use" because Target's labels violated the Food Drug and Cosmetics Act.)

[175] *Dessert Beauty, supra* note 160 (cancellation petition failed where a reasonable jury could find that the registrant's labeling did not violate the Food Drug and Cosmetic Act, or that such violation was immaterial).

[176] *General Mills, supra* note 158, at *3.

[177] *CreAgri, Inc., supra* note 169, at 633.

[178] Id., at 631–632.

[179] See, for example, *Satinine, supra* note 153, at 967; *General Mills, supra* note 155, at 967.

[180] *CreAgri, Inc., supra* note 168 at 631–632 ("While it may be possible to conceive of a situation in which violation of a law in connection with a trademarked product would have no effect on the rights inuring in that trademark, the nexus between a misbranded product and that product's name, particularly one designed for human consumption, is sufficiently close to justify withholding trademark protection for that name until and unless the misbranding is cured.").

[181] *Cash Processing Services, LLC v. Ambient Entertainment, Inc.*, 320 Fed. Appx. 494 (9th Cir. 2008) (affirming district court's grant of preliminary injunction to owner of the mark Mustang

Ranch over objections by defendant that the plaintiff's predecessor's use of the mark had been illegal.).

[182]*Anaya Hill v. Roll Int'l Corp.*, No. CGC-09–487547, (San Francisco County Super. Ct. March 30, 2010).

[183]Id.

[184]Id.

[185]"The Seven Sins of Greenwashing," found at http://sinsofgreenwashing.org/findings/the-seven-sins/ (last accessed September 30, 2010).

CHAPTER 16

The Financial Reporting Impact of Intellectual Property Activity

James Donohue

Charles River Associates, Inc.

Mark A. Spelker

J. H. Cohn LLP[1]

I n addition to considering the strategic and legal implications of intellectual property (IP) activity, decision makers will also have to consider the resulting financial accounting and reporting consequences.[2] While often an afterthought, IP activities frequently require financial accounting entries and disclosures that are reflected in company's financial statements. How intellectual property activity is treated depends on many factors, including how the transaction was structured and documented. Changing accounting guidance, which has increased IP-related guidance and disclosures, also complicates this area. Understanding how IP activities are accounted for from a financial reporting perspective can be an important consideration when evaluating intellectual property transactions.

IP Activity

In many organizations, IP activities are occurring every day in various areas. While much focus is often on obvious IP activities, such as patent licenses or sales, IP activities also include many less obvious items. For example, daily research and development (R&D) work can have various financial accounting–related consequences.

While perhaps impossible to list them all, general categories of IP activities can include licensing and sales activity, R&D, IP filings and prosecution, litigation activity, settlements, mergers and acquisitions, and donations or abandonment. Each of these categories can include various components that require some form of financial statement recognition. For example, licensing activity could include the receipt of up-front and ongoing royalty payments that will immediately, or eventually, be recorded as revenue. The entity paying the up-front and royalty amounts might record the payment as an expense, or perhaps in some circumstances, capitalize the costs on the balance sheet as an intangible asset.

Another way to view these IP categories is to consider the IP life cycle. The life cycle of a patent, for example, would begin with the R&D work that is done to develop the concept. Legal costs would be incurred to file an application and perhaps obtain an issued patent. Various application and maintenance fees would be incurred as well. The issued patent could be involved in various IP events during its lifetime. Some patents might simply sit in the portfolio and protect a product, while other patents might be licensed or sold individually, as a portfolio, or as part of the larger business group or organization. The patent may also be used in a patent infringement litigation that could result in a variety of outcomes, including litigation expenses, a settlement, a damage award, or the finding that the patent was invalid or not infringed. Finally, the patent might be donated, abandoned, or, like many patents, simply expire uneventfully.[3]

These IP life cycle activities could each require some form of financial accounting recognition in the owner's financial statements. Given the complexities of financial accounting for each of these activities, we use the life cycle to illustrate the potential financial accounting treatments and accounting guidance that could be relevant to each intellectual property event. In the following sections, we first review some examples of relevant IP accounting guidance and then review how some public companies have accounted for certain IP activities.

Relevant IP Accounting Guidance

Accounting guidance that is relevant to IP ranges from broad concepts statements to specific guidance that explicitly discusses IP-related activity. While clearly not all inclusive, common IP accounting guidance includes[4]:

- Financial Accounting Standards Board (FASB) Concepts Statement No. 6, Elements of Financial Statements.
- Statement of Financial Accounting Standards (SFAS) No. 2, Research and Development (FASB ASC 730).
- SFAS No. 5, Accounting for Contingencies (FASB ASC 450).
- SFAS No. 141(R) (revised 2007), Business Combinations (FASB ASC 805).
- SFAS No. 142, Goodwill and Other Intangible Assets (FASB ASC 350).
- SFAS No. 144, Accounting for the Impairment or Disposal of Long-Lived Asset (FASB ASC 360).
- SFAS No. 157, Fair Value Measurement (FASB ASC 820).
- SEC Staff Accounting Bulletin 104, Topic 13 Revenue Recognition (FASB ASC 605).
- Emerging Issues Task Force Issue No. 00-21, Revenue Arrangements with Multiple Deliverables (FASB ASC 605-25).
- Emerging Issues Task Force Issue No. 08-7, Accounting for Defensive Intangible Assets (FASB ASC 350-30).

FASB Concepts Statements are intended to establish objectives and fundamentals that could support the development of financial accounting and reporting standards. While Concepts Statements do not establish GAAP, they are often useful tools when analyzing accounting issues.

FASB Concepts Statement No. 6 defines the core elements of financial statements: assets, liabilities, equity, revenues, expenses, gains, and losses. "Assets are probable future economic benefits obtained or controlled by a particular entity as a result of past transactions or events."[5] An asset has three essential characteristics: (a) it embodies a probable future benefit that involves a capacity, singly or in combination with other assets, to contribute directly or indirectly to future net cash inflows, (b) a particular entity can obtain the benefit and control others' access to it, and (c) the transaction or other event giving rise to the entity's right to or control of the benefit has already occurred.

With respect to intellectual property, the definition of an asset can become relevant when deciding whether payments for intellectual property rights will be considered assets or expenses. For instance, the purchase of license rights or a patent portfolio could fit this definition and be deemed an asset. A patent portfolio could embody a probable future economic benefit that could contribute to future cash flow to the buyer. The buyer could obtain that benefit and control others' access to the patent portfolio. The purchase of the patent portfolio could be subject to an agreement and payments that have already occurred.

Revenues are defined as "inflows or other enhancements of assets of an entity or settlements of its liabilities (or a combination of both) from delivering or producing goods, rendering services, or other activities that constitute the entity's ongoing major or central operations. Revenues represent actual or expected cash inflows (or the equivalent) that have occurred or will eventuate as a result of the entity's ongoing major or central operations. Similarly, the transactions and events from which revenues arise and the revenues themselves are in many forms and are called by various names—for example, output, deliveries, sales, fees, interest, dividends, royalties, and rent—depending on the kinds of operations involved and the way revenues are recognized." For example, revenues derived from licensing patents are often paid in cash and called royalties.

Staff Accounting Bulletin (SAB) No. 104, Topic 13 (ASC 605) discusses revenue recognition related accounting guidance and includes some specific references to IP. In general, SAB No. 104 (ASC 605) addresses the need for revenue to be realizable and earned. Revenue is considered to be realizable and earned when all of the following criteria are met:

- Persuasive evidence of an arrangement exists.
- Delivery has occurred or services have been rendered.
- The seller's price to the buyer is fixed or determinable.
- Collectibility is reasonably assured.

SAB No. 104 (ASC 605) is often cited when evaluating IP licensing income. When IP is licensed, the licensors often represent and warrant that they are licensing a valid patent that they will defend and maintain into the future. Although this could be considered a future obligation, and thus require the deferral of revenues, a SAB No. 104

(ASC 605) example suggests that this common representation and warrant is not considered a separate deliverable and would therefore not necessarily delay the recognition of revenue.[6]

SFAS 141 (ASC 805) and SFAS 142 (ASC 350) were issued in 2001 and, among other things, materially changed financial reporting and disclosures for goodwill and intangible assets. These statements are generally credited with increasing intangible asset disclosure and requiring additional intangible asset recognition and impairment testing.

SFAS 141 (ASC 805) focused on financial reporting for business combinations and specifically addressed the need for better information regarding intangible assets. For example, SFAS 141 (ASC 805) provided explicit criteria for recognition of intangible assets apart from goodwill in a business combination and expanded intangible asset disclosures. Under SFAS 141 (ASC 805), intangible assets were recognized as assets separate from goodwill when they arose from contractual or legal rights (regardless of whether it was separable from the entity), or if it was capable of being separated from the entity and sold, transferred, licensed, rented or exchanged. SFAS 141 (ASC 805) also provided specific examples of intangible assets (which included many forms of intellectual property) that should be recognized as intangible assets when acquired in a business combination. Since the intangible asset guidance in SFAS 141 (ASC 805) required a business combination to be applicable (i.e., intangible assets are, by and large, only recorded as assets after they are acquired), the mergers and acquisition boom of the last several years effectively placed billions of dollars in IP and other intangible assets on corporate balance sheets.

SFAS 141(R) (ASC 805) was issued in December 2007, and with respect to intangible assets, generally carried over the above fundamental concepts from SFAS 141 (ASC 805).[7] Some notable exceptions included in-process research and development (IPRD), which is now recognized as an intangible asset (IA) and remains an asset until it is either found to be impaired or fully amortized. Prior to SFAS 141(R) (ASC 805), IPRD was fair-valued at the time of the acquisition, but immediately expensed on the income statement.

SFAS 142 (ASC 350) addresses financial accounting and reporting for IAs after a business combination, and for IAs acquired individually or in a group.[8] SFAS 142 (ASC 350) discusses specific IA concepts, including initial recognition and measurement, useful life, amortization, and testing for impairment. IA financial statement presentation and disclosure are also discussed in SFAS 142 (ASC 350). Determining whether to impair an indefinite-lived trademark, for example, is addressed in SFAS 142 (ASC 350).

SFAS 144 (ASC 360) addresses financial accounting and reporting for the impairment of finite, long-lived assets, which would include IP and other IAs. For example, a patent portfolio or a license agreement with a finite life that was acquired and recorded as an asset on the balance sheet would be subject to SFAS 144 (ASC 360) impairment tests. The impairment tests described in SFAS 144 (ASC 360) require a two-step process. The first step compares the IA's carrying value with its projected undiscounted cash flows to determine whether an IA's value is recoverable. This first step is often done when events or changes in circumstances indicate that an asset's carrying value may not be recoverable (sometimes referred to as "triggering" events").[9] If not recoverable (i.e., the carrying value is greater than the undiscounted cash flows), the second step compares the IA's carrying value with its fair value to determine the amount of the impairment.

The Securities and Exchange Commission staff has also commented on IP events during various speeches. These speeches are a potential accounting resource and typically provide specific examples. For instance, a December 10, 2007, speech by Eric West, Associate Chief Accountant, Office of the Chief Accountant, U.S. Securities and Exchange Commission, discussed accounting for litigation settlement.[10] Litigation settlements are a common IP event and often include multiple elements. The speech included a discussion regarding the need to identify and consider each accounting component associated with litigation settlements. The hypothetical example used in the speech included litigation settlement, covenant not to sue, and patent license (granted and received) components.

With respect to the patent license received component, the speech noted that the recognition of a patent license as an IA "depends upon, among other things, whether the company has exclusive use of the patents or the right to sell or transfer them. When a company doesn't have these rights, we believe that it may be more appropriate to characterize and value them as a prepaid royalty."

For the patent license granted component, the proper treatment could depend on how the licenses are expected to be used. If the licenses provided are expected to be used by the licensee in its operations, it may be appropriate for the licensor to " . . . recognize revenue or income with a corresponding increase in litigation settlement expense. However, if the licenses are given as part of a litigation defense strategy and don't have value to the . . . " licensee, the recognition of revenue by the licensor would be doubtful.

The same speech also suggested that Emerging Issues Task Force (EITF) Issue No. 00-21, "Revenue Arrangements with Multiple Deliverables" (ASC 605-25) is useful when allocating fair value to each element. The speaker suggested that it "would be acceptable to value each element of the arrangement and allocate the consideration paid to each element using relative fair values" and that a residual approach would be acceptable if one of the elements could not be valued. The speaker also commented that many companies were not able to reliably estimate the fair value of the litigation component.

EITF 08-7, "Accounting for Defensive Intangible Assets" (ASC 350-30) addresses the subsequent accounting for intangible assets that a purchaser does not plan to use, but will instead hold to prevent others from using (known as a "defensive asset"). A classic example would be the purchase and retention of a patent or trademark in order to keep the asset away from a competitor.

While buyers have historically assigned little value to defensive intangible assets, the guidance within SFAS 157 (ASC 820) and SFAS 141(R) (ASC 805) require the buyer to measure a defensive IA at a fair value that considers the highest and best use of the asset. Since the highest and best use for many market participants could be defensive, the asset would have to be fair valued accordingly. EITF 08-7 (ASC 350-30) provided further guidance related to defensive IAs and required that an acquired defensive asset should be accounted for as a separate unit of accounting. It also suggested that nearly all defensive assets should have a finite useful life.[11]

Accounting for IP Business Activities

IP issues present themselves in a wide variety of business activities. For example, IP must be developed or acquired and eventually used by the business in some matter. This use could be in the form of a sale or licensing transaction, a litigation matter, or the eventual disposal of the IP. The following sections review the accounting for these various intellectual property business activities.

Developing IP

Developing IP typically involves R&D activities. R&D activities can include many types of costs, including, but not limited to, materials, personnel, and contract services related to developing an idea or product. If deemed research and development, the entity incurring the costs would expense such costs when incurred. The internal R&D activity utilized to develop the idea in a patent application, for example, would be charged to expense. The expense would reduce earnings, and not end up as an asset on the balance sheet. The relevant financial reporting accounting guidance in this area would include SFAS No. 2, Accounting for Research and Development Costs (ASC 730).[12]

In contrast, if the entity acquired the R&D activity as part of a business combination, as opposed to developing it internally, the fair value of that R&D activity is now placed on the balance sheet as an IA that would be subject to future impairment testing and amortization.

This accounting treatment paradox is due to SFAS No. 141(R), Business Combinations (ASC 805). As noted above, SFAS No. 141(R) (ASC 805) requires that the acquirer recognize all tangible and intangible R&D assets acquired in a business combination as assets. Prior to SFAS No. 141(R) (ASC 805), acquired R&D costs were fair valued and expensed at the acquisition date if such costs had no alternative future use. This change will essentially place billions of dollars of IPRD on the future buyers' balance sheets.

For example, in 2008, prior to the adoption of SFAS No. 141(R) (ASC 805), Barr Pharmaceuticals, Inc. was acquired by Teva Pharmaceutical Industries Ltd. for approximately $7.5 billion.[13] In this acquisition, nearly $1 billion of the purchase price was allocated to the estimated fair value of IPRD. Pursuant to the relevant guidance at the time of the transaction, this IPRD was expensed at the acquisition and did not remain on the balance sheet.

In contrast, SFAS No. 141(R) (ASC 805) will essentially place billions of dollars of IPRD on the future buyers' balance sheets. For example, in 2009, Pfizer acquired Wyeth for $68 billion. Almost $15 billion of the purchase price was determined to be IPRD and was recorded as an indefinite-lived IA. Going forward, this IA will be subject to impairment testing. For example, in 2010, Pfizer recorded an impairment charge of $1.8 billion, which was primarily related to the IAs (including IPRD) acquired from Wyeth. Once a R&D project is completed and goes to market, Pfizer will begin to amortize the project's fair value. For example, in December 2009, one of the acquired drugs received regulatory approval and was therefore reclassified from R&D to developed technology rights.

The acquisition of Targanta Therapeutics Corporation in 2009 provides another example. Targanta Therapeutics was a stand-alone biotechnology company that was acquired by the Medicines Company. Prior to the acquisition, when Targanta was a stand-alone entity, Targanta spent over $100 million developing various drugs and expensed these costs as research and development. However, when Targanta was acquired, the Medicines Company determined that the fair value of the R&D assets acquired was $69.5 million and recorded that amount as an intangible asset.[14] Future R&D expenditures incurred by the Medicines Company related to the acquired technology will be expensed and the acquired asset will be subject to impairment testing and, when the products reach the market place, amortization.

The treatment for acquired IAs apart from an acquisition is the same. A patent application or issued patent that is purchased alone would typically be deemed an IA that would be capitalized on the acquirer's balance sheet. The amount recorded as an asset on the balance sheet would be based largely on the cost of purchasing the patent application or issued patent, but could also include legal and filing fees related to acquisition of that asset.[15] Since patents have finite lives, the total cost of the acquired patent would be amortized over the useful life of the intangible asset. It would also be subject to SFAS 144 (ASC 360) impairment testing.

To be clear, this same concept would apply to other types of IP as well. For example, internal costs related to developing trademarks or trade names are typically expensed, while the cost of purchasing a trademark would be capitalized and recorded as an asset on the balance sheet. Perhaps the most glaring example of this concept is illustrated on the Coca-Cola Company balance sheet. While the Coke brand is recognized as perhaps the most valuable brand in the world, since it was internally developed, as opposed to being purchased, the multibillion-dollar fair value of the Coke brand is not on Coca-Cola's balance sheet.[16]

IP Transactions

Once the entity owns the IP, it is often involved in some kind of an IP transaction. As discussed throughout this book, IP transactions can include various forms of licenses and sales that range from the simple outright sale of a patent to a multiple-component licensing and settlement transaction involving thousands of patents and various entities.

SALES AND PURCHASES A patent sale generally involves assigning the patent to the buyer in exchange for some form of compensation. For example, in 2002, Unova sold approximately 150 patents and patent applications to Broadcom Corporation for $24 million. Unova recorded a gain on the transaction, which was reflected on the income statement. While the purchase of a patent portfolio could be capitalized in various circumstances, in this particular transaction Broadcom expensed the entire purchase price immediately. The reasoning for recording the purchase as an expense rather than as an asset was that

Broadcom did not have plans to (1) utilize the portfolio in its ongoing operations, (2) generate future cash flows using the portfolio or (3) resell the portfolio. Pursuant to SFAS 144 (ASC 360), Broadcom therefore decided that it was not possible to reasonably forecast future cash flows related to the portfolio and recorded an impairment change to write off the asset immediately after the acquisition.

Broadcom treated a subsequent $18 million patent and patent application portfolio purchase involving Cirrus Logic in a similar manner. Since Broadcom acquired the Cirrus Logic patents for defensive and settlement purposes and Broadcom was unable to estimate future cash flows from the patents, the $18 million was expensed as an SFAS 144 (ASC 360) impairment charge immediately after the purchase.[17]

A review of publicly available filings involving patent acquisitions reveals that expensing versus capitalization of patent acquisitions varies based on individual facts and circumstances. As noted in the examples discussed above, Broadcom expensed the entire purchase price immediately. Conversely, Acacia Research Corporation, which acquires patents with the intent to license or sell them to another party, has capitalized patent acquisition costs and amortized them over their useful lives.

Another portfolio purchase example involved Novell, Inc.'s 2004 purchase of a patent and patent application portfolio during Commerce One's bankruptcy proceedings. This purchase was intended to enhance Novell's portfolio of IP and to strengthen its ability to defend against patent claims against open source products. Novell capitalized the $15.5 million purchase price as an intangible asset and established a 10-year useful life. Novell subsequently contributed these patents to a joint venture and used the portfolio value to fund a portion of its contribution to the joint venture.[18]

RPX Corporation, which provides a subscription-based patent risk management solution by purchasing patents that are potentially a threat to its clients, capitalizes patent purchases at fair value. RPX acquires patents assets that are or could be asserted against current and future clients. In exchange for a subscription fee, RPX licenses the acquired patent assets to its clients to protect them from infringement assertions related to the acquired patent assets. Through December 31, 2010, RPX Corporation has purchased over $250 million in patents and recorded them as IAs. The fair value of the patent assets acquired is generally based on the fair value of the consideration exchanged and includes the legal and other fees associated with the acquisition.[19]

LICENSING   Companies often choose to license their patents and other IP in exchange for up-front or future royalty payments. These licenses typically provide royalty revenue to the licensor and represent an expense for the licensee. The basic question for most licensors is when to recognize revenue.

Revenue recognition accounting guidance is extensive and includes both broad concepts and specific guidance. For example, FASB Concepts Statement No. 5 (ASC 350-30-25-4), states that " . . . revenues are considered to have been earned when the entity has substantially accomplished what it must do to be entitled to the benefits represented by the revenues." While it is difficult to summarize the authoritative accounting guidance that governs revenue re-cognition, in general, in order to recognize revenue from IP licenses, the reve-nue must be deemed realized or realizable, and be earned. As discussed earlier, for revenue to be considered realizable and earned, all of the following criteria must occur: (1) persuasive evidence of an arrangement exists, (2) delivery has occurred or services have been rendered, (3) the seller's price to the buyer is fixed or determinable, and (4) collectibility is reasonably assured. [20]

For illustration, e.Digital Corporation recognizes revenue from patent license agreements when (1) the patent license agreement is executed; (2) the amounts due are fixed, determinable, and billable; (3) the customer has been provided rights to the licensed technology; and (4) collection of the resulting receivable has occurred or is probable of occurring. Such immediate recognition is possible largely because e.Digital has performed all of its obligations under contract and the customer has access to the licensed technology.[21] Outstanding obligations or the need to provide something in the future would generally defer the revenue recognition.

License agreements sometimes provide for the calculation of a royalty based on actual sales dollars or on a per-unit basis. Unless these payments can be esti-mated on some reliable basis, revenues under such agreements are generally recognized after the royalty amount is known and collectable. For example, Aca-cia recognizes revenue from these types of licensing agreements in the quarter following the quarter of activity, provided amounts are fixed or determinable and collection is reasonably assured. Delaying revenue recognition until the quarter after the sales activity allows for the receipt of licensee royalty reports prior to the recognition of revenue.[22]

Companies must also be mindful of the license agreement's term. Even if a com-pany actually receives an upfront royalty payment and has met its obligations under the agreement, it cannot recognize revenue until the start of the term stated in the license agreement.[23] The length of the term can also influence when up-front pay-ment are recognized as revenue.

For instance, in 2008, Qualcomm Inc. entered into significant license and set-tlement agreements with Nokia Corporation. The agreements covered various wireless standards and resolved all litigation pending between the parties. The li-cense agreement provided Qualcomm a nonrefundable up-front payment of $2.5 billion, ongoing royalties, and the assignment of various Nokia patents. Qualcomm recognized $560 million in revenues in 2008 and is recognizing the remaining un-earned revenue during the 15-year term of the agreement. In addition to recording earned and unearned revenues, Qualcomm also recorded a $1.8 billion intangible asset due to the assignment of the patents from Nokia. The estimated fair value of the patents assigned was determined using the income approach based on pro-jected discounted cash flows during an estimated 15-year useful life. The $1.8 bil-lion intangible asset is being amortized on a straight-line basis over a 15-year period.[24]

Nokia, which prepares its financial statements in accordance with International Financial Reporting Standards, planned to recognize the $2.5 billion (€1.7 million) up-front payment to Qualcomm over the contract's period and, accordingly, recorded most of the up-front payment as a prepaid expense. With respect to the patents they assigned to Qualcomm, Nokia also valued them using the discounted cash flow income approach, but unlike Qualcomm, concluded that the fair value of the patents was not material.[25]

IP TRANSACTIONS: SETTLEMENTS   IP settlements are also common, and typically create the need for some form of financial accounting and reporting. Since settlement agreements often resolve various issues among the parties, the settlement of litigation and a future license for example, settlement agreements often contain multiple accounting elements that could require separate accounting treatment. For example, Qualcomm and Broadcom entered into a significant settlement and patent license and nonassert agreement in 2009. Like many IP settlement agreements, the agreement contained various elements, including the settlement of existing litigations and the transfer of patent rights between the entities. Pursuant to the agreement, Qualcomm agreed to pay Broadcom nearly $900 million, some of which was paid in 2009 with the remainder to be paid in the future. As discussed in Qualcomm's public filings, the determination of the appropriate accounting treatment for such an agreement depends on many factors, including the ability to value the assets received. Given the difficulty in reliably estimating the value of the individual elements in the agreement, Qualcomm treated the agreement as a single element for accounting purposes and essentially expensed the fair value of payments owed under the agreement immediately. The difference between the $783 million expensed in 2009 and the total payments due under the agreements represented amounts accrued in prior periods and imputed interest (the future payments were discounted to fair value using an appropriate discount rate).

Broadcom, which was to receive the nearly $900 million in payments from Qualcomm, allocated the payments due under the agreement to multiple accounting elements. Broadcom recognized a gain from the settlement of litigation related to intellectual property of $65.3 million (the approximate value of certain litigation settlements between the parties). The fair value associated with the transfer of intellectual property rights, and the settlement of other outstanding litigation, was estimated to be $825.9 million, and was to be treated as a single unit of accounting and recognized as revenue during the four-year performance period called for in the agreement.[26]

Another large settlement involved Medtronic, Inc. and Dr. Gary Michelson in 2005. In exchange for total consideration of $1.35 billion, Medtronic settled various litigations and purchased spine-related IP and other assets from Dr. Michelson and a related entity. Since the agreement settled litigations and transferred various IP rights and other assets, it was also considered to have multiple accounting elements. $550 million of the $1.35 billion was assigned to the settlement of past damages and, accordingly, expensed in 2005. $627.5 million of the total purchase price was assigned to acquired technology intangible assets, which included a large patent and patent application portfolio, and was to have a 17-year useful life. The remaining $175 million was treated as IPRD and expensed at the time of the acquisition. This fair value was assigned to IPRD because some portion of the acquiring technology was still in development and did not have an alternate future use.[27]

Research in Motion (RIM) was also involved in a large settlement that resulted in the payment of over $600 million to NTP in March 2006. RIM had previously accrued a $450 million liability, which included a $20 million intangible asset. During 2006, the Patent Office issued various office actions that rejected all claims in the NTP patents. Largely based on these rulings, RIM did not ascribe any value to the NTP license and, accordingly, wrote off the existing intangible assets and essentially expensed the entire $600 million payment to NTP.[28]

Acquisition of IAs in a Business Combination

As discussed above, SFAS 141 (ASC 805) and SFAS 142 (ASC 350) dramatically changed how IP and other IAs are accounted for in business combinations. These standards resulted in more intangible asset disclosures and more IA value being recorded, at least initially, on balance sheets. IA impairments or write-downs are also more common, especially given the recent economic downturn, since IP and other IAs are no longer buried in goodwill and "under the radar."

When a company is acquired, the acquirer must recognize, separately from goodwill, the identifiable IAs acquired. An IA is considered identifiable if it meets either the separability criterion or the contractual-legal criterion described above. SFAS 141 (ASC 805), and now SFAS 141(R) (ASC 805), specifically identifies various IP assets that would be considered as identifiable including, among others, trademarks, trade names, service marks, trade dress, domain names, patented technology and software. When allocating the purchase price to the various assets acquired and liabilities assumed, fair value is allocated to these categories of intellectual property and other intangible assets.

Accordingly, when purchasing an IP-focused company, it is likely that the target's IP will generally be disclosed and recognized as an IA on the acquisition date. While patents are listed within SFAS 141 (ASC 805) and SFAS 141(R) (ASC 805) as an IA, and are sometimes recognized as a separate category, the fair value of patents is often included within a broader IA category typically called acquired product rights or developed technology. For example, although Macromedia had patents when it was acquired by Adobe in 2005, the fair value of the acquired patents was included within the acquired product rights intangible category.[29]

For some companies, patents and trademarks comprise a significant portion of the entity's balance sheet and are disclosed separately. For example, as of December 31, 2009, Johnson & Johnson had $9.4 billion in trademark and patent fair value on its balance sheet. This included $5.9 million in trademarks that were considered nonamortizable, and $3.5 billion in patents and trademarks that were amortizing over a 17-year weighted average useful life.[30]

Another example that illustrates the impact of SFAS 141(R) (ASC 805) is the Iconix Brand Group, Inc. Iconix is a brand management company that has purchased a number of well-known consumer brands. These brands are licensed to other companies, which pay royalties to Iconix. Since Iconix has largely purchased its portfolio of brands, as opposed to developing them internally, the Iconix balance sheet now largely reflects the acquisition date fair value of the trademarks purchased. For example, trademarks represent $1.25 billion of Iconix's $1.8 billion in total assets. Since nearly all of this $1.25 billion in trademarks has an indefinite life, they will remain on the balance sheet, unamortized at their acquisition cost, absent future impairments. If Iconix had developed these brands internally, its balance sheet would not include the $1.25 billion in trademark assets.[31]

IP Litigation

Companies are often forced to incur litigation costs to defend their intellectual property rights. These litigation costs are typically expensed as incurred, but can be capitalized as an asset in certain circumstances.

Rambus Inc., which is often involved in litigation, expenses litigation costs and isolates litigation costs within the marketing, general and administrative cost income statement line items. For instance, in 2009 nearly $56 million of Rambus's $128 million in total marketing, general and administrative costs were litigation expenses.[32]

Acacia, which as noted above acquires patents with the intent to license or sell them to another party, also expenses litigation and licensing expenses, and isolates them as a line item for investors. Acacia's litigation and licenses expenses were approximately $14 million in 2010 and 2009.

Intermec Inc. capitalizes external legal costs incurred in the defense of its patents when the future economic benefit of the patent will be increased in accordance with Statement of Financial Accounting Concepts 6, "Elements of Financial Statements." For example, Intermec capitalized $4.7 million in legal costs in 2009. These costs were to be amortized to expense over the patents' useful lives or impaired if the future economic benefit were to decrease.[33]

Sale, Abandonment, or Change in Value of IP

Once on the balance sheet, due to a business combination or direct purchase of IP, various IP events could change the fair value of the IP and require additional accounting entries. The sale or the abandonment of the IP would likely require the removal of the associated carrying value from the balance sheet. While an increase in fair value would not be recorded, a decline in fair value could create the need for a write-down.

For IP with a finite life, which would include patents, amortization would reduce the carrying value over a useful life. Useful lives can vary widely based on the facts and circumstances surrounding the particular IP. The useful life is also typically based on the useful life of an entire patent portfolio rather than the useful life of a specific patent. While the legal life of a patent would represent the maximum useful life, economic life, due to changing technology, for example, is typically a shorter period of time. For example, Nokia's public filings note that "acquired patents, trademarks, licenses, software licenses for internal use, customer relationships and developed technology are capitalized and amortized using the straight-line method over their useful lives, generally 3 to 6 years, but not exceeding 20 years."[34]

As noted by RPX Corporation when discussing amortization policy, determining the economic usefulness of an intangible asset requires significant management judgment. For example, since RPX Corporation's business model provides each client with a license (which under certain circumstance can become a perpetual license) to the vast majority of the acquired patent assets, RPX is unable to reliably determine how patent assets are exhausted. RPX therefore amortizes each patent asset on a straight-line basis during a period equal to the shorter of the asset's estimated useful life and remaining statutory life. As of September 30, 2010, the majority of RPX Corporation's patent assets were being amortized over economic useful lives ranging between two and five years.

In addition to amortization, companies often have to write down the value of IP due to changing market conditions. SFAS 144 (ASC 360) requires that IAs be tested for impairment if certain "triggering events" exist and written down when their carrying values exceed their fair values. Various circumstances could cause a decline in the fair value of intellectual property. For instance, competition could increase and result in lower royalties. Technology changes could reduce or eliminate the importance of the intangible assets and, accordingly, cause their fair values to decline. For instance, in 2008, Rambus determined that approximately $2.2 million of "intangible assets had no alternative use and were impaired as a result of a customer's change in technology requirements."[35]

Further, the company could simply elect to exit or have the need to restructure the associated product line and, accordingly, need to eliminate or reduce the carrying value assigned to the related IP. In connection with the restructuring of Nokia's code division multiple access (CDMA) business, Nokia recorded an impairment charge of €33 million during 2006 that related to an acquired CDMA license.

Alcatel-Lucent recorded a €4.7 billion impairment charge in 2008 related to its re-assessment of near-term outlook, its decision to streamline its portfolio and its weaker than expected CDMA business. The items written off included goodwill, intangibles, capitalized costs, and tangible assets that had been recorded on the balance sheet in connection with the 2006 acquisition of Lucent Technologies by Alcatel; €1.3 billion of the €4.7 billion was related to IP and other IAs.

Future Transition to International Financial Reporting Standards

International Accounting Standards (referred to as International Financial Reporting Standards, or IFRS) are becoming the preferred accounting and reporting format for much of the corporate world outside of the United States. The expected transition from U.S. accounting rules to IFRS will further complicate intangible asset accounting. While current IFRS IA accounting requirements are similar to the U.S. accounting standards, there are some key differences.

- Under U.S. generally accepted accounting principles (GAAP), all expenditures related to research and development (outside of a business combination) are expensed as incurred. However, under IFRS, some internally generated intangibles representing development are capitalized if certain conditions are met.
- There are significant differences in the approach to the IA impairment test. As discussed above, U.S. accounting rules require a two-step impairment test that is performed using a "highest and best use" concept. In contrast, the IFRS test is a one-step process and is based on "value in use" or value to the current owner. Under IFRS, if the recoverable amount is below the carrying amount an

impairment loss is recognized (IAS 36). "Recoverable amount" is the higher of value in use and fair value less cost to sell. "Value in use" is future discounted cash flows from an asset or cash-generating unit. As most indefinite-lived intangible assets (e.g., brand name) do not generate cash flows independently of other assets, it may not be possible to calculate the value in use for such an asset on a stand-alone basis. Therefore, it is necessary to determine the smallest identifiable group of assets that generates cash inflows that are largely independent of the cash inflows from other assets or groups of assets, known as a "cash generating unit," in order to complete the test.

- U.S. GAAP does not permit reversal of previously recorded impairment charges. However, an impairment loss for assets other than goodwill is reversed under IFRS provided certain conditions are met.
- Acquired IPRD projects before FDA approval (that are not part of a business combination) are capitalized under IFRS, but expensed under U.S. GAAP.

As part of the formal convergence project to achieve truly global accounting standards, the IASB and the FASB are working together to remove as many of the differences between IFRS and U.S. GAAP as possible. For example, as discussed earlier, IPRD in a business combination used to be expensed under U.S. GAAP but is now capitalized (as it is under IFRS). While currently unclear how these remaining IA accounting differences will be resolved, it is generally expected that the IFRS requirements will prevail.

Conclusion

Understanding financial accounting and reporting consequences is an important factor when analyzing an intellectual property transaction. While in the past IP and IAs were often grouped within goodwill or buried within the financial statements, recent accounting literature is now forcing these important assets to be recognized separately and disclosed from a financial reporting perspective. Significant IP transactions are often disclosed and can influence earnings and various financial ratios. Although accounting ramifications should not necessarily drive IP transactions, decision makers should be cognizant of these issues and consider the financial reporting impacts during the due diligence process.

Notes

[1]The conclusions set forth herein are based on independent research and publicly available material. The views expressed herein are the views and opinions of the authors and do not reflect or represent the views of Charles River Associates, J. H. Cohn LLP, or any of the organizations with which the authors are affiliated. Any opinions expressed herein shall not amount to any form of guarantee that the authors, Charles River Associates, or J. H. Cohn LLP has determined or predicted future events or circumstances, and no such reliance may be inferred or implied. The authors, Charles River Associates, and J. H. Cohn LLP accept no duty of care or liability of any kind whatsoever to any party, and no responsibility for damages, if any, suffered by any party as a result of decisions made, or not made, or actions taken, or not taken, based on this paper. Detailed information

about Charles River Associates, a registered trade name of CRA International, Inc., is available at www.crai.com. Detailed information about J. H. Cohn LLP is available at www.jhcohn.com.

[2]While IP activities can also have various tax-related implications, this chapter is limited to financial accounting and reporting.

[3]While this life cycle example utilized patents, somewhat similar events could involve trademarks, copyrights, and other IP.

[4]The FASB recently issued a codification that simplified access to authoritative U.S. generally accepted accounting principles (GAAP). Where appropriate the new codification reference topic number has been noted after each prior accounting reference. For example, SFAS No. 141(R) (ASC 805), Business Combinations (ASC 805). In general the new codification hierarchy includes topics, subtopics, sections and subsections.

[5]FASB Concepts Statement No. 6.

[6]SAB No. 104 (ASC 605).

[7]SFAS No. 141(R) (ASC 805) applies prospectively to business combination for which the acquisition date is on or after the beginning of the first annual reporting period beginning on or after December 15, 2008.

[8]SFAS 142 (ASC 350) also addresses the goodwill impairment testing process.

[9]Possible trigger events can include significant decrease in the market price, significant adverse change to an asset's use or condition, significant adverse change in legal factors or business client, accumulation of costs significantly in excess of the those projected, operating or cash flow loss combined with history of operating or cash flow losses, and current expectation that, more likely than not, the asset will be sold or disposed of significantly before the end of its previously estimated useful life.

[10]The December 10, 2007, speech included the following disclaimer: "The Securities and Exchange Commission, as a matter of policy, disclaims responsibility for any private publication or statement by any of its employees. The views expressed herein are those of the author and do not necessarily reflect the views of the Commission or of the author's colleagues or the staff of the Commission."

[11]EITF 08-7, "Accounting for Defensive Intangible Assets" (ASC 350-30).

[12]Notably, the costs incurred in acquiring licenses and patents, as opposed to internally developing them, may be subject to capitalization as an intangible asset and subject to amortization and impairment testing.

[13]SFAS No. 141(R) (ASC 805) was applicable to Teva Pharmaceutical Industries Ltd. as of the year beginning January 1, 2009, less than a month after the closing of the Barr Pharmaceuticals, Inc. transaction.

[14]Another $26 million was recorded as goodwill.

[15]Future internal research and development activities incurred after the acquisition of the intangible assets would be expense as incurred. As discussed later, legal costs related to defending the patent are sometimes capitalized.

[16]While Coca-Cola's December 31, 2009 balance sheet does include over $6 billion in trademarks, these are other trademarks that have been purchased over the years.

[17]Broadcom 10-K, 2004, p. 37.

[18]Novell 10-K, 2005, p. 76.

[19]RPX Corporation S-1, 2011, p. 1.

[20]SAB No. 104, pp. 10, 11 (ASC 605).

[21] e.Digital Corporation 10-K, 2009.

[22] Acacia Research Corporation 10-K, 2009.

[23] SAB No. 104 (ASC 605).

[24] Qualcomm 10-K, 2008, p. 92.

[25] Nokia 20-F, 2008, p. 196.

[26] Broadcom 10-K, 2009, p. 52.

[27] Medtronic 10-K, 2006.

[28] Research in Motion 40-F, 2007, p. 123.

[29] Patent fair value also is often included within the IPRD intangible asset category.

[30] Johnson & Johnson 10-K, 2009, p. 56.

[31] Iconix 10-K, 2009, p. 52.

[32] Rambus 10-K, 2009, p. 36.

[33] Intermec 10-K, 2009, p. 53.

[34] Nokia 20-F, 2008, p. F-12.

[35] Rambus 10-K, 2008, p. 63.

About the Editors

Lanning G. Bryer

Lanning G. Bryer is a partner in the New York office of Ladas & Parry and is director of the firm's Mergers, Acquisitions and Licensing Group. Mr. Bryer is an active committee member of several intellectual property organizations, including the Trademark Licensing Committee of Licensing Executives Society (United States and Canada) and the Editorial Board of *The Trademark Reporter* of the International Trademark Association (INTA). He recently served on the International Editorial Board of INTA, and currently serves as Editor-in-Chief of INTA's *The Trademark Reporter*. Mr. Bryer has written and lectured extensively on foreign trademark practice and IP commercial transactions and routinely counsels a diverse variety of corporate clients on the acquisition, financing, and licensing of intellectual property. Mr. Bryer is co-author and co-editor of other treatises published by John Wiley and Sons, entitled *Intellectual Property Assets in Mergers & Acquisitions; Intellectual Property in the Global Marketplace;* and *The New Role of Intellectual Property in Commercial Transactions.* Mr. Bryer also co-authored and co-edited a treatise published by Clark, Boardman, and Callaghan entitled *Worldwide Trademark Transfers.* He is a graduate of Johns Hopkins University and Hofstra University School of Law. Mr. Bryer can be reached at (212) 708-1870 or via e-mail at lbryer@ladas.com.

Scott J. Lebson

Scott Lebson is a partner in the Mergers, Acquisitions and Licensing Group of Ladas & Parry LLP. Mr. Lebson's practice focuses primarily on counseling corporate clients with respect to the acquisition, sale, licensing, and securitization of intellectual property rights and related technology. He is recognized as one of the leading authorities in the evolving field of securitization of intellectual property rights. Mr. Lebson also counsels clients with respect to the filing and recordation of documentation relating to the transfer of patents and trademarks in jurisdictions throughout the world. He is an accomplished speaker and has lectured and written extensively on a wide range of intellectual property matters and is a committee member of several intellectual property organizations, including the Licensing Executives Society, the International Trademark Association, and the New York State Bar Association Intellectual Property Section. He is a graduate of Villanova University and Hofstra University School of Law. Mr. Lebson can be reached at (212) 708-3460 or via e-mail at slebson@ladas.com.

Matthew D. Asbell

Matthew D. Asbell is an associate in the New York office of Ladas & Parry LLP. He considers himself an IP generalist, though he primarily practices trademark law domestically and internationally. With a diverse background in the entertainment industry, information technology, and medicine, proficiency in several languages, and a certification as a Social Media Strategist, he handles complex intellectual property matters, including those arising in the Web 2.0 space, for a wide variety of corporate clients. Mr. Asbell is an active member of the American Bar Association, in which he serves as a Young Lawyer Fellow of the Section of Intellectual Property Law, and as chair of the Internet and Intellectual Property Law Committee of the Young Lawyers Division. He has chaired the Young Lawyers Committee of the New York State Bar Association Intellectual Property Section, and is an active member of several other bar association committees related to intellectual property. Mr. Asbell has authored and co-authored several publications and given presentations on the topics of trademark, licensing, copyright, patent, broadcasting, and Internet and privacy law. He is a graduate of the Benjamin N. Cardozo School of Law, Carnegie Mellon University, and the Episcopal Academy. Mr. Asbell can be reached at (212) 708-3463 or via e-mail at masbell@ladas.com.

About the Contributors

Joshua Braunstein serves as general manager at Corsearch, a leading global provider of trademark search and life cycle solutions with offices throughout the United States and Europe. Since 1996, he has served as director of content, senior manager of research operations, and began his career with Corsearch as a trademark search analyst. Joshua Braunstein can be reached at (917) 408-5128, Joshua.braunstein@wolterskluwer.com, or www.ctcorsearch.com.

Robert Doerfler is intellectual property counsel at SVP Worldwide, where he oversees the worldwide prosecution and enforcement of the company's intellectual property rights. Prior to moving in-house, Robert was trademark attorney at the New York office of Kirkpatrick & Lockhart and worked in litigation at Adams & Adams in Pretoria, South Africa.

James J. Donohue is a vice president in the New York office of Charles River Associates, Inc. He is a certified public accountant and has a bachelor of science degree in accountancy from Villanova University. Mr. Donohue is also a certified valuation analyst and is accredited in business valuation by the American Institute of Certified Public Accountants. Mr. Donohue has been responsible for consulting assignments in a wide range of areas, including intellectual property, damages, valuation, forensic accounting, securities, analyses of professional negligence, and bankruptcy. Mr. Donohue has provided a variety of due diligence services for intellectual property–based licensing and acquisition transactions, including valuations, fairness opinions, and strategic consulting for tax and financial reporting, and bankruptcy proceedings. His experience in intellectual property litigation matters has included assessing the appropriate economic measure of damages in intellectual property disputes. James Donohue can be reached at (212) 520-7116, jdonohue@crai.com, or www.crai.com.

Joseph M. Forgione is the director of trademark enforcement at the Gioconda Law Group PLLC, a New York–based brand protection law firm focused on intellectual property litigation, investigations, and strategy. He previously worked in the corporate legal department at Chanel, Inc., where he participated in brick-and-mortar and online intellectual property enforcement. He holds both a master of laws (LLM) in intellectual property law and a law degree (JD) from Benjamin N. Cardozo School of Law. Joseph M. Forgione can be reached at (212) 786-7550, www.GiocondaLaw.com, or Joseph.Forgione@GiocondaLaw.com.

Joseph C. Gioconda is an attorney and founder of the Gioconda Law Group PLLC, a New York–based brand protection law firm focused on intellectual property litigation, investigations, and strategy. He spent nearly a decade as a partner and associate at Kirkland & Ellis LLP and was most recently an equity partner at DLA

Piper LLP (US), where he was responsible for the Trademark Litigation and Anti-Counterfeiting practice in the firm's New York office. He holds a law degree (JD) from Yale Law School and is the author of numerous articles proposing innovative approaches to anti-counterfeiting and enforcement. Joseph C. Gioconda can be reached at (212) 786-7549, www.GiocondaLaw.com, or Joseph.Gioconda@Gioconda Law.com.

Maureen Beacom Gorman is a trademark attorney with the Chicago law firm Marshall, Gerstein & Borun LLP. She is a former examining attorney with the United States Patent and Trademark Office and has previously written and spoken on the topic of "green" trademark law. Maureen Beacom Gorman can be reached at (312) 474-6643, MGorman@marshallip.com, or www.marshallip.com.

Terry Heckler is founder and president of Heckler Associates, providing a full range of integrated communication design, advertising, and brand strategy services. His firm has been instrumental in many successful start-ups for such brands as Starbucks, New Balance, K2, Jansport, Cinnabon, Redhook, Sage, and Panera. Terry Heckler can be reached at (206) 352-1010 or tsh@hecklerassociates.com.

Barbara Kolsun is executive vice president and general counsel of Stuart Weitzman Holdings LLC, a luxury shoe design and retail company based in New York. Ms. Kolsun started the company's first in-house legal department, as she did previously for Kate Spade LLC and 7 for All Mankind LLC. She is the co-editor and co-author of the first textbook on fashion law, entitled *Fashion Law: A Guide for Designers, Fashion Executives, and Attorneys* (Fairchild Books, 2010). Barbara Kolsun can be reached at (212) 287-0704 or barbarako@stuartweitzman.com.

Elliot Lipins is an associate in the New York office of Ladas & Parry LLP. His practice encompasses all areas of intellectual property. Mr. Lipins's experience includes litigation at both the trial and appellate levels before court and administrative tribunals. In addition to litigation experience, Mr. Lipins has prosecuted a wide variety of patent and trademark matters in the USPTO. Mr. Lipins has successfully represented trademark owners in numerous ICANN arbitration proceedings. He also has experience in trademark rights, including selection, proper use, and enforcement. Elliott Lipins can be reached at elipins@ladas.com.

James Markarian works for Siemens Corporation as senior counsel and licensing manager for North America. He manages Siemens's outbound licensing programs and IP sales, handles incoming licensing matters and IP acquisitions, and negotiates and drafts various transactional agreements (e.g., IP licenses, JVs, software licenses, R&Ds, Agent and Service, Asset Purchase or Sale, NDAs, etc.). In addition, he provides support for Siemens' M&A activities, advises Siemens business units regarding IP asset management and IP issues related to standards organizations, and oversees Siemens's compliance with third-party publishing and music copyrights. He has an aerospace engineering degree from Boston University and a JD degree from Brooklyn Law School, is admitted to the New York and New Jersey Bar Associations (as in-house counsel), is a registered patent attorney with the USPTO, and has a CLP^{TM} certification from the Licensing Executives Society.

Jennifer R. Martin is senior corporate counsel, investigations, with Symantec Corporation. She previously was a managing director at Stroz Friedberg LLC, a technical consulting firm, and senior counsel with the Department of Justice Computer Crime and Intellectual Property Section. Ms. Martin is an expert on computer intrusion and data breach investigations, computer forensics, and electronic discovery. Jennifer Martin can be reached at jmartinloh@gmail.com.

Jeremiah A. Pastrick is the vice president of Continental Enterprises, an investigation and consulting firm that specializes in intellectual property development and protection. As vice president, he oversees all operations of Continental's Investigations and Licensing Departments as well as Continental's Office of General Counsel as they develop and implement strategies to grow and protect their clients' intellectual property around the globe. Mr. Pastrick received a BS in public management from Indiana University and his JD from Indiana University School of Law. Mr. Pastrick's legal studies focused on intellectual property, international commercial law, corporate law, and human rights law. Additionally, during his time at Indiana University School of Law, Mr. Pastrick attended Renmin University of China in Beijing to study the emergence of rule of law in China. He is admitted to practice law in Indiana and is a member of the American Bar Association, the Indiana Bar Association, and the Indianapolis Bar Association. Jeremiah A. Pastrick can be reached at (317) 818-0523 or jpastrick@ce-ip.com.

Dennis S. Prahl is a partner in the New York office of Ladas & Parry LLP, specializing in international protection of trademarks, copyrights, domain names, licensing, and rights of publicity. He also serves as president of LadasDomains LLC, a top-rated ICANN-accredited domain name registrar. Dennis S. Prahl can be reached at (212) 708-1817, dprahl@ladas.com, www.ladas.com, or www.ladasdomains.com.

John Richards is a partner and resident in the New York office of Ladas & Parry LLP. Mr. Richards specializes in chemical and biochemical patent matters, including drafting and prosecution of patent applications in these fields in the United States and abroad. He is also widely experienced in the negotiation and drafting of patent know-how and license agreements. John Richards started work in the patent profession in the patent department of the British chemical company Albright & Wilson in 1966. He joined Ladas & Parry in 1973, becoming a partner in 1982. He is the general editor of *Legal Aspects of Introducing Products to the United States* (Kluwer, 1988) and co-author of *Intellectual Property and the Internal Market of the European Community* (Graham & Trotman, 1993). He is an adjunct associate professor at Fordham University School of Law, where he teaches U.S. and international patent law, and at John Marshall Law School in Chicago, where he teaches a course in international patent law. Mr. Richards has written and spoken frequently on international intellectual property issues, especially in the fields of patents and copyrights in the United States, Canada, India, and the Far East. John Richards can be reached at (212) 708-1915, jrichards@ladas.com, or www.ladas.com.

David J. Rikkers is the senior IP counsel of the Integrated Defense Systems business unit of Raytheon Company. While serving as a Captain in the U.S. Air Force, he was a chief engineer on international procurement programs. He later worked at the Secretary of the Air Force, Office of the General Counsel for Acquisition, the U.S. Court of Appeals for the Federal Circuit and in private practice guiding clients on intellectual property issues.

Mark A. Spelker, CPA, is an audit and technical consulting partner at J. H. Cohn and a senior member of the Capital Markets and SEC Practice. He specializes in public companies and has nearly 30 years of diversified public accounting experience.

Mark spent 15 years with Big Four firms, servicing several Fortune 500 companies as well as many middle market businesses.

Mark also currently works with many emerging public companies. His focus over the past several years has been on biotechnology companies as well as multi-national public and private companies.

Mark graduated from Villanova University in 1982 with a bachelor of science degree in accounting. He is a member of the American Institute of Certified Public Accountants (AICPA) and the New Jersey Society of Certified Public Accountants. Mark has been an adjunct lecturer in the Economics Department of Drew University and the Accounting, Law and Taxation Department of Montclair State University. In addition, he has been quoted in several publications, including *Venture Capital Journal* and the *Journal of Accountancy,* and has appeared in AICPA continuing professional education videos.

Mark Spelker can be reached at (973) 618-6275 or mspelker@jhcohn.com and jhcohn.com.

Kelly M. Slavitt is North American trademark and business counsel for Reckitt Benckiser LLC. Kelly is a transactional attorney with extensive experience identifying, protecting, and monetizing intellectual property. Kelly previously was counsel at General Electric, ran the legal department at the American Society for the Prevention of Cruelty to Animals (ASPCA), and was an associate at Skadden Arps and Thelen Reid in New York City and a Solicitor at Allens Arthur Robinson in Melbourne, Australia. She has a BA, an MPA, a JD, and an LLM. Kelly Slavitt can be reached at (973) 404-2435 or kelly.slavitt@reckittbenckiser.com.

Fernando Torres is a member and chief economist at IPmetrics LLC, a consulting firm specializing in the strategic analysis, valuation, and expert witness assessment of the full spectrum of intellectual property and intangible assets. He is a member of the National Association of Forensic Economics and regularly blogs, publishes, and presents on topics related to intangible asset valuation in a variety of media. Since receiving his master's degree with a specialization in econometrics, his career has spanned from academia to branches of government, private industry, and consulting in Mexico and the United States. Fernando Torres can be reached at (858) 754-9310, @FTorresMSc on Twitter, or via e-mail at ftorres@ipmetrics.net.

Index